OF GODS AND MEN

Folklore Studies in Translation
General Editor, Dan Ben-Amos

Advisory Board

Eleazar M. Meletinsky
Institute Mirovoj
 Literatury AN SSR
Moscow

Tzvetan Todorov
Centre National de la
 Recherche Scientifique
Paris

Donald Ward
Center for the Study of
 Comparative Folklore and
 Mythology
Los Angeles

Juha Pentikaïnen
University of Helsinki
Helsinki

Vilmos Voigt
Eotvos, Lorand University
Budapest

Masao Yamaguchi
Institute for the Study of
 Languages and Cultures
 of Asia and Africa
Tokyo

The generous support of The L. J. Skaggs and Mary C. Skaggs Foundation has made the *Folklore Studies in Translation* series possible.

OF GODS AND MEN

Studies in Lithuanian Mythology

ALGIRDAS J. GREIMAS

TRANSLATED BY

Milda Newman

INDIANA UNIVERSITY PRESS
Bloomington and Indianapolis

Translation of *Apie Dievus ir žmones: Lietuvių Mitologijos studijos*, copyright Algirdas J. Greimas, published in Lithuanian (1979) by AM&M Publications, Chicago.

© 1992 by Indiana University Press

All rights reserved

No part of this book may be reproduced or utilized in any form or by any means, electronic or mechanical, including photocopying and recording, or by any information storage and retrieval system, without permission in writing from the publisher. The Association of American University Presses' Resolution on Permissions constitutes the only exception to this prohibition.

The paper used in this publication meets the minimum requirements of American National Standard for Information Sciences—Permanence of Paper for Print Library Materials, ANSI Z39.48-1984.

Manufactured in the United States of America

Library of Congress Cataloging-in-Publication Data

Greimas, Algirdas Julien.
 [Apie dievus ir žmones. English]
 Of gods and men : studies in Lithuanian mythology / Algirdas J. Greimas ; translated by Milda Newman.
  p. cm. — (Folklore studies in translation)
 Translation of: Apie dievus ir žmones.
 Includes bibliographical references and indexes.
 ISBN 0-253-32652-4
 1. Mythology, Baltic. I. Title. II. Series.
BL945.G7313 1992
299'.192—dc20   91-48034

1 2 3 4 5 96 95 94 93 92

CONTENTS

FOREWORD BY DAN BEN-AMOS AND ALESSANDRO FALASSI — vii
TRANSLATOR'S ACKNOWLEDGMENTS — xi

	Preface	1
I.	Kaukai	18
II.	Aitvaras	42
III.	Aušrinė	64
IV.	Laima	112
V.	On Bees and Women	158
VI.	Gods and Festivals *Vulcanus Jagaubis*	182
VII.	Gods and Festivals *Krikštai*	197

NOTES — 205
NAME INDEX — 227
SUBJECT INDEX — 229

FOREWORD

A Lithuanian in exile, Algirdas Julien Greimas recalls and constructs the mythological world of his people. In this volume he gives voice not only to a dispersed Lithuanian community, but also to many displaced communities and individuals world wide. Exile has become an existential experience in the twentieth century. Wars, political oppression, and colonialism drove millions of peoples from their native lands into new countries, seeking security, freedom, and hope. But in the pursuit of personal happiness exiles lost the protective shield of their traditional cultures. The sights and sounds of their native lands persisted only in faded memories which they recall, cherish, and savor in moments of crisis and self-reflection, transforming their native lands into cultural mythologies. James Joyce wrote about his Dublin while he lived in Trieste, Zurich, and Paris, and it is in the latter of these cities that Algirdas Julien Greimas writes about the mythology of his Lithuania.

Greimas constructs this mythology by searching into the crevices of his memory that are filled with the voices, rhythms, and smells of his childhood and youth, writing an ethnography of recollection. Then he supplements the personal with the cultural memory, or perhaps it is the other way around. Fragmentary allusions from the thirteenth and fifteenth centuries, descriptions of rituals and customs from the sixteenth and seventeenth centuries, and ethnographic documentation from the nineteenth century are interwoven with the aroma of firewood, the echoes of village songs, and the resonating voice of a storyteller. Together they provide the ethnographic and historical dimensions for the structure of mythology that Greimas builds upon the foundations of the Lithuanian language.

Yet the import of this book extends beyond the personal and the ethnic. The quest for cultural definition takes the form of a systematic and erudite search, trying to decipher the meaning of the symbolic world that Lithuanian mythology constitutes. Greimas exposes covert meanings and significations, metaphors and images that make up the intricate connections that are woven into the myths of the Lithuanians. His analytical method has three immediate predecessors: the comparative mythology of Georges Dumézil,[1] the structural analysis of Claude Lévi-Strauss,[2] and his own semiotic theory of structural semantics.[3] But the roots of his quest extend back into the Romantic era. They draw upon the comparative method of Jacob Grimm (1785–1863), who sought to reconstruct the Teutonic mythology that Christianity shattered, and even upon the comparative mythology of the much-admired and ridiculed Max Müller (1823–1900) who, as Ernst Cassirer puts it, considers myth to be "conditioned and negotiated by the agency of language."[4]

For Greimas too, "mythology belongs to the domain of language."[5] By considering mythology to have the same qualities language has, Greimas is making a fun-

vii

damental proposition that affects his theoretical analysis of myth in general and his interpretation of Lithuanian mythology in particular. Theoretically myth has often been discussed not as an independent symbolic form, but in terms of its relations of affinity, contrast, or even contradiction with other basic ideas and categories. Consequently, myth has become the antonym of truth, reason, science, and history; on the other hand it has been regarded as the antecedent, or even the cause, of metaphor, poetry, and art. Its relations with ritual, religion, thought, and ideology are still full of ambivalence, and the categorial boundaries between them are fuzzy. Nevertheless, even in these discussions myth is laden with negativity and is contrasted with the substantive and verifiable reality of values, events, and personalities that the opposing categories manifest. They become the standards against which myth is conceived, measured, and interpreted. They serve as an "absolute reality which forms, so to speak, [a] solid and substantial substratum."[6]

Even when the theoretical discussions shift from a concern with the nature of myth to its function in society, culture, or the life of the individual, its implicit negativity remains. At the basis of these theories of myth is the puzzling question of the relevance of the set of irrational propositions that permeate myth to human rationality. Theories of myth aim at reconciling the rational image of man with these apparently illogical, unverifiable, fantastic expressions by identifying a particular function that myth contributes to human social integrity.[7]

By positioning myth alongside language, Greimas sidesteps much of the philosophical discussion that has surrounded, often clouded, the conception of myth. In contrast, Greimas examines mythology on a semiotic rather than philosophical level. For him it is a symbolic system, much as language is. Myth is subject to the same probing questions and analytical methods that are applicable to language and any other symbolic system.

Greimas is hardly original in his approach, treating myth and language as two symbolic forms that belong to the same category. Rather he builds upon an intellectual tradition that evolved in the eighteenth century with the publication of *Scienza Nouva* by Giambattista Vico, and which enjoyed periods of growth within romanticism and idealism, even before its current florescence. For Vico both the mythologies and the etymologies of native languages tell the histories of the social institutions, most of all those of the nations that share and use them. Myths do not distort the past but contain it. They are the civil, as opposed to the religious, histories of early man. Complex and confounding as they are, Vico's thoughts about myth and language have become a foundation for the interpretation of myth as language, and language as myth, both documenting the history of a people.[8] For him and for the Romantics who followed the diachronic perspective, the question of origins of either semiotic system was the primal issue. Friedrich W. J. Schelling regarded language as "faded mythology," preserving in abstract forms distinctions and qualities that are concrete in myth.[9] Later, Max Müller reversed the relations between the two and considered myth a "diseased language" that emerged as a narrativization rationalizing misunderstood metaphors. But it was Jacob Grimm who erected the monument to the Romantic approach to myth and language in his application of the Romantic ideas to the reconstruction of the pagan mythology of the Germanic tribes that had been shattered by Christianity. He made a comparative study of medieval German and Nordic languages to recover and reconstruct Teutonic mythology. In his salvage research he made an extensive use of folktales, legends, names, proverbs, riddles, superstitions, and an array of customs, rites, and festivals that preserve the meanings and significations of ancient Germanic gods.[10]

The evocations of Jacob Grimm's monumental study in this context is not accidental. From Grimm to Greimas there is a continuous, though occasionally revolutionized, intellectual tradition that places language at a central position in the initial construction and later reconstruction of mythology. Like his eminent predecessor in the explorations of mythology through language, Greimas employs lexicographic analysis in the recovery of myth. Initially Greimas pursued lexicographic studies as a method for the reconstruction of past social life. For him lexicography was not necessarily a discipline of dictionary making, but a way of reaching into the thoughts, lives, and world views of past generations. Around the late 1940s,[11] he became frustrated with lexicography as a method to reach his goals, shifted methods, and began a lifelong study of structural semantics, eventually developing a method and a theory in semiotics that incorporates principles formulated by Claude Lévi-Strauss and Vladimir Propp.[12]

The present volume is a synthesis of Greimas's early method with his later accomplishments. In examining his own Lithuanian folklore, language, and culture he combines native sensitivity for Lithuanian nomenclature with profound knowledge of his people's ancient literary corpus, and brings to bear upon both of them current rigorous analytical methods. Through his lexicographic method he emphasizes the historic dimension of myth analysis, while through his semantic theory he orients his interpretation toward a search of the integration of meaning in Lithuanian culture. Hence Greimas rightly views this study of mythology as an archaeology of culture.

Archaeology provides a methodological metaphor in a dual sense. First, the significance of the Lithuanian deities and concepts such as the *Kaukai* and the *Aitvarai*, *Laima*, and *Aušrinė* is assembled from scattered texts and contexts. These could be folktales and legends, proverbs and riddles, as well as customs, rites, and festivals, that have been recorded either ethnographically or in historical documents and ancient literature. These complementary meanings are the pot shards that make up the whole vessel of culture.

Evolutionary anthropology of the nineteenth century with its doctrine of survival[13] was also a kind of archaeology of culture, tracing surviving customs and beliefs to their postulated stage of human evolution. However, Greimas employs the surviving evidence of Lithuanian mythology in order to construct an integrated cultural symbolic system, rather than to establish an origin of a single idea or sign.

The search for cohesiveness of a Lithuanian mythology as a symbolic system provides the second dimension of the archaeological metaphor. Often the research in this direction is preliminary and incomplete, a program for the future rather than a summation of known evidence. Yet ideally, Greimas would have liked to construct the relations between cultural meanings not only as extending into historical times, but also as they are changing from one historical period to another, from one social and cultural context to the next. In other words, the archaeology of culture metaphor enables us to view mythology as a cultural ideology undergoing transformation in the past, not only in the present. Since each mythic image occurs in a systemic context, related to other symbols and signs known in particular historical periods and cultural contexts, it becomes part of an integrated layer in the history of the Lithuanian people.

As a language Lithuanian mythology forms a semantic code. This is a key concept in Greimas's theory of structural semantics. The idea of mythology itself as a code dates back to the Alexandrian grammarians and the Renaissance mythographers who interpreted myths allegorically,[14] and has continued up to the solar mythology of Max Müller and the sexual mythology that Sigmund Freud inspired. The semiotic and the allegorical interpretations of myths no doubt share the principle of reading coded messages into fantastic narratives; however, the similarity ends there. Past allegorical interpretations have referred to a single cultural domain as the frame of reference of the figures and acts coded into myth, be it ethics, religion, the solar system, or human desires and fears. In each case the reference has been formulated on the basis of a particular belief system or a certain theoretical assumption. In contrast, Greimas establishes the semantics of the mythical concepts and figures empirically, inferring them from their use and occurrence in Lithuanian literature, folklore, and customs. Furthermore, his interpretation is not allegorical. He establishes the position of a particular mythic figure, image, or concept within a semantic paradigm which serves him as the basis for construction of meaning as it is understood within the system of Lithuanian mythology. Within this system both the meanings and their coded signs are interdependent, standing in relation of analogy or opposition, inclusion or exclusion to each other. It is on the basis of such an analysis of the semantic code that forms Lithuanian mythology that Greimas is able to read in it the interplay between such abstract concepts as life and death, destiny and fortune, beauty and happiness. It is as a semantic code that the Lithuanian mythology forms the cultural ideology of the Lithuanian people.

On the basis of the available information it is an ideology of an agrarian society, the farmers-breeders social stratum of the tripartite structure that Dumézil has distinguished in Indo-European society. The ideologies of the warrior and the priestly classes have not been retained in Lithuanian language and culture to a degree sufficient to enable reconstruction.

In conclusion, this volume is a literary, philological, semiotic, and folkloristic *tour de force* in which subjective attitude and objective analysis join in a synthesis, reconstructing the mythology of the past in a way that will be a model for future studies.

Dan Ben-Amos
and Alessandro Falassi

1988

TRANSLATOR'S ACKNOWLEDGMENTS

I would like to thank the following people for their contribution to the translated text:

Professor Wolfgang Wölck for translation of the numerous German passages;

Professor Paul Perron for various suggestions as to the semiotic and Greimassian terms, especially in the Preface;

Professor Marija Gimbutas for suggestions concerning Lithuanian mythological terminology;

Professor Paul Garvin for his support during the project and in the past.

OF GODS AND MEN

PREFACE

Mythology as Object

Mythology as Ideology

The establishment of mythology as an independent branch of the social sciences is associated with Georges Dumézil's name. He waged this battle for decades against amateurs of mythology, who viewed myths as artistic creations of unbridled inventiveness; against historical-realists who searched for mythic facts, not their significance; against a variety of philosophical theories, which offered to explain with a simple sweep of the pen and with the help of only a few categories the mythic thinking of all mankind. This battle ended with a victory, which consolidated this analytical field in the sixth decade of our century.

Dumézil's point of departure is quite simple. He affirms a correspondence between the human and the divine worlds, in which the world of the gods is viewed as a reflection of the mortal world, of man's systems, his basic concerns and longings. Analyzing the religions of the Indo-European nations, Dumézil formulated a hypothesis in which the general social structures of those nations find their equivalent in the structure of the divine world and in the distribution of its functions. In other words, the religion of a nation is the ideology with which a community conceives of itself, and reflects relations between people, and their contradictions—making all of it absolute on the divine plane. Thus, for instance, the three social classes characteristic of Indo-European society—priest, warrior, and cultivator or herder—correspond to three spheres of divine sovereignty: the priestly class to the sovereign sphere of magic and the contractual, the warrior class to a sovereignty based on power, and the cultivator class to the sphere of sources and guardianship of all types of "earthly blessings"—food, riches, health, beauty.

Without delving deeper into the separate components of this theory—whether such a distribution of sovereign functions applies to all mythologies, or whether the world of the gods recreates the human system directly, or whether supplementary mediation is needed—the general importance of Dumézil's contribution must be stressed. His research, which confirms his initial hypothesis, permits us to understand (a) that gods and other mythic beings are not the result of human "fantasy," but figurative means of explaining the meaning and order of mankind and the universe, (b) that the mythic manner of thinking is not random and accidental but occurs within the framework of an organized system of divine activities and functions, and (c) that mythology is called upon to express the political ideology, as it is widely understood, of the community analyzed.

From such a conception of mythology, there flows yet another, especially important, methodological assertion: mythology is not, as has been commonly thought, a collection of a nation's myths but is rather an ideological structure, capable of being manifested in any "literary" form. As a comparativist searching for correspondences among mythic structures in different Indo-European nations, Dumézil found myths recorded in Rome as historical events, in India as separate episodes in epopee, in Ireland as legends, and so forth. In other words—to thus characterize the scientific methodology of mythology—mythological analysis cannot begin with an a priori definition of "myth" as a predetermined literary genre, or with the creation of a corpus of narratives called "myths" and its analysis, as is still done by the descriptive procedures of nineteenth-century scholarship; rather, mythic narratives are only one source out of many with which one can attempt to reconstruct mythic structure.

Mythology as Philosophy

Claude Lévi-Strauss in a completely separate area—American Indian mythology—applied and extended Dumézil's methodological procedures, even though for his own analysis he chose a different point of departure. His 1955 article, "The Structural Study of Myth," published in the *Journal of American Folklore,* is often held as the date of birth of this new branch of science. Focusing on the well-known Oedipus myth, he states that every myth can be read in two ways: horizontally, it appears perfectly clear, as a story without much significance; and vertically—i.e., where the semantic traits of the story, even if expressed with different figures, constantly repeat and are organized into certain meaningful structures—the myth is not apparent, deciphered with difficulty, but it is a meaningful text. The basic analytic task in mythology, therefore, is first of all to work out the procedures necessary for the reading of mythic texts, with which mythology will then be disclosed as the totality of all the histories which humanity narrates, recounting in that manner its essential anxieties, weighing all the philosophical problems that arise.

Lévi-Strauss extends the problematic Dumézil raised: where Dumézil noted only the expression of the ideology of a society, Lévi-Strauss now discerns in it the expression of a general philosophy of culture. Concerned not so much with the forms of organized religion but with the mythologies of so-called archaic communities, Lévi-Strauss identified the basic dimensions along which humanity conceives of culture. Here there is passage from raw food, characteristic of all living beings, to cooked food, a passage from the naked state to that of being clothed or adorned—these are always thresholds which man crosses, each time denying his nature in order to achieve culture: thus universal themes are encountered, perhaps, in almost all mythologies. It is possible, of course, not to agree with one or another of Lévi-

Strauss's statements or points of evidence; his contribution, nevertheless, helps to elucidate even more what can be described as everyday cognition—the characteristic form of figurative conceptualization that humanity utilizes to resolve basic ideological and philosophical problems.

In an attempt to answer why a surface reading of myth is not understood, even though its deep meaning is not problematic, Lévi-Strauss offers the collective-unconscious hypothesis as an explanation.

While the problems dealt with by mythology are universal and the means of figurative expression, as with the spoken language of every ethnic community, even though relative, do not belong with the capriciousness of individuals but form a common treasure of that society, the content transmitted by the form of mythic narration circulates among the people even though the actual forms of expression are not freely understood or not understood at all. It is possible, of course, to accept or reject this hypothesis—it does not change the procedures. There only remains the same basic problem: the reading of the myth. The mythic text, as any other narrative of man, can be understood only when the addressee has the appropriate semantic code at his disposal which allows him to decipher the given text. In other words, to understand myths, it is not sufficient to have an exhaustive collection—one must also prepare a corresponding dictionary of myths which will be of help in reading them.

Mythology as Culture

The semantic code appears thus as a necessary condition for a definitive formation of methodology in this field. It is understandable, therefore, why a new generation of mythologists is making an attempt to return to Dumézil, according to whom mythology, as semantic structure, is independent of the texts with which it is expressed. As a consequence, the concept of mythology is extended even further when it is identified with the cultural totality of the community as recorded in the frames of a given time and space. Studying ancient Greek mythology, Marcel Détienne turned his attention no less to mythological narratives than to the "scientific theories" of that age, agrarian pamphlets, descriptions of botany and zoology, alimentary regimens, use of perfume and precious stones, and so on, regarding these areas as localized figurative logics which mythic thinking utilizes. The problematic formulated by Lévi-Strauss—according to which mythology is deduced from the totality of myths with the help of a semantic code—is reversed by the new tendencies of this scholarship, which identify mythology with the semantic code that is capable, when necessary, of generating mythic narratives. We shall not evaluate here the various tendencies of some of the methodological differences which have recently appeared in mythology and which are the signs of vitality of this branch of science since its common base remains sufficiently valid and continues to be acceptable to all mythologists: mythology is the cultural expression of the community; as cultural text, it can and must be read and explained in terms of its internal organizing system and not by external a priori categories.

Such a schematic and rather superficial depiction of the basic traits of present-day mythology is presented to inform the reader of the epistemological and methodological framework this book uses in attempting to describe mythic phenomena and analyze methodological problems. We do not feel that a critical view of the author's capabilities and his competency should be used as a pretext to condemn the mythology. Moreover, a nonacknowledgment of mythological theory—or simply a lack of acquaintance—should not be a reason for rejecting the partially worked-out description or localized description of the investigator. To the reader of Lithuanian folktales and mythology who is acquainted with the work of Jonas Balys and his achievements in this field, it should be clear from the outset that the concept of mythology as "mythology from essence" in his statements, appropriate to nineteenth-century pseudo-philosophical and pseudo-scientific considerations of this type, has nothing in common with the formation of mythology as a separate branch of the social sciences during the past fifty years.

The Problems of Lithuanian Mythology

Ethnology or Cultural History?

Mythology understood in such a broad sense can present itself as a means for analyzing the cultures of various societies. Mythology can be considered one of the fields of ethnology for the description of so-called archaic preliterate cultures. Mythology also becomes one of the basic components of cultural history for the description of ancient historical cultures and their reconstruction. Even though its essence as anthropology—as the study of man—is not changed, mythology nevertheless is compelled in both cases to utilize different modes of approach, different data and sources. In ethnological mythology a large role is played by analysts—or their mediators—who have direct contact with a living community, while historical mythology has to be content with existing, unverifiable data and attempt to fill in the gaps in sources with coherent hypotheses.

In this sense, our chosen object of analysis is complex. The data for the study of mythology of the Lithuanian nation are historical as well as ethnographic. On the one hand, there are the written sources: sparse allusions to pagan religions of neighboring nations—and later of Lithuania—in the chronicles and annals of the thirteenth to the fifteenth centuries, and the significantly more abundant descriptions of degraded rituals and customs in the sixteenth and seventeenth centuries. On the other hand, there is the carefully gathered ethnographic material from the nineteenth century to the present day in which it is possible to identify the vestiges of ancient beliefs and customs which have survived within the framework of a dominant religion, Christianity.

It should not be forgotten, however, that every collection of "data" is always subject to the purpose for which it was gathered: this aim may be explicit, for example, as in the form of scientific hypotheses, but it can also be implicit, determined by the dominant ideology of the time. The ethnographic archive created through the efforts of compatriots is thus heterogeneous, obedient to the tendencies of several ideologies. Since Herder's and Goethe's time, the cherished myth of "folk creation" compelled collectors to turn their attention to the "beauty" of Lithuanian folktales: hence, for example, the abundant collections of lyric songs, which have relatively little in common with mythology and antiquity. Another myth of "folkculture" and "folkishness" followed—springing from the first and frequently merging with it—as the expression of the "nation's genius," which provided adequate collections of tales, proverbs, and sacred customs. The dominant folkloric theories—especially the distribution of folklore into literary genres—favored "major" genres at the expense of lesser ones.

These few observations should by no means diminish the importance of the ethnographic material, but rather direct our attention to its heteroclitic nature. This means, on the one hand, that only a very small amount of this material can be used for the historical analysis of mythology. On the other hand, this type of archival exploitation cannot help but raise the problem of determining which field of study the material can be used for: science emerges from the definition of its object and elaboration of its methods and not from data that have been gathered by chance. For that reason, the collected data based on the descriptions of village life in the second half of the nineteenth century—with work and festivals repeated in the annual cycle, themselves recorded within another cycle of individual life: weddings, baptisms, and burials—can be considered as belonging to a field of sociology of closed archaic village communities, characteristic to all of Europe at that time. The socialistic Rumanian regime, which left the entire ancient Marmara lands uncollectivized as if it were some American Indian reservation, created ideal circumstances for such a sociology to flourish. This quite legitimate scientific domain, of course, has nothing in common with the mythological investigations we are suggesting. There is misunderstanding only when the folklorist-sociologist claims to be, at the same time, both a critic of oral literature and an investigator of ancient Lithuanian mythology: this is a mixing of scientific "genres."

Mythology or Religion?

It should not be forgotten that Lithuanian mythology is inscribed as one of the formative elements in general comparative Indo-European mythology. For the investigator, of course, this is of great benefit: comparability of mythic structures—that is, the possibility of identifying the similarities and differences among mythologies—helps to form hypotheses, defining what, namely, must be looked for, helping, as well, to reconstruct ancient religious rituals changed to forms of games or pranks, and so forth. Nevertheless, the dependence of Lithuanian mythology on a broader, more general mythological zone, imposes certain restrictions on the analyst. Dumézil, as we have mentioned previously, turned the attention of mythologists to an especially important dimension of mythic conceptualization characteristic for Indo-Europeans: the ideology of sovereignty, and more generally, the distribution of world power. There is clearly no point in searching for such ideologies in nineteenth-century closed village communities, even in mythic thought. The ideology of sovereignty encompasses the condition of developed national societies differentiated into social classes. In other words, if we define religion—even though such a definition is not necessary—as a specific mythological form, distinguished by the existence of systematized and hierarchized ideologies with their corresponding social institutions, then the presence or absence of Lithuanian religion depends on the conception we have of the ancient Lithuanian nation, as politically manifested in its organization of the state.

The problem is more serious than it appears on the surface. According to the predominant opinion of the folklorist-mythologist, the ancient Lithuanians worshipped "heavenly bodies," "the divine powers of nature" and other such "creations of fantasy." Such an understanding of mythology has nothing in common with the national religion, which can be compared with the religions of other Indo-European nations. Similarly, not too long ago the dominant view presented Lithuania during the Middle Ages as a classless society of free men, with a quite loose, almost nonexistent political organization.

In recent times, archaeological and historical investigations in large part have corrected such primitive views of ancient Lithuania. Archaeological excavations reveal the consolidation of a material culture characteristic of the entire territory of ethnic Lithuania—crops, agricultural implements, and technologies—which allows one to assess the intensive circulation of goods and people of that age, possible only with minimal political organization, to guarantee safe passage. These divisions and problems correspond in the same period to the emergence of Western Europe from barbarism and to the formative cultural beginnings of the Middle Ages. The same research indicates another, no less important conclusion concerning the process of religious revolution extending from the sixth century to the end of the tenth: the formation of a common base of material culture corresponding to the unification of religious forms as manifested by the universal consolidation of cremation. The myths of Sovijus and Šventaragis thus correspond to historical facts as corroborated by archaeology. Historical investigations, on the other hand, gradually disclose the foundations of social and political organization of the Lithuanian nation which permitted it to develop into a state: even though the general concept of feudalism does not allow us yet to see beyond the specific traits of Lithuanian society, nevertheless, it points to the existing unity of the Lithuanian nation of that time, socially differentiated and hierarchically organized. Therefore, it is on such social bases that it is possible to think of the Lithuanian religion as similar to other Indo-European types of religion. The expansion of the Lithuanian state, even, in a certain sense, of Lithuanian imperialism as manifested in the thirteenth and fourteenth centuries—difficult to explain by economic or demographic domination—had to be based at least on ideological cohesiveness and resilience: if we view religion as the figurative expression of the ideology of that time, it is possible to suppose that for the formation of the state and its expansion there had to be a corresponding period of "religious flourishing." Such an economic, social, and political context leads us to believe that the need for the reconstruction and description of Lithuanian mythology is urgent and well-founded and is eagerly awaited by Indo-European mythologists.

History and Structure

There has been much progress in the past few years in archaeological methods. From disparate scattered elements it is possible to reconstruct not just tools, statues, or buildings but entire sites and settlements, which can be used to make determinations about the cities of antiquity, their social, political, and religious institutional forms. This has had an unquestionable influence on historical methodology. Through analogy, it can be stated that the description of an identifiable mythology in the ancient or badly understood past is nothing more than a reconstruction which, with the help of separate mythic fragments, scattered slogans and random pieces, seeks to restore a coherent organized entity. Nonetheless, such reconstruction cannot—and does not seek to—reconstruct the totality of a historical period with its characteristic internal contradictions and heterogeneous elements. Reconstruction of mythology means no more than the description of a given, logically enclosed, structured state. If it is possible, for instance, to identify the reconstructed Lithuanian mythology with the religious and spiritual culture of the Grand Duchy of Lithuania of the thirteenth and fourteenth centuries, then it is apparent, on the one hand, that during the historical period in Lithuania there acted other separate cultural forces and influences, and, on the other hand, that the partial forms of those same mythic structures can be encountered in the superficially Christianized Lithuania of the fifteenth and sixteenth centuries, that mythic outlines can be found in the ethnographic sources of the nineteenth century. St. Anne's church in Vilnius, for instance, is Gothic, even though it was built at a time which can no longer be considered as belonging to the Gothic Age: the Gothic concept and the historical Gothic period are two separate academic objects of study.

Furthermore, the similarity or difference of the expressive plane must be considered secondary if at the plane of deeper content semantic identity can be established. Forms of female clothing and modes of wearing it, for instance, can change in the course of history: these changes can be judged insignificant if the principle of wearing itself—the identification of separate ages and classes of women through clothes—remains constant and corresponds to the structural requirements of the cultural system described. In other words, the definitive aim in the reconstruction of mythology, is to recreate, in spite of the variety of figurative forms and variations, the autonomous semantic world. Such a semantic world as described by a mythologist, evaluating it with the eyes of a cultural-historian, probably corresponds to what could be called the dominant ideology or culture of the period.

Methodological Concerns

If mythology is a type of cultural archaeology, then the methods with which it carries out its excavations must theoretically help to reconstruct the entire vase from several fragments, to trace the entire plan of the city from a few remaining walls. In other words, from the methodological perspective, one must evaluate the recorded mythic facts as an integral part of a wider whole into which it enters. Every mythic object or episode has to be worked out in accordance with a hypothetical model capable of explaining not only that object or episode but also other phenomena associated with it. Mythological reconstruction is thus an ongoing creation of hypotheses, the verification of which, as in other branches of science, presently acknowledges only internal coherence as criteria. The hypothesis can be falsified eventually only by the introduction of new, unexplainable or contradictory facts.

Oral Literature Texts

Reconstruction of Lithuanian mythology thus involves first of all, the search, identification, and description of separate mythic elements and an attempt to inscribe them into wider mythic structures and dimensions. These elements, in turn, can be manifested in various forms of oral literature.

Historical and ethnographic sources present us with a certain number of as yet unexplained "true" mythic narratives: for example, the myths of Sovijus, the founding of Vilnius, the flood. Reliable methods already exist in comparative Indo-European mythology for the interpretation of such myths, which are based, as we mentioned, on the basic principle of myth reading—the reconstruction of the semantic code. In comparison, the small number of such unambiguous myths—attributed to the late realization that they should be recorded—compels the mythologist to raise a question about their general nature: If Lithuanian mythology has survived at all and can be reconstructed, then, namely, in what forms are the mythic narratives and other mythic configurations manifested in the Lithuanian context?

One form that has conserved myths is the group of so-called wondertales. It is sufficient to randomly compare some of the Lithuanian variants of such tales with the widely known Western European versions, so that the essential differences between them become apparent. Here are a few examples: whereas Tom Thumb in the common wondertales is manifested as a nimble little fellow, using his cleverness to save his brother from the cannibal, the Lithuanian Tom Thumb, even though he also plays here a narrative trickster's role, is a mythic being born from an old woman's farts, or from an old man's chopped-off thumb, playing his basic pranks in the belly of the bull or the wolf. Whereas the narrative about the revenant who appears to his or her betrothed belongs to the general apparition theme in the French or English versions, the Lithuanian version introduces mythic elements, and tries to weigh philosophically the relations between the living and the dead. The well-known story from antiquity about the father who longs to marry his daughter, in the Lithuanian context finds a correspondence not only in the avoidance of incestuous relations between the father and daughter but especially in the many variants about the brother's and sister's incestuous life, thus resolving in a mythic manner the problem concerning the passage from blood relationship to a kinship based on contractual relations.

All this, of course, is not appropriate with regards to the classification of the oral literature genres elaborated during the nineteenth century, based on which folklorists frequently "know" what is a myth and what is a wondertale. At a symposium specifically organized around this problem, Dumézil answered my query that all his life he had attempted to find explicit criteria that would enable him to distinguish these two genres but he has as yet to find them. Such valorization of Lithuanian tales, on the other hand, contradicts the theory of the migration of tales and motifs prevalent during the nineteenth century (and even today survives in some places), according to which all of Europe's tales arrived, across mountains, deserts, and oceans from faraway India. Separate studies need to be undertaken to investigate this complicated problem. Suffice it to say, that in this case three separate things and three different problems are confused: the universal nature of narrative structure, common to all mankind; the problem of migratory motifs whose signification and place change from one narrative to another; and the utilization of these structures and motifs in mythic content and mythic configurations.

While we agree, at least in part, with Dumézil's opinion that wondertales can be explained as outcomes of myth simplification, or sometimes even as their complete desemanticization—which are manifested, first of all by the disappearance of the anthropomorphic proper name, and then by a change in their mythic functions through the introduction of magic objects and unusual accomplishments—we nevertheless feel that in separate, well-founded cases we have a right to evaluate certain Lithuanian tales as degraded myths and attempt to explain them on the mythic level, restoring thus to some of the characters their "true" mythic names and determining their divine functions. The rather complex Aušrinė Myth reconstruction, for instance, is based on such theoretical and methodological principles.

The problem of so-called legends is of a different nature. While in cases of myths and wondertales, the mythologist must be concerned with the entire, comprehensive narration, requiring interpretation, legends most often offer only separate bits, they narrate only individual events which touch on one or another mythic or "story-like" being or its characteristic trait. A useful procedure in this case is the opposite of the former; instead of analyzing the given narrative by segmenting it, the mythologist must try to reconstruct the entire narrative from separate fragments, logically reorganizing the scattered fragments into a comprehensive whole. For instance, the description of *kaukai* (chapter one) which recounts the conditions and circumstances of their birth and their demise, separating their life in the forest from their domesticated activities and so forth, can be placed here. This corresponds to the American ethnologists' much-liked "biographical" type of cultural description.

Nevertheless, the only pertinent criterion which can enable us to characterize legends as a separate literary genre seems to be that of veridiction, of "belief." Such a definition is based on quite indistinct "belief" criteria: these are narratives in which the narrator as much as the narratee "believes" in the reality of the beings or events. First of all, belief is not a categorical but a relative concept: people ordinarily believe more or less in something, and do not believe or disbelieve—"Lord, I believe, help me in my disbelief!"—this is a well-known supplicant's prayer, which could compel "believers" into such genre definitions. Recently questionnaires given to Indian students revealed that they in part, approximately 35 percent, believe and partly—approximately 65 percent—do not believe in the sanctity of cows. Consequently, cows, for the same "believer" are both sacred and not sacred, as laumės [fairies] for the Lithuanians in the nineteenth century perhaps existed, and perhaps did not.

Even if we agree that in a closed society in a certain historical period it is possible to divide narratives into tales in which no one believes and into legends which everyone believes, such a distribution changes in the course of time: whereas Mažvydas [Mosvidius], author of the first Lithuanian catechism written in the sixteenth century, believed that *kaukai* "actually" existed, attributing cooperation with them to the area of "black magic," nineteenth-century narratives portrayed them as living only "in another parish" or at some other time, for instance, that of the old man just mentioned. For the researcher concerned with mythological reconstruction such a criterion as veridiction is neither pertinent nor efficient. Thus, the description of mythic beings according to how they appear in such and such a genre of oral literature does not hold up to criticism.

Ritual Texts

It is necessary to differentiate this purely "folkloric" material from documentation created through the efforts of researchers who observe, question, and describe a given society: these include the descriptions of their labors and festivals, customs and beliefs, dances and games. These data differ from the former in that even though they are approached by the mythologist most often through linguistic form, the observed community is captured and recorded now not in its verbal narrative expression but in its somatic behavior, manifested by gestures and bodily movements, which for the mythologist are no less significant than verbal expression. The problematic of reciprocal relations between the two—verbal and somatic—dimensions of expression by which society reveals itself and becomes meaningful, which previously one had attempted to analyze within the comparatively narrow frames of relations between myth and ritual—is especially complicated and difficult to analyze. The descriptions of rituals and beliefs, for instance, appear to the mythologist, on the one hand, as elements of a semantic code with which mythic narratives can be analyzed. On the other hand, the separate rituals and beliefs remain unintelligible and meaningless until he is able to interpret or record them within the general mythological system. The identification of this dialectic relation between significant narration and significant behavior does not as yet constitute a definitive explanation: it should especially not become an obstacle for the in-depth analysis of either of the dimensions taken separately.

During the past several years semiotic theory has accustomed us to evaluating rituals in the same way as we do stereotypical behavioral chains called customs, as specific nonverbal texts which can be analyzed with the same methods used in analyzing oral narrative texts. Furthermore, closed, highly structured societal customs, taken as a whole, form their own characteristic normative system, which allowed the Rumanian ethnologist Mihai Pop to speak of a "grammar of customs," the description of which he considers one of the basic tasks of the folklorist. In other words, crossing from the plane of oral literature to the plane of the description of customs-beliefs-rituals, we find the same general problems encountered in the analysis of mythic texts and in the reconstruction of their common mythological system, which, in turn, must be analyzed progressively, taking into account the close and stable relations between both dimensions of mythic expression.

We are dealing with such ritualistic texts and with difficulties linked to their interpretation in an attempt to understand, for instance, the significance of cyclic, annually repeated festivals. Ethnographic descriptions generally separate them into work and calendar festivals. However, even a cursory glance makes it clear that such a division is not well founded; although, on the one hand, agrarian festivals and the rituals that mark them are not linked to the stable Christian calendar due to seasonal alternatives, on the other, livestock festivals which have no real basis for being considered separate from the former, coincide, at least in part, with the church holidays *Jurginės* and *Sekminės* (St. George and Pentecost). From a mythological perspective, both are first of all linked to one or another type of work, of animal or field-guarding deities. Therefore the first task is to reconstruct the relation between the gods—of whom there often remains only a list with a few annotations—and the festival rituals which allowed people to communicate with those gods. That is the primary classification, within which every area of agricultural activity has a dimension of mythic signification covering it.

Moreover, all agricultural activity must be considered as a general process, continued over time, into which are inscribed the separate phases marked by the rituals. For instance, the annual process of rye cultivation, has not only introductory—inchoative—aspects (ploughing, sowing) but also a continuous—durative—aspect ("attending to the rye") and finally, closing—terminative—aspects (reaping, *gabjauja*). Such an evaluation of every sphere of agrarian activity not only permits the mythologist to create a complete ritual text, its structure similar to oral narrative texts, but also allows for the discovery of similarities, which are repeated in autonomous ritualistic segments, and facilitates the interpretation of their global signification. Furthermore, every such agricultural process is also cyclical and repetitive, so that the linking of one year's cycle of work with the labors of the coming year also requires the setting into form of a particular myth. Within the same isotopy of rye cultivation this is manifested, on the one hand, by the bringing back and safekeeping in the granary of *jevaras* ("sheaves of rye") and by the construction of the mythic *jevaro tiltas* (bridge of jevaras), linking both years; and, on the other hand, of *gabjauja* as the festival of the filling the granaries, which echoes another festival involving the "opening of the seedbin"—Gandrinės. Thus, ceremonial texts not only have a characteristic, internal structure, they are combined with one another, organizing a unified conception of "work and festival."

The suggestion we have just made that a separate god is ascribed to each area of agrarian activity—to entrust, for instance, the cultivation of flax to Vaižgantas—is, of course, only a methodological simplification. One sphere of action can belong to several gods, and, conversely, one god can have an extended sphere of action. We encountered this very phenomenon in our description of the celebrations at harvest time. The protection of the drying grain crops from fire comes under the rule of the fire god *Jagaubis,* whereas the agrarian aim of the operation—transformation of grain into food—depends upon the goodwill of the "Javų Dvasia" [spirit of the graincrops]. The ritual text, as we see, can be formed from different segments which express the contractual relations—of entreaty and thanksgiving—with separate deities.

The existing descriptions of calendar festivals themselves partly fulfill such a segmentation of the text. The relations between the elements of the Christian and pagan festivals appear to be very weak. In the Christmas holidays, it is Christmas Eve as well as the second day of Christmas that are mythologically significant, not Christmas Day itself. The nightly visitations by the serenaders, the swings set up for the young girls, the third Wednesday after Easter (Ledų Diena) are segments which seem to have nothing in common with either Easter or with each other. Sėkminės [Pentecost] is a cattle holiday, as well as "Rugelių lankymas" (visiting the rye), and "rytagoniai," a festival specifically for young girls. Comparing such festivals with, for instance, the Roman festival calendar, we get the impression that often they can be interpreted as more or less successful syncretizations of a few "pagan" festivals. A logical procedure for their description should include, first of all, the deconstruction of these festivals with their distribution into separate ritual programs, and after that the individual programs should be combined into complete homogeneous ritual texts. Only at the very end, with the help of this new reconstruction, as was attempted for instance in the Krikštai festival, can the authentic festivals, long ago integrated into the ancient Lithuanian religion, be reconstituted.

The difficulty of fulfilling such a methodological program accurately is contained in the phenomena noted earlier in the case of oral literature—of the desemanticization of ritual texts. Ritual practices, at one time meaningful to the entire community, were changed in nineteenth- and twentieth-century descriptions into "customs" (for example, Christmas customs), "games" (swinging), or "pranks" (sprinkling). Just as wondertales often appear as degraded forms of mythic narratives, so customs, in many cases, can be explained as stereotypic repetitions of rituals that have lost all meaning. In each of the cases mentioned, the understanding and readability of these tales remind us once again of the need to formulate a semantic code.

The Mythological Dictionary

In reading the ethnographic descriptions of Lithuanian festivals, what catches the eye is not so much the importance of the feast itself, but the variety of foods prepared for the occasion, especially the adaptation of the food to every festival, since there exists a strong link between the dishes prepared and the festivals celebrated. The identification of these correlations allows us to speak about the existence of a characteristic system of alimentary "customs," from which the mythologist can deduce the ritualistic, mythic significance on which they once were based.

Authors who were interested in the relations of the ancient Lithuanians with their gods, seeking answers to such questions as whether the Lithuanians had altars, what offerings they made and how they offered them, in our opinion did not sufficiently concentrate on the elementary features of the offerings themselves, namely, (a) that the deities' preferred animal or food product is offered to them (a black goat, white pig, rooster, etc.), (b) that the offering represents one of the forms of conviviality between the people and the gods, manifested by the sharing of food between one and the other (spilling of drink, crumb strewing, inviting serpents to taste the food), and (c) that (evaluating it with the eyes of a positivist) the amount allowed to the gods, in such an offering, is comparatively small—their divine nature is often "nourished" not necessarily with a large amount of food during the time of the offering but rather with the smoke and odors of the offering. It is apparent therefore that the participation of the human community in the sacred offering is manifested by the collective utilization of the allotted food which, with the rituals having been changed into customs, corresponds to the feasts described by ethnographers.

The importance of the alimentary code as one of the modes of sacred expression can be greater or smaller in one or another religion: let us note, in passing, that the separation of Christianity from Judaism was manifested by the first Christians with violations of the alimentary prohibitions of the Jewish religion (see Peter's visit to the centurion Cornelius at Caesarea). It seems that the Lithuanian festival food customs can be considered one of the methodologically productive means for identifying the spheres of action and sovereignty of the various gods, of determining their relations with the beings of the zoological and botanical planes. Thus that the food at witches' feasts is without salt, that during the cattle festivals no meat is eaten, that during the conclusion of threshing the rooster offered to Jagaubis is eaten by men only, and the pig's tail, in another case, only by the mistress of the house—these are always mythic signs which belong to a common cultural code. During Christmas Eve striped peas, holy bread, sikiai [flaxseed cake], garnis cakes baked in the fire—these are only a few randomly selected illustrative signs which the mythologist must learn to read. The ceremonial ale—ordinary, warm, used for rinsing, in certain cases mead or "green wine," "blood of the bride," čvikinas—these are separate elements in the isotopy of refined liquids whose significance in ritual practices is undeniable.

The utilization of the alimentary culture plane for the expression of the sacred value system is not an exception but more likely an example illustrative of the formation and functioning of mythic forms of expression. Therefore, the mythologist, instead of repeatedly speaking, for instance, about the "worship" of heavenly bodies, first of all should examine the presence in this phenomenon of the often identifiable cosmographic plane of expression of mythology. Having carefully described the more or less significant "heavenly bodies," their characteristics, nature and origin, their perpetual movements—every one of them has its "path" along which it continuously "travels"—their comings and goings, the mythologist could understand without any trouble how such a cosmographic plane serves to express reciprocal relations between the gods, their harmonious life together and their conflicts, which every year are marked by repeated festivals. Unfortunately no such analysis of the cosmographic code has been attempted until now.

Similar observations can be made about the expressive planes which encompass the health and illness problematic. The morphology of the human body—where every organ, from the little finger to the head, including the liver, lungs, spleen and heart, has its symbolic meaning and role—is a type of microcosmic geography which expresses the entire problematic of man as a complex, unified being. Let us not forget that even the Church of the Middle Ages acknowledged for man not one but several souls—human, animal, and plant. In such a human body there live independent beings—illnesses: all kinds of kaltūnai and boils, which grow and spread, rise and fall, emerge through the eyes or through the nails, or kill off the person. A typology of diseases—which is lacking—is associated with the gods who govern or spread them or are capable of driving them out of the human body. In addition, certain illnesses are treated with ritualistic invocations, others with a variety of medicines, potions, and ointments. The preparation of these medicines, the choice of their ingredients—the entire so-called "folk medicine"—is not of fortuitous consequence; just as the festivals with their obligatory foods and dishes create a system of "customs," we can speak as well about healing "customs," which reflect ancient ritual healing practices, based on correlations between the deities and their favored or despised plants. Only a mythic botanical code understood in this manner—in which a large role is played by all types of devilweeds and worts—would be an important element for the description and reconstruction of Lithuanian mythology. Even though it is an important working tool for the mythologist, *Lietuvių kalbos žodynas* [known as the Academic Dictionary of Lithuanian—fourteen volumes have appeared] can be used only in small part to meet such expectations, since it serves another purpose. For that very reason, there is an urgent need for a mythological dictionary which would be a key to the cultural past of Lithuania.

Mythology and Poetry

The confidence nineteenth-century scholars, and the mythologist belongs to this group, placed in science, their reliance on "facts" and on the attainment of scientific "truth," cracked and finally crumbled after several Einstein-like revolutions in a variety of fields. After having lost all certitude and learned some humility, we readily admit that the facts belonging to one or another branch of science are selected by us. Assertions are created within our theoretical frameworks, and in the description of various human phenomena, despite the use made of the most rigorous methods and logical models, intuition often plays a leading role. As the noted linguist Roman Jakobson constantly repeated, a good linguist can only be a person with deep poetic feelings.

Such a spiritual disposition is needed even more when investigating mythology since, after all, mythology is the figurative form of cultural expression. Mythological language, on the social plane, is equivalent to poetic language on the individual plane. Therefore, it is understandable why in the past several decades the notable development of mythology has occurred together with a renewal of interest in poetic—and in all literary—language.

There exists an inherent misunderstanding over facts, even conclusions, between the true folklorist and the doubting mythologist. The folklorist, forgetting that "reality" is only that which is "believed," that it involves two people speaking about objects or words and is a consequence of agreement between them, strews it with "facts" and "events" and calls it "reality." Thus not only poetry but tales and myths are viewed from an exalted position as "creations" and "processes" of fantasy. Unaware—or perhaps unwilling or not able to know—that poetic, as well as mythic, language is not any poorer but only different from scientific language, the search for truth and its manner of expression, he regards figurative imagistic thinking as "imaginary," refusing to give it "reality" status. This is done as though a person's thoughts could not be considered as actual fact and, at the same time, become an object of scientific investigation, as if—let us go to absurd lengths—waving a hand would be a more "real" phenomenon than shouting "come here." Reality is not distributed and cannot be posited by halves—or by quarters—acknowledging objects but not thoughts about objects, acknowledging one's own thinking and discarding other "imaginings." Our 100 percent positivism, which has nothing in common with idealism, is thus an expression of a rejection of subconscious naiveté.

The mythologist does not have the right to separate "true" thinking from "false," confident that by appearance even the "most foolish" thought or saying has its own cause and can be explained. Mythology differs from "real" science only in that its object is not the world and its things, but what man thinks about the world, the objects and himself. In that sense, it must be acknowledged that the mythologist breathes a somewhat more rarefied air.

Fantasy is his reality, his chosen object of inquiry. Nevertheless, fantasy in the Lithuanian imagination is nothing more than thinking with images, not with abstract concepts. It is not an invention of nonexistent and unknown objects, if only because this language expressed in images and representations provides a means for communication, that with its help people reach agreement and understanding. With the exclusion of rare autistic cases unable to live in communities and closed off in separate institutions, imagistic, figurative language is universal, a common expression of all men, and it is used as much by the poet as by the shoemaker and—even though it might seem paradoxical—it is often more intimate for the shoemaker than for the poet, who belongs to a stratum of society more used to an abstract way of thinking: thus, what the poet holds as "invention," for example, for the shoemaker will more often be "a figment of the imagination."

The common opinion that fantasy is able to invent anything and speak any which way—is nothing more than one of the myths of romanticism, of unrestricted individual freedom. Positivism, which succeeded it, only interchanged the signs, replacing a plus with a minus and killing the desire of the individual to tear himself away from stereotypic norms of thought. Irrespective of these alternating ideological connotations in history, figurative language appears to be a compromise between individual freedom and social necessity. It is possible to consider the abundant collected works of Frazer—in the field of mythology—or of Bachelard—in the field of poetry—which point to the universality of mythic and poetic figures, and their membership in a common "fantasy" of humanity from several perspectives. The strictness of their theses must, it seems, be tempered by introducing variations, explaining the relativity of cultures in time and space, though the common "vision" about fire and water, of earth and sky as a figurative base remains unproblematic.

Linguistics, on the other hand, ascertained long ago that the formal means by which one or another living language changes the meaning of its words, is not only common to all spoken languages, but that mythology and poetry use the same metaphors and metonyms, as does our shoemaker. Mythological imagery is not different in essence from the figures of everyday language not only in form but partly in content: every linguistic community has proverbs, riddles, adages, and, especially, abundant oral stereotypes—in the East, the phrase is—the figurative reserves are the witnesses to a common national "memory."

One definition of language characterizes it as the possibility of utilizing one reality plane to speak about another: natural languages, for instance, utilize the plane of sounds not so as to express sounds, but to speak about the whole world. Figurative expression in this sense appears as the primary, autonomous language, recorded in everyday language and acting within its frames: the vocabulary of beekeeping belongs to general language insofar as it is used to speak of bees and their cultivation; but it becomes "language," that is, an autonomous code of expression, when it is used as in Lithuanian culture to speak of love and friendship, of people living together in harmony, of the woman's obligations and responsibilities. It is not important what such metalinguistic configurations—or figurative isotopies, or, in Lévi-Strauss's term, "concrete logics"—are called. Even though local in nature, they are social, constrained forms of imagery, having nothing in common with our folklorist's often-mentioned "products of fantasy."

One of the authorities of the French school of psychoanalysis, Jacques Lacan, has written in the introductory pages of his book, in motto form, the following advice to his students: Do crosswords! If you want to understand what goes on in the mind of man, what is inscribed in the memory of a nation, it is not enough to have abundant sources, strict methodological rules. While we acknowledge the importance of intuition, still we must yet trust imagination and from time to time exercise it by doing crosswords and reading detective novels.

Author's Note

This collection of separate studies is the result of a decade-long interest in Lithuanian mythology. Without claiming to have reached any definitive conclusions, the author attempts to raise partial problems and offer partial solutions. Reconstruction of the entire mythology is possible only after a lengthy and thorough collective effort. Different sections of this book are meant, first of all, to illustrate the methods used in mythological analysis at the present time, applying them to analysis of Lithuanian texts. Therefore, the descriptions that are provided represent only the first phase of the reconstruction.

The unavoidable use of secondary sources due to lack of access to archives is one of the reasons which may help explain any possible inaccuracies and erroneous interpretations. Faced with the dilemma of doing nothing or being content with existing incomplete resources—the more difficult, thankless path was chosen. Of course, this should not be a pretext to cover inadequacies in the present work. On this occasion the author also wishes to express his gratitude to fellow Lithuanians for their assistance in acquisition of texts, provision of books, and any corrections and suggestions.

I

KAUKAI

The Origin and Life of the Kaukas

Kaukas and Aitvaras

That the confusion of these two guardians of goods and providers of wealth is not a fact of the nineteenth century, a period which can be held as "folkloric," is indicated by the following text of Praetorius, in which the author in the seventeenth century already felt the need to specify the basic traits which allow the differentiation of the *kaukas* from the *aitvaras:*

> Jetziger Zeit nennen die Nadraver diese Barzdukkas auch Kaukuczus, die sie obigermassen beschreiben and halten davor, dass sie den Leuten Getreydicht und Reichthump zuschlappen; jedoch das sie dies von Aitwars, den man hie sonsten Alf heiszt, unterscheiden und zwar (1) wegen der Wohnung. Den die Barsdukai wohnen unter, der Aitwars aber über der Erden; (2) wegen ihrer Gestalt. Diese Barzdukken sind als Menschen anzusehen der Aitwars aber als ein Drach oder grosse Schlange, dessen Kopf feurig; (3) Die Bezdukken thun den Leuten, wo sie sich aufhalten, keinen Schaden, sondern bringen ihnen Nutzen, der Aitwars aber bringt ihnen auch Schaden. (4) Die Speise ist auch verschieden, den Kaukuczen geben sie Milch, Bier, oder ander Trinken, den Aitwars aber muss von dem Gekochten oder Gebratenen und zwar das Erste, wovon sonsten keiner was geschmeckt hat, gegeben werden.[1]

> [Nowadays the Nadravers also call these Barzdukkas Kaukuczus, whom they describe as mentioned before and claim that they bring people grain and wealth. They are distinct from the Aitwars, however, who are otherwise called Alf around here, for the following reasons: (1) Because of their dwellings. For the Barsdukai live underneath, the Aitwars above the ground. (2) Because of their features. These Barzduks look like people; the Aitwars, however, like a dragon or a big snake, with a fiery head. (3) The Bezduks brought the people, wherever they live, no harm, but good; the Aitwars, however also harm them. (4) Their food is also different. The Kaukuczes get milk, beer, or other drinks, but the Aitwars must be given the very first of what is cooked or roasted, before anyone else has tasted it.]

Noting in passing, that *kaukai* in the Praetorius text are referred to in the plural, while *aitvaras* is continually held as a deity in the singular, it is possible to record the following oppositions which differentiate these two deities:

(1) *kaukai* are *chthonic* beings, while *aitvaras* is an *air* being;

(2) *kaukai* are anthropomorphic beings, while *aitvaras* is a zoomorphic being (dragon or snake);

(3) *kaukai* are beneficent beings, while *aitvaras* is a complex being, benevolent as well as malevolent;

(4) *kaukai* are consumers of *raw food* (vegetable or at least vegetarian dishes), while *aitvaras* consumes both the *cooked* or *roasted* food.

Taking into account these basic differences noted in the seventeenth century, it is possible now to review the later ethnographic data of the nineteenth and twentieth centuries in order to determine the degree to which they confirm earlier texts as well as the degree to which they offer new explanations and an enlargement in our perspective. With that aim in mind, we will first analyze each of the deities separately, comparing them again when we have carried out both descriptions.

The Chthonic Origin of Kaukai

The first argument which can be used as a basis for the chthonic origin of the *kaukas* is lexical in nature. There is an entire series of suffixed derivatives grouped around the common root *kauk-: kaukolas, kaukolis,* and *kaukoulys* mean a clod of dried-out or frozen ground (*Lietuvių kalbos žodynas*, cited hereafter as *LKŽ* [Academic Dictionary of Lithuanian]), the same as the nominal verb *kaukuoti* which means "to break up clods of soil." By analogy, the first figure of *kaukas* that can be obtained corresponds to some of its representations: "kaukas forms a ball, the size of two fists." (LKŽ, Stk.)

Yet another meaning can be added to the word *kaukas* and its derivatives: a certain type of aromatic rootberry is called *kaukas, kaukelis,* or *kaukoris* (Mandragora officinarum). *Kauko šukos* [kaukas' comb] is the name of the plant which in appearance is reminiscent of a five-finger configuration; its magic power is connected to the underground world, "Comb yourself with them but don't break off even a little piece—or you will know what's in the earth." (LKŽ, Trgn.)

The fact that the permanent dwelling of *kaukai* is underground explains also the magic measures used by housekeepers who, if they wish to have *kaukai* in their homes, "would make cloaks out of a single thread and bury them in the ground beneath the corners of the house. . . ."[2]

With these first lexical and ritual facts, one may accept without any great doubt, since it does not contradict them, the mythic narrative of E. Gisevius[3] about the origin of *kaukai*, according to which the king's son Drąsus, having tried in vain to learn how to sculpt figures of men and beasts out of clay, one fine day noticed that something had started to move in the piece of the clay, from which there finally rolled out a great number of the kaukai led by their king, who had bowed deeply before him and disappeared forthwith.

It goes without saying that *kaukai*, born from the earth, most often choose cellars or granaries as their dwelling site: if they live in garrets and threshing rooms, as it is sometimes thought, the transference of their dwellings can be easily explained either by the influence of their functions as providers of grain and hay, or as a later merging with *aitvaras*. However, *kaukai*, by nature, are far from being household deities.

Kaukai and Barstukai

Indeed it appears that before their contract with people, the dwelling place of *kaukai* (or the diminutive form *kaukučiai*) was the forest. Lexical evidence once again helps to form the initial impression. Thus, for instance, the names of certain types of mushrooms or mushroom groups are compound words which contain the element *kaukas: kaukogrybis* is a type of mushroom (Phallus impudicus); *kaukatiltis* refers to a particular place where there are a great many mushrooms; *kaukaratis* is a circle of mushrooms: "don't build a fire on the *kaukaratis* or the *kaukeliai* [dim.] might come to spend the evening." (Trgn.)

Certain sixteenth and seventeenth century ethnographic sources, while they confirm the forest nature of *kaukai*, introduce additional confusion that emerges due to the synonymy of the *kaukai* with the *barstukai*, on the one hand, and the *barzdukai* and *bezdukai*, on the other. Praetorius once again attempts to determine strict differences between the one and the other:

> Einige Nadrauer haben auch einen Unterschied unter den Kaukczys und Bezdukkus. Diese wohnen eigentlich in den Wäldern unter den Bäumen, die Kaukuczei aber in den Scheunen, Speichern, auch Wohnhäusern. Beide aber nennen sie doch Barzdukkus, weil sie auff eine Art, zu mahlen was den Barth betrifft, gestalt seyn.[4]

> [Some of the Nadravers also differentiate between Kaukczys and Bezdukks. These normally live in the forests under the trees, the Kaukuczei, on the other hand, in barns, storehouses, even in homes. Nevertheless, they still call both Barzdukkus because of their similar features, especially their beards.]

It would appear that the single general name of *barzdukai* encompasses both *kaukai*, who live near people, and *bezdukai*, the forest dwellers.

The word *barzdukas* still in use in modern Lithuanian does not raise special difficulties. It is somewhat harder to accept the explanation by Praetorius that it is the bearded aspect of these chthonic dwarfs that motivates their name. At least, it seems, no one—unless perhaps in a quite understandable wish to bring them closer to their German kin—confers beards on the *kaukai* in their primitive state: having identified them with the clod of earth on the basis of their general form, we must proceed progressively to reconstruct their figurative aspect, which is much more primitive, less finished, less human, further removed from the conventional European representation of gnomes.

By contrast, due to the phonetic proximity of the word "barzda" [beard] the name *barzdukai* appears to be an easily understood reinterpretation of their other name, *barstukai*, noted by almost all sixteenth-and seventeenth-century authors (Lasicius, Strijkowski, Sudauerbuchlein, Hartnoch). Thus, for example, Lasicius, following Maletius closely, writes about "Barstuccas, quos Germani Erdmenlin, hoc est, subterraneos vocant"[5] [The Barstuccas that the Germans call Erdmanlin, that is to say underground] and who, according to him, are servants of the god *Putscetum*. People would turn to this god to send them "Barstuccae, quibus in domibus ipsorum viventibus, credunt se fieri fortunatiores"[6] [Barstuccae, because they believed they would be richer with these Barstuccae living in their homes]. Even though the etymology of this word seems to be uncertain (it is possible to regard it as a verbal noun derived from *berti* [to scatter] and from its frequentative form *barstyti*, which in turn, metaphorizing it a bit, allows for the meaning "distribution, scattering of wealth"), all the texts, which belong to the period between the major national religion and the "degraded" folk beliefs, support the following:

(a) *barstukai* belong to a deity hierarchically above them;

(b) that deity—whose name we write for the time being, according to Lasicius, as *Putscetum* (Lat. accusative)—lives, together with *barstukai*, under the elder tree (*Sambucus*);

(c) the offering made to him (or them) consists of bread, milk and ale;

(d) prayers to *Putscetum* request that *barstukai* be sent to the people and that they bring fortune and gain.

Kaukai: Consumers and Providers

Their nature does not change whether the food products are first given to the god *Putscetus* as an offering, or are given directly to the domesticated *kaukai* as food: with the exception of ale—which, as is known, is a ceremonial drink—these are always natural products of the earth, namely, a product of agriculture—bread, and a product of cattle breeding—milk. Since they are *raw* and vegetable in nature, they are, as we have seen, contrasted to *cooked* preparations, which the *aitvaras* feeds on.

As consumers of vegetarian foods, *kaukai* are also providers of earth's products: they increase the yield of grain (equal to the *bread* they eat) and of hay (equal to the *milk* they drink); if they sometimes bring clothing, then this gift, which belongs to another, separate activity sphere, appears to be of a considerably later origin. In contrast to *aitvaras*, who because of the syncretism of his functions with those of *kaukai* can also bring the same goods, the *kaukai* never bring money. *Kaukai* in this manner are manifested very clearly in their role as mediators, acting within the structural frames of mutual exchange between the earth and the people.

The concept of *provider* of wealth used at a later period to describe the basic function of these deities corresponds very imprecisely to the *modus operandi* of *kaukai*. In contrast to the *aitvaras* who provides material wealth directly by transferring it through space, the blade of hay or several grains brought by a *kaukas* is sufficient assurance of a never-ending treasure. The *kaukas* brings no material wealth but rather the so-called *skalsa*, which can be described as the mythic property of useable objects which causes them to be inexhaustible or consumed slowly. When it is said today, for instance, that stale bread is *skalsi*, this means that one can eat it until he is satiated and there will still be plenty left. Also, "skalsink Dieve" is an optative formula of appeal: we ask God that the food we eat never run out.

It is said that *kaukai* are "naudos skalsintojej"[7] — or, even more specifically, that *kaukas* is *skalsas*,[8] that he himself is, in essence, the principle of that constancy of useable goods [*nauda*], that property which makes them inexhaustible. Just as the earth, untiring and inexhaustible, out of which he has emerged, dispenses her abundant resources, the *kaukas* is the manifestation of the constancy of the earth's dynamic force.

The Mythological Framework of Kaukai

The Praetorius text just cited raises two types of difficulties: it distorts the common name of *barstukai*, the deities under analysis, which is verified by many authors of the sixteenth and seventeenth centuries, offering in its place a much more easily explained *barzdukai*, which brings them closer to the German Erdmännlein; it also introduces the *bezdukai*, distinct from *kaukai*, as household deities, calling these same beings by this new name if they live in the forest.

All these authors (Maletius, Lasicius, Praetorius, Sudauerbüchlein) are in agreement that *barstukai* (for Praetorius—*barzdukai*) and their guardian god *Putscetus* live under *elderberry* bushes.[9] Praetorius even explains that this tree or rather bush is otherwise called *bezdas*, a fact which is confirmed by modern lexicography, with the only difference being that it refers to two types of odors: the one, *Syringa*, which is fragrant, and the other, *Sambucus*, which spreads an unpleasant odor, are often confused and called by one and the same name (LKŽ). Only the second type, which grows in the forest, is of interest to us, along with the derivatives of the same family: the verb *bezdėti* [to fart] and the noun *bezdalas* [a fart] confirms the very nature of the *bezdas-sambucus* smell.

These data explain that the *bezdukas*, a forest parasynonym of kaukas, is named both for his dwelling—the elderberry-bezdas bush—and for its characteristically unpleasant odor.[10] Recalling that a rootberry having a certain odor is called *kaukas*, the figure of the *kaukas*, already compared to a clod of earth, is now supplemented by new traits of an olfactory nature.

The name of the god *Putscetus* "qui sacris arboribus et lucis praest" (Lasicius), or *Putscaetus* "deu(s), qui sacros lucos tuetur" (Maletius), which we identify as the ruler of the *barstukai*, also causes difficulties. Supported by the most banal definition, the typical stereotype of the Renaissance, which specifies that this divinity is the guardian of the forests and sacred groves, ethnographers, it seems, were in quite a hurry to identify him with *Pušaitis, a name formed out of the root of the word *pušis* [pine tree].

Maletius's spelling, of course, does allow one to recognize without difficulty the Lithuanian suffix -*ait-is* in the Latin -*aet-us*. At the same time can the root of the word even be identified with *puš-is*? Either the grapheme group -*tsc*-, if *e* follows, can be read as *š*, in which case then it is not possible to identify the Lithuanian suffix -*aitis* in the Latin -*etum*; or this suffix corresponds to the Latin -*aetum*, but in that case *c* before *a* must be pronounced as *k* and the cluster -*ts*- preceding it then will correspond to the phoneme *š*. In other words, there can only be two Lithuanian interpretations of this name: the god referred to can be either *Pušėtas or *Puškaitis. To these types of inaccuracies, which can be explained by means of graphemes, there can be added the semantic weaknesses of the etymology. It is not clear why a god whose name is motivated by the root of a word that means pine tree [*pušis*] would choose to live under the elder bushes when all around there is no lack of pines; it is equally difficult to imagine what mythic relationship could be perceived between the pine tree and *kaukai*. Rather than the literary stereotype from the Renaissance, the definition offered by Strijkowski (1582) appears to be more convincing: he sees *Putscaetus* as a god of the earth. This definition is superior by the simple fact that it corresponds to the chthonic origin of *kaukai*, which we are trying to establish. Only this latter interpretation allows one to understand somewhat the Lasicius text according to which people turn to *Putscetus*, not only to ask him to send them the *barstukai* that bring riches, but also "precantes eum ut placatum efficiat Marcoppolum, deum magnatum et nobilium, ne gravi servitute ab illis premantur"[11] ["Implore him to appease *Marcoppolum*, the god of the mighty and the noble, so that they (the people) will not have to put up with unbearable servitude"]. Though not much is known about *Marcoppolum*, it is not difficult to imagine *Putscetus*, the god of an earth not broken by the plough, living beyond the boundaries of cultivated fields, perhaps even a god of clearings, mediating and interceding for people with the god of the big landowners; and conversely, we cannot understand on what basis "the guardian of the sacred groves" could intervene.

It is possible then to offer as a hypothesis a new etymology. If the names of *Pušaitis* (or *Pušėtas*) are rejected, and the name of *Puškaitis* is accepted, then its root, *pušk*-, could belong to the same family as the verb *pušk-uoti*,[12] "to breath deeply," or the noun *pušk-as*. Such an etymology would allow us to unite all three figures of *Puškaitis, otherwise reconcilable with difficulty, into one mythic representation of a god who is an incarnation of that earth which breathing deeply [*puškuodama*] and spreading scents with the assistance of *bezdai* [farts] gives birth to chthonic outgrowths: *barstukai-bezdukai-kaukai*.

The Cultural Contract

We must consider it then an established fact that *barstukai-kaukai*, as chthonic beings, live in the forest in accordance with their nature where they serve the god *Puškaitis, who appears to be the guardian of the farmers: by sending them his subjects, the *kaukai*, he increases, or at least conserves, their resources and mediates by protecting them from exploitation by the upper classes. Living in the woods, *Puškaitis, is spatially separated not only from those he guards but also from the agrarian deities (such as *Žemėpatis*, the guardian of the animal herds or *Laukpatis*, the guardian of the fields), which belong directly to Dumézil's third function. He differs from them further in that his guardianship is never direct, but mediated, effected through the help of intermediaries: he either intercedes on behalf of the farmers with *Mar-

coppolum, a deity, who could possibly belong to Dumézil's second function, or hears out their prayers by sending them *bezdukai,* who, transforming themselves into *kaukai,* will act directly as the guardians and providers of goods. Thus **Puškaitis* may be considered a god who belongs to "natural space" (manifested in the form of the forest) as well as an emanation of nature which breathes life into nature. He also is part of those wild forces that are capable of acting toward the "cultural" world only through mediating procedures.

Praetorius, while compiling an exhaustive list of sorcerers capable of communicating with various aspects of the sacred, differentiates among them a class of pagan priests who know how to carry out the "acculturation" of the *kaukai:* "Kaukuczones oder Baržtukkones vermochten die kleinen Erd-oder Goldmanner, die Kaukuszus zu beschworen, das sie sich an diesem oder jenem Ort aufhalten sollten."[13] [Kaukuczones or Barztukkones were able to conjure the little earth or gold people, the Kaukuszus, to settle in this or that place.]

Moving in this manner from the information presented by Lasicius to the Praetorius text, it is possible to observe in the acculturation process of the *kaukai* a certain number of changes: in place of a contractual relation with the god **Puškaitis,* determined by offerings accompanied by prayers and manifested by the sending of *kaukai* to people, in the Praetorius text we can note the disappearance of a god and the appearance in his place of a sorcerer-mediator, who, having knowledge of a magic formula, compels *kaukai* to choose one, and not another, "cultural" settlement. Nevertheless not only do the two descriptions not contradict one another but, more likely, they supplement each other: the presence of the god **Puškaitis* by no means interferes with the existence of a sorcerer and his use of effective forms of prayers and rituals. Only one more thing is needed: the above-mentioned texts do not specify the formulas or rituals with which the attachment of the *kaukai* to the household are carried out, neither their precise form nor content, thus obligating us to analyze the subsequent ethnographic data for additional information in this area.

We find in the ethnographic texts, as expected, signs of "religious degradation": the already noted disappearance of the deity from the text corresponds to the disappearance of the sorcerer-mediators within the lower levels of folkloric facts; the actors who enter into the cultural contract are, on the one hand, the *kaukai,* and, on the other, the mistress of the farm. Mythic operations accurately described compensate in that case for the disappearance of representatives of the sacred.

A fair number of ethnographic texts recount without significant digressions the domestication of the *kaukai.* The fact that these texts do not contradict each other allows us to count them as complementary and to apply the procedure of string analysis, arranging all the pertinent information syntagmatically thus reconstructing their unified and complete history.

The Story of the Domestication of the Kaukai

(1) The first appearance of *kaukai* in the farmstead is manifested in a totally unexpected place with the discovery of a worthless trifle or simply, a *woodchip.*[14] On the

part of the *kaukai*, this represents a discreet offer of a contract: with the acceptance of these "gifts" by the farmer, the first contractual relations are entered into.

(2) Seeing that their gift has been accepted, the *kaukai* may manifest themselves: they then appear sometimes dressed in rags, sometimes entirely naked.[15] Or they can be heard lamenting and weeping: "I'm naked, you're naked. Who will dress us?"[16]

(3) Then the mistress of the house, if she wishes to domesticate the *kaukai*, who quite often come in pairs, must try to dress them properly. For this task she chooses a Thursday which falls on the *waning* of the moon and begins to sew a garment of *flax*. This garment—sometimes a simple cloak or shirt—must be made overnight, from Thursday into Friday, and its production must incorporate all the phases of the preparation of flax: if some more rationalistic observers are satisfied by pointing out that the mistress of the house (or her daughter) must spin, weave, and sew the garment that night,[17] other texts do not count the practical possibilities of these operations and offer a complete program for the transformation of flax, which begins with the sowing and continues with the reaping, threshing, drying, spinning, and so on up to the sewing of the garment.[18]

(4) The garment made in this way forms the *wages*,[19] one of the elements of the contract that joins the entire family to its *kaukas*. It is necessary to emphasize the fact that the terms of this contract are especially strict. If, for instance, the mistress of the house is unable to make the garment in one night, then the benevolent *kaukas* changes back into a naked *kaukas* and empties the granary and threshing floor of the barn for someone else's benefit.[20] The same happens if the terms of the contract are carried out in excess, if, for instance, the mistress of the house out of a deep sympathy calls on the tailor and orders the clothes through him,[21] or more generally, if in addition to the garment set out by the contract, she prepares other kinds of gifts: then the *kaukai* start to cry, lamenting their fate, and forthwith disappear.[22]

(5) The fulfillment of the contract consists of mutual gifts. The *kaukai* bring to the household *skalsa*:[23] the blade of grass they bring is worth a full cart, a few kernels stands for several bushels of grain. For her part, the housekeeper feeds the *kaukai* by leaving out an appropriate vegetarian meal for them every night.[24]

(6) With any break in the provision of food, or especially, if in jest dried-out manure[25] (which is an inverted food form) is provided in place of the agreed-upon food, the contract is broken and the ire of the *kaukai* is raised: they then seek revenge, setting fire to the granary, or even more peculiarly, they perish in the fire themselves.[26]

Elements of Interpretation

(1) The fact that the *kaukas* manifests himself, first of all, with the gift of a *woodchip* proves not only his forest nature as a provider. In contrast to the *aitvaras*, whose initial contact with people takes place in a similar manner, except that he leaves a lump of *coal*,[27] the *kaukas* announcing his presence with a fragment of wood, emphasizes his membership in a sphere of cosmology different from that of the *aitvaras*. Indeed, the woodchip placed by a *kaukas* or the coal left by an *aitvaras* are not the actual gifts, but the promise of gifts, certain indexical signs indicating what

one or the other can provide through the transformation of these "natural" signs into "cultural" objects. Coal, a pure and "natural" object produced through the help of fire, allows one to foresee its transformation into a "cultural" object—into gold coins, which *aitvaras* will bring; the woodchip is also a "natural" result of the earth's production: the products will be supplied later in its place, to be "culturalized" through man's labors (grain and hay). This allows us, therefore, to establish a homologous ratio between two parallel series:

$$\frac{\text{Earth}}{\text{Kaukas}} : \frac{\text{dried-out wood (woodchip)}}{\text{grain}} :: \frac{\text{Fire}}{\text{Aitvaras}} : \frac{\text{burned-up wood (charcoal)}}{\text{gold coins}}$$

(2) Thus, the fact that the *kaukas* arrives *naked* at his place of domestication and that his integration into civilized society occurs figuratively when he becomes clothed indicates that the acculturation contract is found in the *vestimentary culture isotopy* and that the crossover from the *natural state* to the *cultural state* takes place with the help of the semantic categories[28] *naked* vs. *clothed*. This not only encompasses the domestication but the actual humanization of *kaukai* (since crossing from the savage state into the domestic state takes place in an entirely different isotopy); the clothed *kaukas* at once joins the human community. Now it can more easily be understood why this change in status, which is a change in his nature as well, is accompanied according to Praetorius by a name change—why *bezdukas* becomes *kaukas*. We can even legitimately ask ourselves whether such a transformation is accompanied as well by a change in the guardian, whether *bezdukas*, who is protected by the god of "nature" *Puškaitis*, does not cross over, when becoming *kaukas* into the jurisdiction of some type of "cultural" deity.

(3) If the passage of the *kaukas* from a natural state to the cultural state can be explained at the deep structure content level as a logical transformation, realized through the use of the discrete terms of the category *naked* vs. *clothed,* then the manifestation of this passage appearing on the surface level of narrative structures is figurative and represented in the form of a process, which encompasses the preparation of the cloth and the sewing of the garment.

To clothe the *kaukas* does not mean to dress it simply in a child's shirt:[29] on the contrary, it means in the form of a symbolic summary to represent the entire complicated procedure of flax preparation, a procedure which in other texts is called *Lino Kančia*[30] [the Torment of Flax (Linas)]. This Torment—to which alone one should devote a separate study to appreciate the importance of the vestimentary plane in Lithuanian culture and religion—consists of an entire series of the most varied tortures which the flax must experience: trampling, bone-breaking, soaking in the deadly waters of the pond, and finally burning, which appears in our text in three different forms:

(a) First of all, as *metaphoric allusion:* "He has endured the Torment of Linas" is said about a person who has had a difficult life.[31] The Torment, which lasts an entire year and is renewed year after year, takes on in this manner the dimensions of man's life. Actually such a torment surpasses man's strength, since "not even the Devil can endure the torments of flax."[32]

(b) *Lino Kančia* is encountered in story form in which a man promises his soul to the Devil with the condition that the latter will first suffer through all the phases of the Torment: the Devil agrees to turn into a flax seed but manages to endure the torments only up to the trial by fire: when he starts to burn, he drops everything and runs away.[33] We see that these attempts by the Devil are not some kind of extended metaphor, but, conversely, a *mythic operation* of great complexity and extreme difficulty, which can be carried out only by a representative embodied as flax of an appropriate divine sphere which corresponds to the meaning of the myth. Meanwhile an entirely different sacred sphere in the story is represented by the Devil.

(c) Nevertheless *Lino Kančia* most often appears as a narrative situated within the frame of another, broader story in which it has a distinct function: as an effective magic formula, capable of stopping the malevolent activity of an opponent, here none other than the Devil.[34] A man who has started to narrate the Torments of Flax—which, as is known, is unending since even the tortures of the flax are many and varied—compels the Devil against his will to hear out this entire story without end thus interrupting—until the cock's first crow, which announces the end of the Devil's power—his already begun persecution of a victim. Consequently, the story appears to be an *uninterrupted* and *unending* narrative: as a narrative it appears as if it were a certain canonic formula: the fact that it cannot be interrupted invests it with a magic power whose nature is contrary to the nature of the Devil; finally, as an unending narrative it formally expresses the infinite distance which separates Nature from Culture, the state of being naked from that of being clothed.

In the group of tales to which we are referring, the magic formula conveyed by the Torments of Flax has a characteristic *separation* function: it serves to protect the human world of the living from the intrusion of the Devil, the ruler of the world of the spiritual-dead (i.e., *vėlės*).[35] However, as to the case of the domestication of the *kaukas*, which is of interest to us here, the same procedure expressed through the retelling of the Torment is manifested conversely as a *unification* function, as a possible passage from Nature to Culture, transforming "natural beings" into "cultural beings," such as, namely, the clothed *kaukai* become.

From these observations it is possible, hypothetically, to draw two inferences. *Lino Kančia*, as we have seen, only appears as either a retelling of a mythic operation—the Devil's metamorphoses into Flax—or as a canonic formula possessing magic powers. It appears self-evident that the description of the domestication of the *kaukai* should not be taken literally, that it should be viewed as a ritualistic, perhaps somewhat degraded, formula, with which *kaukučionys*, sorcerers, who knew how to settle the *kaukai* among people, at one time would magically carry out the domestication. On the other hand, the Devil's unsuccessful attempt to endure the Torments after having turned into flax clearly indicates that the Torment as such forms a functional, relatively autonomous sacred sphere and that Linas itself is only a material incarnation of a deity who represents this sphere and guarantees magic power through the formula of a symbolic transformation which was used, in this case, by the sorcerer, or in his absence, by the mistress of the homestead. This deity, mediating between Nature and Culture, manifested on the vestimentary culture plane, could only be *Vaižgantas,* the god of flax, whose feast and its rituals have been quite extensively described by Lasicius.[36]

Another Origin of Kaukas

Kaukas and the Boar

Up to now we have attempted to reconstruct, step by step, the entire history of *kaukai,* beginning first with their chthonic nature—which became clarified, among other ways, through the multiple meanings of their name, in turn allowing for the comparison of their appearance to the image of a clod of earth or rootberry called by the same name—then describing their underground or above-ground life in the forest and, finally, placing their socialization fulfilled through mediating procedures on the vestimentary culture plane.

Man could ensure the help of the *kaukai* by turning to **Puškaitis,* the ruler of the *kaukai* who, as has become apparent, is not so much a deity of the forests as the deity of *uncultivated earth,* breathing primitive energy and vitality and, in every case, found beyond the boundaries of the social and cultural world: in this context kaukai appear as a spontaneous emanation of this earth, her outgrowth.

Thus it is even more interesting to ascertain that next to the already described forms of acculturation of the *kaukai* there exists yet another way of enticing them and ensuring their guardianship, namely, to hatch them out of a boar's testicles. There is frequently encountered in our rather abundant folkloric material—we have already underscored this—quite a bit of ambiguity and contradiction which goes as far back as the sixteenth century, due to the confusion of the appearance and functions of *kaukas* and *aitvaras.* This problem was analyzed quite adequately by Basanavičius,[37] who, at least in this area, set down sufficiently distinct differences between the *kaukas* and the *aitvaras.* Therefore, we will not return to them, maintaining as definitive two separate origins for the *kaukas* and the *aitvaras*: if the former can roll out of a boar's testicles then the latter can hatch, under similar circumstances, from a rooster's egg.

The procedure for the acquisition of a *kaukas* (or, sometimes, two *kaukai*) is quite simple—one must slaughter, on exactly the same day as he was born, a seven-year old boar,[38] cut off his testicles and in one way or another hatch them. The actual hatching—which should correspond to the acculturation phase—in our text is neither completely nor uniformly described: sometimes one must put them in a warm place (on a stove),[39] sometimes place them under a rooster[40] (a mixing with the origins of the *aitvaras*), or again—and this is more significant—place them on some fluff inside a hole created in a pillar of the porch doorway—and, boarding up that opening, to wait until the newborn himself announces, rapping and tapping, that he has now hatched. This last version can have the significance of an allusion: it is as if the wood points to the forest origins of the *kaukas* and the porch doors—the passage from the "natural" exterior to the "cultural" interior.

The Boar and the Rooster

The relationship between *kaukas* and the *boar,* which could not have been foreseen earlier, can be explained only by inscribing it into a double network of relations, only by taking into account, on the one hand, the parallelism between the *aitvaras* and the *rooster* and, on the other, the relationship between the *kaukas* and the *earth.*

The choice of the rooster and the boar as "fertility symbols" at first glance is self-explanatory: the rooster is well-known as a polygamist, and the boar, in his own way, has exceptional impregnation capabilities. It is necessary to add that the name of the boar—*kuilys*—is derived from *kuila,*[41] "rupture," "hernia," and this is added lexicographic evidence of his procreative capabilities.

However, it seems more interesting to ascertain as much in the case of the boar as in the case of the rooster the notable inversion of signs in the semantic categories *male* vs. *female* [of the animal species]. This inversion, which contends that the *male* and not the female can give birth to the mythic being, can be explained as the negation of "natural" process and affirmation of the "supernatural." The assertion that the *male* alone can give birth to a supernatural being logically requires us to assume not only the presence of a *female*/birthmother, but foresees another normal possibility of birth, as a result of the union of male and female elements.

It appears that the female element, balancing the male element—the boar—actually exists: it is the earth, out of which, as seen in the first part of this description, the *kaukai* appeared to originate. In addition, without attempting to analyze the figure of the *aitvaras* more closely, it is possible to establish a strong connection between the *aitvaras* and fire, which appears as one of the basic elements that form his nature. Keeping in mind that fire is of female gender and that, on the other hand, the rooster is closely tied to the concept of fire,[42] it is possible without further hesitation to establish the following correlation:

$$\frac{\text{Kaukas}}{\text{Aitvaras}} : \frac{\text{Earth}}{\text{Fire}} : \frac{\text{boar}}{\text{rooster}}$$

which explains the dual origin of both mythic beings—they can be born separately from either the female or male element.

Kaukas—"glands," Kaukė—"pestle," and Kaukas—"boil"

Even though the image of the boar as a being who roots around in the earth is quite suggestive in itself, it is not sufficient for establishing a stable, complementary relation between the boar and the earth. Lexical data can once again be of help: for instance, the word *kaukos* (s.f.pl.), "glands," "pig's jaw," can be added to the exposition of the nuclear figure of *kaukas* itself; this figure, similar in appearance to a clod of earth, distinguished by an unpleasant odor, is supplemented now with the help of this new image by the new features: *softness, dampness.*

These same features are found in the word *kaukė* (and its synonymous derivative *kaukorė*) which means "pestle to pound bacon" or "wooden dish to hold mashed fat and bacon"(LKŽ). We must take this opportunity to direct our attention to the rather interesting distribution of meanings encountered here, according to which the opposition *feminine and/or plural* vs. *masculine* is correlated with the opposition *contained* (object) vs. *containing* (object). Such a distribution seems to represent a separate case in the more general interpretation offered by Hjelmslev, appropriate to Slavic languages.[43] In our case, this differentiation of meaning not only explains that, on the one hand, we find the masculine *kaukas* as "household deity," "a clod of earth," "rootberry" and so forth, and, on the other hand, the feminine and/or plural words such as *kaukai* as "child's shirt," *kaukos* "jaws," *kaukė* "pestle" but also that it can be used as an interpretive model for the comprehension of other facts in the same series: for instance, if we consider *kaukolė* or *kaukė* "carnival mask" as the "containing object," then we can certainly ask what could be the corresponding content of the "contained object."

In light of these facts, perhaps we can better understand yet another opposition which becomes more distinct from a comparison of the *kaukas* to the *aitvaras*, involving a specification of all the illnesses which one or another can inflict: if an *aitvaras* infects one with *kaltūnas* (Plica polonica) then a *kaukas*, made angry by people who have shown him the finger, can start a boil[44] [*kiaul-niežis*] (*LKŽ*), which is a synonym for *kaukas*. The shape of these boils is spheroidal, filled with glandular, fatty matter, both soft and wet; we see that the image of *kaukas* as a "boil" is similar in every respect to the appearance of *kaukas* as *dievukas* [little deity], which we are attempting to disclose here little by little.

Storm, Hail, and Summer Lightning

In this way thanks to lexical data, the "natural" kinship between *kaukas* and his apparent father, the boar, and more generally, the entire swine family, come to be resolved. However, it still remains for us to analyze the sources which disclose the relations between the earth and the boar (or sow).

Animal fat, as is known, is a "fertility symbol" and it is with the help of this symbolism that its use in agrarian rituals is commonly explained. For instance, in the rites of ploughing the first furrow in the spring, the farmer goes to the fields carrying lard and bacon provided by the wife, who reminds him to eat some himself and not to forget to apply some to his plough:[45] thus the ploughman together with his plough which pierces the earth are, as we see, both smeared with pork fat.

There is more. In a very important spring festival—Jurginės [St. George's Day]— a special ceremony is held to raise the rye [*kelti rugius*], that is, to help them grow;[46] during the ceremony people circle the fields in a procession, "jurginėja," burying shells from Easter eggs and *bones from the ham*[47] at the boundaries.

Another text[48]—disregarding the actual date of the ceremony[49]—presents other details that concern this ritual: the bones of the Easter ham (no mention of the eggs) must be buried not in one place but at *all four boundaries* [ežia]. In such a manner, the setting of boundaries for the fields, with the purpose of protecting them—this ceremony's significance—is carried out twofold: circling of the field together with the burial of the ham bones at all four of its boundaries. This constitutes then a fencing off of the field, its boundary-setting procedure, in which the bones of the pig play either the role of the guardian of the fields, or serve the function of an offering to the god-guardians of the fields.

The second précis offered by the text indicates that the aforementioned ritual which is meant to guard the fields from *hail* can also be used against *thunder*. However, if protection against misfortune brought on by hail seems to be entirely understandable, defense against thunder requires some explanation.

The word *perkūnija* [thunder] as a derivative from the name of the god *Perkūnas* defines a common atmospheric phenomenon: the sound effect (thunderclap) and light effect (lightning), together with its damage-rendering consequences.

To protect the fields from thunder means nothing more than to protect them from the consequences of thunder. These consequences, in turn, can appear only after the earth is reborn: we know quite well that the spring activity of *Perkūnas* is beneficial, that with his first thunderclap he "unlocks the earth," making her fecund.[50] The devastation caused by *Perkūnas* can only be manifested later, and not through thunder or lightning, but through their consequences. These consequences can be malevolent, keeping in mind now only the grain fields, only in the form of rain or, namely, the "ruined," negative forms of rain.

The first of these negative consequences is the *storm* [audra], that is, the abnormal, boundless—both in amount and intensity—type of rain. Lasicius already directs our attention to this agrarian activity of Perkūnas, even citing an appropriate Lithuanian prayer for this occasion with which the farmer addresses him: "Percune deuaite niemuski vnd mana, dievvu melsu tavvi *palti* miessu."[51] The Lithuanian text indicates that a flitch of bacon is an appropriate offering to appease Perkunas, but the Latin translation of that text inaccurately explains further that the issue is the protection of the fields and not, for instance, one's personal protection from lightning: "Cohibe te inquit Percune, neue in meum *agrum* calamitatem immittas."[52]

The moisture which falls from the sky appears in two forms: *rain* or *snow* and their mixing is called sleet [*darga, dargna,* or *dargana (LKŽ)*]. It is characteristic that the sow which otherwise seems a rather hardy creature responds very poorly to sleet and cannot stand it. She reacts, first of all, with diarrhea[53] and vomiting,[54] which are physiological reactions; the sow responds "psychologically" as well, starting to "čiudytis," that is, "to act peculiarly, mocking and sneering."[55] This protest of the sow—or more likely of the *boar*—against the mixing of the waters of the sky with snow, which affirms their relations with rain, is reminiscent of yet another ironic reaction of the sow to the mixing of rain with the sun: it is said that "the sow is laughing," if it starts to rain while the sun is shining.[56]

The other two forms of "ruined" rain are *hail* or *ice* and *summer lightning* [*amalas*]. The word *amalas* is polysemic: as "lightning without thunder" it refers to the initial cause of the phenomenon, which provokes a rain of a sweet, sticky liquid (Lat. mellis ros; *LKŽ*); when "amalas krečia" or "amalas meta" [57] [lightning strikes], then the earth is sprinkled with that liquid and the crops are "ruined," as well as fruit trees at blossoming time; the result of the jolts by amalas is a crop disease (Lat. aphis) called by the same name *amalas* (or *amaras*): in the polysemy, *amalas* also means *fog* (both meanings correspond to French *nielle*): "(miodowa rosa) iszejn isz wundenum isz ipiun ežerun migla tokia yra paskuj krynt unt žola yr medžiu gadindama juos diel to szalip upiu ta liga tunkiuausiej matoma."[58] [Fog comes from the lake and river and then falls on the grass and trees, ruining them. Thus this disease is seen mostly near rivers.]

A separate study would be necessary to describe the diverse phenomena covering the entire polysemy of *amalas*.[59] For now let us limit ourselves to the types of damaging wet material that attack the fields and destroy the harvest.

In conclusion we can say that the request made while burying the pig's bones touches all aspects of the harmful waters that fall from above: the heavy rains, manifested in the form of a *storm* and the two types of "ruined" rain—*hail* as the union of rain with cold, and *lightning* [amalas], the mixing of water with fire and heat. Such a formulation is confirmed by rain's useful purpose: "amalas . . . nevodij kad lytus nuplaun tuoj nukritus (amalui) . . . "[60] [rain washes away amalas]. Nevertheless, the earth, the female partner of the heavenly waters in the fecundation process, also plays a guardian role. Here, for instance, during Ledų diena [Wednesday after Easter] (and somewhat later during Joninės [St. John's Day]), it is forbidden to "disturb" the earth[61]—and similarly, when *amalas* attacks the grain crops, it is necessary to sprinkle earth on them that has been brought over from the crossroads and the lightning will immediately vanish.[62] Thus, here again the elements of our description are grouped together: on the one hand, there is the earth, and on the other, the sow performing in the role of guardian and mediator in relation to the waters of the sky.

The Sow and the Cloud

We have just made an attempt to explain what at first glance appears as a strange connection between the sow and various malevolent forms of water that threaten the harvest: *storm, hail,* and *lightning*. Now it behooves us to extend the problematic somewhat and review the ethnographic data which touches on the relations between our mythic creature and the waters from the sky, especially those between the *rain* and its source, the *clouds*.

At first glance it seems that there is a simple antecedent relation between the sow [kiaulė] and the rain: *kiaulmiegis*,[63] for instance, is the sound sleep [miegas] before rain. But this connection will very likely be more narrow: we know, for instance, that the common relation of two occurrences following one another in a given time frame is often explained as a causal relation. Therefore in legends, the appearance of an enormous sow, immediately followed by a *storm*, means that there exists a strong reciprocal connection and not a simple contiguous occurrence in time:[64] if it would be too much to say that the appearance of the sow provokes the appearance of the cloud, then at least it "forecasts" the cloud.

It should be noted in this situation that the connection between the waters of the sky and the earth is, within the framework of the world view of Lithuanian myths, more complementary than oppositional. For instance, the rainbow which appears after the rain is called *dermės juosta*[65] [sash of harmony]: its function is to absorb the overflow of rainwater and to return it to the sky, thus restoring the original equilibrium. In this context, it becomes easier to understand the Lithuanian belief that lakes are actually clouds that have descended from the sky to previously chosen sites.

In the legends about the origin of lakes, the sow appears in just this manner in her role as the explorer, helper and herald. At first either the sow appears entirely unexpectedly[66] or a barrow falls directly out of a cloud[67] and begins to root around in the earth, preparing a place for the descending cloud.

After establishing this close tie between the sow and the cloud, it can be understood why shepherds would pray to the little cloud to float by, promising a piglet in the name of the Ruthenian neighbor to the East.[68] On the other hand, there being no essential difference between the waters of the earth and the sky, the offering of a white piglet to the god *Upinis*[69] mentioned by Stryjkowski, as a request for clean and clear water, can be inscribed into the same context.

Now we can explain the intensifying adage (of the same type as 'white as snow', for instance) which sets out the entire misunderstanding: "you know as much about the cloud as a pig,"[70] is an expression turned antiphrastic, no longer comprehending the mythic tie between the piglet and the cloud. A somewhat earlier text, which, conversely, states that the pig "knows a great deal about where the cloud goes,"[71] reconstructs the mythic truth.

From the ethnographic material available at this time it is difficult to say how far this comparison between the sow and the cloud can be drawn. It seems to us that it would not be possible to come to a definitive identification of these two mythic beings, as some texts apparently would like to suggest: even though here, for instance, the strange atmospheric phenomena in which rain starts to fall while the sun is shining is explained by people as either that "the sun is crying,"[72] or that "the sow is laughing."[73] In place of a metaphoric relation, it is better to regard this as a metonymic relation: the sow, due to an identification of characteristics common to both, it seems, is a partial substitute for the cloud.

Kaukas: Earth and Water

In every case, as the defender of the cultivated earth from the malevolent rain, as the prophet of beneficial rain and the driver of clouds, the sow, without a doubt, has close ties to the waters of the sky and appears as their representative on earth and on the surface of the earth. As to the agrarian *Perkūnas*[74]—who fecundates the earth, i.e., the goddess Žemyna,[75] for the first time—the boar, in a certain sense, stands in for him, assuring with the wise distribution of the waters the growth and prosperity of all that are born of the earth.

Taking into account this close tie between the sow and the waters of the sky, which, while liquid in the form of rain, turn solid during the time of hail and viscous in the case of lightning, it is now possible to supplement the primary nuclear figure for *kaukas* born of the boar. As much as the development of *kaukas* in two phases—

from the boar's testicles and their comparison to the mythic beings born from them, as well as the utilization of the word *kaukas* in the naming of its related forms (pig's glands, boils)—this basic figure of *kaukas* derived from the boar, while it preserves on the visual plane the same shape of a spheroidal, unfinished, uncontoured mass, nevertheless, in the portrait of the *kaukas* we are attempting to reconstruct as originating from the earth, is supplemented by new features which are characteristic of its "content," a content which is formed of a liquid, damp, soft, viscous substance, which does not necessarily correspond to *kauke* as "clod of earth" but in which it is possible to identify the *kauke* as "rootberry."

Thus, to the attempt to explain the opposition of *kaukas* and *aitvaras*, by homologating it with the opposition *earth* and *fire*, we can now add a new category: *water* and *air*. We have observed from the very beginning, and we will later find, that Aitvaras is a creation of *both air and fire*: and it is becoming apparent that *kaukas*, in turn, is formed of two other basic elements: *earth* and *water*.

$$\frac{\text{Kaukas}}{\text{Aitvaras}} :: \frac{\text{earth + water}}{\text{fire + air}}$$

This only confirms the dual nature of those two beings, so different in their characters but in the course of time, due to the similarity of their functions, becoming confused and finally identical.

The Complex Figure of Kaukas

Putting together all the data in the description of *kaukas* as child of the earth and *kaukas* as son of the boar, it is possible now to attempt to reconstruct its original image. This many-faceted figure of the *kaukas*, nevertheless, has nothing in common with its conventional representation which we find in later texts, marked by the influence of Germanic folklore: it is most certainly not a long-bearded, happy-faced, elf sporting a jaunty red cap.

We have already noted that the grammatical opposition *masculine* vs. *feminine* and/or *plural* corresponds to the semantic distribution of meaning of the category *containing* vs. *contained*. Now we can imagine the *contained* content of the *kaukas* figure as one composed of a soft and damp substance, a mixture of earth and water. This distribution of meanings, although not absolute, still allows us to regroup the many meanings of the word *kaukas* and its derivatives, and in this manner to determine the so-called "nuclear" figure of *kaukas*, i.e., the general configuration of essential traits, which makes possible and accounts for all the meanings of a word scattered during the processes of formation into a variety of "figurative meanings."

(a) The spheroidal form of kaukas
To the customary inventory of images of "clod of earth," "root," "glands," "boil," we can add the word *kvaukė*,[76] "head," and "makaulė," a phonetic variant of *kaukė*, and especially *kaukolė* [skull], and *kvaukolė*,[77] words whose first—figurative—meaning, and—second—literal meaning, refer to a spheroidal, *hollow* figure.

The word *kvaukis*[78] (s. mob.), designating a woman or man who "ties a scarf leaving the forehead bare" (*LKŽ*), is often applied to *laumės*,[79] suggestive of a kinship with these female-gender deities and reminiscent as well of the sow which differs from the other animals by not having horns. The derivative *kaukarikas*[80] and compound word *kauk-delis*[81] meaning "back of the head," complete the oval, spheroidal appearance of *kaukas*.

(b) Spheroidal form + long nose
The same word *kvaukis*, (s. com.), which describes the owner of a round and bald forehead is also used to name a person with a long nose,[82] a feature which apparently will be common to both *kaukas* and *laumė*. This exaggerated elongated outgrowth in the shape of a hook, which is attached to a spheroid figure, permits and explains the metaphoric namings of *kaukas* as *kvaukes*[83] "wooden shoes" and as *kaukas*[84] "fishing hook."

It appears that this last figure explains as well the significance of the word *kaukė* as "carnival mask." We will return to this point later.

(c) Spheroidal form + long nose + thin and elongated body
A round, shapeless head, decorated with a knobby outgrowth, sometimes can possess a thinned-out elongation; and actually *kvaukė*[85] also means "a fish resembling a tadpole," and *kaukas*, as we have noted, is a fishing tool which ends in a hook. On the other hand, a pipe with a long mouthpiece is called *kaukis*,[86] and *kaukutis*[87] is a child's toy, "'vilkutis" [top]. Finally, *kaukorikas*[88] is "a child with a large head."

The fact that such a figure can be clothed with *kaukos*,[89] a "child's shirt," doesn't essentially change its schematic appearance. It is true that in a certain sense, it is already an anthropomorphic figure, but it is still rough and unfinished, barely developed out of its primordial elements—earth and water—and it finds itself halfway between Nature, which is non-human, and Mankind, whom it is approaching prepared to serve.[90]

Kaukai and Vėlės

Kaukas and Kaukė

The unfinished, rudimentary figure of the *kaukas* cannot help but suggest a comparison to a word in the same family, *kaukė* [mask], which, according to the proposed hypothesis, is in the relation:

$$\frac{\text{containing}}{\text{contained}} :: \frac{\text{kaukė}}{\text{kaukas}}$$

Oddly enough, this common word can be found in modern Lithuanian in only one, somewhat older, example of the intensifying proverb "dried out as a Christmas mask."[91] In spite of the frequent use of masks in the rituals of Christmas and

Shrovetide, surviving in some areas until the first decades of the twentieth century, the word *kaukė* was replaced rather early by two loan words: Ruthenian *lyčyna*[92] and Polish *lerva*.[93] The actual borrowing is easily explained by geographic and cultural proximity, even though the verbal loan does not necessarily imply a mythic semantic borrowing as well:[94] on the contrary, even though both of these words have separate origins, the similarity in the differentiation of their meaning is surprising. The "meanings" of *lyčyna* and *lerva* differentiated into two subclasses are as follows:

    I. (a) kaukė [mask]
         (b) face (mocking sense)
         (c) scarecrow, spook, loathsome creature
         (d) dirty, untidy, good-for-nothing person
   II. (a) *lyčyna*, something very small, a parasite, larvae
        (b) *lerva*, a living being, in its first developmental phase

The two basic meanings—*lyčyna* and *lerva*—probably appeared as so distant from one another to the authors of the *Lietuvių kalbos žodynas* [Academic Dictionary of Lithuanian] that two separate entries were made for them. However, if we assume that these two foreign words have a common localized semanticism inherited from the word *kaukė* and that this latter word is related to our *kaukas* then the semantic area covered by these two words seems to be consistent and coherent. The mask, as a rough or degraded face, covers a sub-humanity which raises horror and terror, hides an embryonic being unable to reach a human status.

We will not develop here an exposition about the general significance of carnival masks, or the significance of "foreigners" and "animals" (supra-or sub-cultural beings) which these masks represent in a narrow sense. There is quite a bit already written about this in anthropology texts. Nevertheless, we should emphasize in passing that the masks of Shrovetide attack the *bergždinės*[95] [barren women] in Lithuania as in other countries, that in the Shrovetide rituals we find "lino tęsimas"— riding about the fields urging the rebirth of the flax (whose connection with the *kaukai* are well known), as well as "bitelių vežiojimas" [driving about of the bees], at which time water is sprinkled: these are all "fertility rituals."[96]

Kaukas and Kaukolė

The impression is created that beings covered with *kaukės* [masks] represent embryonic, unfinished life forms, prior to the actual birth of man. Therefore, it is possible to assume that those beings, having temporarily risen to the surface in the time span bounded by birth and death, and having manifested themselves in terms of a "human life," again return to their ancient pre-birth state, and continue their existence in the semblance of *vėlės*, i.e., "the spiritual dead," awaiting the real death-peace.[97] This helps us to understand Lasicius who considers *kaukai* to be "spirits of the dead."[98]

This somewhat unexpected statement is corroborated in part by lexical data: the polysemy of the word *kaukas* includes among its meanings "the unbaptized dead

Kaukai

child."[99] It seems that in this case we can observe a conflict of two religious world views. In Christianity, an unbaptized child has not yet been born into human life; and such a child, having died, belongs to another, non-Christian, or better—anti-Christian sacred sphere.[100] Such a child is thus a double *kaukas*: *kaukas*, as yet unborn, and *kaukas*, as already dead.

This identification of *kaukai* with the spirits of the dead—if Lasicius' assertion could be based on other facts as well—sufficiently explains the derivation of the word *kaukas* from *kaukolė, kvaukolė*[101] [skull]. In this context it is possible to understand the commonly held belief that the life principle is contained in the head of the deceased, and if one wishes to prevent the spirits from returning then it is necessary to cut off the head of the corpse, since *kaukolės* are capable of rising from the graves at night, rolling about in the graveyards, smashing into one another, and raising holy terror.[102] Even though they appear to belong to a later period, such beliefs confirm the existence of a sacred area in which the future of *kaukas* encompasses a variety of representations of death.

Vėlės and Vaižgantas

In the cult of the dead, which was still flourishing until recent times, two types of rituals can be differentiated. One type is dedicated to the deceased individual and, beginning with a feast prior to the funeral, is repeated in constantly lengthening time intervals (third, sixth, ninth, and fortieth day, according to Lasicius). Other rituals are annual and are consecrated to the memory of the members of the community (family or village).

There is no need to go into the details of those ceremonies. We will only note that during the funeral feast [*šermenys*] every one of the participants at the meal throws a few crumbs from each dish under the table for the deceased, but that which falls unintentionally from the table is left on the floor for the individual *vėlės*, "desertis, ut ipsi loquuntur, animis quae nullos habent vel cognatos vel amicos vivos"[103] [". . . who have neither living relatives nor friends"]. Afterward, when everyone has left the table, the crumbs are swept up like fleas with a broom. In another part of the Lasicius text, which has nothing in common with this citation, the author, commenting on the god of the dead, *Veliona,* indicates that the dead are fed a certain type of wafer, which is crumbled and scattered in four separate directions, called *Sikies Vielonia permixlos,*[104] which in present-day Lithuanian would be: *sikės velionio peniukšlas* (*sikės*—the food of the dead).

In the descriptions of the third day of the ritual of the autumn festival, called *Ilgės* or *Ilgiai*[105] in honor of the god Vaižgantas, the guardian of flax, the same *sykies* appear again in which the officiant after the ritual drinks, "è sinu eijcit à deastris, si qui sint VVaizgantho comedendas"[106] [Invites the dead to come out of the tombs and take a bath for the feast]. And knowing that *sikės* or *sikiai* are prepared from *flax seeds,*[107] we unexpectedly find the relationship of the flax god Vaižgantas with the dead: Vaižgantas, whose role we can identify from the acculturation of the barstukai and their transformation to *kaukai,* is a god born *out of the earth* in the form of flax who is tortured, killed, and resurrected *out of the earth;* now we encounter him accompanied by secondary deities, which are fed *sikės,* the characteristic food of the vėlės, whose direct use in feeding the deceased we have already discussed. The question arises: Who are these escorts of Vaižgantas: *vėlės* or the *kaukai*?

Vėlės and Veliona

The autumn festival of *Ilgės,* corresponding somewhat to All-Saints Day, would last for ten days;[108] three were entirely given over, according to Lasicius, to the cult of the dead. During the time of the festival: "mortuos è tumulis ad balneum et epulos invitant":[109] apparently this is a feast for the dead, where tables are laden with food and drink intended solely for the dead, where the number of towels and shirts laid out corresponds to the number of the invited dead. After preparing the feast, the living return to the house and "triduum compotunt."[110]

Somewhat later, nevertheless, the same Lasicius, once again unintentionally and in any case without any connection to the festival of Ilgės, returns to the cult of the dead. This time he comments on *Skerstuvės*,[111] the "sausage preparation festival," or rather, the festival which takes place on the day of the butchering of the pigs, when the meat for the entire winter is prepared and salted.[112] Even though Lasicius does not indicate the date of this festival, it is quite apparent that it can occur only during the fall; the insertion of a Lithuanian citation into the text inaccurately translated into Latin as so often happens with him confirms this fact. During the time of the festival, according to Lasicius, people turn to the god *Ezagulis* in this manner: "Vielona velos ateik musump und stala," a formula which Būga[113] interprets thus: "Veliona, vėliuõs ateik pas mus į stalą" [Veliona come to our table veliuos]. This text, if we wish to place it within a more general context, requires a rather extended commentary.

(a) The word *velos,* interpreted by Būga as *vėliuõs(e)* is the plural locative of the word *vėliai* "the feast of the dead," which is derived from the word *vėlė.* If *Veliona* is invited during butchering time [skerstuvės] to attend *Vėlines,* then the feast of *Skerstuvės* has to fit into the general frame of *Ilgės,* during the three days consecrated to the cult of the dead.

(b) The fact that the deity is invited to the table to take part in the mourning feast does not surprise us: such participation by the dead during the funeral feast is an entirely normal phenomenon. What is more surprising is that the feast to which the goddess *Veliona* is invited has dishes prepared from the easily spoiled parts of *pork.* The connection between vėlės and the pig can be determined only through the mediation of the *kaukas,* only on the basis that it is both a "spirit of the dead" and miraculously born out of the boar's testicles. One more argument, it seems, can be added to the confirmation of this thesis. A rather reliable observer, Jucevičius (1846)[114] notes that the *kaukai*—who, as we know, are 100 percent vegetarians—"during the night were given an offering of barrow's intestines stuffed with a mixture of blood and flour." The uncommon offering of this kind of sausage could only be made infrequently, when pigs were butchered, namely at the time of the fall festival during the period of *skerstuvės*. Although by a thin thread, this connects *kaukai* with the *pig*, and the *pig* with *vėlės*.

(c) Lasicius mentions *Veliona*, the Goddess of the Dead, in two places: both times she is referred to in the male gender even though the Lithuanian ending *-a* contradicts this. In the first case, it is said that "offerings are made to him when one wants to feed the dead,"[115] and this permits us to compare this cult of the goddess Veliona directly with the "feast of the dead" already mentioned.

The explanation of the second text is more difficult. Since Lasicius did not know the Lithuanian language, he introduced a complication when he referred to one deity from the start by two separate names: during the time of *skerstuvės* people turn to the god Ezagulis and invite the goddess Veliona to the feast prepared in honor of the dead. Is it possible to overcome this difficulty? Is it possible, for instance, to say that the first name, even though it is of a different gender, is only the epithet of the second? *Ezagulis,* actually, can be easily transcribed into modern Lithuanian as *ežia-gulys,* recalling that *ežia* marks the boundaries of cultivated fields,[116] within which the bones of the Easter ham are buried so as to protect the fields from hail and thunder. It follows that if *ežiagulys* can be explained as the epithet of Veliona, indicating her customary settlement, then offerings to Veliona in the form of bones of the *pig* turn her into a protectress of the fields against the malevolent rains that destroy the harvest.[117] This secondary function does not interfere with her continuing to be "the Goddess of Death" and being invited to the table set with *pork* dishes to honor the dead, especially if we take into account the general conviction of mankind that the dead are the guardians of the living.

Even though the problem which emerges due to the confusion of male and female gender still remains to be resolved—this is due to the fact that *Veliona* in both cases is considered to be a god and not a goddess, and not because there are two separate gods: *Ežiagulys* and *Veliona*[118]—historical data confirm rather the possibility of seeing in the boundaries of the field or its remote parts the dwelling of *Veliona* and those she protects—the dead.[119] It is known that the burial of the dead in cemeteries is a relatively recent custom and that, for instance, the Prussian prince Georg-Friedrich in 1578 on December 6th in Tilsit issued a decree to the Lithuanians which stated "sawa numirusiu kunus ing pusta lauka laidaie" [bury the bodies of your dead on the other side of the fields], and to equip certain enclosed areas for this purpose—*schwentorius* [churchyards].[120] In that manner, the intimate ties between the living, the dead, and nourishing Earth were severed.

Provisional Conclusions

In ending this brief survey of the life of the *kaukai* we must make a few observations about the significance of this type of work, its methods, and the results that have been achieved.

(1) One of the primary goals of Lithuanian ethnology should be the complete and accurate reconstruction of Lithuanian mythology as a national Lithuanian religion.

(2) The methods for such a reconstruction could be compared with the methods of archaeology which restore castles, cities, and entire civilizations. From separate shards, found in different sites and strata, pots and vases are reconstructed, from separate bricks—entire buildings. The transference of these methods as worked out by scholars such as Georges Dumézil or Claude Lévi-Strauss to the analysis of Lithuanian mythology does not proceed without difficulty. Lithuanian ethnographic material, even though especially rich, has not been prepared for this type of scientific endeavor. Therefore, the first phase is possible only in terms of a monograph—the reconstruction of separate structures but not of whole villages or cities.

(3) The description of kaukai thus is only the stirrings of one very narrow area of mythology. However, following structuralist postulates, the phenomena, whatever they might be, cannot be described in isolation but only in relation to other phenomena. Therefore, in this case, we began with the differentiation of the *kaukai* from the *aitvarai*, confused with one another in the most recent ethnographic layers, then dug down to the barstukai in order to separate two types: *bezdukai* and *kaukai* and so forth.

(4) This entire class of secondary deities belongs to more or less different sacred spheres, which are represented by gods of a hierarchically higher class: **Puškaitis, Vaižgantas, Veliona,* and so forth. Approaching these deities, several major religious problems present themselves whose definitive solution within the narrow descriptive frames of the *kaukai* may not even be possible.

(5) On this occasion, the question of the *reliability* of this type of reconstruction emerges: what role in the description can be ascribed to "pure facts" as far as the internal coherence of deductive methods is concerned for understanding the general principles and modes of organization of mythology.

(6) Let us take the description of the appearance of the *kaukai*. There is no doubt that *kaukai* are not the bearded gnomes of an academic painting but the abstract, rough, unfinished forms of modern sculpture. Almost no doubt is raised by their acculturation process as forest-dwellers, or by their chthonic and gland-water origins. However, the reliability becomes less when we attempt to explain the kaukai as souls of the dead. Given two possible explanations—(a) the identification of the kaukai with vėlės as a late phenomenon, belonging to the time period when mendicants and all types of apparitions could be referred to by the general name of *kaukas* and (b) the earth-water origin of the *kaukai*, their infra-human nature, allowing one to compare them with the diminished life of the spirits of the dead—we have chosen the latter. In spite of the scarcity of documented material and the gaps which we hope will be gradually filled, the relationship of *kaukas* with *kaukė* [the mask] and *kaukolė* [the skull] plays a decisive role.

(7) The same type of reliability gradient can be recorded when we speak about the higher gods. The status of *Puškaitis* as a god, his relations with the *barstukai-kaukai*, even the etymology offered for his name appear to be satisfactory. The case of *Vaižgantas* is even more interesting: even though there is less known about him on the level of pure "facts," the personality of Vaižgantas—not only as a god-civilizer, but as a type of Lithuanian Dionysus—appears enriched with this description, even

though the degree of reliability of the description could be increased, supplemented by new ethnographic findings. Meanwhile the figure of *Veliona,* while becoming somewhat more distinct, still remains quite blank: her figure may become more distinct before long through new, more comprehensive descriptions of the cult of the dead. There is no lack of such descriptions. The portrait of the *boar,* although his role appeared to be an important one, is not complete.

(8) We are not offering this description as the simple truth. At this time, it is more important to form a sufficient catalogue of hypotheses, more important to raise a series of problems than it is to solve them. In scholarly research it is not enough to have an abundance of data, one must know what to look for. Let this attempt at a description of one sphere of mythology encourage other descriptions or criticism of this description.

II

AITVARAS

Introductory Remarks

"Tai wisa kruwai pati welina ira" [All that is devilry]

In chapter one we chose as a point of departure a Praetorius text[1] which permitted the strict separation of the *kaukai*, chthonic and water beings, from the *aitvarai*, air and fire beings; this opposition seemed convenient since it made it possible to classify a large number of ethnographic facts, mostly recorded in the nineteenth and the beginning of the twentieth centuries, where name substitutions of these deities and the confusion of their functions occur quite often. The sixteenth and seventeenth centuries present an already degraded status of the national religion, though one in which syncretism with the Christian religion has not yet occurred, which helps to explain a large number of subsequent facts as well and allows one at the same time a return to mythic times for the reconstruction of a coherent mythic system. Our point of departure was thus a strategic choice necessary for every investigation of this type.

The representatives of the dominant religion of the period who were concerned with apostolic and ministerial duties held to a point of view which is very characteristic in this respect: while they acknowledged, even though in the form of an entreaty, the existence of the dominated religion:

> Forsake, dear Lithuania, your prayers to the kaukai, aitvaras, žemėpačiai . . . [2]

they were forced to place all these deities belonging to the still active "anti-religion" under the general term of *welina* [devilry].[3] It is easy to imagine how much such an official teaching, in an epoch where the practise of the ancient religion, its cult and rituals weakening by themselves, added to the confusion of various sacred spheres and their amalgamation.

The "False" Aitvarai

Therefore, any interpretation of ethnographic documents must eliminate from the corpus all facts in which deviations or changes of religious functions can easily be discerned.

Here for instance, one often encounters the *Velnias* figure [the devil] referred to by the name of *Aitvaras*, who having changed into a boy stands to serve the farmer in a variety of ways—most often through craftiness and deceit:[4] such a pseudo-aitvaras without a doubt is attached to the extensive cycle of wondertales which depict the devil as man's friend. It is apparent that in this case the partial intersection of the functions of Aitvaras and Velnias as *providers of services*, which they both manifest, made it possible for the expansion of the activity sphere of Aitvaras.

In other texts, the functions common to *Laima-Dalia* crisscross with the no longer easily differentiated action spheres of Aitvaras, and thus the role of the *provider of a good harvest*[5] is attributed to him. It is not surprising then to encounter the reverse phenomenon as well—the attribution of fields to the activity sphere of Laima and calling them *Laimykas*.[6]

The name of *Aitvaras* sometimes is used for the representative of one type of laumė [fairy], more widely known by the name of *Slogutė* [nightmare].[7] The confusion in this case, it seems, can be explained by the fact that the manifestation of the real aitvaras has as a consequence the worsening health of the mistress of the house, and that, on the other hand, a serious illness with complications, more widely known by the name of *kaltūnas*,[8] is also called *aitvaras*.

It is necessary to include the original image of *Aitvaras* characteristic of the region of Dubingiai,[9] where this name covers an entire unexpected functional disposition.

(1) Aitvaras appears there as a type of *antikaukas:* he not only does not provide the people with goods, his activity is characteristic in that "he takes away *skalsa*."[10]

(2) He cares for the horses and in general "rides and nurses the animals," which, as is known, belongs to one type of activity sphere of the *laumės*.

(3) The circumstances that lead to his birth give him special properties. "He is born only of woman through the fault of man. If the man urinates *while the moon is out* and returning to the house lies with the woman—an aitvaras will be born."[11] This grants him an image of *a lunar being*, born out of the union of the moon with a woman, and inscribes him in this manner into a sacred sphere in strict contrast to the sacred sphere of the "Varuna-type being" of the real aitvaras.

These various manifestations of the "false" aitvaras, which can be identified according to types of deviations of religious functions, are enumerated here only so that we can exclude them from our field of analysis. We would like to turn our attention at the present time to a very important and as yet little developed area of religious and mythological analysis—the description of their diachronic transformation.

Magic Relations

Even though all the Lithuanian gods, lumped together, are "pati welina" [devilry itself] Mažvydas, nevertheless, makes a distinction between the gods such as *Perkūnas* [god of thunder], *Žemėpatis* [master of the earth] or *Lauksargis* [guardian of the field], who, although false, still are honored—if the expression can be used— "normally," and the deities who are given only to "qui *ad malas artes* adjiciunt animam" and "Eithuaros et Caukos Deos profitentur suos."[12] The aitvarai and the kaukai are thus separated from other gods, since their relations with people belong to spheres of sorcery and magic as they were understood at that time. It is evident that from the middle of the sixteenth century these two deities were already compared and treated on one plane, and that this undoubtedly contributed to their subsequent confusion. This process in Praetorius' time had not been fully developed, since it did not interfere with his making comparisons between the kaukai and the aitvarai and establishing strict oppositions for their separation.

The Spheres of Action of Aitvaras

Ruler of Culinary Culture

The parallelism between kaukai and aitvarai established by sixteenth-and seventeenth-century authors is based not only on the specificity of the "magic" nature of their relations with people but also with a comparison of their functions: as "Namiszki Diewai" [household gods],[13] the one and the other are considered as helpers of man and *providers of benefit*. Only in moving away from these comparisons—which, as we have already mentioned, correspond to one moment in the historical transformation of the religious organization of the Lithuanians—is a differential study possible based on a search for their similarities and differences.

Using this principle, we could have exploited Praetorius' opposition in which the kaukai, consumers of *raw* food, differ from Aitvaras, the consumer of *cooked* and/or *roasted* food.[14] Actually, the food of Aitvaras consists of two dishes: *omelets*,[15] as roasted food, and *porridge*,[16] as boiled food. If porridge, the daily food of the farmer's family, is a cooked dish *par excellence*, the omelet is distinctive from at least two standpoints: it is often a ceremonial dish offered to honor guests, but it is also food of avian origin, thus emphasizing its relation to the airborne nature of *aitvaras*.

If Aitvaras is the exclusive *consumer* of food, the preparation of which requires the intervention of fire, his activity as *provider* is based on the same principle: contrary to the kaukai, who provide natural goods through *skalsa*, the food products provided by Aitvaras[17] are the results of a transformation which occurs with the help of fire—or at least through direct contact with fire and heat. Therefore, the basic food products supplied by him are, above all, those which contrast Aitvaras with the kaukai:

(a) Aitvaras provides *curds*[18] while the kaukai provide *hay*, which allows for the production of *milk*.

(b) Aitvaras provides *flour*,[19] while the kaukai are content to provide *grain*.

Other useable goods provided by the *aitvaras* are products transformed by contact with fire:

(c) *Meat*,[20] for instance, is "cooked" indirectly when it comes into contact with the smoke in the smokehouse.

(d) *Ale*[21] is the result of fermentation, i.e., internal heat.

Thus, Aitvaras, as a "household god," can be compared with the kaukai: like them, he maintains close ties with people. These bonds, being of a circular nature, turn him into both an addressee and addressor of cooked and/or roasted food values.

Nevertheless, Aitvaras, at the same time, differs from the kaukai: when kaukai appear as mediators between the nourishing earth and people, guaranteeing only the *skalsa* of the products provided, Aitvaras, who absorbs, transports, and *vomits*[22] the goods into a place provided for them, no longer appears as mediator but as a transformer since he himself is the principle of fire: it is within his innermost space with the action of fire that the fermentation and cooking process take place. Therefore, if we consider kaukai as peculiar messengers or servants, acting within the spheres of higher deities, such as **Puškaitis* or **Vaižgantas,* then in the hierarchic scale of divine beings, Aitvaras must be placed not in the same class as the kaukai but where we find his "guardians": he himself is the *ruler of culinary culture* just as, for instance, Vaižgantas is the *ruler of vestimentary culture.*

It seems that these differences in social standing can best explain the difference in treatment by sixteenth- and seventeenth-century observers: next to the *kaukai*, noted in the plural, appears the singular *aitvaras*;[23] next to the lower-case letter for kaukai, *Aitvaras* is honored with an initial capital letter.[24]

Ruler of Precious Metals

Our decision to treat the two functions of Aitvaras separately—that of provider of *consumed values* and that of *treasure-hoarding values*[25]—is based not only on the fact that certain ethnographic texts differentiate a type of aitvaras—the *monetary aitvaras*[26]—which in some areas is even called by a special name, *pūkys,*[27] but more importantly on the knowledge that the characterization of his nature and the determination of his personality raise totally different problems.

The *monetary aitvaras* can be easily identified by his form when flying—he looks like a *red-hot poker,*[28] or most simply he is *fiery,*[29] or he reminds one of a shooting star: "kada žvaigžde lak, švist par dangu, saka žmones, eisvars su pinigais lak"[30] [when a star flits across the sky, people say it is aitvaras flying off with gold coins].

This fiery image of an Aitvaras bearing coins—and the coins here are, of course, "gold"—must be identified with *burning coins*: "with my own eyes I saw aitvaras flying and the coins burning."[31] On the other hand, the expressions "coins are burning" or "treasure is on fire" are used in referring to the *flame*[32] or the *ball of light*[33] which rises from the ground in the place where buried coins are to be found. Furthermore, "When the coins are burning, it is said that the gold is airing out";[34] in other words, *burning coins* are nothing more than that vital force itself, manifested in the form of air and fire, which in solid form appears as gold coins, just as wax, for instance, may exist in either a solid or melted state yet still remain wax.

Now it is becoming clear why the other names by which *Aitvaras* is called— whether *Švitelis* or *Žaltvikša* (better: *Žaltviska*) are also used for *ignis fatuus* [the flickering gaseous flame which wanders along the marsh ground].[35] The identification of the *aitvaras* with this flame, which in turn is only a gaseous form of gold, compels us to imagine this deity as the fiery force capable of facilitating the transformation of precious metals as longed for by alchemists of the Middle Ages.

Taking into account the fact that *Aitvaras* can be purchased in the form of *coal,*[36] that he sometimes manifests his presence among people through gifts of coal pieces[37] that nobody needs, in other words, that he can exist as a lump of coal, reduced in the process of burning to this minimal form of existence, and can be reborn anew, from his ashes, luminous, in the shape of precious gold, and recalling, as well, that he is often represented as a *bird,*[38] it seems that when one basic element is placed next to another a case gradually emerges, not complete but which new investigations could most certainly enrich, allowing for the reconstruction of a comparatively distinct image of a Lithuanian *Phoenix.*

Two mythic figures — ruler of culinary culture and ruler of precious metals (or stones) — can, depending on the cultural and mythological context in which they are recorded, either be differentiated, or combined and manifested in the form of one actor who performs dual functions: the rule over fire presents a general basis for such a merging. Regardless of which of these hypotheses will be chosen for the interpretation of the archaic Lithuanian religion, it must be noted that in an epoch of an already degraded paganism and syncretism with Christian beliefs, Aitvaras reduced to the status of "household deity" combines within himself both roles — provider of food and coins.

Nevertheless, even with such a rudimentary figurative correspondence, the fact that Aitvaras provides money, which until then had been hidden in the form of "buried treasure," contradicts, although only in part, his nature as a household god. It is well-known that in ancient agrarian societies the circulation of values — and parallel to it the circulation of money — was perceived as a closed system in which acquisition by one member of the community of such value was possible only through the compensation by another member of the community either with the same property or by forfeiture or loss of money. In such a context the appearance of a *buried treasure* could be seen only as an introduction of the element of disorder, and its acquisition, arousing passion and fear surrounded by various interdictions, always appears as an introduction of anxiety-producing extrasocial values into a stable communal life. When we evaluate it from this standpoint and take into consideration the transcendental origins of the coins, Aitvaras appears as an asocial being.

This feature is revealed even more clearly when we encounter texts which in place of customary, degraded, and universal ethnographic facts reflect ancient beliefs and religious practices. We have in mind, namely, the procedures with which it was possible to prevent the aitvaras from bringing coins: upon seeing him it was sufficient to "rip open one's nightshirt"[39] or according to other versions show him one's "naked ass"[40] and having done that, to hide as fast as possible in the *garret;* if one manages to hide, the aitvaras will immediately spill the coins, and if not, if the supplicant is not protected by the roof, the aitvaras "covers him with scabs that do not heal."[41]

The general significance of this mythic *praxis* is quite clear: in an appropriate ritual behavior Aitvaras, on the one hand, is compelled to surrender to man's will, and on the other, not allowed to harm man. Nevertheless, it is a surprising fact that the insult done to Aitvaras when exposing one's "naked ass" or one's sexual organs — more or less symbolically — forces him to submit to injunctions and to relinquish the coins: this contradicts his behavior, when upon finding that the food prepared for him has changed to excrement[42] — a provocation similar to the first — he decides to suspend his services and often even resorts to revenge. The interpretation would be considerably easier if it were possible to assume the existence of two separate types of aitvaras.

This contradiction is not the only one: when the aitvaras who provides food, seeks revenge against people by setting their houses, in which he himself has lived, on fire, the monetary aitvaras, as we have seen, is unable to seek revenge if a man is in the house guarded by the same roof which he had no qualms about setting ablaze in the first case. His revenge is then entirely different—he covers the person with scabs.

However it might be, we cannot deny the strict opposition which exists between Aitvaras and the roof of the house, or more precisely, the deities that guard the house. Aitvaras as the embodiment of asocial fire—since his relations with *Gabija,* the goddess of the hearth, are not the best[43]—seems more and more a deity external to the social zone of the settlement, external to the enculturated sacred sphere.

Aitvaras and Perkūnas

The fiery character of Aitvaras is so distinctive that it helps to elucidate anew man's relations with one of the principal deities—Perkūnas, who, as god of thunder is also the proprietor of a certain type of fire. The well-known fact that lightning often strikes houses and sets them on fire, is hard to coordinate with the personality of Perkūnas as a beneficent caretaker of mankind. One of Praetorius' texts obliterates this contradiction: according to it, people "believe that where lightning strikes, whether it sets something on fire or not, there must have been one of the Prussian gods in the house, even if only *aitvaras*. If it strikes him then *he sets the house on fire,* if not, then the thunder and lightning cause no harm to the house."[44] In other words, Perkūnas has nothing to do with the fire; it is Aitvaras who causes it. An explanation follows: "Aitvaras is struck by Perkūnas, that is, by thunder since he behaves poorly toward people. Since he is punished because of men, he seeks revenge by setting the house on fire." Even if this interpretation may appear to be overly anthropocentric, other texts as well as the stature of Aitvaras himself, as we will see, allow us to imagine that this is actually a very ancient, cosmogonic type of battle between two mighty protagonists[45]—the image of Aitvaras, as provider of goods, is now so changed that it is possible to regard it, if not as an enemy of mankind, then at least as a vindictive god with a rich temperament.

The Manifestations of Aitvaras

His Double Embodiment

It is an interesting fact that Aitvaras at one and the same time can be represented in two entirely different forms: on the one hand, a *bird*[46] and on the other—a peculiar *air serpent*.[47] In the first case, he most often appears as a *rooster*—sometimes *red*,[48] most likely because of his fiery origin, but more generally as *black*[49]—at the very least as a *black heron*,[50] as a *crow*,[51] as a *raven*,[52] or more commonly as a *wondrous little chick*.[53] Numerous observers say that they have seen it as a *serpent*, similar to a grass snake having the form of a *poker* or *hay pole,* with a variety of bright, hard-to-describe colors, spreading in the treetops during fall evenings or in the summer before sunset; the front part corresponding to a head is often fiery and thicker and the back, more slender, moves not by weaving back and forth but by pushing itself up from the ground.[54] We see that neither one nor the other of these rather summary descriptions corresponds to the *žaltviska* form of the wandering flame.

An attempt can be made to create an inventory of features common to both figures and with such an inventory thereby try to reduce the two images into one personage—a similar procedure allowed us to state that the kaukas, represented as a bearded dwarf with a red cap, is only a modernized form of the archaic kaukas. Such a list would contain not only the air and fire characteristics they share but also the fact that both of the aitvarai are "born two times": the first time in the shape of an egg, and the second, in the shape of a zoomorphic being. These features, nevertheless, are perhaps too abstract and prevent us from seeing the general configurations, especially since the appearance of both aitvaras figures in one and the same narrative[55] is entirely possible, and doesn't shock either the narrator's or the listener's ears. To these two autonomous figures—or three, if one counts the flame—there is no corresponding distribution of functions: the miraculous bird places gold under the pillow, aitvaras-kirminas [the serpent] transports coins, and *žaltvikša* [the flame] itself is the burning coins.

We can offer two noncontradictory hypotheses as an explanation for this phenomenon. According to the first, a historical hypothesis, we can say that in the case of the aitvaras we are dealing with one specific phenomenon in the historical development of a religion: syncretism of several divine functions does not prevent the deities from maintaining their autonomous figures. According to the second, a typological hypothesis, we can state that aitvaras belongs to a separate category of mythic beings distinguished by a variety of manifested forms, that as a god, while maintaining his invariable essence, he can be manifested in a variety of shapes. Aitvaras in this sense would be similar, for instance, to Velnias [the Devil], with the difference, however, that Velnias has his basic anthropomorphic form and can change into a variety of different beings while Aitvaras has no such basic form.

His Dual Origin

It was easy to identify the dual origin of the kaukai when we were analyzing their nature, or better yet, the dual possibility of their acquisition. The first of these possibilities is the determination of contractual relations with mythic beings who live in the woods beyond the boundaries of cultural space. The second possibility permits the acquisition to take place within the frames of the household, within cultural space, but the acquisition operation itself takes on a miraculous, if not a magical nature: the kaukas is acquired by hatching it out of a boar's testicles.

This second capability, as we have seen, corresponds to the miraculous birth of the aitvaras from the seven-year-old egg laid by the *black rooster.*[56] This delicate and complicated procedure similar to the hatching of the kaukas differs by one strange feature to which we will return later: the appearance of aitvaras, in this case, is accompanied by the prolonged illness of the mistress of the house.

If we discount the possibility common to both the kaukai [pl.] and the aitvaras of buying them in a foreign, heretic land[57] — most commonly in Riga or Königsberg, and mention briefly the numerous texts in which the appearance of the aitvaras remains without explanation: "Aitvaras *attached* himself to a man, it is not known from where"[58] — another "normal" acquisition possibility of aitvaras is that of *finding*. The place where aitvaras is found is most often a *roadway,* or more specifically, *crossroads,*[59] that is, a place where all roads meet, where all foreigners wander, where adventures of all sorts take place. One especially interesting text further specifies and describes in detail such a place: the farmer returning home finds the aitvaras in the form of a "drenched, black chick" "under the wild pear tree."[60] We will return to this text several times.

However it might be, comparing both types of acquisition:

$$\frac{\text{kaukas}}{\text{Aitvaras}} \simeq \frac{\text{boar's testicles}}{\text{rooster's egg}} \simeq \frac{\text{contract}}{\text{find}}$$

it is easy to see that corresponding to the contractual, that is, the social and cultural acquisition of the kaukas, is the adventurous, accidental type of acquisition of Aitvaras.

The Transcultural Factor

"Finding," as one type of acquisition of objects of value, is a phenomenon often encountered in mythology. We had occasion earlier to attempt an interpretation of this phenomenon:[61] it seems that the idea of an *ex nihilo* appearance of objects of value is unacceptable to archaic thought, in which every found object must necessarily have been left by some unknown addressor, existing beyond the boundaries of the social sphere, and that the fact of the find itself could be explained only as a *gift,* depending on the addressor's sovereign will. Applying this mentality to our analytical case, we will see that the appearance of Aitvaras by means of a find is in symmetrical and inverse relation to the acquisition of the kaukai, which occurs with the help of a contract. Actually, in the case of the kaukai, the active factor, which defines future relations between them, is man (by clothing the kaukas, he enters into an agreement with him); in the case of Aitvaras, it is the reverse — man's role is nonexistent and the entering into a relationship depends solely on an unknown but active factor, which brings the aitvaras.

We have already seen[62] what transcultural role must be ascribed to "the buried treasure": its discovery is an incursion of extrasocial values into a closed society. The identification of this "treasure" with Aitvaras, who behaves only in accordance with his sovereign and capricious will, helps us to understand the rules which treasure seekers must follow: their behavior has to correspond to the inverse behavioral form of Aitvaras. There must be at least two excavators of the coins, not one — i.e., to symbolically create a microsocial image, they cannot be "jealous of one another." The most significant negative desire interferes with their finding the coins, in contrast to Aitvaras, who is a jealous deity.[63] One story of this type shows a man who chooses a dog for his friend and in that manner finds and uncovers the money: if he had taken his wife with him, the narrator comments, it would have turned out entirely differently.[64]

The Returning Coins

We must not forget that Aitvaras, an arbitrary power, a jealous and antisocial deity is also the ruler of *pareitiniai pinigai*[65] or *pareičiokai*[66] [returning coins]. These are, of course, the coins which barely spent, immediately return to their owner, sometimes even bringing back with them all the other coins in whose company they had *found themselves*.[67] If we keep in mind that the circulation of money is based on a tacitly agreed upon fiduciary contract, we can imagine what disorder, what mocking negation of the social order based on the principle of exchange, is created by Aitvaras' introduction of the returning coins.

If we wish to understand this phenomenon, and, refusing to be content with the explanation that this is a "magic operation," try to imagine the functioning of the returning coins as a certain *modus operandi* characteristic of Aitvaras, we will have to note that their movement depends on a special power of Aitvaras for establishing unbreakable bonds between some object chosen by him and a subject, an inseparable relation between the two that is of the same type as we have encountered in the cases of *casting a spell* or *inflicting an illness*.[68]

We must note one of the procedures indicated by Volter on how to get rid of the returning coins—since, contrary to *kaukai,* who bring good luck to the home, people very often are concerned with how to rid themselves of the Aitvaras. According to him, "one must give them away at less than face value, then they will stay with the one to whom one gives the money."[69] Recalling that the *returning coins* are a negation of the fiduciary order, we see that this order can be restored by negation of the same order carried out in a different form: the negation of a negation of order is the affirmation of that order.

Another procedure, parallel to this one, is of a more general nature and is added to the list of techniques for getting rid of the aitvarai: the returning coins must be placed for three weeks in a row at the crossroads, then aitvaras will disappear;[70] sometimes it is enough to place them there only once but to "shit on them"[71]—this is a form which only doubles or consolidates the placement at the crossroads, since excrement, as everyone knows, is an inverted form of *gold*.[72]

Several Lexical Facts

Even though the etymology of *aiktvaras* or *aitivaras* is considered to be unknown or faulty,[73] there is no doubt that it is a compound word *aiti + varas*, whose elements taken separately, are easily identified and can function autonomically. The noun *aitas* means "a restless individual" or "rake," "Herumtreiber"[74]—we see that it is a semanticism which corresponds in a universal sense to the traits of the *Aitvaras* character itself.

At first glance, the meaning of the verb *aitauti* (or *aitouti*) appears more unusual, even though it is obviously derived from the root of the noun. *Aitauti* according to the *Lietuvių kalbos žodynas (LKŽ)* [The Academic Dictionary of Lithuanian] means:

(1) "To quiet, soothe, appease"
Ex: "Go and quiet [*nuaitauk*] that child, so he doesn't scream all through the field." (Srj.)
(2) "To bribe, to appease"
Ex: "If we bribe him [*aitauna*], he will not go to the police, but when he gets mad, then he will betray us." (Rdm.)

Taking into account all the findings that we have assembled about this deity's willful, jealous, vengeful, unpredictable behavior, we see that both of the core meanings of the word *aitauti* correspond entirely to the behavior which we expect from people when they enter into relations with Aitvaras and wish to remain in his good graces. Because of his excessive and capricious character, one must do everything to quiet and appease him: while he is in essence amoral and behaves only in accordance with his angry and vengeful mood, if one wants to accommodate him it is necessary to soothe and bribe him. If relations with the kaukai are based on justice and principles of mutual trust, then in the case of Aitvaras, we are dealing with a well-known type of deity with whom relations can be maintained only by hypocritical and artificial measures in order to achieve good results.[75] We must strictly separate deities of the *Varuna* type—implacable, vengeful, autocratic—from deities of the *Mithra* type— the overseer of harmony and agreement.[76]

Aitvaras or Kaltūnas

A new activity sphere of Aitvaras is unexpectedly uncovered when we learn that "in Prussian Lithuania there is a belief that the aitvaras is capable not only of bringing all types of goods, but can also tangle all the hair on a person's head, to inflict *kaltūnas*."[77] Along with this finding, the efforts of the researcher are rewarded when he succeeds in finding that in spite of its absence from the dictionary (*Lietuvių kalbos žodynas*), the word *kaltūnas*, a borrowing from Slavic languages used for an illness known by the name of *Plica polonica,* is only a substitute for the ward *aitvaras* (dial. *atvaras*) which means according to Ruhig, "der Alf" and "Haarzotten, Mahre, Mahrzopt eines Menschen" [hair tassels, tufts, braids of a person].[78]

Even though our information is as yet quite inadequate, it already allows us to determine that this illness of the aitvaras is much more complicated than what the authors just cited say about it: it is not just an ailment involving hair, its activity encompasses the entire organism. On the contrary, we can say that *kaltūnas* is an *internal disease* localized within the organism, while the *tangling of hair* is only one manner of its manifestation, that in the normal process of development it starts to exteriorize: "*the kaltūnas rose to the surface* (the horse's mane became coiled, knotted, tied in knots, not only tangled and plaited) so he will not go blind."[79] People even differentiate three types of *kaltūnai*: "The *kaltūnas* is threefold—of the hair, of the nails, and of the intestines,"[80] even though this latter specification is not entirely correct.

Actually, according to our data, the external manifestations of *kaltūnas* are of three types:

(1) the most characteristic is, of course, the *kaltūnas of the hair*: "may *kaltūnas* tangle your hair,"[81] is said when one wants to bring bad luck on another's head.

(2) *Kaltūnas of the nails* is also a terrible disease: "the nails never heal from *kaltūnas*,"[82] but it spreads to the *hands, your hands are covered with kaltūnai*" (full of fissures and cracks).[83]

(3) Finally, *kaltūnas* "coming to the surface" affects the eyes: "the eyes are afflicted with *kaltūnas*, they have been unhealthy for a long time,"[84] whose significance is supplemented by the following example: "you are a real kaltūnas, *your eyes shine through your hair*."[85]

This comprises a totality of the common external manifestations of *kaltūnas-aitvaras*: if we attempt to visualize and to sketch out their global configuration we would have a type of *branching tree,* whose terminal points would be marked by the illnesses. V. T. Mansikka explains the procedure by which one attempts to determine if a patient really is sick with *kaltūnas*. For that purpose, a spell involving melted wax, cast into a full bowl of water and held over the sick one's head is used: "Wenn die auf solche Weise enstandene Wachsfigur *Verzweigungen* hat, so wird das als ein Zeichen dafür angesehen, das es sich um Koltun handelt."[86] ["If the figure of wax, created this way, has branches it is taken as a sign of a case of koltun."] We should record the eruption of this elemental power into the extremities following the branchings of the body as one of the forms of Aitvaras.

Generally taken, such a perception of disease is not special to *kaltūnas*: whether it be an old-fashioned *growth* or a modern *cancer,* illness is often represented as a living being, which has crept into the interior of a person's body, gnawing at his insides, moving around, either yielding or wanting to leave.[87] The affliction of kaltūnas-aitvaras is thus, above all, his settling within man's organism. This explains the phenomenon which originally appeared peculiar—the wife's illness when hatching an aitvaras.[88]

Another separate text about aitvaras bought in Riga from a German is even clearer in this sense. Having sold the aitvaras, the German gives advice on how to behave with it: "When you return to the gate, sitting in the cart, call to your wife, saying: "Wife, oh wife! *Come raise the gate so that the devil can crawl into your heart!*"[89]

This text, confirming the wife's dominant role, is interesting from yet another standpoint: it clearly identifies the homestead and its gates with the housewife's body and the crawling into her interior, into her heart. Aitvaras, you see, enters the house in a double form: as a deity, he makes himself at home in the homestead—in the granary or in the garret of the cottage—and as an illness, he settles in the heart of the housewife. This phenomenon of doubling again does not surprise us: *possession by the devil*, for instance, can be explained in no other way than, on the one hand, the devil's remaining the Devil, and on the other, the same devil's crawling into the person's body. Thus we must call on a certain *participative relation* to help us explain even the present British constitution: the Queen of England is a sovereign; even though she delegates almost all her power to Parliament, there is no diminution of her absolute power; she remains the absolute ruler of England. Aitvaras thus remains Aitvaras, even though his emanation, kaltūnas-aitvaras, settles within the person.

The aitvaras-kaltūnas, which today we would unquestionably place with psychosomatic illnesses, applies almost exclusively to human beings, although people share this with one type of animal—the horse. Even though the external manifestations of *kaltūnas* among horses are the same as those among people, nevertheless, in their case new specific elements appear. We saw, for instance,[90] that when *kaltūnas* "does not come to the surface" in the form of a tangled mane, the ailing horse *goes blind*. We should add *lameness*[91] to *blindness* as a second means by which one may recognize that a kaltūnas refuses to leave the horse. These two forms of contra-manifestations which indicate that *kaltūnas* has finally settled within the organism are especially significant. In mythology antiphrastic expressions of this type are often encountered: a *blind* person is in reality *clairvoyant* (or, if his eyes are weak or nearsighted, then they have an especially overwhelming power), a *lame* person is distinguished by great *speed* (or can magically transport himself to another place). This interpretation is confirmed by a statement that, contrary to people, whom *kaltūnas* weakens, *horses with kaltūnas* are considered to be especially strong.[92]

Thus if *devils*, normally envisaged in the form of man, often have *weak eyes*, if they are often *crippled*, Aitvaras, though belonging to the same tribe of gods, can be embodied as a horse, identified with the primordial steed.

This figure of an Aitvaras-possessed steed is thus so much more unexpected since the horse, as a mythic being, probably belongs to an entirely different sacred sphere, in strict opposition to Aitvaras. Here, for instance, if one wants to safeguard goods from Aitvaras, this advice is given: "Take an old *horseshoe* and nail it to the cottage entry way with the points facing upward";[93] that is most probably so that it could kick more easily defending itself against an attacker. This custom is not the only example: if one wishes to do battle with the aitvaras, who in the form of a rooster vomits grain into a trough standing next to the granary, one is advised to "make a whip of *horsehair from the tail* and . . . with it flog around the trough and the trough itself."[94] Thus, the horse is a powerful antagonist of Aitvaras: if Aitvaras is sometimes embodied as a horse, then this can happen only after a victorious battle.

Aitvaras and Apidėmė

Having become more closely acquainted with the nature of Aitvaras and his various manifestations, we can now attempt to analyze a quite conservative text which has carefully preserved its mythic traits.[95] This is the retelling of a misfortune which happens to one farmer, who returning home finds "under the wild pear tree" "a little black chick, drenched and trembling from the cold" and, feeling pity for it, brings it home. The chick soon manifests itself as an *aitvaras*: he started to carry off the potatoes, grain, coins. The farmer, a God-fearing man, doesn't know how "to rid himself of the aitvaras." Meanwhile "people would see how at night a *glowing pillar* would descend behind the farmer's hut and started to gossip that he keeps the devil." The entire community finally decides that the man must move from the house, leaving the aitvaras in it. Then he "sold everything, crops, animals, whatever he could do without, and bought himself a place a mile away and moved there. When he was hauling the last wagonload and there was nothing left in the cottage, *he set fire to all four corners of the cottage:* Burn, you rascal; I will get my money back later for the *field.*"

This abandonment of the home and the fire set by the owner himself can be compared with another ethnographic fact: we already know that Lithuanians did not rebuild a house set on fire by Perkūnas at the same site.[96] We also know from other sources that the house actually is not set on fire by Perkūnas, but that he is only battling his old enemy Aitvaras, the real culprit behind the fire.[97]

The situation as described in our text is a reversal in a certain sense of the religious interpretation of the sixteenth century: in the first case, Aitvaras sets a house on fire, forcing one to abandon it; in the second case, the farmer himself, on the advice of the village community, decides to abandon it and to set fire to it himself. Thus, it is not difficult to understand that even though the arsonist differs in the two cases, the basic cause—Aitvaras' presence in the household—in both cases is the same. Aitvaras is the real cause of the fire and of the change in residence.

Apparently, the farmer was naive when he imagined himself capable of killing the aitvaras in the fire. Indeed, with the cottage barely on fire and the farmer sitting in the wagon ready to go, "in the back of the cart, a black chick, shakes out his feathers," and sings:

> From corner to corner
> Burn the hut to the ground [to the last stick.][98]
> From here we'll go on further
> And it will be better for us.

The farmer is forced to transport the little chick with him to his new residence.

If we delve deeper into the text, we note a strange, conceptually illogical detail—two quite separate problems are compared in one sentence: after "Burn, you rascal!" there follows, "I will get my money later for the *field.*" The field about which the matter revolves has a special name, *apidėmė,* which today means "a plot of land between two homesteads," and "a small amount of land between cottages."[99] In the sixteenth- and seventeenth-century juridical texts written in Russian and Polish, *apidėmė* maintains its Lithuanian form—since it is naming a specific Lithuanian entity—with the explanation when translating or commenting that it is "the former site of the homestead."[100]

The same word is encountered in the list of Lithuanian gods compiled by Lasicius during the same epoch in which *Apidome* is briefly characterized as "mutati domicilij deu(s)," that is, as "god of a change in domicile."[101] It is becoming apparent that the farmstead and the plot of land belonging to it in our text, abandoned and set fire to because of Aitvaras, were called *apidėmė,* and that they are left in the guardianship of the goddess *Apidėmė*. The necessity of this guardianship is implicit, and not for sentimental reasons only, as is supposed by Jurginis,[102] but especially for religious ones: this abandoned plot is the domicile of the deities who guard the family hearth, the abode of the ancestors, which cannot be left without protection.[103]

Lasicius, summarizing in three words the divine function of *Apidėmė*—which we are trying to verify and substantiate—adds a supplementary sentence meant to explain the cause for the homestead's abandonment: "nato cuiusuis generis, *vel coeco vel debili pullo,* actutum sedes mutantur."[104] At best, we can consider the explanation to be elliptical: birth of a *blind* or *lame* animal is a sign whose consequence can only be a change in residence, and not a deep grounding for such an important decision.

The comparison of this phenomenon to the manifestations of kaltūnas in horses can add to an understanding of aitvaras: we have observed that kaltūnas-aitvaras' refusing "to leave" the organism of the horse, manifests itself as a *blindness* or *lameness*. This allows us to compare three series of facts already described:

No.	Themes	Cause		Consequence of Cause		Consequence
1	Aitvaras-fire	Aitvaras	→	(fire)	→	change in residence
2	Aitvaras-kaltūnas	Aitvaras	→	blindness lameness	→	Y
3	Apidėmė	X	→	blindness lameness	→	change in residence

These three causal series are parallel and, taking them two at a time, have at least one common trait. If Aitvaras (series 1 and 2) is the cause of two consequences, both a change in residence (series 1) and blindness and/or lameness (series 2), and if both these consequences appear together (series 3), then we can say—considering it to be a *strong hypothesis*—that these two consequences are consequences of one and the same cause—Aitvaras. Actually, it is not difficult to acknowledge that the birth of a blind and lame animal—most likely a colt—can and must be considered a sign of misfortune: the prophet of this misfortune is Aitvaras settling in the homestead. Thus, for his part, he forces people from their ancient settlements, leaving them, nevertheless, in the guardianship of the goddess Apidėmė.

Aitvaras and Kirnis

Our attempted analysis of the variety of functions and manifestations of the aitvaras, although clarifying the diverse nature of its figure, nevertheless raises perhaps even more difficulties than it brings satisfactory explanations. Even though two separate functions of Aitvaras are identifiable—ruler of culinary culture and ruler of precious metal—we were unable to find two separate figurative equivalents for them. Aitvaras' semblance as a bird is quite apparent in its zoomorphically realistic figure, which differs strictly from the figure of Aitvaras as a "serpent-haypole." The unclear contours of the latter, which coincide with no living being, make it impossible to postulate two activity spheres, at least with the facts we have now for these two representations. The magic activity of aitvaras who inflicts kaltūnas and the variety of his manifestations open up entirely new, unforeseen aspects of his personality, which eventually might not correspond with any air deity figure in the "natural world." However, this has nothing in common with the appearance of the Aitvaras-bird. We can thus try without any claims to a differentiation of its functions to imagine the *aitvaras-bird* as a mythic being, different from the elemental *cosmic god—Aitvaras*.

We have already noted that such an Aitvaras is an asocial creature, found beyond the communal boundaries, somewhere by the public road or in the forest. These two places for discovery complement each other, since the roadways usually run through the woods, separating one settlement of people from another. However, the place for such a find still remains undetermined. Only one text—praised by us for its abundance of mythic traits and used to describe the goddess *Apidėmė*—clearly identifies the place where an aitvaras is found: the farmer, returning home, that is, *on the road*,[105] finds it under *the wild pear tree*. This place for a find becomes significant when we take into account the ending of the narrative: the soothed aitvaras finally agrees to retreat under condition that the farmer will bring him back to the same place. He "carried the Aitvaras to the same pear tree under which he found him, and after that he didn't return again."

Those inclined to believe this version of the events will notice the parallelism between our aitvaras and the forest life of our previously described *kaukai—barstukai*: both the one and the others, before coming to stay with people, are forest dwellers, residing under a tree—in one case under the elder tree, in the second—under the wild pear tree. The differences, of course, are clear: in the first case people pray to *Puškaitis* to bring them kaukai, in the second case—the aitvaras through deceit invites himself to live with man.

Having ascertained these facts, the next step for the mythologist is to search among the ancient Lithuanian gods for a god of the forest who would correspond approximately to the role of *Puškaitis*. Once again the catalogue of gods compiled by Lasicius comes to the rescue; in it the only god who meets our requirements would be *Kirnis,* mentioned twice, about whom it is said that he "guards cherry trees next to the fortress by the lake. If one wishes to appease him, then slaughtered roosters must be placed among the cherry trees and wax candles burned there."[106]

The definition provided for the god *Kirnis* consists of two parts: in the first part he is characterized as *guardian of the cherry trees;* in the second part *the ritual* for his worship is described in a condensed version.

A cursory glance is sufficient to show that the two parts of the definition contradict each other: the god described in the second part belongs to a class of gods who must be "appeased." It is entirely incomprehensible why it should be necessary to appease the guardian of cherry trees with blood offerings and with what seems to be a complicated liturgy. Conversely, Aitvaras, or a being resembling him, requires appeasement. Recalling the parallelism with *Puškaitis, living under the elder tree, it will suffice for now to retain from the first part of the definition only the fact that *Kirnis*, like *Puškaitis, has his own dwelling bound with some kind of tree of the forest. As so often happens in the descriptive mythological texts of the outside observer, the determination of functions is less reliable than the description of the rituals.

Glancing at the rituals tied to the cult of *Kirnis*, we can ascertain that:

(a) living sacrifices are offered to him in the form of *roosters*: the rooster, as we know, is not just one of the manifested forms of the aitvarai, but is also the one who gives him birth.

(b) *wax candles* are burned in his honor: this is entirely congruent with the fiery nature of the aitvaras.

Consequently, the second part of the definition corresponds to the "appeasement" required by the god who—whatever his name might be—could eventually be the ruler of the aitvaras-birds.

Etymological Difficulties

The first part of the definition raises difficulties not only because *Kirnis* is considered to be the guardian of the cherry trees—a stereotype characteristic of the Renaissance—but in part because of the choice of tree—a cherry tree. This is almost too pat: the word *kirnis* means "kryklė vyšnia," *Prunus cerasus,* and *kirnė* is the "wild cherry belladonna," *Atropa Belladonna*.[107] It would follow that the deity "Vyšnia" [meaning "cherry"] guards the cherry trees, the same as, for instance, a deity Liepa [meaning "linden"] guards linden trees.

In *Lietuvių kalbos žodynas [LKŽ, The Academic Dictionary of Lithuanian]* we find yet another word *kirnis,* meaning "swamp, bog,"[108] next to its parasynonym *kirna,* "a place of fallen trees and wood debris," illustrated by the example "by the lake there are *kirnos*, a place of wood debris, willows and osier beds, shrubbery, undergrowth";[109] other forms are *kerna, kernavė* [marsh or bog]. At first glance, the etymology of the god *Kirnis* is more reliable when the proper name is derived from a place name; it is a general rule which can be used to ascertain names of people as well as, perhaps, names of gods.

If *kirnis* is a god of bogs and swamps then his relations with the aitvaras are confirmed even more: not only because a place called by his name corresponds to the most anti-cultural space—*žaltviska,* that is, the flame in the bogs and marshes—but also because the aitvaras bought in Riga, when we investigate it, appears to be a "tree stump in the swamp,"[110] and he still sets fire to all the cottages in the swamp of the village and so forth.

If our conjecture is correct then Lasicius, a conscientious observer but also one who did not know the Lithuanian language, demonstrated more than was necessary: after recording the name of the god *Kirnis* and checking its meaning, he could only get a very simple answer: *kirnis* is the wild cherry tree, since the Lithuanians of those days did not care to tell the Christian foreigners about their gods. For Lasicius this was enough to make *Kirnis* the guardian of cherry trees.

The reader should understand that the aim of our discussion is to compare our analyzed text with the observations of Lasicius about *Kirnis*: in spite of the large number of equivalents, the existence of the cherry tree interferes with the manifestation of the wild pear tree.

The Wild Pear Tree

We must not forget that our *little black chick* was found under a wild pear tree where he returned after being with man. *Grušia* or *kriaušė* [pear tree] is not an ordinary fruit tree and, even though its mythological significance is not yet apparent, its importance in religious thinking is unquestionable. The following Christmas song can serve as an example whose motifs unexpectedly remind one of the ritual described by Lasicius:

> In the middle of the field, *the pear tree* is in bloom
> Alelium, kalėda [Christmas], *the pear tree* is in bloom
>
> In the tree *a candle is burning*
> Alelium, kalėda
>
> Oh, three little sparks fell out,
> Alelium
>
> Oh, and there came great wonders
> Alelium.[111]

Easter songs are mentioned as well, in which a maiden gathers in a silken scarf the silver dew under the pear tree:[112] in both cases they are most probably hymns of ritual origin, whose remaining fragments are not easily given to interpretation.

The mythological elements which have been preserved in wondertales are much clearer. Here, for instance, there is a story about *the Black Gentlemen*.[113] A man who has left home to look for work spends the night under a *pear tree* growing by the side of the road. The little pear tree, whom he thanks for the night's lodging, advises him to look for work with the *black gentlemen*, requesting that he ask them if she will bear fruit before long. After various adventures, the man returns to the pear tree having learned that she will bear fruit *"when the coins buried beneath her roots are dug up."* Murderers attack the man who has dug up the coins and pluck out his eyes (the absence of a cause indicates the mythic character of this fact): birds flying over and perching on the pear tree explain that *under the pear tree* there grows a grass "which can *restore the plucked-out eyes.*"

We see that under the same pear tree where the farmer with whom we are already familiar had found the chick-aitvaras, a second seeker of fortune finds buried coins, the ruler of which we know is Aitvaras; furthermore, under the same pear tree grow blades of grass that can return the plucked-out eyes—the relationship of the Aitvaras with *blindness* is also well-known.

Aitvaras 59

Another tale[114] relates how a man found his fortune: advised by an unknown voice, he digs a hole next to *the pear tree* and under an overturned stone finds *fortune* in the form of a man sleeping soundly. The latter gives him two *gold coins* sending him to the market with instructions to buy and then sell the first object he likes. The man buys a *hen,* which lays an *egg,* and he gets "nine brick houses in town" and "nine thousand" for it. The gentleman who bought the hen explains that *"the hen lays diamond eggs."*

Even though indirectly, we find under the pear tree a whole series of "aitvaras-like" elements: both the gold coins and the hen-aitvaras which lays the diamond eggs. As ruler of precious metals, Aitvaras is also, as in other mythologies, *a ruler of precious stones.*

Thus the wild pear's close ties with Aitvaras are unquestionable.

Aitvaras—Ruler of Birds

There is a clear characteristic separation in these two stories of the deity herself— manifested in the form of "black gentlemen" or an "unknown voice"—from the space she inhabits, where we find the wild pear tree along with the coins that are buried there, and under its shelter a chick or hen who lays diamond eggs. The wild pear tree in no way can be identified with the deity itself, just as we cannot identify **Puškaitis* with the elder tree. These are strong arguments which indicate that the god *Kirnis* cannot be identified with the same-sounding name of the wild cherry tree [kirnė].

A second characteristic common to both texts—along with the song fragments— is the maintenance of comparatively good relations between people and various manifestations of Aitvaras. It would appear that the stories have preserved an even more ancient representation of these relations: the deity which rules the wild pear tree is more likely benevolent and is so out of free will. The cult surrounding *Kirnis* is becoming better understood as well.

In the second story *Aitvaras* appears to be confused somewhat with *Laima*,[115] but the causes for the confusion become apparent: the poor fellow looking for help can turn to two types of "laimes," either to the Mithra-type *Laima* locally bound with the *linden* tree, *liepa,* or to the Varuna-type *Kirnis* (one of the divine forms of Aitvaras), related to the wild *pear tree.* The words of the song about the young man finding fortune are becoming better understood: "Prijojau liepa, ir žalia grušia"[116] [I rode up to the linden tree and the wild pear tree].

In conclusion we must say this: the localization of aitvaras as a bird in the woods under the wild pear tree beyond the bounds of cultural space is, by our calculations, within the framework of mythological reconstruction, a *strong hypothesis.* Can the deity in whose jurisdiction this tree exists and on whose rule the aitvarai-birds depend be identified with the god *Kirnis?* The question still remains open, even though a good number of arguments have been gathered as a basis for this thesis. It seems that only in this manner is it possible to ascribe distinct functions to *Kirnis* and explain the meaning of the description of his cult.

Aitvaras—A Cosmic Deity

The Etymological Semanticism of Aitvaras

It would be wrong to suppose that the enthronement of *Kirnis* as ruler of the aitvaras-birds would make him an autonomous god having nothing in common with Aitvaras and his other manifestations: we often encounter this among mythological deities of a higher class for whom separate cults are organized or who are honored by various, separate names. The cult of *Kirnis* could just as well be explained as a certain instance of mediation which allowed people to communicate with cosmic powers unconcerned with mankind, as an instance in which it would be possible in an epoch of religious degradation to conceptualize in some way an Aitvaras, characterized by primordial features, as a provider of goods of the kaukai class.

The character traits of Aitvaras which we have tried progressively to identify in this study are repeated in the etymological analysis of his name. Būga[117] has compiled a large word family, which is not only Indo-European but Baltic as well, around the stem *var-* (which is the second component of the compound word *aitivaras*). In this latter case we can group the basic meanings of the word as determined by Būga in the following manner:

(1) two sememes, expressing *processes*:
   (a) *var-yti* [to drive, distill]
   (b) *vir-ti* [to boil]

The first meaning is a description of a rotational movement, occurring in position (comp. *varyti samagona* [to distill brandy]) or propelled forward (comp. *varyti vaga* [plough a furrow]; *įvaryti kaltūna* [to inflict, to drive in, kaltūnas]); the second meaning is the denotation of the same movement (comp. *versmė*, "source of water") accompanied by a thermal process (comp. *virti košė* [boil cereal]);

(2) one sememe as *agent of the process* (comp. Latvian *vara, vare*, "power," "force")

(3) one sememe as the *result of the process* (comp. *varis* "metal")

Reviewing the small number of compound words whose second component is *-var-as*, we can explain more precisely the significance of aitvaras:

(1) Comparing *aiti-varas* with *aki-varas*, in which *-var-as* signifies *power* as the agent in the process, we note these differences:

aiti-varas	aki-varas
centrifugal force	centripetal force
exteriorizing force (directed outward)	interiorizing force (directed inward)

(2) Contrasting *aiti-varas* vs. *geivaras* "barely alive man"

klivaras "exhausted man"
liovaras "sluggish man"[118]

we find an opposition already mentioned between the agent of the process and the result of the process with the only difference being that *varis* is a positive result while *geivaras* or *liovaras* are negated results of that process (as the ailing housewife is a negative "result"). The affirmative or negative appraisal of the result belongs to the first element of the compound word.

Aitvaras and Vėjas

We are already familiar with the first element of the compound word *-ait-as*: it means "restless individual." Therefore to the global meaning of the second element, understood as a "rotational centrifugal force propelled forward," we must add "perpetual, random movement" components. Such, roughly, would be the spiritual portrait of our Aitvaras.

Taking into account that it is an air deity, its comparison with *viesulas* [the whirlwind] presents itself even more strongly because in stereotypical expressions such as *aitais nueiti, aitu keliais nueiti*[119] [go astray], *aitas* is easily interchanged with the word *vėjas* [wind]. You see, the *whirlwind* also has his "road": "if a whirlwind comes into the path of a man then a little devil can obsess him"[120] since the whirlwind spinning is nothing other than the small wind deities, commonly called *velniukai* [little devils], but which have other names—*puščiai*,[121] *svodba*[122] or *veselia*.[123] Their ruling head, *vėjas* [wind], is represented generally in a human form, as an "old man" with thick lips,[124] "storlūpis,"[125] who with one small uplifting of his long whiskers blows the roofs off the cottages.[126]

Even though this anthropomorphic form does not as yet allow *Vėjas* to be identified with Aitvaras, it does not interfere with our search for traits common to both of them to determine their kinship. One such trait is their negative stance with respect to the *knife*. We recall that the mane of the kaltūnas-ridden horse must be hacked off with a stone and not a knife, otherwise the horse becomes blind or lame. *Vėjas* can be killed—or at least wounded—only by hurling a knife at him.[127] One time while drying the rye harvest on the threshing floor and being bothered by the wind and hurling the knife through the doorway, a man found the "ground sprinkled with blood," and following the drops of blood he found in the forest an ailing old man, whose face had been "cut open by a knife."[128] As much as *Vėjas*, Aitvaras appears to belong to a certain, specific sphere of a divine culture which pits itself against the use of the knife as an implement of war: in this sense both of them are compared with *Velnias* [Devil], whose biggest crime is the theft of the knife from Perkūnas.

We could find more traits common to both Vėjas and Perkūnas [Thunder] but it would raise a variety of problems requiring separate studies for the identification of the god *Vėjas* (Sanskrit *Vajū*) or *Vėjopatis*.[129] It will suffice only to mention that next to his anthropomorphic figure, *Vėjas*, the "Aeolus Žmudzki" (Aeolus of Western Lithuanians) living "on a cloud in the sky" has yet another, perhaps more ancient form: he is represented as a "beast of the sky" who "from under his nails or fingertips emits the wind."[130] This *Vėjas* in the semblance of a beast in the sky is compared in turn by the same informant with *Gavėnas*, about whom it is said that "when he sharpens his knife, wind emanates from his fingernails":[131] here once again a comparison offers itself between the wind emanating from his fingernails with the fingernails spoiled by aitvaras with kaltūnas.

Aitvaras and Perkūnas

This incorporation of *Vėjas* into the problematic of *Aitvaras* is not an isolated excursion into the space between the sky and the earth but involves a wish to reveal the autonomous sacred plane in which the specific power of Aitvaras would be as significant as his activity and form. In that respect the introduction of *Vėjas*, manifested in the form of a heavenly beast, helps us to understand that the nonrealistic, partly zoomorphic, partly elemental cosmic appearance of Aitvaras is not some kind of exception in the imagery of Lithuanian deities but just the opposite. Aitvaras has equivalents; he is not alone in the world of Lithuanian gods.

It would be wrong to suppose, on the other hand, that the basic activity of the gods, that their primary responsibility, would be to be concerned with people. They have enough problems of their own, lead their own lives, are friends and enemies among themselves, conduct unending battles—thus illustrating the history of the world. We had need, for instance, to deal with the battle led by *Perkūnas* against *Aitvaras* even though we did not quite understand its cause. It is more interesting to emphasize that Perkūnas does battle not only with *Aitvaras* but with *Vėjas*: there are strict directives pertaining to Perkūnas' thunder: the fact that one must avoid the draft, "čiongo,"[132] or one must not run so as to stir the wind,[133] indicates that people understand this battle quite well. A more syncretic explanation that this is only an eternal battle between *Perkūnas* and *Velnias* is, as we see, a simplification of the history of the divine world.

On the other hand, sovereign gods—or gods making a claim to an even partial regional sovereignty—have not only the hierarchic problems of maintaining their rank or gaining new spheres of power, but also the problems of the entire cosmos and the governing of all its elements. Here, for instance, *Vėjas* during his spare time can blow the roofs down, destroy the homesteads, in due course provoke *svodbas*, but the *brother of Vėjas*, whose head so bursts with pain that he even has it fettered with "iron bars,"[134]—if he should begin to blow then he not only would die himself but "wys ką išžlaužitų, ne twertu ni žole, ni medis"[135] [he would destroy everything]. We can see what *boundless power*, threatening a cosmic catastrophe, is concealed in these gods persecuted by Perkūnas.

Meanwhile, *Vėjas*, in turn, leads a separate battle with *Marių Karalius*[136] [King of the Seas]: the waters of the sea blown out by him on returning drown his three sons.[137]

Only in the context of such a cosmic battle is it possible to understand the battle of *Perkūnas* with *Aitvaras*: "Perkūnas chased the aitvaras. Aitvarus tried to hide—in the hills, in the waters, in the lakes. Perkūnas chased him, upturned the hills and struck the water with his power, wanting to kill the aitvaras. Perkūnas threw pieces of the earth at him to slow him down . . . Where Perkūnas grabbed some ground, lakes and pits appeared. Aitvaras spat out the water and filled those depressions. Where Perkūnas hurled the earth, there appeared hills."[138]

This description can be supplemented by another, similar text: "There came such a *storm*, that it carried the water and the earth with it. It is said that Perkūnas was chasing Aitvaras. He swallowed and spat where there was water on earth, all of it together, and dropped and spilled them out unto another place."[139]

It is evident, first of all, that the *storm* described in these texts is no longer the *whirlwind* of the little devils—"velniukų veselija" led by *Vėjas*—but a cosmic battle between two gods of comparable strength: even though *Aitvaras* is chased by *Perkūnas* and temporarily overpowered, he doesn't give up and the battle is destined to continue for ages. It is apparent, as well, that this is a battle between two sky-air beings on earth, using as weapons the elements that form the world: "earth" and "water." These two elements are not only implements of the battle, but during the time of the battle the earth's surface relief is formed with them, thus creating the hills and lakes. In a certain sense, their battle is the original chaos—the *storm* after which the contours of the earth become revealed. Only as a consequence of this battle will Perkūnas be able to fecundate the earth—Žemyna, who will then cover herself with a clothing of "greenery."

The place of Aitvaras in the world of Lithuanian gods is slowly becoming more distinct: he belongs to that first, primary generation of gods—gods who are imagined to be in the shape of giants, monsters, and beasts of the sky, whose defeat permitted the creation of the first order in the world.

III

AUŠRINĖ

This study will attempt to develop and elucidate to the extent possible one aspect of Lithuanian culture—its viewpoint concerning life and death and the concepts of fate, fortune, youth, beauty and material benefit that are associated with this viewpoint. The means by which we hope to approach this problematic involves the utilization of ethnic cultural data, preserved by folklore in the form of folk beliefs and customs.

The method which will be used to reconstruct the figure of the goddess Aušrinė and her sphere of action is simple yet perilous. We will select one out of a thousand Lithuanian folktales, and attempt to read it not as a tale but as a myth, searching for the significance which is contained beneath the surface of the text. Such a reading does not, in essence, differ from the analysis of poems, the desire of the psychoanalyst to understand his or her patient, or a solution to a crossword puzzle. The chance of making a mistake is hidden in every corner of the text and the boundary between intuition and "fantasy" is not always clear. Mythic truth is safeguarded only by the comparability of the text with other texts, both similar and different, and by its internal coherence.

The tale we have chosen is taken from the M. Davainis-Silvestraitis collection published in Lithuania (Vilnius, 1973) *Pasakos, Sakmės, Oracijos* [Tales, Legends, and Orations]. The tale itself is called "Saulė and Vėjų Motina" [The Sun and The Mother of the Winds] (pp. 309–13); it is characteristic since it marks especially well the distance which separates two—"surface" and "deep"—modes of reading.

To allow readers to orient themselves, the entire text will be presented first, with the separate segments repeated later, one after the other.

> There were three brothers. To one brother, Joseph, two suns always appeared—in the morning at breakfast and in the evening at vespers; otherwise he could not see the second sun. He asked his brothers to let him go search for the second sun. The brothers blessed him and sent him on.
>
> He came to another land with great forests. He listens—there is an uproar in the forest. He is curious to know what is going on there. He looks—a lion, a hawk, an ant, and a wolf have killed an ox, but don't know how to divide it. The lion notices there there is a fresh [meat] man and calls him to come closer:
>
> "Man, be kind, divide that meat for us." The man cut off the head, and gave it to the ant:

Aušrinė

"You are small, you can eat away at all the little holes!"
He gave the sinews to the lion, the bones to the wolf, the ribs to the hawk.
"Is everyone satisfied with the division?"
"Very beholden!"
Each one gave him a bit of hair, the ant his whisker, and the hawk—a feather.
"If there is trouble, reflect on the things we have given you, then it will be so."
He went further into the forest and wished to eat—he reflected on the wolf. He changed into a wolf, caught a ram and ate it. He reflected on the hawk—changed into a hawk, and quickly traveled to a foreign land. He set out to fly to the mother of the winds. He enters her cottage, paying his respects to God.
"By all eternity. What are you looking for?"
"I am searching for the second sun!"
"I will roll a ball [of yarn], follow that ball, you will come to my mother."
He snapped the yarn with his beak, being a hawk, and traveled very far. He came to the mother of the winds. The mother placed him to guard the orchard:
"If you protect the orchard, then tomorrow you will know the sun!"
She gave him a sword, and he went to the orchard. In the middle of the night, there came a man to whom the trees were like twigs. The giant reached through the fence, uprooted a tree, and carried it off. The man raised the sword and chopped off the arms of the giant, who went away. After an hour, there came another, trampling the forest under his feet. He leaned on the fence, again to uproot the apple tree. The man chopped off his head. A third one came—he chopped him in half.

When day came, he went to the mistress and described the troubles of the night. They went to the orchard to look around, and found three giants that had been slain. For that good deed, she gave him three apples. The apples were of great worth.

She summoned her children, the four winds, and asked them:
"Did you see the second sun anywhere?"
The north wind answered:
"That's not the sun. I was there today and saw for myself. There is a maiden on an island in the sea with hair like the sun. She has a manor."
The mother of the winds once again rolled the ball of yarn to him. He placed the yarn in his beak, having changed to a hawk, and traveled to the sea shore. The north wind came to him, and taught him:
"Now, wait until the evening. The maiden's bull will return with three cows from the forest and will swim across the sea to the other side. Hold onto the tail of the bull, it will carry you to the other side. Then dive under when you have swum across, since he will gore you if he sees you. When you come out of the water, you will find a birch stump on that island. Crawl into that stump since the bull will look for you. After breakfast go to the manor, you will find the maiden sleeping. She lies on her stomach. Mount her as you would a horse and braid her hair in your hands. She will say: Let me go! If you don't the earth will perish, turn into the sea. You say: I will swim out on you. She will say this three times. Then she will say: You are mine, I am yours. Then release her."

And the bull returned from the forest with the cows. The man held onto the bull's tail and was carried across the seas. He did this. He later released the maiden when she said: "You are mine, I am yours." They both lived there for many years. He, the smaller one, was her servant. He himself herded the cows every morning across the seas. The bull did nothing to him.

Once he found one hair of that maiden stuck on a thorn and found an empty nutshell. Wrapping the hair up, he put it into that nutshell and threw it into the sea. A ray from the sea became reflected into the sky as the biggest star.

A prince, sailing the seas, saw the novelty. He set his sail directly for that star, came closer, gazed through the spyglass, and found the nutshell. He hurried home as fast as he could. He had an old grandmother witch:

"Tell me, old woman, what is that hair?"

"There is a maiden with such hair!"

"Could you bring her here? I'll cast a gold cradle for you, rock it day and night."

The witch changed to a beggar and went to the maiden, telling her that she had been thrown out of a ship onto the shore:

"I am a poor beggar, I asked them to take me but they put me on the shore here. Perhaps, beneficent lady, you could take me as your servant. I will serve you well."

She accepted her offer. She remained there for a week or two, becoming a true servant. Whatever the maiden said to do, she did it twice as well. The witch, meeting the prince at night, ordered him to cast a gold ship and go where he had found that nutshell. It was to have a silver bridge too.

In the morning at 8 the maiden awoke, and left her manor when she saw the new ship. Such a vessel there had never been. The old woman invited the maiden:

"Come see!"

The maiden had left bareheaded. She started back to get her scarf. The sorceress said:

"I will bring you the scarf."

The husband slept. The witch took a knife and killed the husband. She took out his lungs and liver and threw them in passing into the sea. The lady was not aware that she had done this. She came closer to the ship—she sees that there are no people on it. The sorceress invited the lady to take a look. When she stepped onto the ship, it started to sail. The prince jumped out, grabbed the maiden, took her to his dwelling.

"Don't be afraid, you'll be safer with me than here. I have a kingdom, soldiers."

He brought her to his kingdom. He wanted to marry her in a little while.

"I cannot marry for a year! I mourn for my father, who died not long ago."

She bargained for time as best she could, so he would not marry her.

All the four winds had gathered at their mother's to ask about any news. They look and see that all the apples in their mother's orchard have withered.

"Why is this so, mother?"

"Go look, perhaps our friend who guarded the orchard is dead."

The found him slain. They began to search the shores and the water for his lungs. They saw—a very large crab was dragging them into his cave. They took away his lungs and liver. The north wind dove into the seas and carried off the restorative water and the "gyvuonis." He anointed him, washed him—he stood healthy and whole.

"Where did that maiden go?"

"I don't know. I was asleep."

"You were slain." He searches all the lands—his maiden is nowhere. He asked the wind for directions:

"What shall I do now?"

The north wind:

"Go to her manor. You'll find a bridle and saddle. Saddle the bull, and there will stand such a stallion as has never been seen in all the kingdom. Mount it, and you'll

Aušrinė 67

ride on the seas better than on land. He will carry you to the kingdom where she is. On that day there will be a horse fair, the king will look to buy a stallion. When he starts to haggle you say: 'If buying, buy; I don't have time.' Until the maiden comes.''

The maiden came out and recognized her animal. She took him by the hand and mounted the horse. They rose into the sky, escaped to her manor. The king grieved greatly. He asked his council:
"What should be done now?"
"There are no instructions, nothing."
The maiden upon returning released her bull. The bull knelt down and spoke in a man's voice:
"Chop off my head!"
The maiden did not want to chop it off, but she had to. She chopped the head off—a fourth of the seas disappeared, became land. Her brother emerged from the bull. She cut off the heads of all three cows, who were her sisters. All the seas disappeared, turned to land. The earth sprang to life. She remained the queen of that earth and her husband its king. Her husband atoned for her brother and her sisters. They lived happily ever after.
And that's the end.

I. Wondertale or Myth?

There were three brothers. To one brother, Joseph, two suns always appeared—in the morning at breakfast and in the evening at vespers; otherwise he couldn't see the second sun. He asked his brothers to let him to search for the second sun. The brothers blessed him and sent him on.

An entire series of elements in this introductory segment corresponds to the canons of wondertales:

(1) The presence of *three brothers,* which defines the starting situation.
(2) The departure to *search* for something.
(3) The *blessing* of the traveler.

Other traits of the text are more unusual:

(1) Absence of representatives of the older generation (parents or king), who would play—directly or indirectly—the role of the Sender, indicating for whom, in the name of what values, the mission is to be carried out.
(2) Request for permission from his brothers to travel: usually the three brothers leave together, or one after the other.
(3) The rarity of the hero's name—Joseph.

These unforeseen elements at once attract the reader's attention to that which separates this story from the others. However, the decisive mythic character of the text appears in the choice of the sought-for object: in place of the usual good *fortune,* the desired object here is recorded as the *Second Sun.* The extraordinary hero will seek an object of value of unusual worth.

The first segment, it goes without saying, offers too few facts to make it possible to begin to look for an answer to the question—on which the entire interpretation of this text depends—what, namely, is that Second Sun. We need thus to set aside this problem at least until the fourth segment, where the *North Wind* will offer us his explanation.

Generally taken, it can already be noted that we are dealing with a text in which abundant narrative motifs are tied to mythological data. This enlarges the difficulty and care necessary for its reading.

II. The Just Division

He came to another land with great forests. He listens—there is an uproar in the forest. He is curious to know what is going on there. He looks—a lion, a hawk, an ant, and a wolf have killed an ox, but don't know how to divide it. The lion notices that there is a fresh [meat] man and calls him to come closer:

"Man, be kind, divide that meat for us." The man cut off the head, gave it to the ant:

"You are small, you can eat away at all the little holes!"

He gave the sinews to the lion, the bones to the wolf, the ribs to the hawk.

"Is everyone satisfied with my division?"

"Very beholden!"

Each one gave him a bit of hair—the ant, his whisker, and the hawk, a feather:

"If there is trouble, reflect on the things we have given you, then it will be so."

He went further into the forest and wished to eat—he reflected on the wolf. He changed into a wolf, caught a ram and ate it. He reflected on the hawk—changed into a hawk, and quickly traveled to a foreign land.

Animal Helpers

The second segment utilizes a frequently occurring motif in wondertales known throughout the world, that of animal helpers: this is a characteristic *migratory motif*.

Thus it must be noted at once that when this motif is fully developed, every animal whom the hero had helped to extricate from trouble, in turn, becomes a helper, and its appearance at the necessary moment seemingly creates a separate episode of the story. In that manner, the structure of the story becomes equally balanced according to the principle "you for me, I for you," and is based on an implicit agreement.

In our case, only one helper is necessary for the further development of the story by the narrator—the *hawk*. He will help the hero transmigrate to another mythic space. Applying the methodological principle of *reading,* according to which every text or its fragment has to be read not from the beginning but from the end, one of the basic narrative functions of this segment is clearly revealed: the entire distribution motif seems to be developed only to enable the hero to find a necessary *helper* for himself.

It is clear, therefore, that the manner chosen by our text of a "just division" is neither the only way to introduce the hawk into the text and make him the helper, nor is it obligatory. In tales one or another such bird helps transport the hero from one space to another for any type of service, most often, for the rescue of his children. There emerges then a well-founded question: why is the necessity for acquisition of animal helpers in our story solved by the introduction of a specific, non-obligatory *just division* motif?

The Hero's Qualification

Narrative logic, familiarity with narrative structure, allows us to understand the functional significance of the just division—which is also a repetitive and migratory motif.

The first element for its comprehension involves the distribution model of *spaces* utilized in the text. The hero fulfills his basic feat in the *utopic* space ("in another world": underground, underwater, in the sky): his place of origin, from this point of view, is *heterotopic,* and the transmigration from one space to another is accomplished by crossing *paratopic* space. In Lithuanian tales, as with the neighboring Germans and Slavs, such a paratopic space is most often the *forest* which is found beyond the boundaries of the civilized world, but which has to be crossed when one wants to find another "possible" world. In this space the *trials* of the hero usually take place; after these the hero becomes *qualified* to carry out his future exploits.

Applying this model to our text, it is not difficult to see that the "just division" is a task which the hero must fulfill in order to become a hero. The tasks are various: they can test the hero's power, his cunning and so forth. According to the nature of the task, the listener-reader decides the true *nature* of the hero, together with the nature of the Sender, whose entrusted mission the hero fulfills.

The answer to the question of why our text introduces a "just division" motif will become clearer by itself within the framework of this narrative model: the hero's ordeals, and the competence he acquires as a consequence, concern (*a*) the hero's knowledge of *how-to-act* (*b*) in making *just decisions*. The sovereign sphere, to which the activities of the hero in our text belong, becomes clearer as well: namely, the contractual sovereign sphere of *Mithra*.

The Metamorphoses of the Hero

The contractual structure of this segment is clear: the hero fulfills the just division as requested by the animals, satisfying everyone. For services rendered, he is presented with the "*hair*" of every animal and in that manner he acquires several *helpers* for his future activity.

The status of the helper in narrative structure requires an explanation: the helper in the story can be a separate actor (animal, man, magic object and so forth), but, having such an autonomous figure, he is also an inseparable part of the hero's nature. The French epic hero Roland, for example, has the miraculous sword Durendal, but that means in turn that he is himself an unusual athlete. In other words, possession of helpers is only a figurative means for depicting the basic attributes of the hero's nature.

In our case, therefore, the acquisition of the hair of the *wolf* or the *hawk* means nothing more than the hero's acquisition of basic traits characterizing the nature of the *wolf* or the *hawk*.

The word *hair* used in our text does not fully correspond to the definition "an outgrowth resembling a thread in the skin of man or animal":[1] it can be used to name the ant's *whiskers* and the hawk's *feathers*. It is the most external body part of every animal, its *metonym,* able to stand in for the animal's entire body. Two separate possibilities for the use of the *hair* are self-evident.

First of all, the possession of a hair of another person (a beloved, children, or parents worn in a medallion) determines an obligatory relation between the possessor of the hair and its owner, inevitably bringing them closer: this is only a profane, degraded form of relationship established by means of the hair. In wondertales, possession of the hair and reflection on the being which it represents often calls for the appearance of the being: these two cases are the same in nature, differing only in the degree of imagined effectiveness and strength of the ties with the *hair*. The aforementioned *hawk* in our story was able, for instance, to present his "hair"—a feather—as a gift. Possessing it and reflecting on the hawk, the hero provokes the appearance of the hawk and the hawk, in turn, as it is received in tales, was able to place the hero on his back and transport him to another space.

The function of the *hair* is recorded differently in our text. The strength of the ties that are created between two people is, of course, not in doubt here, although the hero's "reflection on the wolf" or "about the hawk" goes further, calling forth metamorphosis into a wolf or hawk. Here we are dealing with a specific mythic mentality in which the "hair" of every living being metonymically corresponds to its bodily form, with whose help it is manifested on the phenomenological plane of this world. But even such an explanation is not enough. In another variant of "just division,"[2] the hero, having divided the birch between the lion, the ant, and the falcon, receives from each one "po tokia laime" [such fortune] that with its help, whenever he so wishes, he is able to "change" into one or another of these animals. Undoubtedly *laimė* is here a synonym for the *hair*. Our initial explanation is incomplete because it is too close to the traditional body and soul dichotomy: *laimė-dalia* is one of the body-spirit units that make up the person, whose dwelling place can be the human body, but which can also be separate from it, living, for instance, in the swan, lamb, or a well-chosen wife. We will devote a good deal of space in the second part of this study to the *laimė-dalia* problem because of its special importance for understanding the Lithuanian world view; thus, we will not pause here. However, even such a superficial explanation of *hair-fortune* will help us understand one of the basic episodes of this myth—the manifestation of the hair of the "maiden of the sea" in the form of a star.

It is noteworthy that our story does not exploit all possibilities of the metamorphosis offered at the beginning, but chooses from them only two—the transformation into a wolf and a hawk.

The significance of the choice of a *hawk* is rather clear: on the narrative plane it performs an acknowledged function, transporting the hero from the paratopic forest space to the utopic atmospheric space. Since, as we have already mentioned, the acquisition of a helper means the enrichment of the hero with new attributes characteristic of the helper, the transformation of the hero into a hawk invests him with a *mediator's* value between certain human and certain divine spheres. In the mythological sense, the *hawk* is considered to be either the husband of the *cuckoo* or the shape she assumes during wintertime.[3] Taking into consideration the fact that the cuckoo as a fate-determining mythic being belongs as well to the *Mithra* sphere of divine *knowledge,* the hero's trait as mediator is supplemented with knowledge of the means for communicating with the divine world. It is not surprising then that the hero-hawk finds the path to the *Mother of the Winds* [Vėjų Motina] and is received well by her.

It is more difficult to determine the correct function of the *wolf.* He differs from the other living beings—the lion and the ant—in that the metamorphosis procedure as applied to him—in which the hero changes into a wolf so he can eat the lamb—does not seem sufficiently serious and, most importantly, is not as well-founded narratively, as is, for example, his transformation to a hawk. This seems a rather typical case of *hapax*: the mythic figure is preserved by the storyteller, who is not aware of either its meaning or its manner of manifestation. It is noteworthy that in Lithuanian mythology the *wolf*[4]—sometimes an *iron wolf,*[5] sometimes a *copper wolf*[6]—is encountered in what at first glance appears to be rather unexpected surroundings: he is either the lover himself—a seducer, who persuades the sister to relinquish an incestuous life with her brother—or a helper of the hero, who has departed to find "a maiden" or "a princess" in a foreign land or in another kingdom. In one case or another, he appears as an enemy of endogamy and a creator of a new family structure based on exogamy and of marriages determined by *contract*. Our hero, capable of changing into a wolf—or perhaps transformed into a wolf for that purpose in versions unrecorded or as yet unknown to us—represents the very seeker of love based on contractual relations between two worlds.

We will return to the figure of the *wolf* below.

III. The Orchard of Magical Apples

He set out to fly to the mother of the winds. He enters her cottage, paying his respects to God.

"By all eternity. What are you looking for?"

"I am searching for the second sun!"

"I will roll a ball [of yarn], follow that ball, you will come to my mother."

He snapped the yarn with his beak, being a hawk, and traveled very far. He came to the mother of the winds. The mother placed him to guard the orchard:

"If you protect the orchard, then tomorrow you will know the sun!"

She gave him a sword, and he went to the orchard. In the middle of the night, there came a man to whom the trees were like twigs. The giant reached through the fence, uprooted a tree, and carried it off. The man raised the sword and chopped off the arms of the giant, who went away. After an hour, there came another, trampling the forest under his feet. He leaned on the fence, again to uproot the apple tree. The man chopped off his head. A third one came—he chopped him in half.

When day came, he went to the mistress and described the troubles of the night. They went to the orchard to look around, and found three giants that had been slain. For that good deed, she gave him three apples. The apples were of great worth.

Stereotypic Motifs and Mistakes in Logic

This segment utilizes two stereotypic migratory motifs to develop the action:
(1) *A ball to show the way.*
(2) *The orchard of magical apples.*

Both of these motifs are necessary to enable the hero, according to his narrative program, to perform, within the confines of this text, the tasks assigned to him:
(1) To find the way to his goal.
(2) To acquire an object of value—the apple.

It should be noted that in this short fragment there are two prominent mistakes in logic: it seems that the storyteller, lucky to have found conventional motifs which help him develop the intrigue successfully, forgets the mythological aim of the story and no longer concerns himself with maintaining the accurate appearance or nature of his character. We may regard this segment as a good example of the process of degradation of myth into story.

The first mistake is the too-early appearance of the *Mother of the Winds* [Vėjų Motina]. In a normal wondertale we should find one of the animal helpers in this position. Since the action occurs "in a foreign land," it is difficult to introduce the animals here: in their place we would expect some sort of secondary mythic being or deity. The words, "you will go to *my* mother" which are placed on the lips of a character would indicate that the helper's role is played here by the daughter of the *Mother of the Winds*. However, at least until now, we have encountered no wind deity of the female gender in the Lithuanian context. The helper's figure thus remains unclear, which is just as well, since no role is provided for him in the future.

The second mistake is that the slain giants and their dead numbers do not match: the first giant, whose arms the hero chops off, "went away," while the next morning, *Vėjų Motina* finds the bodies of *three* giants. It appears that the storyteller has gotten confused here, utilizing the much-liked *triplication* process of wondertales for the description of the battle with the giants. Having introduced three giants in place of one giant, the victory seems much larger, especially if it is underscored by the fact that the first time the arms are chopped off, the second—the head, and in the third the giant himself is chopped in half. Nevertheless, again, as with the case of the daughter of the *Mother of the Winds,* the storyteller goes astray, allowing his favorite literary genre mechanism to operate, and the personage who should represent the giant class recedes: only his function as the destroyer of the orchard and the characteristic trait of his appearance—his arms—remain. Thus in one and the same text, not far from one another, we find two *hapaxes*: the *wolf* and the armless *Giant*.

The Apple Orchard

The arrival of the hero at the *Mother of the Winds* by way of the road as shown by the rolling ball does not raise special problems. More interesting is the choice of *Vėjų Motina*—and the family of the Winds in general—as the helper in the search for the Second Sun.

At the dwelling of *Vėjų Motina* is found the orchard of magical apples which are "of great worth." The motif and symbolism of such an orchard is common, perhaps, to all Indo-European mythology: at this time we can supplement it with a whole series of Lithuanian variants.

The role of *Mother of the Winds* as mistress of the apple orchard is not accidental. According to Lithuanian beliefs, the *wind* has the power to pollinate the apple trees: "When apple trees, swayed by the wind, creak, then it is said it will be a fruitful year in the orchard since the apple trees creak from a great number of fruit."[7] In Lithuania Minor, it is said: "if you find a *hobble* or *rope* on the roadway, then you should bring it back and hang it on the apple tree, so that the tree will become fruitful and full of apples."[8] The significance of this advice becomes more apparent when we discover that such hobbles found on the roadway are "neither of flax nor burlap, neither woven or spun—they are only the *bonds of the wind*."[9]

We can attempt to identify the magical apple orchard with the *Garden of Paradise*—a constellation which apparently exists "in the winter to the east. In winter time near the middle of the sky, those stars appear as round as a wagon wheel, but can be seen in a wide circle to the East. They all shine bright. The ancients knew much about them, but they did not reveal their cunning to just anyone."[10] Since we have no systematic published facts about the structure of the Lithuanian sky dome, it is difficult to say anything more precise concerning this identification. Determining the relationship between orchards and constellations could help explain one of the fortune-telling customs which take place on Christmas night, according to which a starlit Christmas night is the promise of an abundance of apples.[11]

Next to the same case there can be placed a somewhat Christianized representation of *Paradise* (Christian in that it is identified with the place of life after death): "Paradise, it is said, lies in a land to the East—it is the finest and most beautiful *garden,* in which all kinds of trees grow with the most wondrous and tastiest fruit (gold leaves, diamond apples and so on) . . . where eternal day reigns. . . . [12] Such a representation of a *Garden of Paradise* is close to our text also because two giants guard it: *Auštra* lights the way and *Vėjas* blows back the unworthy.[13] Our apple orchard is also in a similar neighborhood.

Basanavičius' study of the symbolism of apples in Lithuanian mythology[14] is sufficiently comprehensive: we will attempt only to summarize it, applying it to the needs of our analysis.

On the basis of folk song material, Basanavičius focuses first of all on their parallelism, in which "youths walk about their *apple orchards,* (as) maidens in their *gardens of rue.*" Therefore the tying of love's knot is often represented by the "rolling of an apple" or "by the tossing of apples," sometimes inviting in such matters the *wind* as helper:

> I will pick *two apples*
> And send them to my love
> I won't carry them or give them to another
> But blow them by way of the South Wind[15]

or when trying to entice a young maiden, promising her wedded bliss:

> Hard tasks you won't do
> Nor reap rye on the hill
> Only walk about the orchard
> Gathering *beautiful apples*.[16]

In Prussian Lithuania it is understood that *to gather apples* most simply means "to chase girls" or "to sweet-talk the girls."[17]

In conclusion, it is clear that the *apple* is a *symbol of love* and as such, it can have magic powers. Here then, according to examples presented by Basanavičius, are its basic characteristics:

(1) The apple inspires the *desire for love*.
(2) The apple can change one's *gender* (from female to male).
(3) The eating of love's apple makes one *beautiful*.
(4) The apple returns *health* to the ailing.

Love, beauty, and *health* (not to mention the change in gender, which even though it belongs to the same semantic sphere, forms a separate problematic) are the basic attributes which are acquired and transmitted with the help of the magical apples, attributes which in Indo-European mythology most often characterize one of the three sovereign functions, as determined by Dumézil, that belong to female deities (Aphrodite, Freya and so on).

Vėjopatis and His Family

We must return for a bit to one domain in our text, the estate of the *Mother of the Winds*, to add to our knowledge of the Wind family.

It seemed perfectly natural that the fantastic orchard of love apples belongs to the *Mother of the Winds*, that is, in the purview of the wind-pollinator mother. However, her appearance in the mythological text raises problems. We know that Latvian mythology is full of female deities, referred to as mothers, and that *Vejasmate* is one of them.[18] Ukrainian tales as well are acquainted with the Mother of the Winds, next to the mothers of the Moon and the Sun, who distribute the magical apples.[19] Thus in the religion of the Lithuanians, with the exception of what we may perhaps be permitted to call the "normal" female deities (Žemyna, Aušrinė, Laima, Ragana), who correspond as well to other Indo-European deities, it is the deities of the male sex who dominate, and it is *Vėjopatis* who rules the kingdom of the winds (identified by

Praetorius with *Bangpūtis* [blower of the waves]),[20] and not Vėjų Motina. Without rejecting the possibility of Vėjopatis himself having a wife, who might belong to another action sphere not related to the wind, we must look at *Vėjų Motina* not with distrust but with caution.

In Lithuania the well-known wind family consists of *Vėjas* [the Wind], his ailing brother and his four sons: *Rytis* [East Wind], *Pietis* [South Wind], *Vakaris* [West Wind] and *Šiauris* [North Wind].[21] These mythologically necessary sons represent the four cardinal points of the world, but practically speaking it should be stated that they do not blow by any such categorical or geometric formation. In the absence of studies in this area, we must be content with random lexical facts, which indicate a special attentiveness to winds that blow at a 45 degree angle. Among these, for example, are the northeast wind, called *Auštrinis* or *Audenis,* the southwest wind named *Aulaukis* and the southeast wind *Ožinis*.[22] We think that this allows us to identify the North Wind *Šiauris* in our text with *Auštrinis* especially since such an identification corresponds to the direction of his action—which indicates the direction of the sea maiden's dwelling—and with the similarity of their names (*Auštrinis = Auštra, Aušra, Aušrinė*).[23] This case can be expanded with one more piece of evidence that pertains to the healing power of *Auštrinis*: "If your head aches, face the Auštrinis wind, and soon you will be well."[24]

For a better understanding of our text it would be useful to add certain other traits characteristic of the Wind family. One of them is the wind's inquisitiveness: once upon a time the four sons of the wind wishing to see the *bottom of the sea* began to blow the water from the sea and caused a big flood on the earth.[25] With such inquisitiveness there is bound up, as a consequence, the wind's wide-ranging *knowledge* of the geographic and cosmographic sphere: a person who wishes to know where the sorcerer hid his magic treasure, in turn appeals to the Sun, the Moon and the Water, who send him from one to the other. Finally, Water says to him, "I don't know anything, but I can tell you *who does know.* Go to the forest that you see from here and you will find there a very large oak tree. *The throne of the wind is in the oak tree.*[26] Going to *The Kingdom of the Wind* the hero acquires the necessary information.

Thus, one of the basic characteristics of the Wind [*Vėjas*] is his knowledge of the world. It would seem that as much as the pathways of the earth—where the Wind, as we remember, sometimes loses his bindings—the air or the pathways of the sky are in his knowledge: after all the "daughter" of Vėjų Motina gives to our hero the *rolling ball* that leads the way, and the North Wind will later tell him how and where to find the Second Sun.

The Race of Giants

It is worth noting that the hero arriving at the *Vėjų Motina* does not himself create but already finds *a state of war* between the *Winds* and the *Giants.* Being a seeker of love it is only by this title that he will succeed in overpowering the giants, the representatives of power and *violence.* Actually, the magical apples which our hero protects are not themselves the objects of value for which there would be a battle between two opposing lands—the aim of the giants is not to pick the apples but to uproot the apple trees and to destroy the orchard. The giants not only in our text but in the entire mythological world are represented as *uprooters and tramplers of oaks,*[27] *firs,*[28] *hills and flowers.*[29] This is a race which, as we know, had populated the entire world before the "flood": "They had multiplied without measure, and all were evil, they detested and scorned each other."[30]

It would be interesting to describe the life of this race of giants, their labors and exploits: we would find there as well the Lithuanian Polyphemus, the *one-eyed giant,* whose eye the hero pierces with a stake,[31] the giant *Velnias,* who with his voice shakes all the leaves down in November,[32] and the powerful giant born of the maiden impregnated by the Devil.[33] The battles against these representatives of violence undistinguished by large brains are led by both gods and men. We will note here only the battle that is meaningful to us, that of the *giant with the wolf* (or wolves): when the giant sits down or sleeps, the wolves gnaw away his toes and he dies from that.[34]

This episode of the wolf who is capable of killing the giant is interesting in that it is possible to compare it to a similar dual of our hero. The hero, as we have seen, is capable of turning himself into a wolf, but he does not exploit this, just as he will do nothing with the apples which he has acquired with his victory. These are always the narrative's unused possibilities.

IV. Not the Sun, but the Maiden of the Sea

She summoned her children, the four winds, and asked them:
"Did you see the second sun anywhere?"
The north wind answered: "That's not the sun. I was there today and saw for myself. There is a maiden on an island in the sea with hair like the sun. She has a manor."
The mother of the winds once again rolled the ball of yarn to him. He placed the yarn in his beak, having changed to a hawk, and traveled to the sea shore.

The Double Form

Our text finally brings the receiver-readers's long awaited answer to the question, who actually is that wondrous being whom the hero has gone to find. However, the answer of the North Wind, who is an eyewitness, is not direct, but only a negation of her identification with the *Second Sun,* while at the same time, of course, signifying the affirmation of her presence as a separate individual being.

It should be stated that this being, whoever she may be, is manifested in two separate forms. First of all she appears in *human* form as a "maiden" living in her own manor on an island in the sea. In this, however, she does not as yet differ from the Sun, whose anthropomorphic shape can be verified by the fact that they have "the same hair." On the other hand, she is observed in the shape of a *beacon in the sky*: in the beginning of the storytelling she appears before the hero's eyes, morning and

Aušrinė 77

evening, as the second Sun. The hero had been certain that both of these luminary objects belong to the Sun, even though taken together it was clear to him that beneath the shape of this beacon there was concealed a being with a human appearance who was worthy of a search, and who could, as we have seen, be an object of love. In mythic thinking there is no contradiction here: the forms of manifestation do not change the essence of things and one would have to be a hardened positivist to speak of the worship of "heavenly bodies."

Aušra

The identity of the hair of both maidens and their simultaneous appearance in the sky allows one to easily identify the "Second Sun": Lasicius, introducing the Goddess *Aušra* (in the Latin text printed in corrupt form as *Ausca*), characterizes her as "dea . . . radiorum solis vel occumbentis, vel supra horizontem ascendantis" or "goddess of the *rays* of the sun that descend and rise above the horizon."[35] The rays of the sun are nothing more than the hair of *Aušra*.

The recognition of the "Second Sun" and her identification with *Aušra* [the dawn] or *Aušrinė* [the morning star] not only elucidates but makes our text readable in its entirety and explains as well a series of textual facts. Knowing, for instance, that in Christian interpretations of folklore *Aušrinė* becomes identified with the *Blessed Virgin,* it becomes understandable why the hero who has departed to look for her is, rather unusually, named *Joseph*. It is becoming apparent as well why the *North Wind,* otherwise named *Auštrinis,* and not another of his brothers, is familiar with her dwelling and visits her: her manor is in the northeast, where, according to other versions, she "kindles the fire for the Sun [Saulė]"[36] and prepares the way for her.

Saulė and Aušrinė

One of the distinct, irrefutable facts of Lithuanian mythology is the rivalry between *Saulė* [the Sun Maiden] and *Aušrinė* [the Morning Star], but until now there has been no satisfactory global interpretation for this rivalry. The love of *Mėnulis* [Moon] for Aušrinė is one of the most painful, widely-known tragedies in the world of the gods:

> Mėnulis walked alone
> Fell in love with Aušrinė
>   Perkūnas, greatly enraged,
>   Smote him in half:
>   —"Why did you leave Saulė?
>   Fall in love with Aušrinė?
>   Walk alone at night?"[37]

It is as if this text, whose authenticity at one time was in doubt, represents the epilogue of the history of love. It begins, perhaps, with the birth of Aušrinė. In one story the Moon is explaining why he has not risen for two nights and two days:

"Because . . . on the earth in one or another kingdom from humble means there was born such a *beautiful maiden* as has never, anywhere, been born. I became so transfixed I did not rise."[38] In another context it is not the Moon but the Sun who "has not shown for three days": "A *beautiful princess* was born and I gazed at her for one tiny minute,"[39] or, in another variant, "in the middle of the sea there is a maiden named Alena. She is more *beautiful and radiant* than I. Thus I gazed at her and forgot to rise for three days"[40] All these texts are in agreement on one thing: the newly-found maiden is the *princess of beauty*: even though the Sun Maiden becomes silent, it is easy to imagine what she thinks of her competition.

Yet another variant poses the question somewhat differently; it is concerned with why the Sun descends at all in the evening. The answer: "Because there is in the *sea* another maiden who is more *powerful* than I." When she in the evening *rises from the sea*, then I must descend."[41] We see how when we move from one variant to another, the portrait of our beauty is slowly revealed: "beautiful maiden" becomes "beautiful princess," "more beautiful and radiant" than the Sun; this princess of the sea appears as being even "more powerful" than Saulė, and, furthermore, she in the sky dome is manifested in the form of a nightly *beacon*. It seems to us that the identification of the *Maiden of the Sea* with *Aušrinė* when described like this is unquestionable.

The final variant known to us approaches the situation as described in our text. The hero going to *Dievas* [God] to ask "why are the days so gloomy?" finds out from him that "there is a maiden drowned in the seas."[42] And actually before long we will see that our hero will light up the world by lowering the reflection of Aušrinė into the sky dome.

V. You Are Mine, I Am Yours

The north wind came to him, and taught him:
"Now wait until the evening. The maiden's bull will return with three cows from the forest and will swim across the sea to the other side. Hold onto the tail of the bull, it will carry you to the other side. Then dive under when you have swum across, since he will gore you if he sees you. When you come out of the water, you will find a birch stump on that island. Crawl into that stump since the bull will look for you. After breakfast go to the manor, you will find the maiden sleeping. She lies on her stomach. Mount her as you would a horse and braid her hair in your hands. She will say: Let me go! If you don't, the earth will perish, turn into the sea. You say: I will swim out on you. She will say this three times. Then she will say: You are mine, I am yours. Then release her." And the bull returned from the forest with the cows. The man held onto the bull's tail and was carried across the seas. He did this. He later released the maiden when she said: "You are mine, I am yours."

To make *reading* of this segment easier, we must turn our attention first of all to several facts characteristic of narrative structure, especially their use in oral literature.

One such feature is repetition: first the hero's action project is set out in detail, after which it is repeated anew with its execution. In mythic thinking, knowing how to act is more important than the activity itself, which appears as a meaningless, repetitive realization. Our storyteller in a concise "he did this" sums up all the actions of the hero. Therefore in reading there is no need to separate two reality planes—the virtual and the actual.

The second trait is triplication of the heroine's resistance: the Sea Maiden, by repeating her threat three times, allows us to understand that she has done everything she could to resist foreign attack and has the right now in good conscience to yield to him.

The Problem of Spatial Domains

Until now we have seen how our hero acquired his qualifications in the *forest* and became an intermediary capable of communicating with the *air* space. However, the possibilities of his movement, which are manifested by his turning into a hawk and by the magic ball which leads the way and was given to him by the wind as a gift, end on the shores of the sea. The shore is a wall at which the North Wind stops as well, past which even he must use new means of travel. We can thus add to the differentiation of spacial domains offered by our text by providing four different spaces:

/Earth/ ----▶ /Forest/ ----▶ /Air/ ----▶ /Water/

A naive reader may well feel tricked by the narrator: he had the impression that his hero, transformed into a hawk, flies in the skies, that having flown through atmospheric space ruled by the *wind,* he should find himself in "heaven's sphere," and find Aušrinė there. The confusion here is not major—the hero actually finds himself in a peculiar "heaven," or more accurately, in another *utopic world,* only this world in the Lithuanian mythic world is often *watery* in nature. Lithuanian myths of the flood represent the earth as a huge "platter" flung in all directions by the *Wind* and the *Water* and in that manner sunk into the water.[43] It seems that the earth is surrounded by water from all sides—even above—from where else would rain come?—and below—where would the sun descend in the evening behind the mountains and the seas? The Sea is a watery, utopic, sacred world.

However, the possibilities of representing such a world non-anthropologically are poor—therefore even in the middle of the sea there is found an *island* with Aušrinė's manor (or at the bottom of the sea, palace of the princess) as well as her *herd* which every morning must be driven out.

In this space there are new and different rules of the game and the hero can travel there only with the help of the *bull*. The arrival of the hero at the *Marių Pana* [Sea Maiden] herself is thus difficult and complicated, composed of three stages:
(a) swimming, holding onto the bull's tail
(b) diving into water, to avoid being gored by the bull
(c) hiding under the birch stump, while the bull searches.

We will acknowledge that this episode is told in too contracted a manner to be sufficiently clear. We hope that new variants and new analytical information will add to it. The role of the *bull* here is interesting. As the helper of the maiden and the guardian of the island, the bull helps the hero to cross the seas, even though he does not wish that for himself. He behaves in a manner similar to that of his mistress, who fights the hero as much as possible then finally gives in. His role as only the cursed brother of Aušrinė (see segment XI) is thankless: he senses the approach of the rescuer but has to oppose him.

In the battle with the bull two helpers aid the hero in hiding from the bull: *water* which protects him from sight and the *birch stump*—most likely from sight and smell (generally mythic beings smell the person as "fresh meat"). The role of the *birch stump*[44] could be somewhat clearer: as an object in the Devil's sphere, it represents the illusory "devil's world" (man, participating in "the devil's wedding," suddenly "recovers his sight" and finds himself sitting on the stump in a bog). Thus the help of the Devil, as a master of illusion in this watery kingdom, is difficult to understand. It is enough for now to be content with these several fragments.

The Herd of Aušrinė

It does not surprise us, nevertheless, to find the *bull* in the role of guardian of the Sea Maiden; the *ox* is an aquatic being, merged with water. *Jaučių Baubis* (or *Bubalis, Baubaušis, Baublys*) is a deity who dwells in the waters and bogs in the form of an ox, or as a bittern, a guardian of herds and shepherds.[45] Lakes traveling in the form of clouds are led by oxen or are directly identified with the oxen: the names of the lakes can be guessed at by referring to them by the names of oxen.[46]

By no means with these conjectures would we want to identify, for instance, the *Jaučių Baubis* with the *bull* in our text. We wish only to clarify the bull's aquatic nature, thus explaining his proximity to Aušrinė—the maiden of the sea who has her herd of cattle. In another text parallel to our myth, intended to describe the discovery of "a maiden, the most beautiful in all the world," we find her already brought back but still requiring that her cow with twelve calves be brought back as well: this is accomplished by the *bull*. In riddles, where the answer is dew, Aušrinė is presented as a *maiden* who "drove the calves" or "herded the calves" and "lost her keys."[47]

In another narrative group in which the same theme of the search for the sea princess, which we have started to utilize, is developed, the herd of the sea maiden that corresponds to our Aušrinė is composed of *iron cows*, whose number is not fixed and changes from one variant to another (from one cow to twenty-five).[48] The iron cow—or those cows—are herded to the kingdom of the king who wants to marry the maiden and a test is presented to him: he must bathe in the cow's *boiling milk* and thus become *young and handsome*. The king, attempting to bathe, perishes, but the hero finding and rescuing the princess, bathes, becomes handsome, and inherits the hand of the sea maiden and the kingdom of the unworthy king.

This episode parallel to our myth is especially important, first of all, since it allows us to homologate *Aušrinė* and her herd as having the same essential characteristics: the hero gives to *Aušrinė*—the goddess of beauty—the magical apples, which bring youth and beauty, while the milk of the iron cows in her possession has the power to renew and beautify people. However, it is even more important since with

Aušrinė

its help the Lithuanian *iron-cow* figure finds equivalents in basic Indo-European mythologies. It goes without saying that these episodes taken together give added weight to our interpretation of the Aušrinė myth.

In our attempt to develop and formalize somewhat the methodology of Indo-European comparative mythology, we had occasion earlier to examine Dumézil's analysis of this myth, or rather the comparative procedures of three—Indian, Roman, and Irish— myths.[49] Dumézil regards the Indo-European mythic figure of the royal *Cow* as one of the elements in the ideology of sovereignty of these nations. In India there is the *Cow of Plenty:* the newly appointed king must catch her and with her milk feed his entire nation; this is his qualifying test as a king. A similar role is played in Rome by the *Imperial Cow,* which is the symbol of Roman power and the plenitude and abundance it will bestow on the nation. An entirely opposite role is played by the *Wooden Cow* in Ireland: by not honoring or feasting the poets of his domain, the king is disqualified from his status as king, is forced to milk the *Wooden Cow,* and dies, having drunk the poisonous milk. The Lithuanian version is obviously closer to the Irish: the Iron Cow provides boiling milk, and the king, having bathed in it, is also disqualified, not having displayed sufficient gratitude for all the exploits carried out for him by the hero; according to the Lithuanian version, the throne belongs not to the blood heir, but to the *worthiest warrior* who travels the true path.

Unexpectedly another essential trait of *Aušrinė* becomes apparent: she is not only the embodiment of Beauty and its distributor to mankind, but in a certain sense, she participates indirectly in the distribution of the sovereignty function. It should be noted that in place of *iron cows* one variant of this narrative group introduces the *mare of the seas* (more rarely—mares)[50] in the same way that in some texts there appears the horse or the *silver horse* in place of the bull.[51] Such a confusion of the zoomorphic representations of the beings of the sea is not accidental—the causes will soon become apparent.

Aušrinė—The Mare of the Sea

The second part of this segment is given over to the conquest of *Aušrinė* herself, which involves, based on the counsel of the *North Wind,* quite an unusual procedure. The role of the *North Wind* is major here: it is characterized by *knowledge* of her nature and *ability* to manipulate her. And he is able to act, it is clear, because he is acquainted with one of her innate forms, namely *mare of the sea:* "Mount her as you would a horse, plait your hands in her mane," he advises the hero. Only by accepting this hypothesis of Aušrinė as mare of the sea does our entire text become intelligible and readable: "I will swim out on your back" answers the hero to the Sea Maiden, when she threatens to turn the earth to water. The storyteller forgets on this occasion to add that the *bridle and saddle* are in the maiden's "chamber." He will tell us this later. (See segment X.)

This new shape of *Aušrinė* is not as unexpected as it seems at first. In one legend the prince stops by *Mėnesis* [the Moon] to ask the way to the maiden he is searching for, who lives "beyond the river of milk, beyond the forest of honey, in a tall granary, above the swan." The moon agrees to help: "I know, *I'm going that way,* I can take you there," and gives him a beautiful horse, who carries him across the river of milk, through the forest of honey. Nearing the manor, big enough "for three lifetimes," the horse gives him his final advice, but the narrator intervenes and explains to the listener: "the horse, or that moon turned to a horse."[52] Such a manifestation of Mėnulis in two forms, anthropomorphic and zoomorphic, creates no difficulties for Lithuanian mythic conceptualization. As proof, we cite a widely known riddle: "On a Wednesday, on a Saturday, there was born a *colt of god* with a gold bridle and silver horseshoes (the moon),"[53] although this may not please our positivist folklorists who perceive in riddles only the origin of games.

It is now possible to present a chart of all the possible *forms* of Aušrinė connected to the spatial domains that she utilizes—the fundamental *elements* of nature:

$$\text{Aušrinė} = \frac{\text{Maiden}}{\text{earth}} \simeq \frac{\text{Star}}{\text{sky (air)}} \simeq \frac{\text{Mare}}{\text{water}}$$

In this perspective, the narration of our segment is becoming transparent. The threats of the maiden—"Let me go! If you don't, the earth will perish, turn into sea"—would be perilous if the hero, inspired by the *North Wind,* did not know that with the earth changing into the seas, Aušrinė herself turns into a mare and if he had not from the beginning taken a riding position, making her threat ineffective.

From a narrative point of view, the program seems to have come to an end: the goal of the hero, the Second Sun, is reached. Having acquired the magical apple in the first phase of his activity, which granted him the will and capacity to love, he now conquers his beloved, finally uniting with his longed-for object of value, which had been the basis for his entire program of action. "You're mine, I'm yours" appears as an often-encountered, canonical formula,[54] registering in a contractual manner new matrimonial relations reminiscent of the Roman "Where thou art, Caius . . . "

VI. The Exaltation of Aušrinė

> They both lived there for many years. He, the smaller one, was her servant. He himself herded the cows every morning across the seas. The bull did nothing to him. Once he found one hair of that maiden stuck on a thorn and found an empty nutshell. Wrapping the hair up, he put it into that nutshell and threw it into the sea. A ray from the sea became reflected into the sky as the biggest star.

The Servant of Aušrinė

In a certain sense, this segment appears as the epilogue to our story: the retelling of the *action* up to now turns on the description of the *situation*. "They both lived there for many years" marks a calm, stable condition after the events: all that is missing is "and I was there . . . " which usually ends the story.

The newly created situation corresponds to the morganatic state of marriage; from a domestic viewpoint Aušrinė and our hero form a wedded pair, and from a social

Aušrinė 83

viewpoint she is the *Princess of the Sea*. Nevertheless, he remains her *Servant*. This mésalliance, it seems, corresponds to the cosmological relations of the two beacons of the sky-dome: the "radiant Aušrinė" appears in the sky with a Servant "smaller" than herself. "The star of the dawn rises before the first rays of the sun. And the ancients would watch to see whether that star always rises with her *servant*. If the servant rises before her and precedes that star, well, then the old masters say: 'Oh, the year will be good.' The master will have to follow his family (he will send for her, it will cost dearly). But if he sees *Aušrinė* first, with the *Servant* following, then all the masters are joyous: 'Well, then glory to God, the family will have to obey us, since we always have to bow to them!'"[55]

Next to the atmospheric explanation of the relations between Aušrinė and her *Servant* applicable to the farmers, our text appears to be an *etiological legend* which accounts for the origin of the Servant of Aušrinė and his duties—to herd the cows across the sea (the sky) every morning to the pasture.

Aušrinė in the Sky

Our text does not end, however, with the explanation of the origin of the *Servant*: into this settled state new events suddenly emerge with which our hero seemingly crowns all his activity. At first glance the new activity seems to be inscribed into the sign by chance; at one time the hero "finds" a hair, at another time he "finds" a nut. Instead of viewing this passivity of the hero as a mythologic deficiency, as some ethnographers do, his activity inscribed on the horizon of fate (comp. to the entire French epoch which was regarded as "gesta Dei per Francos"), it seems to us, is rather a sign of the myth's antiquity.

The significance of the hair found by the hero, as a metonym for *Aušrinė's* nature, is sufficiently clear to us. We will, however, confess our ignorance as to why the hair was "caught" on the thorn: since a rationalistic explanation is insufficient, perhaps we can look to its being mentioned as an allusion to the throne of the *Blessed Virgin* decorated with roses.

The symbolism of the *nut,* in which the nucleus is contained, the embryo from which plants, animals, and people develop, is quite clear. We must not forget that the human race emerges after the *flood,* if it can be expressed this way, from a nutshell: God, seeing the last two elder-giants drowning and at the time chewing on some nuts, cast down one shell which the old people used to save themselves and who later gave birth to the second species of inhabitants on the earth—man.[56] The same role as the nutshell may be played by the *acorn shell*: even though the name of the gods "Liubegeldae" still remains obscure and unexplained, their activity is quite accurately depicted by Lasicius in the Lithuanian citation: "Liubegeldae per mare porire sekles gillie skaute." Correcting for spelling, it is clear that "per marę perirė sėklas gilės kiaute" [seeds cross the seas in the nutshell], is corroborated by the Latin explanation: "in putamine glandis."[57] As was the case for seeds, so it is for both people and the stars in the sky: their origin is "aquatic" and their intermediary is the nut or acorn shell.

It is enough then for our hero to place the hair of Aušrinė that he found into the hollow shell, and throw it into the depths of the sea, so that the hair, radiating, "would appear in the sky, as the *biggest star*." Here then is a complete description of the procedure by which Aušrinė was "elevated" into the sky and began to radiate there in the shape of a star. Thus this is also a good lesson in elementary philosophy for those folklorist-mythologists who still continue to write thick volumes about "heavenly gods"—on improved versions of the worship of "heavenly bodies"—as if these were a separate, homogeneous class of gods. According to Lithuanian religion everything that happens in the sky is only a reflection of life at the bottom of the sea and, in general, phenomenological manifestations in various figurative forms are only variations of nominal reality.

From a narrative viewpoint, this ascent or *exaltation* of Aušrinė into the sky as fulfilled by our hero corresponds to the final facultative task of the hero, which is frequently followed by the common acknowledgment of him as hero, his glorification. The digression from canonic formulas of narrative structures is especially significant here: in place of fighting for his own acknowledgment, the hero's final efforts seek to announce to the entire world the beauty and honor of his princess.

In this manner the first part of our analyzed text thus far appears not only as a completed myth, but also as a *double etiological myth*: the myth of the appearance of Aušrinė's Servant and the myth of the ascent of *Aušrinė* herself into the sky.

VII. Another World

A prince, sailing the seas, saw the novelty. He set his sail directly for that star, came closer, gazed through the spyglass, and found the nutshell. He hurried home as fast as he could. He had an old grandmother witch: "Tell me, old woman, what is that hair?"

"There is a maiden with such hair!"

"Could you bring her here? I'll cast a gold cradle for you, rock it day and night."

The witch changed to a beggar and went to the maiden, telling her that she had been thrown out of a ship onto the shore: "I am a poor beggar, I asked them to take me but they put me on the shore here. Perhaps, beneficent lady, you could take me as your servant. I will serve you well."

She accepted her offer. The old woman remained there for a week or two, becoming a true servant. Whatever the maiden said to do, she did it twice as well. The witch, meeting the prince at night, ordered him to cast a gold ship and go where he had found that nutshell. It was to have a silver bridge.

One Myth or Two?

We have seen that with the hero's becoming a *Servant* and with the ascent of *Aušrinė* into the sky, the narration as recorded in the first part of our text is completed. With this segment it is as if an entirely new history begins, with a new hero—or rather the *antihero* prince. Without considering at least for the moment whether we are dealing with one myth or with two myths linked together, we can try to determine the parallelism that exists between these two narratives:

Joseph sees Aušrinė	The Prince sees Aušrinė
(the second sun form)	(the star and hair forms)
J. wants to *find* her	P. wants to *kidnap* her
J.'s helper is the *North Wind*	P.'s helper is the *Witch*
J.'s battle is *loyal*	P.'s battle is *not loyal*
(using force)	(using deception)
J. *remains* with Aušrinė	P. *transports* Aušrinė
Aušrinė's *exaltation*	Aušrinė's *enslavement*

The activity programs of both the hero and antihero are similar, and develop according to one and the same general narrative schema; however, the mode of action of these two heroes, their helpers, their relations with the longed-for object of value—Aušrinė—are diametrically opposite. Since the activity occurs not in the human but in the divine world, we can suppose that according to the means of action used by the hero and the help given him, it is possible to determine, even if not fully, those mythological sacred spheres to which each one belongs.

Ragana

Although the entire *Wind* family has voluntarily come to help Joseph, the prince selects as helper a being related to him by blood—the old woman *Ragana*. And yet, even though it seems that the old woman's help for her grandson should be more natural than the entire alien help of the *Wind* [Vėjas], the prince gets this help from her only when he promises to cast a gold cradle—a payment based on the principle of *exchange*. On the other hand, the manner of activity of Ragana is one of masking, "turning into a beggar." Instead of appearing as what she is, *Ragana* appears as she is not: such a verbal, gestural and somatic manner of communication is called *lying*. In the world of Lithuanian tales both of these traits characterize the well-known "kingdom of the devil."

Even though, from the sixteenth century on, she is verified as a goddess of the *forest* and compared with *Medeina* (= *Modeina*), *Ragana* (= Ragaina),[58] whose manifestations are abundantly displayed in our story texts, seems up to now a very enigmatic being, and her physiognomy is by no means apparent: the distance between the etymology of her name (comp. Latv. *paraguone* "a woman seeing into the future," *pa-redzet* "see into the future, conjure")[59] and the forms of her stereotypic activity seem enormous. What is even more interesting is her basic characteristic—her *knowledge*, which orients the future because it is supplemented by knowing *how to act*: when the prince sees only the hair in the nutshell, the old woman *Ragana* knows, i.e., "sees through" and sees who hides under that hair form; she plans the future as well, foreseeing not only her own actions, but also the actions of *Aušrinė*. The manner of her actions corresponds to that of the many "čerauninkai" of the kingdom, i.e., to the actions of *sorcerers* who, unlike *seers* who only guess the future, can orient the future in one direction or another.

Among the various tales in the world concerning the activity traits of witches, we will mention here only those which are directly associated with the figurative value system of the text we are analyzing. First among them are those actions which involve incompatibility of their world with water: *witches* do not have power "on the sea," states one narrator directly;[60] to protect a child from a witch who wishes to kidnap him, he is put out in a boat on the sea, and the *witch* must try in all manner of ways to lure him onto the shore—otherwise she cannot take him.[61] The examples can be multiplied, but that would go beyond the scope of our study: it is clear that the mythic zone which Ragana represents is entirely hostile to *Aušrinė* and to her kingdom.

If Ragana reacts passively to her fear of water then we must not forget that one of the most important activity spheres of her servants, the women-witches, is the "spoiling" of *cow's* milk. If we take into account the significance of the herd of *Aušrinė*, this harmful activity is a covert battle against Aušrinė and the values that she represents. Out of such a world then comes the prince who once "sailing the sea" observes "a novelty."

Kalvelis (?)

If we attempt to apply the principle that the hero may be recognized by his deeds, we notice, first of all, that there is a paucity of "deeds." His activity is manifested in only one area: promising the old woman to *cast a golden cradle* and somewhat later on her orders to cast a *gold ship* and a *silver bridge*. Consequently the prince is a caster of precious metal—or, better put, a goldsmith.

Such a portrait of the prince cannot but be compared to one of the oldest (approximately 1261) verified Lithuanian gods, whose name—*Kal-ev-elis* = *Kalvelis* [the smith]—and etymology (a deformation of the selling of *Teliavelis* from the Malala chronicle) had been reconstructed long ago by K. Būga,[62] corresponding to one of four major Lithuanian gods cited by Dlugosz, who interprets it as the Roman *Vulcanus*. The case of *Kalvelis*, of course, is incomplete: the chronicle only mentions that he forged the *Sun* and hung her in the sky. We will try thus to supplement it with several folkloric facts.

The devil's ties with the forge and the smith's with devilry are unquestionable. In *Fearless John*, a corpus of 33 variants of the story, we had occasion to meet the real Velnias—and not some little devils playing tricks in bad taste—placing a bet with the hero in his *underground smithy* on who could hammer the anvil as deep as possible into the ground.[63] Another hero, Meškiukas—the child of the Lady and the Bear—"descended *underground*. There he found a land . . . a smithy. He went inside, the smith is hammering. When *the smith strikes the anvil with the hammer*, a little German appears (devil *is forged*). The Little Bear looks and says: 'This is a great place!' "[64] It is said about a dodging, sly person that "he is shod by the devils."[65]

The underground blacksmith figure of the *Devil* [Velnias] is quite clear. It seems however that the smithy's secret—"earlier on earth the blacksmiths were the devils of hell"—namely, how to weld iron, was betrayed at one time, either through deceit or in good faith, by some *Kalvis*[66] and from that time on the relations between *Velnias* and *Kalvis* become unclear: thus *Kalvis*, after his death, drives all the devils out of hell. God then decides "to take the blacksmith into *heaven*, and drives the devils back into hell."[67] Another time a hero, placing a bet with *Velnias*, scares him by saying that his blacksmith brother *Kalvis* lives in heaven.[68] Even though their context is rather late and Christianized these two examples illustrate the power of Kalvis over devils. The final example worth mentioning tells of a blacksmith in his smithy who, having forged a picture of *Velnias*, laughs at him. As a consequence of the Devil's revenge, the blacksmith, doomed to be hanged, is saved only by promising not to make fun of him any more.[69] These ambiguous relations between the Devil and the Blacksmith indicate that *Kalvis*, although appearing in later folklore, preserves his mythic figure.

There seems to be no point in pausing any longer at the relations between the *witch* and the *blacksmith*—they are abundant and varied, but bring nothing new to our concerns. Only the weapon used by Ragana mentioned somewhat later in our text is of interest—the knife. This implement made by the blacksmith is detested by Perkūnas,[70] who often strikes it, and is especially feared by the Wind [Vėjas]—since every unseen *wind* can be wounded or killed with a knife.[71]

The question of whether our *prince* can be identified as the god *Kalvelis* from the existing facts cannot yet, it would seem, receive a final answer. That is not, however, the basic task of our study. It has seemed useful to add the especially important case of *Kalvelis* to the analysis of Lithuanian religion particularly since the tendency has arisen in later years to solve it somewhat too hurriedly.[72]

VIII. The Kidnapping of Aušrinė

In the morning at 8 the maiden awoke, left her manor when she saw the new ship. Such a vessel there had never been. The old woman invited the maiden:
"Come see!" The maiden had left bareheaded. She started back to get her scarf. The sorceress said:
"I will bring you the scarf."
(The witch slays the hero.)
She came closer to the ship—she sees that there are no people on it. The sorceress invited the lady to take a look. When she stepped onto the ship, it started to sail. The prince jumped out, grabbed the maiden, took her to his dwelling.
"Don't be afraid, you'll be safer with me than here. I have a kingdom, soldiers."
He brought her to his kingdom. He wanted to marry her in a little while.
"I cannot marry for a year! I mourn for my father, who died not long ago."
She bargained for time as best she could, so he would not marry her.

Narrative Organization

The introduction of the antihero and the development of the new program—the kidnapping of Aušrinė—complicate the narrator's task. He must not lose sight of the basic fate of the hero, but, at the same time, he must also develop a second intrigue. From a technical viewpoint, he fulfills this rather well in a linked form, by interweaving the episodes of both programs: his jumping from one story to another, using short episodes, does not diminish the attention of the listener. The order of arrangement of these episodes is roughly as follows:

(1) The kidnapping of Aušrinė (enticement)
(2) The slaying of the hero
(3) The kidnapping of Aušrinė (bringing home)
(4) The hero's resurrection
(5) The rescue of Aušrinė

It is difficult for the analyst to follow all the alternations of domain and action; he is forced to neutralize the requirements of this discursive form, pairing episodes (1 and 3; 2 and 4) so as to reconstruct the homogeneous narrative segments.

The Epiphany of Aušrinė

In the preceding segment we saw *Ragana* placing an order with the Prince-Kalvelis for a golden ship with a silver bridge: even if one understands the general significance of such an order—the desire to entice Aušrinė into the boat to kidnap her—the form of the deception itself remains unclear. To understand it, the parallelism already disclosed between the activities of the two primary personages—hero and antihero—can be of help. Just as the hero exalts Aušrinė by elevating her to the sky, so the antihero, in turn, offers her an unusual staging for the exaltation: *a golden ship with a silver bridge descending from it, and standing on it, a bareheaded beauty*—this is the sunrise epiphany of Aušrinė, a temptation against which no female heart will hold back.

We find this type of deceptive design in another story, as well,[73] even though it appears in a strictly separate context: the sea maiden here is kidnapped not for "evil" intentions but for good, the author of the kidnapping is the hero himself who has to bring her back to his king. Of course, this is another one of the narrator's chosen *perspectives* and *moralizations* of the described events which divides the actors into positive and negative types. What is characteristic in this story is that *Kalvis* appears as the hero's helper, who kills *Ragana*, who chases him. Be that as it may, with the hero riding to the shore of the sea, his wondrous colt orders him to rip open his stomach, take out his intestines, and bury them so that no one will find them, and then after throwing his "entrails"[74] into the sea, sit on them and swim. In the middle of the sea, the foal's entrails change into a *golden ship*, onto which later the sea maiden will be enticed. Once again sailing to the middle of the sea, "the golden ship" returns to her original state, changing back into the foal's entrails. The story continues: the maiden, taking offense, takes the beads from around her neck and scatters them into the sea (the *beads* or *pearls,* as we know, are the *dewdrops* scattered by Aušrinė).[75] Thus the hero must return to collect the *beads*, bring back the *stallion* of the sea with the nine *cows*, bathe in their milk, become very *handsome*, and, well, marry the maiden of the sea.

We are recounting this history not for our pleasure but to show that the general theme in whose frames the *golden ship* motif appears does not differ essentially from our analyzed text, that the motif itself, irrespective of its several transformations, must be tracked as a parallel version of the epiphany as described in our text. Only after accepting this can we now introduce the mythic fragment registered in the Malala chronicle, according to which the god *Kalvelis* forges and hangs the *Sun* Saulė in the sky. Already having three versions of one and the same motif (along with the transformation Aušrinė-Saulė), we can now at least imagine the general frames of the myth of the origin of *Saulė* and its general mythologic atmosphere. Alas, the case of *Saulė* in Lithuanian mythology has not yet begun to take shape.[76]

IX. Death and Resurrection

The husband slept. The witch took a knife and killed the husband. She took out his lungs and liver and threw them in passing into the sea. The lady was not aware that she had done this.

(The prince brought Aušrinė back.) All the four winds had gathered at their mother's to ask about any news. They look and see that all the apples in their mother's orchard have withered.

"Why is this so, mother?"

"Go look, perhaps our friend who guarded the orchard is dead."

They found him slain. They began to search the shores and the water for his lungs. They saw—a very large crab was dragging them into his cave. They took away his lungs and liver. The north wind dove into the seas and carried off the restorative water and the "gyvuonis." He anointed him, washed him—he stood healthy and whole. They ask:

"Where did that maiden go?"

"I don't know. I was asleep."

"You were slain."

Death

Our segment consists, as we have mentioned, of two episodes which describe the hero's death and his resurrection.

The process of his death must be divided into three separate phases:

(1) The slaying,

(2) Throwing of the lungs and liver into the water,

(3) Their dispatch into the cave of the crab.

Death is not an ordinary crossing from one state to another. It is a complicated procedure which passes through autonomous stages. It can be represented as an algorithm of two logical operations realized on the semiotic square:[77]

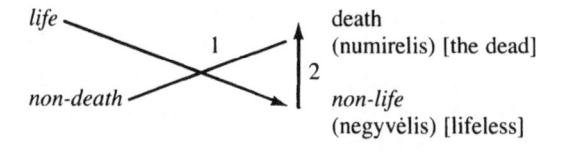

```
     life ╲      ╱  death
            ╲  ╱   1  (numirelis) [the dead]
             ╳         ↑
            ╱  ╲    │ 2
     non-death ╱    ╲▶ non-life
                       (negyvėlis) [lifeless]
```

The significance of this schema will gradually become more evident after a more detailed analysis of the segment.

In Lithuanian anthropological thinking the *lungs* and *liver* are considered to be the most important organs of the body, in which a person's health, strength, and life are concentrated. It is not surprising, for instance, that in one tale the father, angry at his youngest son for his deceit, orders that "he be driven to the woods and *chopped* up, buried in the ground, and as a sign his *lungs* and *liver* brought back."[78] In this case, the lungs and liver are proof that the son is no longer alive. This is appropriate only to humans and not to beings of a higher type—raganas [witches]: one such witch had been burned with summer straw until "there remained only her *lungs* and *stomach* (most likely her liver)" (they floated in the bog, which is why that bog is called The Bog of the Lungs).[79] An even more amazing happening is described in a legend about a maiden who knew how "to capture three vėlės [shades] traveling on the road."[80] With the hero successful in finding the maiden and asleep from fatigue, her witch-mother, "ripping open his stomach, pulls out his lungs. The daughter runs inside. She looks and sees her mother, carrying the lungs across the dirt floor. She grabs them from her mother, puts them back and sews him up. And again he sleeps as he had slept. (This is repeated *three times*.) Ragana desperately wants to throw those lungs into the kettle in which water had been boiling." In rescuing the hero from death the maiden has indicated that she "knows how to capture *three* vėlės traveling the road (and those vėlės—by returning the *lungs*, placed back the material soul)."

This especially interesting text identifies the *lungs* with "dušia," the pre-Christian concept of "material soul," which as yet does not acknowledge a dichotomy between the body and the soul. It also accurately characterizes the concept of vėlė: *vėlė* is "dušia" that has left the body "traveling on the road" to death, just as the lungs, carried across the mud floor by Ragana, "travel" to the boiling water, in which they are destined to boil, to disappear. *Vėlė* can also appear in the form of a "breath, spirit," or "vapor," but its principle of life is contained in the lungs, and its life has to end, as in our text, in *water*.

It is noteworthy that this life-principle which we have just identified as vėlė or the material "dušia" can be manifested in another figure—that of *dalis*. It is well-known that the *bedalis* [poor, shareless] man can live from his wife's dalis, or even from that of a lamb or a dog given him as a gift. Furthermore, the *dalis* can be transferred, passed from one being to another. Here is a description of the process by which the *dalis* of a slaughtered cow is transferred to people: "She placed the *lungs, liver*, and meat (of the cow) in a boiling pot. After cooking them for a little while, she cuts off a piece and gives it to her children, her husband, and she herself tastes it: she looks and sees . . . that *her children, her husband,* and *she herself* have a share."[81] Without raising the question of whether *dalis* can be identified with the vėlė-*dvasia* [spirit]—that will require a separate study—we must underscore the fact that the dwelling site of the *laimė-dalia* principle can be the lungs and the liver.

We see that the *liver* (*kepenys, kepenos, kepsniai,* or *jėknos*) is not separable from the *lungs* when describing a person's or animals's essential life principle. The *liver*, as the etymology of this word indicates (comp. *kep-ti* [to cook]), is the vital center of warmth:

"The liver really heats up when thrashing with flails,"[82] but it is also the site for the expression of man's temperament: "My liver is heating up (I am angry) and he still continues to annoy me,"[83] human strength is found there as well, the roots of man's efforts: *jaknintis* means "to try," "to work with effort," "to strain,"[84] his health is contained there as well: "bedbugs scatter from his liver" is said of a weak, ill person.[85] The *liver* thus becomes the site for moral values, a synonym for *conscience*: "The injustice you have done me will be on your liver, i.e., conscience."[86]

It would be too early as yet to attempt a differentiation of functions between the lungs and the liver to determine the specific attributes of the liver. It will suffice to remember that Greek mythological facts, for instance, do not differ here from the Lithuanian: Greek gods are immortal, as immortal as their livers; the eagle, for instance, feeds on the liver of the shackled Prometheus, but since it is immortal, the eagle feeds on it forever.

In our text the aforementioned "large crab," elsewhere called directly the *King of the Crabs*,[87] has as his realm the bottom of the sea. Dragging the hero's lungs and liver into his cave, he drags them to a certain death, and the *North Wind* only at the last minute saves him from perishing. The *crab's inverted locomotion,* his glance directed to the land of the living as he drags the vėlės to death (comp: *vežys vež-ti*), makes him especially suitable to the role of guardian and procurator of this kingdom of death.

The crab behaves similarly not only in our text, but in other tales associated with the Sea Maiden: "the horse says to the fool, slay me and throw a piece of my meat into the sea (another variant mentions throwing "babakai," and we know what kind of "meat" that refers to). The crab will come to eat the meat, then you catch him and tell him to summon all the crabs to take out the dowry of the princess of the sea. . . . "[88] The crab is the guardian of the "dower chest" of the *Sea Maiden,* her "treasure"—or at least of the keys to the chest[89] in which the witch keeps her imprisoned. Finally, in the crab's command there is found an *egg* with which it is possible to cover the glass hill on an island in the sea, and thus revive the entire kingdom,[90] or an *egg* in which there is contained "the soul [dušia] of the king without a soul."[91] But we will examine the *egg* later.

There is no return from this world of death, which is strictly separated from the living and not only from those people who upon discovering its secrets must die,[92] but also from the gods: the Winds' sons, who wish to investigate the secrets of the sea depths and attempt to blow the waters from the sea, perish in the waves.[93] Between this world of death and the world of the living there is an intermediate zone settled by beings who are neither truly "living" nor "dead." This is the world of vėlės, raganas (whose lungs and liver are not afraid of fire), sorcerers, and devils.

These are the initial features with which we can begin to characterize the Lithuanian conception of "life after death."

Resurrection

The murder of the hero, as we have seen, is a dual procedure: first he must be slain, and then his "vėlė"—the lungs and liver—must be thrown into the sea so that the crab can put an end to him. Thus the operation of his resurrection from the dead is composed of two parts: first his "material soul" must be found and placed back in his "body," and after that an attempt must be made to revive the organically psychic whole.

In order to revive a lifeless person [see semiotic square]—or, in any lesser cases, to heal the sick or make the invalid healthy—two types of therapeutic waters are needed:

(1) The *healing* (or *curative*) water [gydantis-gydomas] is called here *gijantis* [restorative] water

(2) The *living* [gyvasis] water here is *gyvuonis*.

Our text, which has a distinct mythic nature, introduces a mythic personage in the role of the seeker of the water—the North Wind. Other narratives which utilize the healing and life-giving water motif are of a more narrative nature, and their hero is most often a silly fool searching for medicine for his ailing father. According to the genre requirements of wondertales, the mythic qualities of the hero are thus transferred and invested in his helpers. In the role of such helpers we find first of all, the *blue ox* lying by the sea indicating that the water can be found "on the other side of the sea."[94] Another helper is the *Wolf,* who carries the fool to "another kingdom,"[95] or who, in another case, kills the swallow's child so that if she wishes to revive him she is compelled to search for and bring back the healing and life-giving waters.[96] Next to the primary helpers, as we shall see, the logic of the story develops an entire secondary helper series of birds, among whom, besides the swallow, we find the crow, as well as the hawk, familiar to us from our text: they bring the *water* by way of the *air.*

In this group of stories, which should be studied comprehensively, the activity of the therapeutic waters is manifested by:

(1) The *invalid's recovery* (the story begins with a common expression: the father is *ill*).

(2) The *restoration of beauty* (on the king's head there grow *angry-looking sores*).

(3) *Rejuvenation* (the old father is reborn "youthful and whole, lively and swift").[97]

Next to these areas of influence we must add:

(4) The *recovery of sight* (the hero's plucked-out eyes are healed), which of course, belongs to another narrative group.[98]

Our hero, anointed by the healing waters, stands "healthy and whole." This stereotypical formula, which we use mechanically every day ("sveikas, gyvas, Jonai!") is more significant than it appears on the surface.

In order to understand the mythic procedure of "resurrection from the dead," it is necessary, first of all, to apply a general methodological rule based on the old principle "he who can do more, can do less": when dealing with a number of the variants of the same text, one must choose as a base that variant which more comprehensively and extensively recounts the facts or events under analysis. In our case, the recovery of the invalid or the removal of that which is ugly from his body (sores) seems to be a weakened version of a much more significant rejuvenation procedure with which the old father is reborn "youthful and whole."

It becomes apparent that the man chosen for rejuvenation must first of all be "chopped up into little pieces," and only after that, after being anointed with the healing waters, does he heal up into one entity and become *whole* [sveikas]. Such a motif of a man chopped up and thrown in separate pieces down a chimney is widely known in all of European folklore:[99] it is a characteristic manifestation of the power of the Devil as an actor in the zone of "neither the living nor the dead" mentioned earlier. In this zone, he can chop up bodies and put them back together again.

Returning to the concept of *health* [sveikumas], we should not forget one of the basic meanings of the Lithuanian word *sveikas: sveikas* means "whole" or "integral" ("whole number" for instance differs from fractional numbers). The function of the healing water is thus to return to the individual his "health," i.e., his integrity, which guarantees his identity as a person.

Such a *sveikas* [whole] person must yet be made *gyvas* [living]: that purpose is served by the living water [*gyvasis vanduo*]: with the healing waters man is restored "su-gija" and with the living waters he is revived "at-gija." The essential ingredient of life, we see, differs from the essential ingredient of health. It is not surprising, then, that even our text commonly names this life-giving water very accurately as *gyvuonis*. The word *gyvuonis,* according to LKŽ, means:

(1) The flesh under the finger nail; the innermost part of the horn
(2) Stinger (of a bee, wasp)
(3) Snake's tongue
(4) The inner part of a boil (geluo)
(5) Life ("life is also pulled out of the bee with the stinger"; Valkininkai, Eišiškės district)

All of these meanings have one common denominator: *gyvuonis* is that central point, root, site, within which the rudiments of life, its very principle, is contained.

Gyvuonis is most often changed in other texts to the living—*gyvasis*—water, but that does not change its basic meaning. This water is not a therapeutic means, a medicine, with whose help life is returned to the body; it, itself, is *gyvasis*—the living water; *it, as water, is life,* that elemental ingredient of life, which returns to a "healthy" body.

Therefore, it is becoming better understood why our text—whose archaic characteristics, when compared to other variants, are constantly becoming clearer—in place of the commonly used healing [*gydantis*] water calls this primary, health-restoring water *gijantis*: health, as life, is an element of similar nature whose existence in the body guarantees the individual's integrity. These two additions remain in the organism and make the person "healthy and whole." As elemental matter, however, each has an independent existence and their dwelling is the bottom of the sea.

The further development of a story, in which a simpleton departs to find the healing and living water, often introduces the sleeping beauty motif. The hero often finds the necessary waters there with her, but not content with that he "gets it into his head to fulfill his needs, that fool."[100] As a consequence of "taking care of business," a son is born to the princess, and sometimes a cursed kingdom rises to the surface at the same time.

The simultaneous acquisition of living water and the creation of new life is not accidental. Without posing the question of whether we can view the motif of the sleeping princess as a transformation of the marriage of our hero to the Maiden of the Sea (see segment V), we must record the fact that the appearance of new life (and with it, eventually, all mythic phenomena connected with *birth*) in the Lithuanian world view is homologous with the acquisition of living water, that both phenomena belong to the same philosophic-sacred sphere.

Here it is again appropriate to mention our partially analyzed group of stories (see above) whose hero, instructed by the king to bring him the *Princess of the Sea*, somewhat later also brings her *iron cows*, in whose boiling milk the prince bathes, then perishes, while his helper-hero, conversely, becomes unusually *handsome*, marries the princess, and inherits the kingdom.

The aim of this reminder is to turn our attention to the unambiguous analogy which exists between the effects of the living water and the results of bathing in the milk of the Iron Cows: this analogy confirms—and strengthens our evidence for—the possibility of substituting the motif of iron cows for that of the living waters. The hero of one story, returning the Princess of the Sea to the king, is dispatched on a new mission, since he "knows of one such *water,* that if you (king) would anoint your face with this water, then you would become much *younger,* and if you would anoint the the face of your young queen, then she would be twice as *beautiful.*" The hero departs to the seaside and there forces ravens to go to the "bottom of the sea": "You must bring me one bottle of that water that *can raise a dead man,* and another bottle of such water that when *a man's face is anointed with it he becomes twice as handsome.*"[101]

Even though the narrator becomes somewhat confused here when enumerating the functions of the two waters, it is important in that the healing and life-giving waters motif is introduced in the same place where we find the motif of the rejuvenating milk in several other variants. Both motifs, when viewed as parallel *modi operandi,* belong to the sacred sphere covered by Aušrinė and her herd.

The problematic of life and death, health and illness is also encountered in narratives which describe battles with the *Dragons* [Slibinai]. Here again it is as much lack of space as shortage of comprehensive data that prohibits us from delving deeper into questions about the nature of dragons, which would allow us to attempt to describe their aquatic origin and solve the problem of their degradation into "negative types." It will suffice to touch on only one aspect of their case that is of importance to us.

Irrespective of the aim for which the leading hero clashes with the *dragon,* the entire difficulty involved in his overcoming the invincible dragon is to find his vulnerable spot, his "Achilles heel." This vulnerable spot is the dwelling site of his *sveikata* [health] and *gyvastis* [life energy].

One hero orders the maid kidnapped by the dragon to inquire with cunning of the dragon:

> "Go and ask the gentleman where his *sveikata* is."
> The Dragon gives himself away:
> "My *sveikata*: in the ninth kingdom lives my brother; if someone should slay him, then I too would not have my health."

The hero, of course, slays the dragon-brother, from whose insides there falls an *egg* with which the first dragon is "destroyed."[102]

A similar history occurs to the *king without a soul* [dušia] whose soul the hero must find if he wishes to kill him. His soul is found in the lake, in that lake—a stone, in the stone—a rabbit, in that rabbit—a duck, in that duck—an *egg*, which is the king's soul.[103]

Another dragon, when asked, "Where is your *gyvastis* since you are so *strong* that no one can kill you?" answers, "My *gyvastis* is far and deep: in the sea on an island there is a bull, in the bull, a dove, and in that dove, an *egg*, and in the egg—my *gyvastis*."[104]

The hero of another story, the son of the *Storm* [Vėtra], departs to find the *death of the King of the Sea* and finds it "on the red sea, on an island," in a chest under the oak tree, in which there sits a duck, and in the duck an *egg* and with that egg he slays the King of the Seas.[105] Another variant of the search for the *death* of the dragon is even more interesting from a mythological viewpoint. The dragon, questioned by the maiden, first gives a series of deceitful answers: the first time his *death* is in a glass of *water;* the second time in the *linden tree* where the nightingale sings (and the linden tree, as we know, is the sacred tree of the goddess *Laima*). The truth, of course, is more complicated: in France, after one has eaten 12 *oxen* and downed 12 "pitchers" of *water* one may attempt to wrestle the dragon; while wrestling, a duck would fly out, and that duck was torn apart, an egg would fall out, with which it would be possible to slay the dragon. This complicated procedure, like others similar to it, which indicate the deep origin of life-death and the difficulty involved in reaching it, ends here with an unexpected result: when the dragon has been slain "suddenly *those seas are no more,* only dry land remains,"[106] an outcome which is reminiscent of the end of our narrative.

In all these examples we are dealing either with *Dragons* or with *Kings of the Sea* who are associated in one manner or another with water: taking into consideration their identical life elements, there is no difference between their two forms. However much this concerns the life principles themselves, just the opposite seems to be the case: two separate types of *egg-souls* [siela] can be distinguished, on the one hand, *sveikata* and dušia [health and the material soul] and on the other *gyvastis* [life] and death.

The concept of *health,* by comparison, is rather clear. We know, for instance, that when a person *sneezes* and no one says to him "To your health," his "dušia" goes to the devil.[107] It would seem that upon sneezing the man's "spirit" flies out of his lungs, and one can hold it back only by mentioning its essence and name. However it might be, only his "dušia" crosses over to the devil's power. In other words, man loses his "health" but by no means does he die from this. The same thing occurs with the three black crow-sorceresses who wait for a man to cross the courtyard so that when he *sneezes* they can say to him "To your health!": then they will be able to "cast a spell" on him.[108] No less significant is another belief, according to which a man who runs as a wolf, toasting his neighbor and saying to him "to your health!" can pass on this "characteristic," making him a *werewolf*—it is enough for him to answer "thanks."[109]

With this explanation of the Lithuanian concept of health as the integrity of the individual guaranteeing the maintenance of his "spirit" in the same state, the ancient polite form of address "Jūsų Sveikata" [Your Health] (Daukša, 1599) or "Tamstos Sveikata" (Daukantas)[110] becomes comprehensible as well. These were later progressively changed to the Polish "Jo Mylista" [Your Kindness]. It recovers its full meaning even today in its usage among the Lithuanian highlanders: "I read in the papers that you [Sveikas] sometimes visit America," Jonas Balys writes me.

Gyvastis and *death* on the other hand, are only two aspects of the same phenomenon. Just as the bee, who loses *gyvuonis* [the quick] together with its stinger, or the snake, whose death-bearing tongue is called *gyvuonis,* so man, living under the sign of death and dying when life runs out, hangs by a thread which connects him to the *primary element* of life and death.

These rather lengthy digressions from the basic theme are intended not only to help explain the significance of the ancient Lithuanian stereotypical expression "sveikas ir gyvas"—which today is more often changed to the everyday "labas" [hello]—but rather to help create as full a picture as possible of the logically structured *system of values* which comprise in the Lithuanian context one of the primary areas of philosophical thought. For its clarification an entire chain of previously analyzed binary concepts may be offered, organized according to the principle of homology:

Elements Lexicalization	Sveikas	Gyvas
Abstract concepts	Sveikata	Gyvastis
Symbolic forms	Gijantis v. (healing water)	Gyvuonis (living water)
Somatic forms	Lungs ("dušia," "vėlė")	Liver

The abstractly formulated elements of *sveikata* and *gyvastis* [health and life] are "placed" in the *egg figure* in mythic language. They are symbolically expressed in the form of one of the four elements which make up nature—*water.* In the corporeal world of living creatures, they find a place for themselves in the *lungs* and the *liver* which the crab drags into the sea depths—the land of life and death.

If to this system of values expressed on several figurative planes we add the magical *apples* and the milk of the *iron cows* which cover the values of love, beauty, and health, we will have a more or less complete picture of the sacred sphere in which Aušrinė and her family reign and which, in the form of a semantic code, dominates our text.

Before we finish analyzing this episode, we would like to add an excerpt from another story in order to show how our gradually worked-out semantic code increases the readability of the world of Lithuanian "tales."

The story itself is widely known: it is the history of a king whose children are born during his absences while at war. Out of envy his wife's sisters report to him that his wife has given birth to puppies and kittens. What is interesting here is the unexpectedly inserted episode about the expedition of the children, already grown and raised in secret—two brothers and a sister—to search for a "talking bird, a singing tree and *golden water*"[111] to decorate their manor. When the brothers turn into "pillars of coal," one after another, and when the sister departs to search for them, the "talking bird" points out a spring whose waters will revive her brothers and helps her finally to find the golden water. "Further on that *golden water, oh, how it shines like the sun in the sky.* Go and place a bottle beneath it, *a drop of it will fall in,* then you will have a bottleful. Bring it home to your orchard, uncork the bottle and it will shine as brightly in your orchard as here." And when they came home they "let that water out of the bottle—it again *rose high in the air,* shone yellow and bright."

In light of our text, if it can be stated in this fashion, great wisdom is not needed to identify that golden yellow water high in the sky shining like the sun with our already familiar Aušrinė. To her already well-known transformations—from the mare of the sea and maiden of the sea to the star in the sky with the help of her hair—can be added the identification of the *beacon* of the sky with *water*: the "golden water" hanging in the air, drops one *drop,* from which in another place, there once again appears a luminous body in the sky. Since we know from other texts that *dew,* that heavenly water, is only the scattered *beads and pearls*[112] of Aušrinė, it is understandable why at a certain time of the year *rolling around* in dew heals and protects people from all kinds of illnesses, but especially from diseases of the skin.[113] The *apples* offered by Aušrinė, the *milk* of her cows have then the same characteristics. It is understandable as well that to heal the fool whose eyes had been plucked out by his brothers, it is sufficient for the raven to just "run his wing through the dew," touch his eyes and he is able to see anew.[114]

There remain several as yet undiscussed textual facts which directly concern the narrative itself.

The first of these is the hero's death, which corresponds to the *withering of apples* in the orchard of the *Mother of the Winds*. As a narrative means for restoring communication between the Sender and the dispatched hero, this is not an uncommon phenomenon in Lithuanian stories. The Sender finds out that the hero has fallen into misfortune, for instance, because the *water* in the glass which he has left behind turns red,[115] or that the hero's knife stuck in a wall begins to bleed.[116] In these cases—just as with the withering of the apples—one or another figurative object metonymically represents the hero himself and a transformation of his state changes the status of the metonym. The metonymic object cannot thus be fortuitous: as with the hair which we analyzed earlier, it must represent either the hero's *body* or a trait which characterizes his *nature*. We have seen that in our case the hero's qualification is manifested by an acquisition of the apples, which confirms him in the role of the seeker of *love* and its provider. The withering of apples is a "natural" signal that he has found himself in danger.

As we have seen, the gift of apples formed the opening narrative episode of our text, marking the hero's trial and his qualification. In the second part of the text, allotted to the rescue of Aušrinė, the same function is fulfilled by the segment we are studying. We can then rightly ask in what area the hero is qualified here, and which additional features he acquires on that occasion. The first, superficial answer is provided by the narrator himself who explains in the last segment of the text that the hero has "atoned" for the brother and sisters of Aušrinė. This somewhat Christianized explanation allows one to understand that the hero, passing through death and resurrection, has "redeemed" or "ransomed" the enchanted herd of Aušrinė. However, the mythic content of that "redemption"—if we take into account the fact that the ideology as recorded in our text is entirely different—cannot be Christian. We will return to this problem when we analyze the narrative conclusion.

The third observation touches on the hero's sleep: our hero—like other heroes in similar circumstances—"sleeps soundly" when the question of his life and death is being weighed.

The heroes of Lithuanian tales should not be thought of as being heavy sleepers. They do not sleep when there are matters which involve the events, tasks, or exploits of this life. They sleep only when there is talk of death, or of life in death. Sleep is the form of another and different life; another life which occurs while man sleeps, comprehended only from remembered dreams. It is understood thus that life in sleep and life in death do not differ in essence one from the other. "La vida es un sueño," we are fond of repeating after a famous Spaniard. But *sapnas,* a dream, in the ancient Lithuanian language meant "sleep"[117] (comp. Latin equivalent *somnis*). This parallel form of life is no worse than "actual" life. We can understand, then, why when matters turn to "serious things," i.e., life and death, the narrative leaves the hero sleeping soundly and starts to develop on another level parallel to life.

X. The Rescue

He searches all the lands—his maiden is nowhere. He asked the wind for directions: "What shall I do now?"

The North Wind: "Go to her manor. You'll find a bridle and saddle. Saddle the bull, and there will stand such a stallion as has never been seen in all the kingdom. Mount it, you'll ride on the seas better than on land. He will carry you to the kingdom where she is. On that day there will be a horse fair, the king will look to buy a stallion. When he starts to haggle you say: 'If buying, buy; I don't have time.' Until the maiden comes."

The maiden came out and recognized her animal. She took him by the hand and mounted the horse. They rose into the sky, escaped to her manor. The king grieved greatly.

The king asked his sorcerers: "What should be done now?"

"There are no instructions, nothing!"

The Appearance of the Steed of the Sea

This segment does not raise any further comments for various reasons: first of all, our attention in reading this text is concentrated solely on *Aušrinė*, on the world of her values and the events that directly concern her, since we have neither space nor sufficient information to analyze the kingdom of her enemies. On the other hand, the reader will already have become accustomed to our manner of textual reading and the many observations useful at the beginning of this procedure are now taking on a repetitive character. We will attempt thus to note only a few of the more interesting facts.

(1) In the organization of this segment, we recognize a previously discussed narrative procedure in which the introduction of the virtual program, the activity project, occupies the same, if not more, space than the representation of the activity itself: the advice of the *North Wind* is qualitatively more important than the hero's deeds. The actual narrative program is quite ordinary here and consists, in summary, of arrival and departure, which describe the actual rescue only elliptically: the hero, as in other similar situations, appears very little, allowing his *helpers*—the wind and the bull—to act in his place.

(2) Several details indirectly supplement the rough image formed of the kingdom of the kidnapper of Aušrinė. The date chosen for the rescue is not an ordinary *market day* as is stereotypical for tales, but the day of the *horse fair*: horse trading, their commerce, is rather closely associated with the *blacksmith trade*. The prince looks to buy a stallion, and the operation for purchasing available to him is that of *haggling*. It is known, for instance, that Thursday, a favorable day for commerce[118] in the opinion of Lithuanians, is called *swindler's day*[119] or *devil's day*.[120] In that manner, the prince is indirectly inscribed into the Devil's sacred sphere and is contrasted to our hero, who declines to haggle "If buying, buy, I don't have time" even though such an answer, on the advice of the North Wind, will prolong the time, provoking the appearance of the Maiden of the Sea in the market square. The same traits of the prince are confirmed finally in the last scene of this episode, in which he calls together the council of "sorcerers" of his manor to ask for their advice.

(3) One mythologically interesting fact is the transformation of the *bull* to a *stallion*. Although it is carried out by a well-known procedure in the story world—by the placement of the *bridle* (sometimes a saddle, in the same way, for instance, that witches are turned into mares)[121]—this new form of the bull is significant. We had observed that the *Sea Maiden* has an anthropomorphic form as far as she is associated with life on the island, with land, but that she also is the *mare of the sea*—a

form which she would acquire when the earth turns to water. We encounter a similar alternation of forms in the bull's personality as well: the bull, as the head of *Aušrinė's* herd, is associated with the island and the pasture, but he also is the stallion of the sea who crosses water far better than land and who flies through the sky. The final segment of the text will explain that this *stallion of the sea* can have a human form, since he is the brother of *Aušrinė*. These various, clearly separate forms in mythic mentality, with which one and the same being is manifested, can thus create quite a tangled mess for the average narrator: we have observed how in the various variants of our often-used group of parallel stories the iron cows compete with the sea mares, the oxen with the colts.

XI. The Beginning of a New Era

The maiden upon returning released her bull. The bull knelt down and spoke in a man's voice: "Chop off my head!"

The maiden did not want to chop it off, but she had to. She chopped the head off—a fourth of the seas disappeared, became land. Her brother emerged from the bull. She cut off the heads of all three cows, who were her sisters. All the seas disappeared, turned to land. The earth sprang to life. She remained the queen of that earth and her husband its king. Her husband atoned for her brother and her sisters. They lived happily ever after. And that's the end.

The Beheading

The most distinctive fact in this last segment is the transformation achieved through the beheading procedure, which causes Aušrinė's herd to change into a family with human form and the water to change into earth.

The *beheading* procedure itself does not surprise the reader of tales. It is an often encountered means of metamorphosis used to "change back" cursed beings, returning them to their human forms.[122] Of course, the mythic procedure does not correspond to the facts of our empirical world, but in essence it does not differ, for example, from the kissing of a toad—a condition whose fulfillment can rescue a princess cursed into a toad. This, generally taken, is one of the elements in the conception of destiny, one of the forms of *fulfillment of fate*: the form and condition of life as determined by fate can be changed only by an incursion of an externally contingent event.

However, our text offers a much more complicated interpretation of this metamorphosis. The explanation, "We were cursed until our heads were chopped off"[123] is not sufficient here: the beheading procedure can be applied and become effective only *because* the hero has already "atoned" for the suffering. A certain contractual situation has been formed between the fate of the patient and its agent which can be expressed by the logical formula: "if . . . then . . .": the hero must acquire and transmit certain values which his opponent lacks, a deficiency, which he must fill in, the liquidation of which is marked by acquisition of a new form.

Aušrinė

The logic of the text thus offers only one possible interpretation: the beheading and the metamorphosis of the Aušrinė family *coincide* with the acquisition of new values that characterize her brother and sisters, *health and life*.

The Earth Sprang to Life

In the episode describing the conquest of the Sea Maiden (segment V) we had opportunity to read about *Aušrinė's* threats to turn the earth into water: she had already appeared there as the capable author of her own transformation and of the elements of nature associated with her. Thus, it is not surprising that here—contrary to ordinary narratives, where the hero usually carries out the beheading himself—the bull turns to *Aušrinė* to fulfill what on the surface seems quite an unfeminine task. Except for *Eglė,* queen of the serpents, *Aušrinė* alone has the *power* of all metamorphoses.

The family of *Aušrinė* thus regains human form. However, this transformation is inseparably bound with the changing of water into earth. The two elements of nature correspond to two divine forms:

$$\frac{\text{zoomorphic form}}{\text{anthropomorphic form}} \simeq \frac{\text{water}}{\text{earth}}$$

The existence of earth and mankind is thus associated with the representation of the mortal forms of the gods.

The process of conversion of the seas into land is also characteristic: the seas are divided into four parts, according to the number of divine beings; they are converted into land progressively, parallel to the beheadings. However, only the final operation in fact is significant: "All the seas disappeared, *turned into land.*" Just as a man chopped into pieces becomes whole [*sveikas*] when anointed with the restorative water, so an entire collection of dry pieces placed into one pile makes up *the earth.* The following sentence is not surprising: "the earth sprang to *life.*" Just as man, first made *whole,* acquires life with the help of the living water, so the "universe" starting to *live* becomes an integral part of a single "earth-mankind" concept. *Earth is earth only as it is inhabited.*

It would be possible to develop this idea further by providing as an example another myth according to which humanity arose from a union of the last descendants of the race of *Giants* with *Earth.*[123] We will return to this theme at another time, in our discussion of the history of the Lithuanian *flood* associated with Laima. It will suffice now to clear up only one characteristic feature of this episode: the perfect equivalence of the Aušrinė family as an organic totality, with the integral concept of *earth-mankind.* The divine family of Aušrinė acquires human form so that it can look after and protect both the new-found earth and her inhabitants. In that sense, without considering yet who in reality are her brother and her sisters, we can maintain that the Aušrinė family belongs to a category of gods called *žemininkai* [earthgods].

The hierarchic relations of the *Aušrinė* family are also clearly defined: if a quarter of the earth "belongs" to each brother and sister, *Aušrinė* undoubtedly "remains the *queen of the earth.*" It is difficult to assess the problem of the social status of our hero, her husband. Even though the text clearly states that he was elevated from a *Servant's* role to that of a *King,* we can ask if this belated wedding is not the result of a mechanical application of a schema in narrative tales which provides a wedding and a "happy life" as a canonic ending to stories. Of course, the texts of well-known songs come to mind here in which Mėnulis falls in love with Aušrinė, creating a domestic drama in the world of the gods. There are even tales in which the King of the Seas, *Mėnulis,* is held to be the father of *Aušrinė.*[124] Under the influence of Christianity, the assimilation of *Aušrinė* to the *Blessed Virgin* provides arguments to support her unmarried state. However that might be, this problem is of great importance to all of Lithuanian mythology: without the incorporation of Mėnulis, we will see, we cannot even complete the analysis of Aušrinė. Thus additional, in-depth studies are needed if we want to make a stronger case for one or the other hypothesis.

We will end the analysis of this segment with an attempt to develop the figures of the Aušrinė family by inscribing them into the general Lithuanian teleological problematic.

The Triad of Baltic Gods

One of the basic tasks in the reconstruction of Baltic religion involves, of course, the creation of an inventory of the major, primary gods and the distribution of their divine functions. This quite controversial problem has occupied a rather broad analytical area, as much Prussian as Lithuanian, and possibly in part even hindering the development of other analytic questions regarded as secondary. Undoubtedly, after Romantic optimism and the positivist skepticism following it this problem will have to be reconsidered anew in its entirety. The attempts of Jaan Puhwel[125] to defend the authenticity of the Prussian pantheon appear as an important first step in this direction. Nonetheless, we can ask which theoretical strategy is more suitable in this case, or whether, before any attempt at a synthesis is made, it would be more worthwhile to first enlarge on the mythologic case of the different gods and their divine spheres.

Our knowledge of the ancient Prussian religion is based primarily on material in Simon Grunau's *Preussische Chronik:*[126] whether it is viewed as a serious religious source, or as a compilation of Scandinavian gods dressed in Prussian clothing—this belongs with the mythologist's view of Prussian religion. According to Grunau, this religion was dominated by three major gods—*Patrimpas, Patulas, Perkūnas.* If one takes into account earlier descriptions of the Uppsala sanctuary recounting that three primary Scandinavian gods were also worshipped, then this repetitive triadic principle of divine structure served as one of the most powerful arguments for the inauthenticity of the Prussian gods and for the manner of compilation of Grunau's descriptions.

Our perspective on this already aging debate changes strictly with the efforts of

Dumézil developed for comparative Indo-European mythology, which offer a *trifunctional ideology* model for the comprehension and description of Indo-European religions. The triadic principle of organization of the dominant gods becomes the common structural core of all Indo-European religions, and the existence of the three fundamental Prussian gods, rather than a defect, becomes obligatory, attesting to the archaic nature of such a conceptualization of gods.

According to the model offered by Dumézil, there can be identified in Indo-European religions not three dominant gods but three *sovereign spheres* in which the gods who represent these spheres are inscribed and in large part correspond to the three social classes which exist in these nations: priests, warriors and cultivators. The first sovereign sphere is most often represented by two deities: the sovereign god of contracts *Mithra* (in Hindu religion) and the sovereign god of magic *Varuna*. The warrior class corresponds to the sovereign god of power *Indra*, and the third function usually is represented by an entire series of often-paired gods who are occupied with the direct guardianship of the agrarian class.

Our problematic concerning *Aušrinė* and her family, at first glance, undoubtedly enters into the sphere of the third sovereign function.

According to the Grunau *Chronik*, Patrimpas, who is depicted on the flag of Vidovutis next to two other gods, is described as "ein man junger gestalt ane bardt, gekronett mit sangelen und frolich . . . und der gott vom getreide."[127] His second portrait is in the sanctuary: next to it in a large jug covered with sheaves of grain is kept a *snake*, which the *waydolottinnen* [priestesses] nourish with milk.[128] He finally is characterized as "ein gott des gluckis in streitten und sust in anderen sachin."[129]

To our amazement *Patrimpas*, one of the major gods, whose name without question relates him to *water*[130] and its symbolism, is characterized in the descriptions of Grunau according to the following attributes:

(1) according to the *crops and milk*, as the guardian god of agriculture and cattle-breeding;

(2) according to the *snake* kept in his honor, as the god of health and life;

(3) according to these two spheres, he, finally, is characterized as the god of *good fortune* [laimė]. It would appear that *Patrimpas*, besides the sovereign function directly attributed to him, according to which he would correspond to the Indian *Mithra*, also attaches to it the third divine sphere, in which he manifests himself as the guardian of that sphere. This hypothesis—if Lithuanian mythology data were to confirm it—would reveal the original position of Baltic religion in Indo-European mythology.

The Lithuanian Triad

It is difficult to create a list of primary Lithuanian gods: the early information in chronicles is quite fragmentary, and inventories of gods dating from the end of the sixteenth century copied from one author to another, confuse the Prussian gods with the Lithuanian. It is possible, nevertheless, to try to group these few facts and create some type of general representation concerning this question.

Indian gods	Indra	Varuna	Mithra
Prussian gods	Perkūnas	Patulas	Patrimpas
Lithuanian gods			
Malala (1261)	Perkūnas	Kalvelis (= Teljavel)	Andaj (?)
Volynija Chr. (13th c.)	———	Kalvelis (= Teljavel)	Andij (?)
Dlugosz (15th c.)	Perkūnas (= Jupiter)	Vulcanus	Aesculapius
Striykowski (17th c.)	Perkūnas (in his place: St. Stanislaus)	"eternal fire" (in its place: "cannon")	"black forest," where there are "giwoitos" [snakes] and "ziemiennikos"

Ancient sources which, in one manner or another, provide a list of gods (or the cult sites) but do not mention one or another of them, are as we see of two types: thirteenth-century Russian chronicles and fifteenth-and sixteenth-century Polish "histories." The preservation of the name of the sovereign god Perkūnas of the second function based on power is characteristic of both types of sources (the Volynia chronicle, of course, does not mention him, but in the list there remain two undeciphered gods, *Nunaday* and *Diviriks*, and at least one of these might be the epithet of Perkūnas). The fact recorded by Striykowski that Jogaila [Jagiello], upon changing thrones and religions, had erected the church of St. Stanislaus, the patron of Poland, on *Perkūnas's* site is undoubtedly used to inscribe this deity in the list of sovereign gods. The god in the second column representing magical sovereignty and corresponding to the Prussian underworld god *Patulas*, is more problematic: if *"Teliavelis"* of the Russian chronicles is corrected to *Kalvelis*,[131] its further identification does not present difficulties: Dlugosz interprets him as *Vulcanus*, as both god of the underworld and of fire, and Striykowski, by determining that even before the founding of Vilnius, the *eternal fire* lit by *Šventaragis* was worshipped at the same site, and that when it was extinguished a cannon foundry was equipped at its site, further consolidates the position of *Kalvelis* within the triad of Lithuanian gods.

The Lithuanian Patrimpas

The third god, representing contractual sovereignty, raises enormous difficulties. The repeated *Andaj*, or *Andij* in Russian chronicles, remains obscure: the attempt by some mythologists to explain it as a poorly recorded or poorly copied vocative *Angiai! Angi!* form can be taken only as a subordinate argument to be added to other aspects of his portrait which have been determined by other means.

The Roman interpretation of Dlugosz—*Aesculapius*, adding that the Lithuanian practice of snake worship [*aspides*] applies to him—can only mean that within the cultural content of the fifteenth century there existed in this god's knowledge characteristic matters of health and illness. Striykowski's description of the founding of Vilnius and the ternary distribution of cult sites associated with it supplements and confirms the interpretation by Dlugosz. According to it, next to the eternal flame founded earlier, Gediminas had established two additional, separate cult sites: along with the Perkūnas statue mentioned previously, he dedicated the *black forest* not far from there to the gods and, according to pagan custom, settled priests there who prayed for the knights cremated at the site, and who raised and nurtured "*Gywoitos y Ziemiennikos . . .* iáko Bozki domowe."[132] Along with the snakes already mentioned by Dlugosz, Striykowski also incorporates into this third sacred sphere, the cult of the deceased princes and an entire series of "*Žemininkai*," whom he describes as "household gods." Praetorius presents somewhat later a list of gods called "Namiszki Diewai" [household gods]: Žemėpatis, Žemyna, Laumelė, Gabjauja, Giltinė, Drebkulys, Bangpūtis, Aitvaras, and kaukučiai [pl.][133] This list, created in an entirely different corner of Lithuania a century later, should be regarded neither as exhaustive, nor as precisely corresponding to Striykowski's concepts of *Žemininkai*. Nevertheless, it allows one to form a general understanding of their spheres of responsibility and guardianship.

A conclusion presents itself: without going into further detail or searching for perfect equivalents, we can easily see that the deities within the purview of the Lithuanian Mithra as well as their attributes of power and action, correspond along general lines to the sphere of action of the Prussian *Patrimpas*. With this comparison, which cannot be the consequence of chance or borrowing, one trait common to both Baltic religions must be noted—the placing of the gods of the third function within the sphere of contractual sovereignty. Our attempt to open up this sphere somewhat— which as we saw, appears as the weakest point in the schema of the dominant Lithuanian gods—has yet a further aim: to contribute to the determination of the general structure of Lithuanian theology.

Dievaitis Mėnulis

So far there are no claimants to this sovereign post of a Lithuanian *Patrimpas,* unless it is possible to count *Dievas* [God] himself: this is a theonym by which one of the major Lithuanian gods might have been called, one, I would say, of the most positive gods, since only such a name could have been chosen by Christianity as the Lithuanian name of the one Christian God. The problem is substantial. Unfortunately, its solution at least until now has been directed down the wrong path by mythologists working within the framework of a Christian worldview, who took this opportunity to search for one dominant pagan *God*.

The case for such a *Dievas*—as one of three primary gods—could be fulfilled, for instance, by *Dzievaicis*, the name by which *mėnulis* [moon] was called in the region of Dzukija at an earlier time (*mėnulis* there is a literary word, previously entirely unknown[134]), or *Deuoitis*[135] as recorded by Lasicius worshipped along with Jūra [sea].) This is an interesting hypothesis which at this time does not concern us directly.

Conversely, it seems more important to analyze the activity sphere of *Mėnulis*, which is directly combined with the value system in our text: to understand the gods, we must first evaluate their semantic contours, rather than their names or their forms. The mythologist's interest is especially piqued by the comparatively large number of *prayers* which have come down to us, by means of which one may address the *new Moon* as it appears: no other Lithuanian deity can make such a boast, and Balys with sixty such prayers in his archives (and how many more there are in the archives of Vilnius in Lithuania?) has a basis for positing the importance of the *lunar cult* in Lithuanian mythology.[136]

Balys presents seven well-chosen examples of such prayers. By supplementing them somewhat with data from elsewhere, we can attempt a fairly thorough analysis of this small corpus, being quite certain that a larger sample would yield nothing essentially new.

(1) Addressing *Menulis* as provider of *health*:

> "Grant me *health*, godliness to you" (Anykščiai)
> "A full moon for you, *health* for me" (Šeduva)
> "Grant him a circle [full moon] and *health* to me" (Antalieptė, Tauragiai)

(2) *Mėnulis* appears as guarantor of *beauty and youth:*

> "Brightness for you, *beauty* for me" (Žeimelis)
> "Lordship for you, *youth* for me" (Anykščiai)

to which can also be added a trait which emerges from them—happiness:

> "You shine all the time, you make us *happy*. We see him and we all are at *peace*, all are happy" (Rokiškis)

The antiquity of the two concepts with which our text is concerned—*health* and *beauty* as well as *youth*—in Lithuanian mentality, and the clear differentiation of these two areas is confirmed by folk beliefs as well. To illustrate, it is necessary to cite Balys' summary of those beliefs in its entirety:[137]

> . . . a man born on the *new moon* will remain his entire life of *youthful appearance*, be *handsome*, not age quickly, although he will be fearful and timid, weak and anxious, fearful of the "evil eye." The man born in the *old moon* is old in appearance, scowling, morose, angry, unattractive and ages quickly, but he will be *healthy* and strong, steadfast, unafraid of evil eyes. Christenings should be held on the *new moon*, then the person will not age quickly, remain *youthful* and *handsome*. On the new moon, the newlyweds will live long and age slowly, but weddings most often should be planned in the *full moon*, then the newlyweds will live *prosperous* lives, and want for nothing.

It is interesting that these two concepts of *beauty* and *health* logically opposed in beliefs are extended along a *time* line and correspond in that manner to two separate phases of the *Moon*: the correspondence of man's *birth* to these phases predetermines his *fate*, his adaptation to the deity's changing form (in setting the date of a christening or a wedding) allows him, in a certain sense, to direct his fate in the desired direction. The change in the *Moon's* phases, his "life," becomes thus the archetype for the conceptualization of human life:

> New Moon, young man
> Heavenly prince of the earth
> For you to wear away [crescent moon] for us to get gray (Tauragė)

(3) *Mėnulis* is also the guardian of the *dead*, and he can either bestow or at least help to find "life after death":

> May God grant you the full moon, and us the *kingdom of Perkūnas* (Rokiškis)
> Grant him a full moon, and us the *kingdom of Perkūnas* (Antalieptė, Tauragiai).

The concept of the *kingdom of Perkūnas*, as the place of life after death, becomes more evident in more modern variants:

> May God grant you the full moon, and me the *kingdom of heaven* (Taut. Darb. IV, 184)
> So that my soul would be with you *after death in heaven* (Kabeliai)

(4) *Mėnulis*, finally, is the provider of *good fortune*:

> Bring us all types of *good fortune* (Rokišis). Bring . . . benefit and *good luck* (ibid.).
> A gold crown for you, happiness and *luck* for me (Taut. Darb. IV, 184).

It is not surprising that such a unified sacred sphere can offer to the deity which represents it *sovereign* titles. Actually in the prayer *Mėnulis* is also called "our dear king" or "heavenly prince of the earth," a "gold crown" is ascribed to him. Compared to our "mortal" existence, the "divine" status granted him means that one addresses him as a "bright little god of the heavens."

The Family of Aušrinė

It is normal to expect to find such a superficially closed mythic sphere distributed among several more prominent gods: every god has his own individual life and does not ordinarily enjoy solitude, while people, in turn, like to know with whom they are dealing, to whom they must turn in every specific case.

The question of Aušrinė and her family emerges here. Taking into account the fact that the system of values deduced along general lines in our text—except for the as yet untouched problem of *laimė*—corresponds to the sphere of guardianship of mankind which is in the power of Mėnulis and that they both belong to the "third function"; taking into account as well the fact that the earth and her inhabitants in our text appear at the same time as the conversion and acquisition of human form by the members of the Aušrinė family—there is reason to assume that a separate part of the earth and separate mythic values "belong" as much to the brother of Aušrinė as to her sisters and that one can regard them as "earth gods" [žemininkai].

First of all there emerges, of course, the figure of Aušrinė's brother. It should be noted that the situation created by our text in which her brother appears next to the heroine-Aušrinė is not the usual one in the world of Lithuanian stories. We know of tales about brothers who depart to search for their sister, about a sister who searches for her brothers: the brother and sister play independent narrative roles. There are stories about a brother and sister who travel together, but these are most often stories that weigh the problem of incest. The brother and sister pair which enters into our text, whose presence is not justified by the requirements of narrative structures, can be understood only within a mythological framework.

Second, regardless of the weak role which it plays in the tale, the personality of Aušrinė's brother becomes progressively more distinct and takes on individual contours. He is the helpmate of Aušrinė, the guardian of the secrets of the sea, ruler and guardian of his three sister-cows. On the figurative plane, the text introduces him in two zoomorphic forms—as *bull* and as *stallion of the sea*—granting him at the end a final, anthropomorphic form. It is noteworthy that as stallion of the sea he becomes part of a deity group which assumes the estimable shape of the horse, capable of appearing in the sea and the sky, thus indicating its dual—both *aquatic* and *air*—nature: not only is *Aušrinė* the *mare of the sea*, but *Mėnulis* as well is born a *colt of the sky*.[138] If we keep in mind the fact that researchers of Lithuanian mythology often encounter only empty names of gods in historical sources with almost no information about their content, the figurative and semantic portrait of Aušrinė's brother is sufficiently clear, even though, of course, there is no name.

Next to all of this, we must add, of course, his basic attributes as provided by our text: as previously mentioned, by "atoning" for the brother and sister, our hero thus qualifies them, thanks to the fulfillment of fate, as guardians of the sphere of life and death.

It is significant that in Prussian religion, next to the major god *Patrimpas,* in whose honor a *snake* was kept in a jug, another hierarchically lower god, *Ausschauts,* is included in a list of ten Prussian gods in a 1530 document,[139] in which he is interpreted as *Aesculapius.* The existence of a sovereign god to whom the guardianship functions of life and health are attributed does not interfere with the presence, next to him, of another more specialized god who acts by the principle of delegating.

Almost all sixteenth-century analysts later mention this god, who is easily identifiable in spite of the alternation in the spelling of the theonym:

Ausceutum, deum incolumitatis et aegritudinis (Maletius)
Auscutum, deum incolumitatis et aegritudinis (Lasicius)
Auschleuts, der Gott aller Gebrechen, Krankheiten und Gesundheit (Lucus David).[140]

Another fact is significant as well: Latvian mythology, generally more fond of female deities, is acquainted with the sky divinity *Auseklis,* who is manifested in the

Aušrinė

form of the morning star and who by his activity and frequent appearance in texts overpowers the rather pallid *Austrina*.[141]

The positions of these two gods are somewhat different: the Prussian god's functions of health and illness are well-known, but there is a lack of information about his life and divine form; the functions of the Latvian god, conversely, are unknown, but there is information about his life, which draws him closer to the Lithuanian *Aušrinė* family (he is the easterly star, he buys a stallion, he is kept imprisoned by the daughters of the Sun and does not rise for three days).[142]

Facts such as these from comparative Baltic mythology allow one to introduce next to these two gods a Lithuanian god, investing him with a theonym and divine functions, on the one hand, based on the examples of the Prussian gods, and on the other hand, following the example of the Latvian god, identifying him as the brother of Aušrinė based on our analysis of the text.

The presence of such a Lithuanian god is first corroborated by Praetorius: "*Auszweitis,* nach Bretkius *Auszweikus,* ein Gott der Kranken and Gesunden von sweikas-gesund, sweikata-Gesundheit."[143]

It seems, nevertheless, that in the case of this Lithuanian god of health, several separate matters are confused.

(1) *Ausschauts,* as Būga has indicated,[144] is the Prussian and not the Lithuanian name of Aesculapius: Balys confuses him with the Lithuanian *Auszweitis* when he records him in the same column. It is possible that the eventual disappearance of the Prussian language during the sixteenth century—some Prussians becoming Germanized and others becoming Lithuanianized—the name of the God *Ausschauts* could have remained for a long time within the recollection of the Lithuanian-speaking East Prussians and been used as a synonym for *Auszweitis*.

(2) Būga, in attempting to determine the etymology of this word, it seems, had been influenced by the *Pa-trimpas* and the *Au-trimpas* forms and noting that the prefix *au-* in the name Ausschauts, offered to derive its origin from **aušaũt* "skolyti" [to loan] in turn taken from *šaut* "šauti, stumti, duoti" [shoot, shove, strike]. The Lithuanian form of this theonym, according to him, would then be **Nuo-šiautas*.

If we take into account not only the phonetic requirements of the language but also its semio-cultural context in order to derive the meaning of the word, we can offer the Baltic language specialists another etymological solution. If we keep in mind the fact that one can easily identify the common root *auš-, aus-*"aušti, dienoti" [dawn, daybreak],[145] just as much in the Lithuanian as in the Latvian theonyms, it is possible to view the Prussian *Ausschauts* not as a root with a prefix *au-* but as a compound word with a double root *auš-šautas,* in which the first part would be common to all three Baltic languages:

Auš-šautas — Auš-šveitis — Aus-eklis

and the second part, corresponding to the etymology offered by Būga, means "šauti," "douti" [shoot, strike]. The form of the Lithuanian *Auš-sveitis* becomes evident in that manner. The second variant of the name—*Aussveikus*, which appears as a semantically-based contamination, poses no difficulty.

The significant contributions of our text to this case are of several types:

(1) It points to the existence of a brother next to the female goddess *Aušrinė*, i.e., a representative of the male gender of the same divine sphere. The problem of *Aušrinė* in Lithuanian mythology in that manner is comparable to the problem of the Latvian *Auseklis*: this makes possible the formation of a general hypothesis concerning comparative Baltic religion.

(2) The appearance of *Aušrinė's* brother helps resolve the problem of the god *Auššveitis* and allows his name to be added to the list of "serious" Lithuanian gods: his name, though incomprehensible at first, when taken separately, becomes transparent in this new perspective. His name, in this manner, also provides this god with a solid mythological backbone.

(3) The identification of *Auššveitis* with the *brother of Aušrinė* confirms what until now had only been based on textual analysis, our conviction concerning his sphere of action with respect to people, namely that he is a deity of health and illness.

Although we have revealed the portrait of Aušrinė's brother, Auššveitis, and explained his divine functions, there still remains to be resolved the question of the three sisters of Aušrinė. Their mythological status is not clear: they do not manifest a special, independent activity, and hierarchically they are subordinate to *Aušrinė*, whose herd they comprise, and to the *Auššveitis*-bull, who is their ruler and guardian. Nevertheless, their transformation from cows to maidens is accompanied by the change of water to land: even though they are lesser deities they are, nevertheless, *deivės—žemininkės* [earth-goddesses].

The devoted reader of Lithuanian folklore cannot help but notice a particular antagonistic relation which joins cows to *raganas* [witches], one of whose basic preoccupations is the *spoiling* of cow's milk. Such a predisposition to harm cows cannot be accidental—it indicates the essential contradiction which separates those beings that belong to two different sacred spheres. Witches harm the cows most likely because in the Indo-European context cows appear as symbols of the abundance of earthly blessings, as symbols of plentiful food. The previously mentioned Indian and Roman *cows* echo one rare Lithuanian legend which tells of "that time" when there existed enormous cows which, unable to fit in sheds, stood in hollows, thus permitting everyone to milk them: people would fill their buckets with milk, "whether rich or poor—no one went hungry."[146] With the passing of those days, the cold freezing all the cows, all that is left of them is their sign—*the teats of the cows of the Laumės*.

Next to these cows of *Laumė* (or Laimė?), representing abundance of earthly goods—*nauda*—we had the opportunity to meet the iron cows of *Aušrinė*. We observed that bathing in their milk is a risky business—it can bring either death or new life, youth, and beauty. The symbolism associated with cows is thus twofold: on the one hand, it is a question of life and death, in other words, a question of *fate*, and, on the other hand, it is a question of a rich or poor life or, simply stated, a question of *luck*.

Returning to the problems of the Aušrinė family, at first glance it would appear that with the attribution of the area of health and illness to *Auššveitis,* another sphere would remain for their sisters—that of life and death. There is certainly no shortage of well-known gods in this sphere. Next to the primary position occupied by the goddess of birth, *Laimė,* one often encounters the *Three Laimės* (sometimes confused with laumės), who determine the fate of newborn infants, or a pair of gods who travel together around the world—*Laima* and *Giltinė*—fulfilling the same functions of forecasting fate.

The problem of *laimės* and *laumės* [fates and fairies], one of the most complicated in all of Lithuanian mythology, requires a separate, comprehensive study. In the meantime, it will suffice to clear up only one essential feature of forecasting concerning the fates: coming to the cottage window where an infant has been born, the *three fates* almost always answer two questions: (1) whether the infant will *live or die* and (2) whether he will be *fortunate* (i.e., most often rich) *or not.* A more thorough understanding of the concept of Lithuanian fortune [laimė] is thus necessary if one wants to determine the sphere of action of the goddesses Laimes.

If we recall the previously analyzed functions of the divinity Mėnulis, it can be stated that the entire sphere encompassing relations between men and gods which is under his guardianship can be rather satisfactorily distributed among the members of the Aušrinė family who have apportioned the newly found earth among themselves. *Aušrinė,* who retains the matters of youth and beauty in her power, remains the queen of the earth and rules other areas indirectly helped now by her brothers and sisters. If the sphere of health belongs to *Auššveitis,* then to his sisters—the three *Laimas* [fates]—belong the sphere of life and death, as well as the good fortune [*laimė*] associated with it.

IV

LAIMA

Laima and Man[1]

Man's Fate

There once was a farmer to whom one night a son was born. As in ancient times, *laimės* roamed everywhere, thus beneath the window one could often overhear them talking about what lot a son or daughter would have. It was the custom to listen by the window. His son has just been born, so he listens; *three women* come and speak:
One says: "The child will grow up and be rich."
Another says: "He will die young."
And the third: "He will live till he is twelve, when he turns twelve years old then Perkūnas will kill him."[2]

Scenarios such as this indicate that the fates predestine [laimės lemia] the newborn's destiny in Lithuanian imagery. Differences introduced by variants are not especially significant. Sometimes the father overhears the fates forecasting, but most often it is the mother or midwife or, in special cases, a traveler staying overnight in the courtyard or on the threshing floor, who then becomes bound to the infant's fate.[3]

Generally, three women gossip about the child's fate beneath the window sill, and only in rare cases does one *Laima* predestine his life.[4] The selection of the site for the scene of this prophecy is normal, stereotypical: the wall of the house represents the *boundary* between two separate worlds, and the window serves as an *opening* which marks the mythic, in this case, one-sided communication: in the dead of night—it is noteworthy that children in mythological tales are born only at night—the overheard conversation or cry is one-sided; it is never "necessary to answer from the inside, because it is said that some kind of *illness* or *laumė* or *spirit* is calling from the grave." In our case as well, therefore, judging from the content of the conversation of the three women, it can be understood "that the laimės had been there."[6]

(A poor man loses his way in the forest. He sees a light in the cottage and entering he finds a lone woman.) The table is laden with drink and food and the beds are beautifully made up with fine bedding. The woman puts him in a bed such as he had never

Laima

thought he would find himself in in all his life. During the night he hears a sound through the window and shouts: "*Laima, Laima*. Hundreds have been born. Hundreds have died and are already with God. But for those born, how will they live?"

Laima says: "Their table is as full of drink and food and they sleep on such a bed as my guest is tonight. . . . "

And he stayed a second night. He enters the cottage in the evening—the table is empty, there is nothing, not a crumb of bread, the bed is bare bed boards, there is no cover. And he lies down on the bare bed boards. (The same scene is repeated with the same question beneath the window sill and a similar and inverse answer is given by Laima. The poor man starts to "lash out" at Laima): "So you beast, you *destined* such a hard life for me."[7]

This second scenario differs from the first in that in place of *three laimės* forecasting the fate of the individual person, one *Laima* appears, who determines the fate of mankind which is distributed into different classes. The changing sites of the activity are also significant: when the three fates "wander" through the human world and communicate according to canonically determined rules, man, in the world of Laima, finds himself accidentally "losing his way," and becomes a witness to events which do not concern him directly. The dwelling of Laima—in the thick of the forest in a lighted cottage—is a widely known stereotype of a degraded mythology: the forest is a non-human, non-cultural world in which one can come upon utopic places and there encounter ancient mythic beings: Ragana, Laumė, Vėjas, often even the Senelis Dievas [Old Man God] in the role of a "hermit." The solitary cottages in the forest are as if the caricatured remnants of an impoverished, ravaged, ancient pantheon.

The variants of this scenario differ from each other only in their use of figurative means: in place of a rich or poor reception of the lost guest we can imagine, for instance, *Laima* herself every night changing her clothes or her appearance and with those changes expressing the alternation of fate.[8] In place of one Laima, it is possible to single out another variant in which every hour *several laimės* enter that same cottage in different dress—ragged, elegant, and in-between—and answer questions that are presented beneath the window by an audible voice. This is a natural tendency towards the confusion of both scenarios.[9]

The comparison of these two scenarios, in spite of the similarity of the procedures and the identical content of the forecast—we will examine them separately and more thoroughly later—raises a rather difficult question: how is the abstract concept of fate actually represented on the figurative plane in Lithuanian mythology, by one deity *Laima* or three deities—*laimas*?

The case for Laima appears solid: beginning with the *Laimele* (= *Leumele*) mentioned by Praetorius at the end of the seventeenth century, many of the eighteenth-century dictionaries (Brodowski, Ruhig, Mielcke)[10] verify the presence of the goddess of fate—or birth—*Laima*, or *Laimė*. *Laima* is thus a mythological being confirmed as much by historical sources as by folklore. The case for three fates is considerably weaker: their existence is supported only by nineteenth-century ethnographic data. Nonetheless, the triple form of the goddesses of fate is confirmed by comparative Indo-European mythology: the Lithuanian *laimės* correspond to the three Scandinavian *Nornen*, the Greek *moirae*, the Roman *parcae*. Jonas Balys, who has presented both sides of the argument, seems to be disposed to back up the claims for *one* Laima even though he does not strictly express it as such.[11]

Rather than be squeezed into the frame of such an "either-or" dilemma, we would prefer to choose another, no less possible, "both-and" hypothesis: the parallel presence of one goddess Laima or of three goddesses laimas does not appear to be unreconcilable. This structure of coexistence of Laima and laimas, conversely, is merely reminiscent of the situation of *Aušrinė* and her three sisters encountered in the first part of this study. Just as Aušrinė, the queen of the entire universe, who has turned over a part of the world in a feudal manner for rule by her sisters, so *Laima*, from only a superficial comparison of our two scenarios, appears to be a hierarchically superior being whose general decisions, concerning entire classes of the newly born, are concretely declared by the three fates who visit the house of birth, forecasting every individual's fate.

It should be acknowledged, however, that the definite confirmation for the three fates' configuration is associated with a difficult problem which would require separate studies to determine clear boundaries between the *laimės* [fates] and the *laumės* [fairies]. If this boundary seems unquestionable in some cases—*laimės*, for instance (even if they are called *laumės*), forecast the fate of the child while the parents, from the time of birth to baptism,[12] keep a lighted candle next to the newborn to guard him against the *laumės* (sometimes called *laimės*) who specialize in the exchange of children—such a differentiation is by no means a common phenomenon. In the area of direct concern to us, we cannot lose sight of the fact that *laumės*—the same as the nornen and moirae—are spinners and weavers and can lay claim to a Lithuanian equivalent status in Indo-European mythology. There is no doubt that the *laumės* who are so widely diffused in nineteenth-century texts are syncretic figures, the result of a confusion of different goddesses. Only an exhaustive analysis of their case would allow one to express an opinion with greater certainty on the question of the constellation of the three laimės.

The often-used stereotype "taip Laima lėmė" [so Laima has predestined] became a pretext for the first investigators of Lithuanian folklore[13] to formulate rather superficial judgments about the "fatalistically oriented" Lithuanian nation. Generalizations of this sort are unsatisfactory even from a philological standpoint: it is inaccurate to explain the verb "lemti" by its present-day meaning and "laimos lėmimas" [its nominal form] is not simply a determination of fate, the pairing of a certain programmatic life with every individual. A cursory overview of the variety of meanings in *Lietuvių Kalbos Žodynas* [Academic Dictionary of Lithuanian] of the word "lemti" indicates that it means, for instance:

> (1) *spėti* [to guess] "You guessed that he would get married and it happened—he got married."(J.)

Laima 115

(2) *burti* [to divine] "Others practice divination, but I don't believe that the spleen could indicate a bad winter."(Trk.)

(3) *linkėti* [to wish] "As many drops of mead as we drink, we wish you the same measure of grain."(Klv.D)

It is noteworthy that all these parasynonyms of the work "lemti," by means of which all of its various meanings are characterized, belong to the verb class called *verba dicendi*. *Lemti* means, first of all, "to declare, to pronounce (on questions that concern the future)." Explaining the basic meaning of the word in this way, even those meanings which are characterized as follows must be explained as meaning not the determination itself but the open declaration of that determination:

(4) *nuspręsti, nutarti* [to decide] "The man decided to have that building demolished."

(5) *skirti, nustatyti* [to determine] "Why did you not take care of the day's work as determined?"

Mythological contexts only confirm this general meaning of the word "lemti": whether there be one *Laima* in her cottage, or *three laimės* at the window sill, in neither case do they "predestine" anything, nor do they determine man's fate; they only pronounce openly ("prophesy" is, after all, only a type of pronouncement) what the newborn's—or newborns'—fate "holds."

This role of Laima—or laimas—as prophet is possible only if she—or they—"know" destiny. *Knowledge*—and not *determination*—is thus the basic trait that characterizes *Laima* as a goddess. Therefore it is not surprising if in the sole text we are acquainted with, which portrays the battle of *Laimė* with *Laumė*,[14] a youth who helps Laimė is rewarded with the gift of *omniscience*. This is the same type of knowledge which can be acquired, as we know, on St. John's Eve with the discovery of the fern blossom, a comparison which unexpectedly allows one to guess what divine powers are hidden in the ritual involving the search for the blossom.

If the essential trait of Laima is knowledge and her basic function is the pronouncement of that knowledge, then it is evident that the fate itself is found elsewhere than with Laima, that it is only the object of her knowledge. In all contexts destiny appears as passage of time, as an unchanging background which has only one characteristic: it is distributed into *fas* and *nefas*, periods of good and periods of bad, one following another. Taking into account several of the known variants, these alternating time periods can be figuratively expressed in several ways: one *day* is lucky, another—unlucky, one *hour* a man born will be rich, another—poor, before the *rooster* crows the child will be a thief—after the rooster crows, a bishop. One or another periodization of time, one or another duration of each time period, is secondary and does not conceal the basic conceptualization of fate, according to which time itself, into which our life is recorded, is good or bad and contains within itself the origins of fortune and misfortune.

This binary division of time can be manifested semantically as well, with the introduction of a third, intermediate term foreseen earlier: next to two extreme poles—the child will live or die—there appears a third complex term: "will live and die" (i.e., for example, having lived twelve years, he suddenly will die); next to the two poles—he either will be rich or poor—there appears a third, neutral term "neither rich nor poor" (i.e., middle). The appearance of second-generation terms does not change the principle of time distribution itself.

Returning to the concept of fate of interest to us, we can consider it to have become somewhat more evident by having disclosed the role of *Laima* in the procedure. Laima, supported by her knowledge, fulfills a rather distinct function: she determines the relation between individual events and the modulated passage of time. By recording such chance events as birth into time, conceptualized as the stable frames of the universe, she gives meaning to man's life: the determination of the relationship between chance and necessity in a certain sense eliminates chance in that it becomes inscribed into the order of the universe.

Time and Gegutė

If Time in its ceaseless movement—"time passes even in an overturned pot" is the ancestral wisdom[15]—gives birth to the concept of necessity, then its categorization, its distribution into alternating periods of *fas* and *nefas*, is the organization of those fragments based on the fundamental cosmic order.

To elucidate such a concept of time more fully, we must briefly touch on a problematic concerning another goddess of fate who is manifested in the shape of the cuckoo—*Gegutė*. Time, which *Gegutė* "knows" and is responsible for, is cyclical as well, only the periods by which it is organized (with whose help the *cuckoo* makes her calculations and enumerations) are year-long intervals. Even though the years repeat one after another, the world's order that is established with this repetition is not guaranteed from the beginning: the uncontrollable powers of winter every year open the gates, free all the elemental forces of nature, "ruin" time, threatening to bring chaos in its place. The functions of *Gegužė* [= Gegutė as the month of May] which become manifested with her first song in the spring, are thus two-fold: on the one hand, she announces the end of chaos and the introduction of a new order,[16] and on the other, she renews the fixity of objects and people, solidifying their activities and changing them into states. Similar to the laimės who present themselves at a child's birth, and who give this event permanence by attaching a life which will be his permanent state, so the cuckoo with her first song freezes the actions of people, much like the projectionist who suddenly stops the rolling of the film, changing it to fate: a man caught at work by the cuckoo's song will work the entire year, a man lying down will be lazy the entire year, the man who has not eaten will go hungry and the man with money when the cuckoo sings will be prosperous.[17] In one case or another—man born or the world reborn—the intervention of fate turns chance into necessity.

If the functions of such a cyclical organization of time—even though obedient to the general model of fate—allow for the portrayal of *Gegutė* as an independent goddess, then her other traits and her other activity spheres share great similarity with

Laima

the personality of Laima and her activity. Just like *Laima*, Gegutė is solitary, without a husband, unburdened by children; just as there appear three laimės next to Laima, so at times in the place of a single Gegutė:

Oh, *three speckled cuckoos* flew over in the middle of the dark night.[18]

A human form is also attributed to the cuckoo:

> On a green birch sitting,
> On a gold throne leaning,
> A silk scarf embroidering,
> A ball of gold rolling,[19]

She is represented, as we see, as a seamstress, and is thus drawn closer to the previously mentioned nornen and moirae.

Time, perceived as a lastingness, is bound by inchoative, introductory aspects and terminative, concluding aspects. We have observed that Laima concerns herself with man's entrance into life, and Gegutė with the renewal of the year, its beginning. But the final act is characteristic to both of them as well: when Laima weighs the questions of death and determines its time, Gegutė not only forecasts with her cuckooing the end of one or another state (herding, bachelorhood, or life's end in general)[20] but her cuckooing, after fulfilling her spring functions, also signifies in all misfortune or death directly.[21] Furthermore, by the poetic means of riddles, Gegutė is bound with man's journey to the grave:

> I took a fork in the road
> I found a spinning wheel spinning
> And on that wheel a cuckoo singing.[22]

With the last example let us record the apparently strange belief of people that the cuckoo cuckooing in the summer turns into a hawk during the winter.[23] When this mythologic fact is compared with the alternation of appearance and dress of Laima, expressing fortunate and unfortunate intervals of time, the metamorphosis of Gegutė becomes more comprehensible: the predatory hawk *Vanagas* corresponds to the ruined time of winter, just as *Gegutė*, having recovered her positive appearance, announces spring.

Thus it is not surprising that Senelis Dievas [Old Man God] walking about the earth in the form of a beggar, not only substitutes for Laima in forecasting the newborn's fate but sometimes usurps the functions of Gegutė as well: grateful for a nice welcome for the night's lodging, he "offers luck" [laimė] to the master of the household, granting that with whatever he begins the day, he will have all his life.[24]

This brief and only partial account of the cuckoo—since the figure of the cuckoo, for instance, as the patron of the female state has not been touched on—can offer no definite conclusion. It can, however, encourage new investigations in this area.

Returning to the narrower, semantic territory covered by the figures of Laima—

and laimas—it now behooves us finally to pose the question of just what is it that Laima—or laimės—forecast, in what categories of meaning their prophecies are manifested. The answer to this question is rather simple: even though our corpus of the two previously mentioned scenarios (with several degraded or somewhat digressive variants) is not relatively extensive, the themes that touch the fates are repeated so constantly that it is easy at first glance to separate the two most important, general parameters of forecasting. The fates operate within the frames of two binary categories:

(a) life vs. death

(b) wealth vs. poverty

These two parameters, regardless of the order of the dialogue of the three fates, taken logically, exist in a hierarchically mutual relationship: first the question of life or death of the newborn must be resolved and only after that, in the case of the child destined to live, can it be determined if he will be rich or not.

This simple taxonomy of destiny is supplemented by two subordinate themes:

(c) Sometimes an unusual fate is foreseen for the newborn, manifested through a separation from his *class*: the fates forecast, for instance, that the child when grown up will be "a thief" or "a bishop" (sometimes "a prince").

(d) In even rarer cases, fate is manifested by man's departure from his social *class* not by a vertical (into a higher or lower status) but in a horizontal, centrifugal sense: a child then will find fortune by leaving his community and seeking his abilities, his "talent"[25] (becoming, for instance, a trader).

It should be noted, however, that these two supplemental parameters most often remain only in the form of rejected possibilities, and there is no tendency in our text to develop them narratively. This is entirely understandable: ethnographic texts reflect the closed society of the Lithuanian village of the past in which stable social relations predominated, based on a conviction that material well-being is the result of the distribution of a non-diminishing amount of "goods" among a constant number of people: the prosperity of one person corresponds inevitably to the impoverishment of another, the entry or departure of a person in such a closed economic system, as much as wealth, is considered an abnormal phenomenon. Therefore, settling aside, at least temporarily, these centrifugal interests of fortune it behooves us to concentrate our attention on a more thorough analysis of two basic parameters—life and death, wealth and poverty.

Life and Death

While in some sources Laima is called "Goddess of Birth,"[26] this does not mean that she contributes directly to the creation of new life or its development: *Žemyna* and *Austėja*,[27] who promote fertility, are independent of her. *Laima* is the Goddess of Birth only in that she participates by pronouncing her words of destiny. Between birth and the beginning of life there exists an interval of time well understood in these communities, during which the infant mortality rate is quite high.

The forecasting of the laimės that the child "will live" is thus an independent act, announcing (a) that he will not die during childbirth *or* immediately after birth, but generally (b) that a certain interval of time is allotted to him, called "life," through which he will pass: "You won't die before your time, you'll live as long as foretold"[28] is the folk wisdom. Another synonym for this fated period is "amžius": a man in the ancient Lithuanian cultural context does not die as is sometimes now held, from some illness, he dies because his "appointed time is over."[29]

The conclusion of such an outlook is logical: man cannot willfully decide to end his predestined life. Here two separate cases must be provided—that of the *untimely* man and that of the *unfortunate* man.

It is understandable that the man to whom Laima has allotted no share, after trying everything, wishes to remove himself from life. Not even having a piece of rope, he goes to the forest to search for "a nice tree branch"[30] from which to hang himself. Another such unfortunate tries in vain to drown himself.[31] A third, finally, tries "to bury himself alive in the ground," but "Wherever he digs—there is stone, wherever he digs—always a stone, a stone, he can't dig anywhere: When it is said there is no fair share, then there is none—I can't even do myself in."[32]

The situation of the *untimely*[33] man is somewhat different: "most often people talk about places where someone has caused his own end. Or if someone has shot or killed a thief, then the *number of years that one would have lived on earth*, that many years he leads others about at night, misleading them. When such an untimely . . . "[34] In this second case, as we see, the problem is solved rather casuistically, coordinating two opposing things: the obvious fact that people nevertheless are killed accidentally or kill themselves, together with the conviction that the life which was ordained for a man must still be lived through. The untimely man exists for the duration of his allotted life till the end—only in a weakened form.

Thus, what is appropriate to the beginning of life is appropriate to its end: man waits, in peace, until his appointed time ends and sensing the approaching end, lies down in his bed, invites—not unlike Louis XIV—his children and grandchildren, relatives and friends, blesses them and dies. The role of *Giltinė* is restricted here: all the representations which introduce her as a bone-rattling, scythe-carrying spectre who rends and tears, are only the later contributions of Christianity. Her basic function is to determine if it is yet *time* to die, or not: in the first case, she stands at the head of the bed of the invalid, in the second—at the foot of the bed: "Once again I kicked Giltine; once again I have eluded death,"[35] says a man arising from a serious illness. And if sometimes it happens that some smart "doctor" is able to put *Giltinė* into a barrel or into an iron coffin, preventing her from fulfilling her duty, misfortune strikes mankind: "from that time no one dies anymore anywhere and that's it. No one is ill much either. Three hundred years or so pass in this way. Multitudes have appeared on earth. They continue to be born, grow up and become old, but nowhere does anyone die. Aged, grey, drawn and pale, they all remain as such and that's all. They started to get angry at the Lord God too, saying: 'God has forgotten us!' "[36] Life and death are constants, not merely inevitable but also necessary for the cosmic order.

When people talk about life and death, they rarely touch upon that which is normal and self-evident. For this reason, it is not surprising that the examples we have of the fates forecasting are almost without exception about unusual prophecies where it is allotted for the child to both live and die. The issue here is not about the allotment of a natural span of time to be lived through, but about a life bounded by a death based on nothing more than the laimes' pronouncement. Such a death, which is contrary to world order, indicates not only the absolute power of fate but the sovereignty of the gods associated with it. From a mythological point of view, this is especially interesting material.

At first glance it would seem that such an unusual forecast reveals the power of fate to determine not only the exact time of death (for instance, "12th day of the 12th year") but its precise character. Thus at least one of my folk "philosophers" allowed the Old Man God (who is none other than "Dzievas—who walked among the people") to appear in place of *Laima*: "When a child was born, then Dzievas told him *what type of death he would die from*—one will hang, another drown, and a third will burn."[37]

However, in a strange way, our analyzed works do not fit such logical thinking. By giving *Perkūnas* such a special executioner's role, they allow early death to be related to only two elements of nature—*water* and *fire*.

The forecast of the fates that when the child reaches a certain age (for example twelve or seventeen years) *Perkūnas* will kill him does not surprise us, since he only confirms one of his basic functions—the supervision of world order and execution of its laws. Folk wisdom, which says, "If it is fated, Perkūnas will find me inside the house,"[38] while adding to this interpretation, nevertheless directs our attention to the fact that *Perkūnas* carries out only that which is *destined*: his power, even though far-reaching, is only that of a fulfilling nature.

The prince—or landlord or father—who wishes to protect his son from such a fate devises a plan to build a hiding place, by digging a deep, stone basement, by constructing a cottage out of thick metal, or by building a strong stone tower. *Perkūnas* smashes the tower, splits the metal cottage in half, floods the basement with "flour." Alas, the child is not in his shelter: he is hiding "in the garden under leaves,"[39] or as he, in jest, explains "under a cabbage leaf,"[40] or he "goes to the high hill, to pray to Dievas [God]."[41] *Perkūnas's* power is insufficient, fate goes unfulfilled and the child doomed to die remains alive.

There is no easy explanation for these events. However, two characteristic features are striking. First of all, the child is guarded not by the father's chosen means of protection, using force against force—inscribed in the same dimensions of the activity—but by the son's innocent knowledge that he must search for rescue elsewhere. Second, the child's prayer to Dievas while lying *on a high hill* indicates not only that the god is not a Christian God, and that he is more powerful than Perkūnas, but that within his power lies the ability to change the judgment of the fate: this is the same *Dievas X* whose laws *Laima*, having knowledge of them, uses to make her prophecies.

Things happen entirely differently when the child's predestined death is that of drowning in his father's "pond" or "well." Protective means are utilized here, as well: the pond is fenced off, the well is covered over, nailed up with an "ox hide" — this only underscores the inevitability of the fate. "There came a terrible storm: Perkūnas struck repeatedly, the wind overturned houses and the rain poured as if from a bucket . . . Everyone was frightened: they look, the child is gone! . . . They find him on the well, drowned on the hide. Thus the saying: "taip Laima lėmė [so Laima has predestined!]"[42]

This variant—interesting because of the introduction of the ox hide most probably as homeopathic means—creates an impression that the child, drowning in a depression in that hide, has, as if voluntarily, accepted death. Other variants do not even attempt to create an illusion of drowning: a child who has drowned in the pond is found dead where the pond has been fenced;[43] a second variant on the well shows the child, all the time "around the well and around the well. He lies down on the cover of the well, into the foam, and the child is found dead."[44]

Thus the fulfillment of the forecast is not directly associated with the fact of drowning itself but with man's death, which occurs with his "union" with *water* or, more accurately stated, with a deity in whose command this natural element is found.

If the forecasts connected with *Perkūnas'* unsuccessful intervention allowed us to negatively characterize "Dievas X" as more powerful than Perkūnas and capable of easily disposing of people's fates, these latter examples introduce a new positive element in the definition of the deity—her close ties with the sacred sphere of water. The first part of this study, which reveals the watery character of *Aušrinė*, the princess of the sea, and *Mėnulis*, her husband or sometimes her father, is supplemented now by new attributes concerning the prophecies.[45]

The final type of destiny has a characteristic conditional form: the fates foretell that the newborn will live until "this little pile of firewood has been burned,"[46] "until this bundle of firewood has been used up,"[47] "until these twigs have been burned."[48] This conditionally assumed promise of life has a distinctive contractual structure formed by a homologous principle: firewood is trees allotted for fire just as man is allotted for death:

$$\frac{\text{firewood}}{\text{man}} \simeq \frac{\text{burning}}{\text{dying}}$$

the relation between man and firewood is metonymic, the same as the relations between the wolf and the hair, the dragon and the egg previously analyzed.

It should be underscored, however, that the contract offered by the fates is based on *belief*: the fated infant, now grown into a man, dies, because he burns the pile of firewood, and he does this not only because he does not believe in the forecast of the fates, but because he does not believe in the power of the fire to cut off his life either. The fact that the fire is none other than the home's hearth *Gabija* is indicated by the last of our three previous variants, in which kindling is placed in the fire not by him but by his wife's mother when he is not present; she and her daughter had seen the chest in which the wood pieces had been hidden: the one who breaks the contract is a stranger to the family circle.

Our "Dievas X" reconstructed gradually here with the help of logical premises, the ruler of destiny and lord of the sacred sphere of water, is manifested now as guarantor of belief—especially that of the sacred fire. Since it is known that *Gabija*, just like the Roman hearth fire, is only a metonym for the fire of the national community which has to be renewed from that common source each year, it is possible to offer a hypothesis which ascribes to our Mithra-like *Dievas X* the cult of the eternal fire—and the sovereign fire as well—lighted for the first time for the cremation of the Grand Duke Šventaragis. But this requires another separate study.

Finally, one more observation needs to be added for the reconstruction of the figure of the god. The well-known tales of unusual deaths show death manifested in either drowning or symbolic forms of burning, but no text tells about the normally expected hanging procedure suggested by our "folk philosopher." The cause for this omission is clear: the hanged man, directly and without questions, not only in Lithuanian but in other Indo-European religions, belongs to the *Varuna-Velnias* kingdom,[49] thus hanging cannot be destined by *Laima*, since it belongs to the sphere of action of another, no less sovereign god. Taking into account the Indo-European triad of sovereign gods, we are compelled to state that setting aside, on the one hand, the sphere of power of *Indra-Perkūnas* and excluding the unanalyzed but foreseen sovereign sphere of *Varuna-Velnias*, there remains only *Mithra* in the function of determining destiny and world order for whom we are in no hurry to provide a Lithuanian equivalent, calling him "Dievas X."

The familiar scenario of the poor man who goes out into the world and finds a cottage in the forest, and in it *Laima*, sometimes develops in an unexpected direction. The poor man, understanding that he has business with Laima, who has not allotted him his *share*, attacks her, demanding that she amend the injury. Laima then often promises him a wife from whose lot he will be able to live happily. Now and them, however, the storytelling continues differently:

> "Stop, stop (shouts Laima), when my sister comes back, then she will put an end to you!"
> (The sister is no one else but *Giltinė*, who answers from the barrel in which she had been placed by our hero;)
> "But sister, I'm here too!"[50]

The history ends in a manner not common to *Laima*—not with the promise of a prosperous wife, but with the intervention of her sister *Giltinė*, who makes the hero "a doctor."

This is not the only appearance of the two sister-goddesses together. In another legend which captures our attention the two of them introduce themselves to the youth who is standing watch for the night by the fire: "and of those old women one was *Giltinė*, the other *Laimė*." They ask him for cracklings. He gives some to Giltinė but does not want to give any to Laimė, and she keeps begging: "The youth became angry, threw a crackling at her which hit her on the lips and that crackling was hot . . . it burnt her lip." She flew into a rage: "Oh, that debaucherer, that bedalis . . . he did not have his share, but now he won't have any at all."[51]

Further adventures of that pair are no less interesting. When they both talk about the future, it appears that *Giltinė* only guesses at it, desiring only what is good for the friendly hero, while *Laimė* alone is able to forecast the fate. To those who have become accustomed to her fearful image, Giltinė unexpectedly appears as a goodhearted being, secretly giving advice to the hero, and helping him to choose a wife with a share.

Another variant, similar in some ways but different in others, represents Laima and Giltinė both seated on a steed, riding, and again weighing the fate of another poor young man. While Laima is telling how she "plans to attack one youth,"[52] he overhears and begins to strike her across her mouth with a rock "so that all her teeth fell out," and in the meanwhile Giltinė, unobserved by Laima, invites him to sit with them on the charger.

In one case Laimė tries to take revenge, threatening to *set fire to* the house of the poor man when they both go "beyond the boundaries of that village": her revenge does not succeed since Giltinė advises him in secret to burn several bundles of straw behind the cottage. In another case Laimė foresees that the youth could find his *share* of good fortune if he could endure having his cottage burn down three times, becoming rich only after these disasters; here Giltinė comes to the rescue, advising him to build a cottage three times out of branches and allow those to burn down.

This image of the *two sisters—Laimė and Giltinė—sitting double, riding a charger with Laimė holding the reins*, is sufficiently typical and archaic: it must be considered the more so when analyzing Lithuanian mythology since the comparison of the sisters as represented in a single scene especially reveals their characteristic traits.

The personality of *Laima*, quite blank when viewing only her role at the time of birth, now becomes more distinct. On the surface she even appears as an "active" being, not satisfied only with knowledge and its announcement: she tries to intervene in man's life, "punishing" him, "avenging" him. If we look more closely, however, her activity is seen to be restricted and specific: she does battle only against poor, *shareless*, people and only so that their fates will be fulfilled, in other words, so that they will be left in the future without "a share" and without "fortune." As inscribed in the pre-Christian frames of morality, her activity is, in a certain sense, a manifestation of *reason* and *justice*.

Even though on the surface she appears "active," in fact *Laima* does not interfere in the fate of the hero without his share: her intervention in both cases mentioned is the threat to *burn down* the hero's house. Even a superficial understanding of the Lithuanian semio-cultural context allows us to affirm that she does not involve herself with the arson, that this role belongs to *Perkūnas*, already encountered in cases of untimely death. It is characteristic that the cottages must ignite at that moment when the two sisters of fate are stepping "across the borders of the village": it is widely known that Perkūnas is a guardian of all types of boundaries and borders. This differentiation of roles between *Laima*, who forecasts, and *Perkūnas*, who oversees and carries out the fate, is confirmed once more.

The representation of *Laimė* and *Giltinė* in two contrasted sister forms reveals the portrait of *Giltinė* at the same time. The poor man, rebelling against *Laimė* and her fated "empty share," gives precedence to *Giltinė*; she, for her part, uses the overheard prophecies of Laima to help people and to rescue them. Giltinė's distinctive traits, as we have already mentioned, entirely contradict her post-Christian view.

Giltinė herself clearly characterizes her basic function: "I am Giltinė. I look after the ailing. I must *separate* out whom to keep, whom to kill."[53] Giltinė fulfills, as does Laimė, the function of destiny. The pronouncement of life and death belongs to both of them, though it only manifests itself at different times: Laimė does so at the beginning, and Giltinė at the end, of life.

It is a mistake to consider Giltinė a "goddess of death": the termination of man's life is as much her domain as is the prolongation of man's life, his recovery. Therefore it is not surprising that the sphere of action of the healer—be he sorcerer or a modern doctor—is inscribed in that interval which is created between Giltinė's standing at the head of the bed and her standing at its foot: "you heal the one, when I stand at the foot of the bed, and if I stand at the head then don't heal that one,"[54] Giltinė advises her doctor-son.

It is not worthwhile, perhaps, to expand too much on this well-known theme— repeated in Lithuanian folklore hundreds of times—of Giltinė's relations with medicine. Let us briefly summarize this rather clear situation:

(a) *Giltinė* establishes the healing institution, agreeing to be godmother to the son born to the poor man and later teaching him "to heal." Several rarer variants provide the future doctor with a godfather—the Senelis Dievas [Old Man God] next to the Giltinė-godmother.

(b) Giltinė's "kūmas" [the father of Giltinė's godchild], whose son is fated to become a doctor, is most often a poor shareless man. Giltinė in this manner seemingly fulfills the prophecies of Laima by offering the future doctor a peculiar "lot," which presents him with a specific social status.[55]

This is, approximately, how the medical institution normally functions. If we take into account the fact that the aim of storytelling, generally, is not to portray stable situations, but to show uncommon deviations from the norm, our existing collection about Giltinė as the protector of doctors provides two cases of the godchild's disobedience to his godmother.

(a) On the individual plane, the doctor, wishing to heal a patient doomed to die by Giltinė (most often a princess or some important gentleman), orders a bed to be made which spins on one leg, thus allowing the head of the bed to be interchangeable with the foot. The fate of Giltinė is eluded in this manner, although such disobedience is punished and the healer is disqualified.

(b) On the social plane, the doctor fools Giltinė, luring her into an empty nutshell,[56] and in that manner stops mankind's normal process of dying. Not only the creation of unjust exceptions, but also such a dismantling of world order is punished.

This overview of her activities can end only with the total rehabilitation of *Giltinė*: she is the sister of *Laimė*, goddess of life and death, with secondary duties as the guardian of medicine. Such a homogeneous semanticism helps to clarify as well the etymology of her name: our "linguistic intuition" leads us to include this name with the entire family of *gelti, gėluo, gėlimas* [to sting], and this allusion again develops normally into the image of the snake: it is quite possible that the snake could be one of the more archaic forms of *Giltinė*, not only in the similarities of the conceptual content, but also in the comparison of the figurative representation of the two cases—the earthly *Giltinė* and the divine *Auššveitis* (see above *Aušrinė*).

Wealth and Poverty

Having discussed rather extensively the initial parameter of the prophecies of *Laima*—or laimės—which frame deliberations on human life and death, we must touch on a second dimension of fate as well: the man destined to live, must still be allotted one or another kind of life, good or bad. We mentioned earlier that our ethnographic sources inevitably reflect the mentality of a closed agrarian society, whose concepts of fortune and misfortune are naturally homologous with the conceptualization of a prosperous or impoverished life.

When viewed from a purely formal standpoint, the binary differentiation of the dimensions of this life can be ascertained in two ways: people can be separated into two categories:

(a) haves vs. have-*nots* [dalingi vs. *be*daliai]
(b) fortunate vs. *un*fortunate [laimingi vs. *ne*laimingi]

The difference between these two dichotomies depends on the type of logical relations between the opposed terms. The have-not [bedalis] differs from the have in that he has *no share* (= no luck): the relation between these two concepts is contradictory. The unfortunate man differs from the fortunate in that he not only does not have any fortune, but misfortune is concretely manifested in his life as well. Opposition between these concepts is based not on contradiction but on contrariety.

Lithuanian mythology exploits both types of logical relations, creating in that manner not only additional questions for the mythologist but new data for his theoretical consideration. The logical structure chosen for fortune [laimė] determines which generation of mythic beings will appear on the figurative plane. In the case of the contrary structure two opposed beings representing fate can be identified without any difficulty: *Laimė* [fortune] (or *Dalia* [happiness]) and *Nelaimė* [misfortune] (or *Vargas* [travail]). In the case of contradictory relations the presence or absence of *Laimė-Dalia*, the problem of having or not having one's fortunate share [*dalis*], is the sole issue; no specific being protects the "bedalis" unless it is *Laima* herself, who, as we saw earlier, makes certain that, God forbid, he not grab his fortune from someone else.

Let us take a few "actual" events.

> Once two brothers lived next to each other, one rich, the other poor. One time the poor man, walking about his fields, sees that his ears [of grain] have been plucked. He goes at night to see who is plucking the ears. A beautiful maiden comes out of the woods, takes the ears and throws them in the fields of the rich one. He catches hold of that maiden and starts to beat her. She says: "Don't hit me, I must do this for him. I am his dalis."
> "Well, if you are his dalis, where is mine?"
> "Yours is covered with blight in the fields."[57]

Here is another, somewhat different adventure.

> There were two brothers, one rich, one poor. The poor one, unable to cope, decides to run away from his master and settle elsewhere (this occurred during the time of serfdom). He moves out, but forgets his axe and returns. He sees that there is a light in the hut; he goes to the hut and looks in. Behind the stove there sits an old woman putting on her leggings. She says: "I am your *Nelaimė*: as you have moved now into another house, so I will go again to be with you."[58] The man became angry, struck her on the head with the axe, chopping her into pieces. Then, stuffing the *Nelaimė* into a basket, and stuffing the basket under a tree stump, he returns home, where life begins to get better for him.

We are dealing here with two different mythic beings who—just as *Laima* in other texts, with the change of her dress changes the destiny of the newborn—differ in their appearance: the benefactor *Dalis* appears as a "beautiful maiden" and the evil-doer *Nelaimė* as an "old woman." The latter, however, is not a deity with distinctive features: even though called *Nelaimė* [misfortune], she can be represented in the form of a "large white man";[59] with a change in her name, she becomes *Vargas* [60] [Travail], appearing at the scene just described. Her sphere of action, on the other hand, remains very limited: as a passive actor, *Nelaimė* is chopped up by the poor man into little pieces or stuffed into a tobacco pipe or into a brandy bottle; she manifests herself more actively only in passing from the poor one to the rich one, as if reconstructing "social justice"—and that, as we know, is not a moral function which belongs to *Laima* or to the sphere of fate. An impression is thus formed that this *Laimė* and *Nelaimė* pair is a rather late and rather artificial construction, created as a figurative expression of the logical parameter of "wealth" vs. "poverty" which is nonetheless unable to compete with the *Laimė-Dalia* problematic.

The figure of *Laimė-Dalia* is entirely different, a fact for which analysts of Lithuanian mythology—foremost among them Balys[61]—offered an independent status, one irrespective of Laima. Her presence is verified not only by an inexhaustible number of texts of tales and legends but also, though considerably less often, by songs:

> A mother walks about
> Searching for *Laimė-Dalia*
> *Laimė-Dalia* answered
> On the other side of the seas.[62]

The question of whether we are dealing with two goddesses or with one Laima manifested by two different modes of action is an especially interesting question from a mythological viewpoint.

To untangle this problem, we must move away from the usual statements that *dalis*—or *dalia* [one's share, lot]—is first of all an abstract concept, one of the means which allows man to conceive of his fate. In the same way that the dying father divides his wealth among his children, allotting to each one his *share*, it is thought that when man is born, *Senelis Dievas*—or *Laima*—allots him his corresponding share. Thus one time, while Senelis Dievas is spending the night at a gentleman's house, "a bird flies over, lands on the old man's window sill, and starts to talk in a never-before heard voice: 'Lord, a son was born to poor parents. What *share will you allot him*?' 'He will be a shepherd to the maiden' was the answer."[63] The share [dalis] allotted by God is thus a formal concept whose content changes. In this case the son's lot is to be a "shepherd."

One of the prayers with which one addresses *Mėnulis* [the moon] reveals even more clearly the concept of *dalis*.

> Young man, young man,
> Prince of the heavens
> Grant me a bit of luck [dalis šcesties]
> For you a crown of gold
> > For you youth
> > For me wealth . . .[64]

The *dalis* prayed for from the "prince of heaven" is not just any type of dalis but *laimės dalis* [a share of good fortune]: *laimė* is a global concept subsuming all of life's possibilities, and man turning to instances of fortune distribution asks for a corresponding share of good fortune. The relation between laimė and dalis is metonymic (*pars pro tota*), although both concepts are isotopic: the last stanza of the poem narrows further and confirms the content of the *dalis*, which is manifested in the form of "wealth."

Let us summarize: the relation between *laimė* and the *dalis*, as whole and part, is manifested on two planes:

(a) with respect to form: *dalis* is only a part of *laimė*

(b) with respect to content: *laimė* encompasses all the possibilities of fulfillment in life, and *dalis* touches only on its material values.

Such a concept of distribution of fortune is not specific to Lithuanian mythology: in India the well-known distributor of fate is the god *Bhaga*, who belongs to the sovereign sphere of Mithra; it could be argued that even the Slavic *Bog*, who was chosen as the only sovereign God with the introduction of Christianity, is by nature also a god-distributor.

In the Lithuanian context this role, if evaluated on the surface, is fulfilled by *Laima*. However, *Laima's* task, as we saw, is not to distribute man's fortune and lot but only to prophesy it. Therefore, in principle, before embarking on a concrete analysis, we must differentiate at least three instances of forecasting:

(a) the deity-distributor—a role in Lithuanian stories often laid claim to by *Senelis Dievas* [The Old Man God] and in the remaining prayers by *Mėnulis* [the Moon].

(b) the deity-prophetess, who announces fate and with it its dalis—this is the Lithuanian *Laima*.

(c) the dalis–alloting deity—this is a figurative form, which can be clothed in the concept of the individual's share, which in Lithuanian has an entire set of synonyms: *burtas, likte, luomas,* etc.[65]

If *Laima* would provide for every man by giving him the *dalis* [share] that belongs to him, if every man would live according to his *laimė* [fortune], mankind would have no problems, and people, gathering in the evening, would have nothing to say to one another concerning this theme. A stable condition is unproblematic, but life, alas, is full of riddles, to which only tales can provide an answer: "At another time the *Lord God* (Ponas dievs) went about telling tales and the *Devil* (Velns) posing riddles."[66] It is in this manner that the wisdom of our ancients explains the origin of philosophy.

Actually it so happens in life: *Laima* allots some people their *share*, and leaves others without. Such an elite distribution has important consequences. First of all, the concept of one's lot in such a case changes its content, it becomes "a fortunate share"—since poverty means not having one's share. Second, as a consequence of an unjust distribution, there appears a separate class of have-nots resolved not to capitulate: they go off to *search for fortune*—a theme of many wondertales—and often to stand in battle with *Laima* while she, often beaten lifeless, is compelled, as we saw, to seek other means.

The first of such means—since *Laima* cannot change her own fate—is the advice given to the poor man to try to live from his wife's *share*:[67] it is enough to find a prosperous wife, so that one's entire family can live from her allotment. This explains, though only in part, why all the tales end with the marriage of the fortune-seeking hero to a princess or even to some rich gentleman's daughter. It is characteristic, however, that the group of stories which weighs not the hero's fate, but the clear, explicit fate of the poor man, pictures the future fortunate wife commonly in the form of a ragged, unkempt girl. A pretty, well-dressed maiden met by the poor man does not offer anything special or good. It is probably her lot to live from a rich husband's share—and the helpers of the poor man advise him to avoid her. This type of inversion appears as a compensating structure to resolve in an ideal manner the questions raised by social and aesthetic inequity.

The ability to circumvent the laws of fate by finding a rich wife extends by itself the functions of *Laima*, granting her a complementary role in the formation of "couples":

Laima

> Don't weep my maiden
> Still your heart
> You'll be *chosen by Laima*
> You'll be my love.[68]

It seems, however, that *Laima's* interest in marriage also has other, conditional, causes in the general structure of kinship:

> Don't let dear Dievas
> For Laima to forecast
> That my maiden will grow up
> In the same village.
>
> But let dear Dievas
> For Laima to forecast
> That at least a mile away
> My deal little Mary will grow up.[69]

The issue here no longer centers on the formation of individual pairs but on the prohibition of endogamous marriage and the search for exogamous means: in the case of incest, which is especially well-represented in Lithuanian folk tales (and which requires a separate, comprehensive study), a place is also provided for *Laima*.

The significance of *dalis* once again changes when it has become more evident that the poor man can live as well from a lamb's share. The history of one such man goes roughly like this:

> There once lived a son with his father, and nothing went well for this son. His father was so *wise* that he was able to tell if a person was *rich or not*. He saw that his son had no share and he *hated him for it* and wanted him to disappear. (The son wanted to marry a girl, but the father, knowing that she had her share, didn't allow it. The son married another, poor one—then the father threw them both out of his house.)
>
> On the road they met an old man leading a lamb. The old man said, "I will give you this lamb, then both of you will be able to live from *his share."* (They become established, make a living, have children.) But the father heard about their *fortunate* life . . . he wanted to know *where they got their share*. Arriving he sees that the lamb walks about the farm and *it has its share*. The father asks that the lamb be slaughtered. The son, thinking that the lamb is old and unnecessary, agrees. He kills it and begins to cook the meat.) Just as it was *cooked*, he gave a piece to the children and they both tasted it; the father looks, the *children now have a share*, and they *both have their share*. (The father becomes angry and returns home.)[70]

Another variant of the same story does not differ in its general economy from the first. There, as well, the poor son has a "wise" father who, having married the son off to a poor wife, drives both of them out. And there they both meet *Dievas Senelis*, who gives them, it is true, not a lamb but a puppy: "Thus from this dog you will have your share." In that variant as well, the father learns about the new fortune of the children, arrives, and kills the dog.

> The animals were let out of the barn in the morning. All those animals began making noises with that dog around: *the dalis attached herself to a cow*. The father sees that *the cow has her share* and asks for the cow's meat. The son, on his orders, slaughters the cow. The *lungs, liver* and other meat were placed in the pot—after having *cooked* them a bit, the wife cut off a piece and gave some to the children, tasted some herself and gave some to the husband: the father sees that the *children, husband* and *wife* all have their share.[71]

If we set aside the concept of the father's *wisdom* for later analysis, and consider the lamb's change into a puppy in the stories as a contamination from other stories which mention the *dog's share*,[72] let us pause briefly at the concept of dalis and its last avatar—its incarnation into animals. While the poor man lived from his wife's share, *dalis* could be held as an abstract religious concept. It is even possible to assume that the lamb, as a living creature, can have its own share: other texts recognize "the share bestowed by Laima."[73] The lamb, on the other hand, can be viewed as a metonym for the wife: in Juška's description in *Svotbinė Rėda* [Wedding Laments]—supplemented by new variants by his commentators—during the blessing of household objects carried out by the daughter-in-law ("gifting them" in succession with towels), along with the many inanimate objects that the daughter-in-law blesses, only one living creature—the lamb[74]—is ascribed directly to her sphere of action.

However, the lamb's (or "dog's") *dalis* appears here no longer as an abstract concept but as an autonomic psychic rudiment able to migrate from one being to another, incarnated directly in a chosen site in the organism—in the *lungs* or the *liver*, which as we have seen earlier (see above, *Aušrinė*) are in turn the sites of *health* and *life*: *Dalis*, as the key element of earthly fortune and happiness is typologically identified with the principles of life and death within the knowledge of *Laimė*. Perhaps the concept of identification here does not entirely correspond to the procedure we wish to describe: *dalis*, as a spiritual rudiment, remains autonomous. It can migrate from one body to another in at least the two ways indicated by the text: through "attachment" (i.e., by "touching") and with the "tasting" of the lungs and liver which have been slightly cooked (i.e., touched by fire), a characteristic pagan "communion."

In this context *Dalis* is a figurative mythological concept.

The previous examples indicate that the personification process of *Dalis* has already begun, that the following stage—the anthropomorphic form—can be easily discerned.

> The poor son goes out into the world and meets the Old Man God, and, when asked, answers: "I don't know myself, where I'm going—I don't have any share, nothing goes well for me. I have nowhere to put myself."
> The Old Man takes him on as a servant and sends him to the "well" for water.

Three birds fly over (in another variant: *three swans*). They remove their feathers and start to bathe. The youth later tells him what he has seen. The Old Man says: "Do you know who that is? *That is your dalis, come over to bathe.*" And he advises him to steal the youngest one's feathers and not return them "until she promises to be your dalis." The poor man fulfills the directives, "And, of course, as God had said, so it had to be: they got married, lived on, and became very wealthy."[75]

The variant in which the birds are specified as *swans* does not differ in any special way from what has just been summarized. It is just somewhat richer in several familiar details. The poor, shareless man [bedalis] leaves his home saying: "I will go, perhaps I will find *my fortune* [laimė] somewhere. The concepts of *laimė* and *dalis* here appear as synonyms. Before finding himself with the "Old Man Hermit," he serves as a shepherd in a manor: the *three sheep* that he receives as wages are eaten by a wolf. The youngest swan's feathers are thrown into the *fire* by the hermit and are burnt up. He says that now those two can "live as a pair." The swan bride seems to be a good *seamstress*, and from that they both make a living.[76]

Another, parallel story no longer tells of beings who lead a double life as both swans and daughters-in-law, but is instead about *three maidens* found in the woods. The rich brother's *Dalis*, appearing in the form of a beautiful maiden, when asked by the shareless brother where he could find his share, gives him this advice: "Go to the forest, you will find a *three-branched tree*, and in that tree you will find three maidens sitting, two will be happy, and the third, scowling: that is your dalis. Then pull that maiden out of the tree, and pummel her until she promises to be your share."[77]

The road we have traveled is rather long: in place of the poor man at the beginning, who acquires a *wife with her share*, now our hero finds *Dalia, whom he takes as his wife*: Dalia is now not a theological concept but a type of personal deity belonging to one individual.

On the other hand, *Dalia* has now acquired an anthropomorphic form, and she often appears not as a single figure, but as a composite of three swans or maidens: this ternary figure is reminiscent of the *three laimės* encountered earlier. It would seem that with a human form *Dalia* moves closer to *Laima*, the only difference being that while the *three fates* represent the totality of all possible "fortune," *Dalia* is only one of the fates, representing with her partitive character one's *share of good fortune* which, as we remember, people pray for when they turn to *Mėnulis*.

> There once was a young man who served a farmer: when the year ended he asked for his wages. The farmer said: "Your *wages have dwindled away.*" He received "several pennies" and traveled on.
>
> At another farmer's the youth asked as a wage "a big rooster." And during the year that rooster dwindled so that he looked like the tiniest chick.
>
> He went to a third farmer, and asked as his wage "that *huge stone*—the stone in the courtyard was very big . . . " While he worked, "that stone dwindled and dwindled, so that by Christmas it was so worn down one could barely see it."[78]

Several observations can be added to increase the text's readability:

(a) The *wages* of the hired worker constitutes his entire wealth, all his goods. The dwindling of his wages is thus his passage over to the impoverished status of the have-nots [bedalis], or the external sign of his status as a poor man. Actually, the narrative ends with the shareless youth marrying the princess, and living from his wife's share.

(b) The *dwindling away* [dilimas], even though it is applied to the characterizations of the disappearance of the entire three year's "wages," in its literal sense applies only to the progressive process of the stone's reduction. The triplication of this destruction is thus only a rhetorical means used to represent total non-success and the significant fact mythologically is the dwindling away of the stone. Other variants of the "dwindling dalis," which preserve only the reduction episode, indirectly confirm this.

Let us take another similar occurrence.

> The youth who serves conscientiously for two years does not get any wages. The third year he says: "I will be with you for one more year, but you will give me the stone which is in the corner of your entryway." In that landlord's entryway there was a *huge stone* which was used to set things on. The landlord promised to give him the stone.
>
> The youth continues to work. "On that stone of his he put on his footwear, took great joy in it, embraced it. Soon he sees and so do the others that that stone is getting smaller and smaller, getting ground down and down. By the end of the year, there is left of it an amount no bigger than a goose egg."[79]

The importance of the case of this stone's dwindling away compels us to posit yet another, quite similar variant:

> Another time there was a son of a very wealthy man, but nothing went well for him: whatever his father gave him or entrusted to him, he lost: neither money, nor animals—nothing would endure. In that father's barn, there was a very *big stone*, so the father, trying, gave him the stone. He took great joy in this stone, climbed on it, put on his footwear on it, took it off. After a few days that too disappeared, who knows where.[80]

These texts can be supplemented with a few observations:

(1) In all three variants the issue centers not just on any stone, but on the *huge stone*, namely, on the "akmo saxum grandius," whose "worship" is recorded by Rostowski, on the basis of late sixteenth-century sources.[81]

(2) That huge stone is found in the farmstead: in the courtyard or threshing floor or entryway, which is the space occupied by the farmer's family, even though its use is not clear and probably forgotten. To say that the stone is there "to put something or other on it" is clearly nonsense.

(3) The relations between the hero and the stone that is given to him appear more

than strange and are more likely those of worship—without mentioning the word "worshipping"; the hero "rejoices" in it, "climbs on it," "strokes it."

(4) One act of the hero especially stands out: in two later variants he likes to sit down on the stone "to put on his footwear." (In such a manner let us remember, the poor fellow, returning home, finds his *Nelaimė*, his misfortune.) Putting on one's shoes is a sign of the beginning of the day—or some new activity—which cannot help but be compared with the goddess of all types of beginnings—*Laima*, the assistant at birth which is man's beginning, but, as we will later see, the assistant to the beginning of mankind as well.

When we read of such specially manifested forms of misfortune, a question presents itself: by whom and for what reason is that huge stone, the poor boy's last hope, ground down? An answer is provided by the culprit herself—*Laima*, who in our previously cited text tells *Giltinė* "that she is waging a battle with one youth" and that she has ground down the stone which he had bargained for as his wages. And we have already explained the "battle" and "revenge" of *Laima* as the supervision of the fulfillment of the will of fate.

There is no need, it seems, for additional commentary that that big stone—which the unsuccessful man bargains for as his last chance, the stone which he loves, worships and strokes, and which is destroyed so that that poor man would not have any share—is nothing more than the final incarnation of *Dalia*, her manifestation in the form of the hardest, most stable material—stone. The hierarchic relations with the goddess of fate, *Laima*, become clear, as does the identity of the one who is capable of dwindling the personal guardian of man—the goddess Dalia.

"They worshipped the stones as gods," writes Rostowski at the beginning of the seventeenth century about the remnants of the ancient Lithuanian religion.[82] The general problem of the Lithuanians as stone worshippers—as well as of stars, forests, or rivers—is resolved by our mythologists in a variety of ways, but their proffered explanations reflect only their own viewpoints about religiosity as a cultural expression. However it may be, the basic mistake, in our opinion, and the resulting difficulties due to it, is their desire to explain the worship of stones as a global fact, without taking into account the separate forms and types of stones and their relationship with one or another deity or sacred sphere. Such an explanatory mode would differ in no way, for example, from a study of the cult of saints in the Catholic Church that would evaluate the veneration of statues on the basis of their wooden or stone composition, making no attempt to distinguish between the "idols" of St. George and those of St. Anthony of Padua.

Thus we, too, having come across the problem of the "embodiment" of *Laima-Dalia* in stone in ethnographic sources, will attempt to search only for that stone in the extensive field of stone figures which corresponds to the already distinct semantic traits necessary for our analysis, leaving other types of stones to more detailed and specific studies.

The Jesuit *Chronicle* of 1600[83] quite painstakingly describes one such type of stone worship:

Alibi lapides non parvi in horreis, in terra defossi, superficie plana sursum versus, non terra sed stramine contecti asservantur, quos *Deyves* appelant, atque ut custodes frumentorum et pecorum religiose colunt.

This text is necessary, in our opinion, if only for its precision, even though the translation is literal and not elegant:

> Elsewhere (= in other places) in the "sandeliai" large stones are kept, dug into the ground with their flat side facing upward, (laid down,) covered not with soil but with straw; they are called *Deivės* (= Deyves) and are worshipped devoutly as the guardians of grain and livestock.

A detailed commentary to the translation must be provided:

(1) The word *deivės* must be considered as a general appellation for mythic beings of the female gender—folkloric sources refer to these goddesses both as laumės and laimės—not by their specific stone names. The use of this word in the plural means that one is dealing with the abundant secondary non-sovereign deities, which belong to the category "household gods" who guard every family and each farm separately.

(2) The function of these goddesses as "guardians of grain and livestock" corresponds to the role and content of Dalia, whom we identified with the concept of material benefit [*nauda*].

(3) As in other Latin texts of that period, the translation of the word *horreum* into Lithuanian creates difficulties. The abstract concept "sandelis" does not correspond to the name of any concrete construction. In the Balys translation,[84] the work *klėtis* [= grain storehouse] is used, making the function of "livestock guardianship" incomprehensible. The means of conserving grain and the structures built for this purpose changed in the course of history: in analyzing the case of the god *Gabjaujis*, when faced with the same problem, we were compelled to identify *horreum* with the threshing-barn [*kluonas*].[85]

(4) A similar problem arises for analysts of Roman mythology: there the altar of the guardian of grain, the goddess *Ops Consiua*, is kept (whether actually or only symbolically is a different question entirely) *sub terra*,[86] dug into the ground, and not as Balys erroneously translates in the text "dug out of the ground." The self-evident assumption utilized by Roman specialists—that such a goddess or her altar dug into the ground corresponds to archaic methods of grain conservation—keeping them in excavated cellars (as potatoes were kept over winter during my childhood in Lithuania)—is not confirmed, it seems, by archaeological research, which has not found any remains of structures of this type.

(5) However it might be, the inexplicable correspondence of this detail in two mythologies—Lithuanian and Roman—underscores the importance of our anlayzed text as well as the context associated with it. Another detail of the same type—an indication that the altar of the Roman goddess was kept covered and was uncovered only a few times during the year on appointed feast days—explains why our goddess stones were covered only with straw and not earth. Whether it is possible to deduce from this—as does Būga, [86a] unaware of the existence of a Roman

Laima 135

equivalent—that those stones were nothing more than household *arae* (altars), is difficult to say.

In our opinion, the question itself should not be stated in the form of a dilemma: Is it an altar or a goddess? Such a sacred stone can also be the site of her embodiment: the place she "keeps to"; it can be uncovered at the time of ceremonies dedicated to her, offerings can be placed on it in gratitude or in supplication to the goddess.

(6) The final comment concerns the stone's form—its flat side turned upward. Būga perceives in this one of the underlying arguments for the interpretation of the stone as an altar. Without contradicting him, but nevertheless turning our attention to the fact that it is a flat form appropriate for offerings, which does not as yet specify our deity since it can be common to many—or all—sacred stones, we would like to compare these flat-stone goddesses to the large stone with the same flat surface, which lay on the hill called Rambynas, which was dedicated to *Laima*.[87] But we will return to this question somewhat later.

All that remains now is to take the final step, to compare the information disclosed by folklore with the material from historical sources, to equate those "huge stones"—i.e., the stone rubble remaining in the farmstead and preserving only in the mythic subconscious certain aspects of their "sacredness"—with the huge stone goddesses recorded by the Jesuits. And to compare, as well, their semantic grouping: dalis as symbol of a prosperous life with the guardianship of grain and cattle. Equating these two planes allows the formulation of a strong hypothesis for the structural identification of both objects, which are separated by a three-hundred-year span.

The final remaining question is the determination of the common name for these beings separated by historical evolution and supported by two types of sources. As we have already stated, the term *deives* utilized by the Jesuit chroniclers is only a general name for the extensive class of secondary deities. The dwindling stones can convincingly be held as one of the characteristic forms of manifestation of *dalis*—or *Laima-Dalia*. We can then ask if from the mid-seventeenth century on, the goddess of luck, *Laimelė*[88] (Glöcksgöttin), whom only Praetorius characterizes as a birth goddess, is not the same "grain and livestock" goddess, i.e., a household goddess guarding the goods, whose *stabas* ("idolum")—or altar—were especially suited for the practice of a private forbidden cult.[89]

Laima and Humankind

Just as the history of humanity's individual life becomes more comprehensible when it is inscribed in the frames of cosmic time, so the destiny of humankind, the direction and meaning of its development in time, cannot help but raise philosophical considerations. As with other Indo-European cultures, Lithuanian mythology offers its own characteristic interpretation of history with this theme, supplementing the general theory of the so-called three ages of humankind with its own variant.

The projection of the elementary categories of time, "past"—"present"—

"future," onto the background of world history makes possible the distribution of time into three periods, one following another—for example, the gold, bronze, and iron ages—and to view their development as the progress of humanity or its degradation. The Lithuanian version of such a concept of history represents it as three racial forms following one another: a once-living race of *giants* is changed into the present race of *men*, after which there will follow a race of *dwarfs*, when people will be so weakened that it will take nine men to slaughter one rooster.[90] Mankind, inscribed in such a conceptualization between two races alien to it, has its beginning and end; it was fated *to be born*, and is fated one fine day *to die out*.

It is not surprising then, that Lithuanian mythology places such a historical-philosophical explanation onto the lips of *Laima*—the goddess of knowledge—if we encounter Laima in texts which no longer describe the birth and death of individual persons but the appearance and disappearance of humankind.

In Lithuanian mythology, these two events are connected to world cataclysms, the flood and the plague: if as a consequence of the *flood*, there appears a race of men, then to a frightened humanity the threat of a *plague* appears as the possibility of the end of the world.

Laima and the Flood

Four versions of the universal flood myth are known to us at this time. We can count as the basic version the text recorded and published in 1888 by M. Davaina-Silvestraitis in his collection of folklore, *Pasakos, sakmės, oracijos* [Tales, Legends, and Orations].[91] There are two close variants of the same myth recorded in 1878 and 1880 and translated into Polish by Davaina. The authors of the collection provide us with short but useful summaries. The fourth version appears unexpectedly three years later in the collection of historical studies by J. Jurginis, *Pagonybės ir Krikščionybės santykiai Lietuvoje* [The Relationship Between Paganism and Christianity in Lithuania],[92] in which the author provides a loose Lithuanian translation of the myth published by T. Narbutt in 1835, stating his own convictions "that it is a literary reworking of the Biblical plot about the flood and the tower of Babel."

Such confirmation by Jurginis—together with the commentators' mutual disregard of two separate sources—forces us to pause and express our opinion on the separate branch of study in the humanities called "source criticism." The historian Jurginis and the folklorist Balys agree on this question, taking a "positivist" position: the works of historians and especially mythologists of the Romantic epoch—but one can also target Renaissance historiography—must be rejected as "invented," "plagiarized," or "reworked" products. Such a positivist outlook, nevertheless, obscures, in our opinion, the "idealism" of their defenders in assessing literary creation: they admit studies based only on facts, and push the whole of artistic creation into irrational recesses, as appearing from nothing—figments of the imagination—or as imaginary creation not obedient to any logic.

On the question of comparing the Narbutt text with Biblical themes, it can be briefly stated that:

(1) The *flood* myth is of quite general, perhaps even universal character, encountered from Australia to Alaska; the Biblical text of the flood is only one of the more general versions of the Mesopotamian flood myth.

(2) The *Tower of Babel* myth, as one means to explain through mythological categories the presence of the variety and abundance of linguistic and national communities, is no less diffused: German scholars have provided four thick tomes of its various versions.

Thus, there is no basis to suppose that the Lithuanian flood myth would inevitably be the "reworked" Biblical myth: the task of source criticism is only to select the possible Biblical elements that appear in it.

The comparison of the Narbutt text with the folk variant offered by Davaina, which would require a separate study, inspires an entire series of observations which can be grouped under four rubrics:

First, concerning the texts of oral tradition, the trained eye can easily discern which elements have been introduced by the literary historian as an "embellishment" of the text. An example of such bad literary writing as, "The waters became quiet, the storm was stilled, and in joy the bright sun started to shine," which marks the end of the flood, undoubtedly belongs to the personal creation of Narbutt. The seventeenth-century French writer Charles Perrault "embellishes" folk tales in a similar way.

Second, and conversely, some textual facts, common as much to Narbutt's as to Davaina's sources, have nothing in common with the Bible, and can neither have been "invented" nor copied from each other. Among these can be mentioned the following:

(a) The fact that the last giants are rescued in the *nutshell*;

(b) The fact that the appearance of the first people is explained as the consequence of sexual relations between the representatives of the race of giants with the earth;

(c) The fact that such "fecundation" is fulfilled on the advice of the "rainbow."

Such textual facts have put down roots too deep into Lithuanian mythic thinking, are connected too strongly with common mythic themes (touching on, for instance, the chthonic nature of humanity): their existence allows us to confirm that all the known variants are versions of one and the same myth.

To the third group of textual facts belong elements which, although of mythic character and occupying the same or similar positions in the development of the text, are nevertheless realized separately in different variants. In this group, the most prominent place is taken by the proper names:

(a) The god who rules the race of giants and tames the flood in the version offered by Narbutt is called *Praamzis* and in Davaina's variants—*Prakorimas* or *Prakurimas*.

(b) Another important actress in the myth, the messenger of the principal god, called by Narbutt "Vaivorykštė Linksminė" [rainbow of happiness,] has several names in the Davaina text—she is "the rainbow" and "Laumė's sash" and "Laima"—a fact which raises serious "philological" problems for the narrator.

Under the second and third rubrics, the facts mentioned—similarities and variations—form the primary object for the attention of the mythologist.

To the fourth group belong those "personalized" textual deformations which reflect not the author's desire to make his narrative more literary but, consciously or unconsciously, express the author's ideology. At first glance it is easy to identify two of Narbutt's dominant tendencies:

(a) Rationalization: if there is concern in the Davaina myth only with the destiny of the two elder-giants from whom mankind will arise, Narbutt does not forget to rescue the birds and the animals. This is a logical—not a mythological—addition: additions of this type most likely allowed Jurginis to create an impression of a Biblical imitation.

(b) The Lithuanianization of the myth: while in the Davaina text there is concern with the general problem of the appearance of mankind (every nation holds itself in mythic thinking to be the center of the universe), Narbutt not only begins to rationalize by providing, next to the elder-giant pair from whom the Lithuanian nation originates, other pairs who become dispersed throughout the world, but he also determines the number of children—nine boys and nine girls—from whom there can arise nine Lithuanian tribes. These nine tribes are necessary so he can continue the development of the mythic history of the Lithuanian nation.

Such tendencies of interpretation based on the ideology of the epoch and the author are comparatively easy to recognize; they do not interfere with the construction of mythic prototype, which for Narbutt served as source for reworking an "improved" version.

Our rather lengthy but unavoidable digression allows us to formulate two types of deductions. First of all, it is apparent that there is need in mythology for its own "textual criticism," differing somewhat from historical "source criticism" and from philological "criticism of literary texts." Applying it to our sources, the usefulness of the Narbutt version and the limits for its utilization become more apparent, as does the basis for selecting the Davaina-Silvestraitis version for analysis of the mythic text, though supplemented progressively with information provided by Narbutt.

" . . . before the time of the floods there were only big people . . . the ancient people called them *giants* . . . and the god, whom they worshipped, had a big palace in the sky. His name was *Prakorimas*. And when he looked down on the earth, he saw such injustice by his people that *Prakorimas* sent two men, whom the ancient Samogitians called *Vėjas* and *Vanduo* [wind and water] to deter them from their evil deeds . . . (When they did not listen), those two men became angry and in the course of 25 days gathered the earth into one pile into their arms like a platter and tossed it in all directions. And so the water flooded the whole world."

Although our basic aim is the description of the personality and activity of the goddess *Laima*, we should, nevertheless, pause at this representation of the flood: only within its frame can the place of *Laima* in the world of the gods, her relations with other gods and, all together, her cosmic functions, be more fully understood. Therefore, the analysis of the myth, whose excerpts are presented here, will not be exhaustive—it will mostly touch on problems held in common with *Laima*.

There is no doubt that the world was once settled by giants: this is verified by abundant and varied folktale sources and confirmed by comparative Indo-European mythology which places the Lithuanian data within a wider framework.

It is evident that the gods of those other times could only be giants. Here, even our well-known *Velnias* [Devil] is represented in some texts as a one-eyed giant, a Lithuanian equivalent to Polyphemus, or as "lapkritys," who denudes all the trees of their leaves with one blow. There is a widely diffused legend about two giants who lend axes to one another across rivers and valleys: in some of the variants they are called *Perkūnas* and his brother. There is no lack of similar examples. It is quite normal then that those two men, called by the ancient Samogitians *Vėjas* and *Vanduo* are considered to be giants in the Narbutt version. We are dealing here, as in Scandinavian and Greek mythologies, with the "ancient generation" of gods, with a race of fellow giants and their rulers. In this environment of primordial gods before long there will appear our goddess *Laima*.

The god whom the giants "worship," but who is also the ruler of the gods of that epoch, is called *Prakorimas* in the Davaina-Silvestraitis Lithuanian variant and *Prakurimas*, or, directly, *Dievas* [God] in the Polish variants.

This peculiar name—*Prakorimas*—accompanied by *Occopiruum* (acc. sing.) mentioned by Lasicius, raises nothing but questions for Davaina's commentators. From the standpoint of meaning, if the second part of this compound name can be interpreted as = *pirm*(as) [first], then it is not such a poor comparison. However, it is not possible to consider this as a deformation of the theonym offered by Lasicius, if only due to the fact that the word *prakorimas*, complete and unaltered, exists in the Lithuanian language, and, furthermore, that it is recorded in *LKŽ*.

The abstract significance of this word corresponds to the functions of the god we are analyzing—that of *destiny* [likimas]. *LKŽ* even provides two citations by Pietaris to clarify this meaning:

"Why do you separate yourselves from the Poles, with whom *Prakorimas* had kept together for so long in one group?" And: "*Prakorimas* instructed us to live in the colder regions of Europe."

These two examples—in which it is possible to discern without great effort even the image of a personified Likimas—are taken from the works of Vincas Pietaris of Suvalkija while Davaina's *Prakorimas* is of Samogitian origin (Raseiniai district of Western Lithuania). Thus the diffusion of the word, used in this sense, is sufficient for it to be counted as pan-Lithuanian.

However, this word has even more ancient roots in history: no longer in its "figurative" but in its "literal" sense, it means "pralaužimas, the removal of honey from the beehive" (Ruhig, 1747; Mielcke, 1800); *prakoriauti*—"to begin to break open the honeycombs" (A. Juška) and *prakorauti*—"to first taste the food and drink given to someone" (Brodowski, 1713–1744). *LKŽ*, citing an entry in the Mielcke dictionary, "The food, drink, given to the king, I taste first, prakorauju," explains that this word defines the widely known service performed in the Middle Ages at the estate of the prince or king by an official called in Lithuanian *prakorauninkas* (Ruhig, 1747).

In order to explain the global significance of this word family from a historical-semantic viewpoint, the common prefix *pra-*, which gives the root an inchoative, beginning aspect, must first be separated out: *prakorimas* as an abstract but personified Likimas [destiny] or *prakorauninkas*, an official of the manor, are both initiators, baptizers, who first start something. The nucleus of the root = *kor*, indicating that the issue centers on the bees' *koriai* [honeycombs] (this confirms the "primary" meaning of *prakorauninkas* as "the taker of the bee's honey"), cannot help but remind one of the major role which apiculture played as the model for the domestic and communal system in ancient Lithuanian culture: it is not surprising that this beekeeper metaphor serves, on the one hand, for the formation of the concept of fate on the divine plane, and on the other, on the mortal plane, to name an important institution of the feudal Lithuanian regime—that of the *taster*.

In our opinion, however, it would be a mistake to consider the *prakorauninkas* as only a civil servant of the estate, although of a high order, whose duty it was to check that the food and drink given to the ruler had not been poisoned. Having had the opportunity to analyze on another occasion the rituals of *krikštijimas*, i.e., "of a beginning," "tasting,"[93] we can be certain that during the *Day of the Serpents* [Kirmių diena] the tasting of the food by the serpents—or their refusal to touch it—signified their blessing in the dual sense of the word: not only—and not so much—to bless the food, but with the help of this introductory ritual, to fulfill the forecast for the future. It is very likely that the *prakorauninkas*, at least in the initial phases of this institution, was a priest who baptized and blessed the food and realm of the ruler.

In such a context, the concept of *prakorimas* in the sense of "destiny" utilized by Pietaris, as well as the theonym recorded by Davaina, become apparent. While agreeing that *Prakorimas* is actually the name of the god who existed before the appearance of mankind, it is possible to recognize in the semanticism (a) his aspect as the initiator, the original god, (b) his traits as one who knows and fulfills destiny, and finally (c) his figure as the world's first beekeeper, who establishes apiculture and raises from those unruly giants "who could not tolerate one another, who scorned one another,"[94] a new race of men who live in accordance with the laws of the universe and of society.

The second variant of the *Prakorimas* name, *Prakurimas*, is also possible due to its connotation of a beginning: *prakurėjas*, according to *LKŽ*, which refers to ancient sources, is "protėvis," "sentėvis" [forefather]. However, our existing data do not allow it to be inscribed into a wider mythic context. Taking into account that it had not been directly recorded by Davaina but that it is a proper name used in a Lithuanian context taken from a Polish mythic source, one can suppose that it is an "improvement" introduced by Davaina himself, without his understanding the meaning of *prakorimas*.

The final difficulty concerning a definitive acknowledgment of *Prakorimas* as the "true" theonym is linguistic in nature: its use as an abstract noun signifying "destiny" in the role of a proper name. Even though it is derived from a figurative image—"breaking apart of honeycombs"—the fact that it expresses an action, and not a state, makes it more difficult to accept its significance as that of abstract fate. *LKŽ*, perhaps, is indirectly to blame here by offering "likimas" as its synonym: using "lėmimas" in its place, makes the connection between the taking of honey, "korių ėmimas," and forecasting, "lėmimas," more reliable, more acceptable to "linguistic intuition." Crossing over from "lėmimas" [forecasting] as action to "likimas" [destiny] as the result of that action, and after that to the personification of "likimas," and finally to a proper name obeys the laws of semantic development. Its complicated history together with the presence in the same domain of concrete words such as *prakorauninkas* which define ancient, feudal institutions, without doubt are indicative of the antiquity both of this concept and of the representations which express it.

The Narbutt text in which *Praamžis*—somewhat Lithuanianized to *Praamžius*—is used in place of *Prakorimas* presents no such difficulties: *Praamžius* is an abstract concept, and its grammatical form is that of a proper noun.

His case, nevertheless, seems somewhat weaker if only due to the fact that it is found only in texts of the nineteenth century: along with Narbutt, it is mentioned by Jucevičius, an ethnographer of the same period, in his narrative about Juratė and Kastytis, and by the end of the nineteenth century it is already found in the *Praamžius* form in "authentic" folklore in the Kalvaitis collection, *Prusijos Lietuvių Dainos* [Songs of the Lithuanians of Prussia] (1905): "My dear little hands, to whom will you belong? . . . If to a young man, then give *Praamžius*, give . . . ,"[95] in which he appears, as we see, in the same role of forecaster of fate. Consequently, even though his documented appearance in literature occurs rather late, there is no basis for counting him as an "invented god": *Praamžius* appears to us as one possibility out of numerous names for the same god *Prakorimas*, derived from the use of *Praamžis* [eternal], which *LKŽ* considers to be an adjective, in the role of an epithet.

Our attempted rehabilitation of *Praamžius* should not be confused with attempts by other mythologists, influenced by Christianity, to find in the Baltic religions one primary god. *Prakorimas* is a god-giant and a god of the giants. The history of religions, when it is capable of embracing a longer time span as, for instance, in the case of India, indicates that religions, like the cultures in which they are inscribed, develop and change, forming separate—or at least separately touched on and described—layers. On the other hand, the conceptualization of the divine universe as a battlefield between two generations of gods is often characteristic of Indo-European mythologies. One of the basic traits of the mythic way of thinking, after all, is the search for the origins and causes of the constituted phenomena and events: the fact, for instance, that at the present time there exist day and night, in mythic thought signifies that at one time there was no difference between night and day, that their separation must be explained by some sort of unusual act of creation or of a battle between cosmic forces.

Therefore the presence in Baltic religion of a triad of sovereign gods does not at all contradict the possibility of identifying other, generally more obscure, gods of an ancient generation, *Prakorimas*, in their midst as well, the same as the myth of Gediminas about the founder of the Lithuanian state and its capital, not only does not interfere with, but even calls forth the memory of the figure of Šventaragis, creator of a dynasty and founder of the cult of the eternal fire: type and archetype supplement and confirm one another.

The identification of *Prakorimas* as the original instigator of destiny and its natural development does not interfere with the presence of the Lithuanian *Mithra*, one of whose basic forms of manifestation, next to the Christianized *Senelis Dievas*, appears to be that of *Dievaitis Mėnulis* [Moon Deity]. This helps us to resolve one important question left without an answer, that concerning the Lithuanian concept of *wisdom*.[96] In the narrative about the *wise* father who knows the true will of fate and hates his son because he does not have his *share*, who persecutes him despite the fact that *Senelis Dievas* allowed him to live from the lamb's share, we undoubtedly encounter two conceptualizations of fate, the father's and son's obedience to two different principles of destiny. It is possible then to formulate the hypothesis that the father's *wisdom* is manifested by the conception of the implacable will of *Prakorimas* and the son's *good fortune*—as a gift of the *Senelis Dievas*—by the acceptance of *dalia* [one's lot].

> When the deity looked down upon the earth a second time from his palace window, while chewing on the nuts of the sky that grow so abundantly in the garden, and seeing the oppression of mankind, he took such pity, thinking to himself: "If only one person could survive the flood."
>
> Then he took the shell from a nut and threw it through the window to the drowning people. It so happened that one old man and an old woman were able to save themselves in that nutshell.

A comparison of this text with the narrative cited by Narbutt does not introduce anything new: Narbutt, as already mentioned, embellishes his text by placing in the nutshell not only several pairs of people—thus explaining the origin of nations, not only Lithuanian—but, reminiscent of Noah's ark, places in it all the representatives of beings, birds and animals. Our text, of course, is not taken up with such details. It is concerned with the general affairs of mankind.

The summaries of two variants recorded and translated into Polish by Davaina-Silvestraitis, conversely, supplement the basic text somewhat:

(a) With the elders sitting down in the nutshell, *Velnias* [Devil] appears and sends a mouse (or turns into a mouse himself) so that it would gnaw through the nutshell.

(b) *Laima* (or *Prakorimas* himself) throws a glove, which turns into a cat and catches the mouse.

This additional information is interesting, in that, next to *Prakorimas*, it introduces other deities, new inhabitants of the divine universe of those other times—*Velnias* and *Laima* (and distances the Lithuanian text from the Biblical model), and it gives us the appearance of *Laima* as helper of *Prakorimas*—or directly his replacement.

The introduction of a nutshell as a means of rescue is also worthy of attention. We have already had occasion to come across this shell in another myth[97] about the ascent of *Aušrinė* into the sky, i.e., her metamorphosis, her new birth. The symbolism is similar here also: the elder-giants sit in a nutshell which is the nucleus from which there will develop a new race of people, with whose help there will be a new metamorphosis of humankind.

> But when the deity *Prakorimas* looked down the third time from his window at those two men, his messengers, who were so angry, he said to himself that they in anger have destroyed the people and they want to ruin the whole world. Then that deity sent to those men the *sash of favor—the rainbow—*to tame them and drive them back from where they had come. Thus those men were driven back.

A comparison of this text with Narbutt's narrative brings to light that which is missing in the latter: in the Narbutt text, *Praamzis* himself, shutting the angry giants away in the "ancient place," does not make use of the *rainbow* as messenger, and the rainbow *Linksminė* [happiness] appears to him only later, in the following episode, with the ending of the flood, "starting to shine a radiant sun." This rationalization characteristic of Narbutt—the rainbow "actually" appears only after the rain—directs our attention to the "abnormality" of the Davaina text—or the too early appearance of the rainbow and her specific mission—which is to appease the god-giants. In other words, the "rainbow" appears earlier than her "sash."

What, then, is this "rainbow"? This is a question that bothers not only the modern commentator, for it also gave no peace throughout the entire narrative to Davaina's informant, who from the very beginning tried to differentiate the three names for this phenomenon: "the first name is *laumės* (laimės) sash. The second is *malonės* (favor) sash. The priests say that it should be called by its *real* name, *vaivorykštė* [rainbow]."

The problem is both complicated and simple. While the "true"—literary or liturgical—name of the rainbow was not known, *Laima* (or *Laumė*) was a mythic being known to all, whose *sash* from time to time would appear in the sky. The appearance of the word *vaivorykštė* [rainbow] complicates matters: this name refers both to the sash and the mythic being to whom this sash belongs. (It is understandable, therefore, why there emerges a new "folk" etymology for *vaivorykštė* differentiating the goddess *Vaiva* and her *rykštė* [rod].)

Even though having decided to call it *Malonės Juosta* [sash of favor] (perhaps a name formed due to Biblical influence) the Davaina informant cannot evade the problem of personifying her by placing onto her lips such expressions as: "You will often see me *with my light* (i.e., with a sash)"; "And I will often gaze upon you with *my eyes of favor* from the sky." The idea that female beings could be called "juosta" [sash] is nonsense. Therefore, as the narrative develops, the informant has to interrupt his history, clarifying that upon seeing a "rainbow in the sky . . . our forefathers say, It's not true. This is not the rainbow but *Laimės juosta*!" adding that *Laimė* left as well other "signs"—*brooms and rainbows*.

It would seem that no additional commentary is necessary here since the narrator himself slowly untangles all the polynomic tangles. Since we are aware of the extension of the name of *laumės* [fairies] into the account of *laimės*, during the whole of the nineteenth century, verifying that *Laimės juosta* and *Laumės juosta* are rival names for the same phenomena known throughout all of Lithuania (*LKŽ*), we can easily separate, on the one hand, *Laimė* and her sash, and on the other, *laumės* [pl] and their brooms.

Returning to our episode, it should be noted that the goddess *Laima* in our myth already appears a second time entirely independent of her "sash." Her actions—the first time she rescues the nutshell from *Velnias*' design, and the second she restores the giants *Vėjas* and *Vandenis* [Wind and Water] to their proper place—are so important that the existing variants ascribe these works to *Prakorimas* (or *Praamžius*) himself. Therefore, Dumézil's statement about the primitive gods of Rome—Jupiter and Fortuna[98]—can be applied to disclose the relationship between *Prakorimas* and *Laima*; both their figures encompass one and the same sphere of divine action, the only difference being that *Prakorimas* remains more in the shadow as a god-sovereign, and *Laima* more willingly associates with her surroundings as his messenger and the prophet of his will.

> (After chasing the giants out), she then said to the old one:
> If you want to have children, then go on such and such a hill and jump from that hill to the other. (They were not young, they went around without their pants, those shameless ones.) They jumped from hill to hill. The one who jumped most would have more children. Thus, the old man jumped as taught by *Malonės Juosta* on the hills. And as many times as he jumped, well, that many handsome grown sons appeared. The old woman, even though grown too old, as many times as she jumped, had that many beautiful daughters. But she was older, she jumped less and she had fewer daughters.

This segment of the text is unquestionably archaic, and we cannot discern any Biblical imitation. In the Bible, humankind is born of Adam and Eve, but here the giant-elder pair does not have children and cannot have them since such children would also be giants and not people. Therefore, the sexual act, as a premise of birth, is here represented as the union of the old man and the old woman—each separately, with the *Earth*. The role of the old man's female partner as he leaps "from hill to hill" is fulfilled by the valley. Difficulty appears only with the old woman, for whom the Earth [*Žemė*], being of female gender, cannot be a partner: the Davaina text thus passes over this episode. According to Narbutt, who conversely supplements our text, the old woman's male partner is "the earth's hillock." Fearing that the listener may not understand this allusion, the narrator adds—"they were not small": in other words, being of the giant's height, they corresponded to the earth's uneven proportions. Finally, removing the last obstacle for sexual relations, he explains: "they went around without their pants, the shameless ones."

The newly found humankind is thus, on the one hand, a continuation of the race of giants, but, on the other hand, its *chthonic origins* (a problem which in Greek mythology has an important place as well: without it, according to Levi-Strauss, one cannot explain the meaning of the Oedipus myth) are also unquestionable. In this sense, our analyzed text is reminiscent of another etiological myth—that of *Aušrinė*, in which recovery of human form by her brother-bull and her sister-cows is tied to the appearance of earth and of humankind. Each of the two myths echoes the other. In one it is *Aušrinė*, in the other *Laima*, who participates in and unites with the appearance of humankind, and in both cases, with a humankind closely associated with the earth.

The role of *Laima* in this important Lithuanian myth cannot be forgotten: she not only participates in the birth of mankind, but the appearance of the first people is possible only by following her "teachings." *Laima* is thus—and the entire mythological context was necessary to show this—the goddess of birth not only because she—or the *three laimės*—assists at every man's birth and forecasts his future, but especially because she guides the birth of all mankind. Cosmologically and anthropologically her activity planes are analogical and her divine stature cannot be identified, as some folklorists would like, with the "good fairy" representations of the story world.

> The sash of favor (and that, as we know, is *Laima*), having taught those oldsters, said: "Well, now *your new world begins* with its little people. But after that, when the people have come to an end, there will be such men, that it will take nine to kill one rooster. And having said that, I will now remove myself from you *to my realm on high* where I had been. You will often see me with such a light as you see me now. And I will often gaze upon you with my eyes of favor from the sky. But do not forget: when you see my *sash, blue in the sky*, with little red, well, then in that year there will be more white bread [wheat] than dark [rye]. And when I appear to you with *more red*, well, then in that year there will be more dark bread and the year will be bad."
>
> And, having spoken those words and *others*, she rose in radiance into the sky. She was covered by the clouds, and she appeared thus for the first time to those oldsters while they stood on the hillside of Varpija.

If we look at this segment of the text—for which there seems to be a shortage of equivalents in the Narbutt version—only from the standpoint of *Laima*, we can pinpoint several of its characteristic traits:

(a) The participation of *Laima* in the birth of mankind is closely tied to another function of forecasting—that of knowledge and prophecy. She herself briefly recounts for the first people the philosophy of the history of the three races of man.

(b) The mission of *Laima* on earth among people is temporary, since her permanent dwelling is "in her realm" "in the sky."

(c) *Laima*, expressing her principal benevolence to mankind, announces that she will continue her forecasting: a rainbow of one or another color will be her "sign," according to which men will always be able to guess their *fortune*, their good or bad years. *Laima*, as one would expect, is concerned with man's material well-being, supplementing, in that manner on the cosmic plane, her role as the distributor to every man his allotted share [*dalis*].

Just as *Laima* can appear as an anthropomorphic being without her sash-rainbow, so the appearance of the rainbow is not, as we have seen, inevitably connected with the end of the flood or rain—even though it is commonly thought that her function is to restore the equilibrium of the elements of nature by gathering the descended waters of the sky and returning them to the sky.[99] *Laima* prophesies good and bad years, and she does this by changing the colors of her sash: a dominant *blue* color with a small amount of red means a good year, and a dominant *red* means a bad year.

Of course, the colors of Laimas' sash are those "seen" by folk culture and do not necessarily correspond to the colors of the rainbow of artists such as Šimonis, which cover the entire color spectrum. Taking into account the especially distinct cultural relativism of this area, the observations by Lithuanian culture of a combination of only two colors of the rainbow—blue and red—should not surprise us.

Only by explaining the chromatic composition in this way can we understand the etymology of one of her names—*vaivorykštė*: *vaivorykštė juosta* is a sash [juosta] whose colors are similar to the colors of the crowberry [*vaivoras*]. *Vaivor-ykštė* used as an adjective is derived from *vaivoras* and belongs to the same derivational paradigm as *pernykštis*, *vakarykštis*, or *čionyskštis* [last year's, last night's, this native]. Such an etymology is offered not only by Būga[100] but also by Davaina's informant, who explains conversely—in terms of mythic thinking—that "vaivorai" had originated from "vaivorykštė [rainbow] and therefore that they are signs left by Laimė, adding as a colorful example the following menacing expression: "I will make you look like vaivora! I'll beat you up so you'll be blue!" (i.e., go from red to blue). A similarity in the colors of the sash does not as yet constitute a basis for the name *vaivorykštė*: while awaiting additional facts, we might add that the intoxicating ability of vaivorai—and of the ledum which grows in its midst—gives people the illusion of transcendence, happiness, and fortune.[101]

Such an interpretation of the color signs of *Laimė*—of the sash and the vaivorai—explains as well the selection of the huge stone of Rambynas hill with a circumference of 15 yards for attribution to her: the stone, according to Otto Glagau,[102] "was of hard *reddish-black* granite with mica" and "the slanting rays that fell on the stone reflected a wondrous golden light." It seems that in the Lithuanian chromatic system—and the etymological argumentation of Būga supplements this[103]—there dominates in this case not the exposition of primary colors and their opposition but a common trait—sparkling.

There should be added to the "signs" of Laimė the *lauminė skara* [fairy scarf], about whose coloration it is known only that it is "striped" just like the sash of Laimė.[104] Therefore the ritualistic nature of its use—the bridegroom would bring it to his intended bride, together with the "shoes,"[105] after a successful matchmaking—indicates that it is used to mark the newly created pair's devotion to Laimė. With the same aim in mind, the newlywed pair would climb the Rambynas hill to pray.

Laima and the Plague

The application of structural method to our analytical object from the start indicates one empty position, which Laima should fill by her appearance and activity: actually, if *Laima*, on the anthropological plane, is a goddess who determines every man's life and death, then on the cosmological plane, participating, as we saw, in humankind's birth, she should be manifested at another occasion—menacing death for humankind.

Therefore the recorded text of Davaina-Silvestraitis does not end with the teachings of Laimė, which are given to a humankind newly created: without any stylistic embellishments it crosses from the birth to the death problematic, from a narration about the flood to the description of the plague.

Mythic mentality, as we have already had occasion to note, is especially concerned with the question "why," and not with "how." In our case, knowing that humankind's history is distributed into epochs separated from one another by cosmic cataclysms, such as flood or plague, helps us in our studies of humanity's search for answers to "Why the flood?' or "Why the plague?" We happen to find two answers to these questions in Lithuanian sources.

The first, the answer given by the Davaina informant, as we have seen in the case of the flood, corresponds to a certain philosophic tendency to explain history pessimistically as a constant impoverishment of mankind, as a degradation process. Just as the race of giants was destroyed by the flood for its "evil," so the newly emerged people, according to this narrator, became "quite evil and lived without justice, plundered, pillaged, vanquished each other." To such a regime based on brutal strength "God sent a terrible scourge—a tempest—people died like leaves falling from a tree."

It is difficult to say to what degree such a moralistic explanation reflects the influence of Christianity. In the conception of history as a changeover of three races, there is no need for moralizing: according to the Davaina text, *Prakorimas* sends *Vėjas* and *Vandenis* only so that they would "contain" the giants, and they themselves, on their own initiative, becoming angry, took and drowned the earth. But that same text, before proceeding to the moral causes of catastrophes, begins its explanation with the fact that before the flood, "once again people multiplied in all corners": it seems then that one of the basic causes of decadence of mankind is, as we have seen, quite a modern problem—the *boundless* multiplication of mankind.

If we consider such an explanation to be persuasively changing the criteria of good and evil in the characteristic morality of moderation of Lithuanian culture as we have seen elsewhere,[106] we are inclined to accept it as more archaic, even more so since other sources confirm it as well:

> After the creation of the universe, when much of the world became populated, the *earth* began to complain to the Lord God that she *could not bear it*. The Lord God heard her out and permitted a *flood*. After that there was another rapid increase of men, the earth asked the Lord God to *ease her burden*. The Lord God sent the *plague*.[107]

Viewed in this manner, the turnover of three races and the problem of cataclysms that separate them appear to be independent of the goodness or evil of mankind. Rather, it is strictly a matter concerning mutual relations between the gods. Let us return then, to the Davaina-Silvestraitis text:

> And at the time of the plague, during the night, in the villages and around the cottages there walked about, as the elders say, *laumės juosta* [the sash of laumė] herself or the *vaivorykštė*. She had changed into an old woman.
> And those *vaivorykštės* had great power over all types of diseases, which they would shake from themselves like mist onto the people. They had woven onto their sash the sign of the rainbow—the same as the rainbow carried herself.
> Whichever man was just and good-hearted, then, to those *laumės* or *vaivorykštės* would appear and would tell of all kinds of *covered things*, where they were going and what they were doing. And from such tales they would come to learn other news of the time: will the plague continue to be so severe, and why are there such plagues and what will happen to us? Will anyone survive? And they would always make this known to the just.

This episode about the plague, like the previous description of the flood, is divided into two parts as it concerns *Laima*. The first involves the characterisation of Laima—her appearance, dress, and action—and the second, her fulfilled prophecies. The prophecies again consist of two parts: the disclosure of "covered things," i.e., her "self-revelation," the uncovering of divine nature and, only after that, of the prophecies themselves. Since the narrator leaves the "covered things" covered, let us return to the first part of this text.

We would like to believe that our reader, having been cautioned, will have no difficulties in grasping the *Laimė* nomenclature: the narrator calls the rainbow at first *laumės juosta* and after that *laumė* herself. Somewhat later, continuing his narrative and supported by the authority of the elders, he adds: "it is not the rainbow but *laimės juosta*," and finally he speaks not about the sash [juosta] but about Laimė leaving her "signs." In spite of the alternation of the names, the similarity in the personage of *Laimė*—on this occasion having the appearance of an old woman and wearing the "lauminė" sash—is not to be doubted.

No particular difficulties are created by the fact that in one place one speaks about one *Laima* and elsewhere about *laimas* in the plural, who wander about the villages: such confusion of singular and plural—if only because the deity must appear in several places at once, but especially because of its incompatibility with our modern concept of the *individual* is a common well-known phenomenon in mythology.[108]

The procedure according to which *Laima* fulfills her deadly task by "shaking diseases from herself onto people like a mist" corresponds to a definition of the word maras as "epidemic," or "infection."[109] We find a similar image in the Vilnius region: "Oh, when cholera walked about earlier, perhaps (even now) flew over the treetops, attacked them and suffocated them . . . "[110] Difficulty arises in part because a somewhat similar procedure is attributed to *Ragana* [witch] or raganos (pl.)—often also considered to be a cause of the plague: "In former times fair maidens on a high hill piled skulls, hair, and horns and kindled fires. The plague appeared wherever the *smoke* had gone."[111] Basanavičius responds to this East Lithuanian text by giving a Samogitian (West Lithuanian) explanation: "As soon as she (Ragana) gets angry over something that concerns people she immediately calls together all the raganas and orders them to shear tufts of wool from underneath the ears of a lamb of some owner and to bring them to her on the Šatrija [hill]. There they kindle the wool and whichever direction the wind carries the *smoke*, there the plague will set on the people or on the animals."[112] In one case the plague spreads like a fog, and in another it passes over with the smoke, but the actual disseminators of the plague, as we saw, are different.

Without obscuring the contradictions—the plague for mankind was such a terrible occurrence that not one but several mythological theories could have been formed to explain it—we nevertheless think that a place for *Laima* in this catastrophe is assured not only because ethnographic sources verify this, but also because this position is guaranteed by the internal logical coherence of her divine sphere of action.

This is confirmed by the nuclear meaning of the word *maras* [the plague]: *maras* is, first of all, the death principle itself, its cause:

> "The sword is mine—the plague is mine" (D1081)
> "The gun has the plague: you fired and the rabbit fell" (T1)
> "That arrow does not have the plague" (when shot, one does not fall immediately) (Grg) (LKŽ)

When we take into account the fact that *Laima* is the bearer and prophet of life and death, the statement that she "contains in her being" the plague and she shakes it on people "like a mist," should not surprise us.[113] The connection of *Laima* with the plague is confirmed as well by another linguistic fact—synonyms for *maras* understood as "collective misfortune": *lykava, likava, lykuva* [pestilence].

"There came such a *lykava* that all the people began to die like mad" (LKŽ, Erž) apparently belongs to the same family as *likimas* [destiny] and expresses with the help of the suffix *-ava, -uva* (sim. *velniuva, brolava*) both the collective and augmentative nature of the manifestation of fate.[114]

Laima and Aušrinė

Laima at the Christening

As the goddess of birth, it would seem that *Laima* should be most often encountered in documents which describe lying-in and christening ceremonies. The *three laimės*, of course, appear beneath the window when a child is born, and they forecast his destiny. However, in descriptions of christenings it is rather difficult to identify the cult of *Laima* or the remains of the rituals associated with it: as we observed elsewhere,[115] allusions were more easily found there to *Austėja* and her honey. Praetorius, although noting that "Bei der Geburt rufen einige Nadrauer noch die *Laime* oder Goettin der Geburt an," somewhat later adds that during the christening banquet "darauf dankt die Pribuweje [midwife] (Alte) Gott und der *Jungfer Mariae*, andere der *Layme*"[116] ["during childbirth some Nadrauers still invoke Laima, or the goddess of childbirth. . . . Thereupon the (old) midwife gives thanks to God and the Virgin Mary, others to Layme"]. It seems that in his time, the Christian figure of *Mary* had taken over the place of *Laima* and her functions.

More important, it seems, is that solitary testimony from a christening song which we find recorded in the twentieth century in the district of Kamajai;[117] we will make use of both of those rather close variants here.

One variant begins with (and the other inserts somewhat later) the description of the preparation of *Laimė* for the christening:

> *Laimė* intended
> To make the ale
> Čiuta, čiutela
> Žalia rūtela [green rue]
>
> All the stars
> To summon
> Čiuta, čiutela
> Žalia rūtela.

The commentary provided by the informant does not raise any doubts concerning the song's introduction of the personage of *Laimė:* "*Laimė* used to be a "seer" [žynė]. She knew everything. Žynės were not laumės, nor witches, they were beautiful and good women . . . When a child was born at night, they would announce behind the window the child's fortune or misfortune . . . "[118] *Laimė* thus is here the same deity of birth and fate with whom we are well-acquainted.

The site of *Laimė's* dwelling is the sky on high: she invites "all the stars" to the baptism feast. The informant verifies this directly: "Those (laimės), says the old woman, were friends with the sun, with the stars." Such a dwelling does not surprise us: we saw somewhat earlier that *Laima*, appearing at the birth of mankind after the flood, again ascends "into the sky" saying, "I will now distance myself into my realm where I had been."

Since each of the existing variants supplements the other, we will provide them here, while attempting to preserve their thematic parallelism. The song [sutartinė] continues:

Only *Saulutė*	Not to invite
Not be invited	*Saulutė* only
Saulutė intended	Wait, *Laimele*,
To take revenge	I'll take revenge
Nine mornings	Nine mornings
The mist misted	I will not rise
....	The other nine
....	Not shake out the dew
On the tenth morning	....
Saulė appeared	....
All the people	....
Awaited her dearly.	....

This insult to *Saulė* and her revenge by not rising for nine mornings is a well-known motif, encountered while analyzing the birth of *Aušrinė*, her first appearance at the bottom of the sea.[119] The sun there, as we may remember, probably does not rise because of sadness or envy and not because of revenge, but that does not change matters.

The rivalry between *Aušrinė* and *Saulė* can be explained on two planes. On the divine plane, it is a rather banal history of love, a battle between the legitimate wife and the sweetheart over the *Dievaitis Mėnulis* loved by both, in which, for instance, *Laima* supports *Aušrinė* [the morning star] and *Perkūnas* supports *Saulė* [the sun]. On the mortal plane, it can be regarded as a reflection of a religious revolution mentioned by some authors, in whose footsteps the cult of *Saulė* was pushed to a secondary position.[120]

The consequence of *Saulė's* revenge for not having been invited to the christening, in one variant is accounted for by two introductory stanzas:

> Arising, rising
> The bright *Saulelė*
>
> Upon rising
> Finds žvaigzdelė [a little star].

The little star, which Saulė *finds* upon rising—as the entire context of the song indicates—is our well-known *Aušrinė*: we recall that one of her hairs in the nutshell thrown to the bottom of the sea is reflected in the sky in the form of a star, marking her new rebirth in the sky.[121]

One of the variants of the song, not content with the description of the heavenly events, extends the narrative, carrying out as is customary for Lithuanian songs, a parallelism between the divine and mortal life. Even though such parallelism cannot always be trusted—otherwise it would be pure allegory—it is interesting to note the homology that is established by the song:

$$\frac{Laima}{mother} \simeq \frac{Stars}{daughters} \simeq \frac{Saulė}{older\ daughter}$$

Without taking this literally, it is possible to emphasize certain hierarchic relations between *Laima*—representative of the older generation—and the Stars as well as Saulė, who belong to the generation of younger mythic beings. One thing is certain: this parallelism does not establish any family relations between *Laima* and *Aušrinė*. Laima, preparing the christening, appears thus more readily, expressed now in terms of the human world, in the role of godmother of *Aušrinė*.

Let us now place this song—which actually is a hymn suited for christening rituals—within the general context of Christianity: during the time of the feast, if one wishes to draw on the good will of *Laima* for the newborn infant, a hymn is sung, in which one turns to *Laima*, reciting her role in another case of divine birth— that of *Aušrinė*. If we take into account the basic attributes of *Aušrinė*—beauty, health, good fortune—it is evident that such an invocation is also a supplication that the divine model be applied to a concrete human case, that the newborn be endowed by *Laima* with the same traits as those of Aušrinė.

The Close Proximity of Laima and Aušrinė

The essential nature of the relations between *Laima* and *Aušrinė* is thus being disclosed, bit by bit. These are established with some difficulty, due to the unambiguous similarity of both of their divine functions (which gave Balys the opportunity, without waiting for the conclusions of this study, to take me to task for the merging of these two deities);[122] meanwhile, when *Aušrinė* is, within the frame of Lithuanian mythology, a *twice-born* goddess—the first time from the depths of the sea, comparable to Aphrodite rising from the waves of the sea, and the second time with her reflection appearing in the divine world of the gods—*Laima*, as we have seen, is the original deity, who belongs to the old generation of gods, fulfilling her duties as the messenger of *Prakorimas* and the prophet of his will, playing a basic role in moments of cosmic cataclysms—the flood and the plague. She is "praamžė," as is *Prakorimas*—participating in the birth of *Aušrinė* and preparing a christening for her.

Since we know that the traits of the godmother often are reflected in the character of the godchild—and we know this not only from the beliefs of the ancient people but also, for example, from the similarity between *Giltinė* and her godson "doctor"—we are not surprised when we observe that *Aušrinė* and her family, in a certain sense, "inherit" some of the attributes of *Laima*. The following enigmatic sentence of Daukantas then becomes comprehensible: "*Aušra* [the dawn] was behind *Laima*, and, it is said, daybreak began with Laima"[123] and so forth. Just as *Aušra* announces the day, so *Laima* prophesies the life of man and humankind: the parallelism of these two cycles is obvious. This functional, but not genetic, proximity between *Laima* and *Aušrinė* can be easily identified in the description of the "altar stone" dedicated to *Laima* on Rambynas hill, whose "rainbow" colors already have caught our attention: "It lay with its lower end pointing south, and the sun always shone at daybreak on it; therefore the flat surface would always reflect the *rays* of the *ascending and descending sun*, since the rays which fell diagonally on the stone would reflect a *wondrous golden light*."[124] Recalling the definition of *Aušra* offered by Lasicius according to which she is "the goddess of the *rays* of the sun that descend and ascend above the horizon,"[125] which corresponds almost word-for-word to the O. Glagau description, it is possible to observe the coming together of two chromatic sources in terms of the effect of the light. If the huge stone mass composed of "a hard reddish-black granite with mica" is the "sign" left by *Laima*, then the "wondrous golden light" is a reflection coming from another source, which is the epiphany of *Aušrinė*. This partial syncretism of our two deities on the manifestation plane is well expressed: *Aušrinė* with her wondrous light reveals, lights up, the massive, primary, divine essence of *Laima*. It is understandable, then why the festival of *Laima* is celebrated together with the festival of *Rasa* [the morning dew], i.e., *Aušrinė*, during the month of the tree consecrated to *Laima—liepa* [the linden tree] in July (now at the end of June).

Earth, People, and Gods

In order to review and evaluate the general scope of this study before concluding, we can observe in it, *grosso modo*, the analyses of two distinct myths carried out separately. The myths, however, even though they appear quite different, from a semantic viewpoint share quite a few traits in their deep meaning.

(a) Each one touches on the problems concerning the *appearance of earth and of humankind*: the *Aušrinė* myth ends with it, the *Laima* myth begins with it.

(b) In each case, the appearance of mankind is connected with the *earth*: in the Laima myth the human race is born directly from the earth, while in the Aušrinė myth the appearance of earth and of humans is one, irreducible phenomenon.

(c) The earth's appearance in both myths is associated with *water*: in the *Aušrinė* myth, water most frequently "changes" to earth, and, in the *Laima* myth, earth emerges from "the flood": in both cases the primary element, the condition for the appearance of earth and men, is water.

On the other hand, the differences are no less distinct. If we glance through the *Aušrinė* myth, it appears that attention is concentrated on the world of the gods. Its basic theme is the "birth" of Aušrinė herself from the watery depths, her final "rescue" and, in all, the "rebirth" of her brother and sisters through acquisition of anthropomorphic form. In other words, the myth narrates *the birth of the gods*, maintaining this birth as a necessary condition for the appearance of earth and of humankind: the newborn gods in this sense are gods of the "human race," the *žemėpačiai* of Lasicius, or the *žemininkai* of Striykowski. [126]

The *Laima* myth, conversely, presents all the gods appearing in it as the primordial ones—not only *Prakorimas* and *Laima*, but also *Vėjas*, *Vandenis*, and *Velnias* [Wind, Water, and Devil]—and is concerned, in essence, with the *birth of humans* and the death that threatens them. However, despite the differences, these two myths do not contradict one another: while they recount separately the strands of divine events, they unite them all into one definite synchronized *epoché*—the moment of appearance of earth, humankind and the earthly gods.

Humanity, born into the care of *Laima*, has thus its own gods: first of all, there is *Aušrinė*, the "queen" of the entire newly created universe, even though hierarchically still distant to Laima, nevertheless, together with her—and especially her "family"—is closely tied to the fate of humanity. The word "close" is too weak to express the relations of these two deities with the earth and its people: their rebirth *coincides* with the appearance of the different parts of the earth (and with the "universe" that they inhabit). The appearance of every one of these deities and of every portion of earth is as if two aspects of one and the same phenomenon.

The facts of ancient Greek culture can help us to better understand this phenomenon. The Greeks, not having an abstract concept of space, imagined the world either as a totality of thrown-about pieces (*meros*), corresponding to the apportioned parts of the body of the earth goddess *Geia*, or as a result of its political divisions into separate parts (*moira*). [127] These separate parts must be understood as the division of a populated earth having its communal organization, its gods with their cults. Such a partly mythical, partly cultural conception—mythology and culture here are not separable—corresponds roughly to two concepts of the newly emerged earth in the myths we are analyzing. In the *Laima* myth, the Lithuanian *Žemė* [earth] can be compared to the Greek *Geia*: the anthropological representation of the earth's body is characteristic to both of them. In the *Aušrinė* myth, the *Žemė* that appears populated with people, distributed into separate parts corresponding to the deities of the Aušrinė family, is reminiscent of another Greek principle of distribution of the earth into geopolitical units, even more since each part [*dalis*] is called by the same name, *moira*, just as the three Greek goddesses of fate are *moirae*. The hypothesis becomes self-evident that the three sisters of Aušrinė, upon acquiring anthropomorphic shape, "change" into the *three laimės-dalis*, which correspond to the Greek moira-parts.

This problem, which goes beyond the Lithuanian mythological boundaries, can be weighed only within the framework of comparative Indo-European mythology, for which Lithuanian data can contribute only a little to an already old debate. In this perspective, for instance, one should regard *Auššveitis*, to whom one part of the "universe" also corresponds, as an equivalent to the Indian god *Bhaga* and his "portion," without taking into consideration now the Slavic *Bog*. The concept of *dalis* as "that which is allotted to someone" can be applied as with the Greeks, to mark geopolitically defined parts of the world or, as with the Lithuanians, to characterize every person's *laimė-dalia* [fortune or allotted portion]. These are two possible concrete manifestations of the *dalia-moira* concept in the mortal world. However, it is understood that on the divine plane she can be "embodied" in either one form as the destiny-distributor deity, or in the form of three goddesses—laimės, moirae, nornen. Why in the Lithuanian context the earth is divided into four parts, one of which is allotted to the male god *Auššveitis*, with the other three going to the sisters of *Aušrinė*, the *laimės* [fates], is a new and separate problem for mythology.

The Distribution of Divine Functions

The separation of the primordial gods from the younger generation of gods already born facilitates our comprehension of the scope of the sacred spheres covered by these deites and of their functional distribution. *Laima*, as we have observed, appears first of all as a rather removed deity, occupied only with the most important matters of life and death. With the formation of a new divine order, even though maintaining her original role, she can carry out only specific interventions in this world, and can play, in a certain sense, only metonymic roles that only in part utilize her essence so that the general sphere of her activity becomes distributed among younger, more active deities.

If we cast a glance at *Aušrinė* and her "family," we can easily recognize the following rough distribution of their functions:

—They have a shared interest in the sphere of *life and death*, and the separate spheres of their action seem only to be reduced parts of the common sphere.

—*Aušrinė* reserves for herself the sphere of *youth* and beauty.

—Within the knowledge of *Auššveitis* are the problems of *health* and illness: as we have observed, this constitutes only an application of the general functions to everyday life.

—Even though the three sisters *laimės* forecast for the newborn a life and death which is independent of them, they are, in essence, only concerned with the question of the allotment of *material goods* [nauda]—fortune and misfortune, riches and poverty.

The areas of beauty, health, and material well-being create one homogeneous sphere which corresponds, in the framework of comparative Indo-European mythology, to what Dumézil calls the third sovereign function. If we keep in mind that they become actualized only with the appearance of humans, it is entirely normal that they should be distributed along with the family of gods that appear with the world.

It must not be forgotten, however, that these separate areas of activity are only *derivative*, secondary, that they are based on one general principle of sovereignty, the sovereign plane of life and death. If we recall that this entire complex of manifested divine powers is attributed at the same time to *Dievaitis Mėnulis*, whose relations with Aušrinė, while controversial—is she his sweetheart, wife, or daughter?—are, undoubtedly, close ones, it should not go unacknowledged that this new family of gods is subordinated in its activity to the authority and sovereignty of *Dievaitis Mėnulis*. Taking into account the fact that the same sacred sphere corresponds to the distinctly manifested functions of the Prussian god *Patrimpas*, we are compelled to state that in the religion of the Balts the third sovereign function is obedient to, and perhaps entirely integrated into, the first sovereign sphere of the *Mithra* nature. Whatever the "true" ancient name of this Lithuanian Patrimpas might be, we must regard the *Dievaitis Mėnulis* as one of the god-sovereigns who inherit power and strength from old *Prakorimas* and who form the "primary" triad of Lithuanian gods.

The Legacy of Laima

Such a comparably harmonious distribution of power and rule among the gods of the new generation cannot but raise, as we have mentioned, the problem of the legacy of *Laima*. As in other mythologies—Roman, Indian—the ancient gods, even though forced out of their dominant positions, remain and attempt to accommodate themselves to the new conditions.

Our proffered hypothesis, which identifies the *three fates* with the three sisters of Aušrinė, can be utilized here to explain one of the means of preservation and maintenance of *Laima*. Taking into account the importance of *nauda* as material well-being in agrarian communities (whose often-used synonym is the word "laimė" [luck]), it is not surprising that the preservation of *Laimė* in the role of guardian of this sphere assures for her a sufficiently honorable place in the new situation. Here she appears as we have seen, either in the form of the *three laimės* or one *Laima-Laimelė*.

The ternary form seems especially significant: when speaking not of one *Laima* but of *three laimės*, the important principle of "distribution" in the conceptualization of fate is emphasized, which serves as a basis for the formation of the figure of *Laimė-Dalia*. However, the symbolism of the number *three* has other connotations: triplication in narrative structure, as we have had occasion to underscore elsewhere, has a distinct totality function, as the exhaustion of all possibilities; it is a unit understood not as *unus* but as *totus*. On the other hand, the number *three* is an odd number, underscoring both the nature of indivisibility and singularity: it is not surprising, thus, that the "odd numbers 3, 5, 7, and 9 are called the *numbers of Laima*."[128] The importance of the number *three* beautifully illustrates the following belief:

> Not with any piece of wood will you protect yourself from the devil, but with a rowan tree. When you hit the devil with the rowan tree *once* (one time), he will immediately say: "Add a *second*!"
>
> When striking the devil, never say: "*One, two*," but if you hit him once and twice then quickly give a *third*.
>
> Or striking always say: "*One, one, one.*" Then you'll overcome him—otherwise not.[129]

In other words, the numbers that are *lucky* are either the number *one* repeated three times, or the series *one—two—three*, said without a break: one *Laima* or *three laimės* are one and the same *distributed, divided,* and *indivisible* divine being.

We have seen what role the genetic principle plays in the conceptualization of the organization of the divine world: thus the idea that gods are born, appear through metamorphoses, that they are united and distributed into families and, according to their ages, into generations, is one of the basic, most frequently utilized means in mythology to represent the divine community. However, one must not forget that mythology, in that sense, is not a once and for all time determined religious system but that it is also a theology, i.e., a constantly expanding collective manner of thought about the sacred and the gods that express it. The fact also remains that the opinions of the thinkers—knowledge and reason—may not be in agreement, may partially contradict each other, may triumph over one another, may gain strength, or may become a common religious property.

The privileged form of such thinking is narrative—often a figurative narration. The narrativization of value systems, as semioticians already know, has its own laws which are based on the necessities of linguistic structure. One such law is the inability of the syntagmatic, narrative form to express complex concepts, the inability, at one and the same time, to say white and black. In theological systems, conversely, concepts of this type—as for instance, the basic element of *life* important to our analysis, which encompasses both life and death, or the concept of *fortune*, which expresses both wealth and poverty—often occupy dominant positions. If we start to talk about such concepts, to analyze them, the words used to express them are placed next to each other, one after another: next to *life* appears *death*, next to *fortune*, its lack, *misfortune*. In other words, every analytical thought deconstructs complex ideas, calls forth the appearance of *binary* structures. The terms organized in such a binary manner, if they are used on the figurative plane—as is common in mythology—easily yield to personification, and create an opportunity for new divine figures to appear. Such a development of the divine world, its multiplication, is obedient not to a genetic but to the *generative* principle.

In the area of direct interest to us, the application of the generative principle can be of help in the understanding of certain aspects of the *Laima* legacy. It is sufficient that the thinking about *Laima*, as about the origin of life, becomes somewhat more diffused when stating questions about life's beginnings and its end, and that *Laima*, as the goddess of birth, which is the beginning of life, calls forth the appearance of the goddess of death, her "sister" *Giltinė*. The same can be said about the evolution of the concept of *laimė*, "that which is allotted to man he can count on": such a *fortune*, valued positively, calls forth its antithesis—the appearance of *misfortune*. It is noteworthy that not by chance in the French language, for instance, the concepts of *espérance* "hope" and *succès* "success" have emerged in its positive sense only in the seventeenth century. It is difficult to say what role the development of such antithetical gods has played in the influence of Christianity which favored dualism. One certainty is that the first pair of gods—*Laima* and *Giltinė*—appear markedly more archaic than the duplication of *Laimė* and *Nelaimė*. *Laima* and *Giltinė*, let us not forget, are not only sisters; the nature of their activities—*Laima* especially is concerned with the fulfillment of fate, and *Giltinė* strives to help people—without doubt is reminiscent of the primordial *Laima*, who carries out the will of *Prakorimas*. Meanwhile, the figures of *Laimė* and *Nelaimė* appear rather as the personifications of two different portions [dalis] allotted by fate.

V

ON BEES AND WOMEN

Auštėja

Name Reconstruction

Despite the present reaction against the nearly universal explanation of gods and rituals in terms of *fertility* by the previous generation of folklorists and mythologists, we should not discount the existence of authentic gods—or more likely goddesses—of fertility. Here, for example, in Lasicius' inventory of gods, we find two "fertility" goddesses compared:

> Sunt etiam deae, *Zemina* terrestris, *Austheia* apum, Vtraque incrementa facere creduntur.
>
> There are as well goddesses: *Zemina*—goddess of the earth; and *Austheia*—goddess of the bees; it is believed that both of them promote growth (as well as multiplication, propagation).[1]

The first task for the mythologist encountering a Latin theonym with a Renaissance spelling is to attempt to reconstruct its Lithuanian form. Savukynas, reviewing an edition of *De diis samagitarum*[2] appearing in Vilnius, analyzes the characteristics of this spelling, objecting with some justification to the production of nonexistent gods when the principles of orthography are not taken into consideration. The proper name *Austheia*, as he correctly notes, may be read in two ways: as *Auštėja*, comparing it with *auščioti, aušouti* "to gossip" "to talk," or as *Austėja*, connecting it with *austyti*, "to open and close the door." He chooses *Auštėja* as a more reliable variant, taking into account the "semantics of the image."

While fully agreeing that the "semantics of the image" in this case has decisive significance, we, conversely, choose the *Austėja* variant for similar reasons, but especially since we understand "semantics" to involve not only the determination of lexical meanings, but, when dealing with mythology, the utilization of an extensive mythological context. Here are the arguments to support our thesis:

(1) The semanticism of *Auštėja*, derived from *auščioti* "to gossip," at first glance does not correspond to the nature of bees: bees are workers and not gossips, further-

more, they enjoy peace, and beehives are usually located "further away from roads and from noise."[3]

(2) Conversely, *austyti* is the frequentative form of the verb *austi* [to weave], and the meaning of *austi*, according to *LKŽ*, is accounted for this way:

(a) to weave (a cloth)
(b) to shuttle back and forth
(c) to constantly open and close doors

All of these meanings have a common semantic nucleus—a zigzagging, repetitive movement, which corresponds to the gathering of honey, the flitting from blossom to blossom, the constant return through "doors" into the beehive, and finally, to weaving itself.

(3) The production of the honeycomb is stereotypically compared to weaving (comp. Išrašė raštelius (audėja) kaip bitės korelius)[4] [The weaver wove the designs as bees their honeycombs] is verified by an abundant inventory of riddles. Next to

> Sėdi panaitė tamsioj seklyčioj
> *Audžia* be staklių ir be nyčių (bitė)[5]
> *Neaustas*, neverptas pasidaro šešianytis (korys),[6]
>
> There sits a maid in a dark chamber
> *Weaving* without a loom or a heddle (a bee)
> *Neither woven*, nor spun, it becomes six-sided (a honeycomb)

which compare the work of the bees with *weaving*, we can find *sewing*:

> Smagi panaitė smagiai *siuva* (bitė)[7]
> Clever maid cleverly *sewing* (a bee)

and *knitting*:

> Gražios panytės.
> ....
> *Mezga* gražias kurbatkytes (bitės)[8]
>
> Pretty little maids
> *Knit* pretty little panniers (bees).

These are synonyms, which indicate the antiquity of this image, reaching back to a technological epoch in which people did not as yet know how to either sew or knit.

(4) If we glance to other Indo-European mythologies, we can be certain that the image of the bee-weaver is neither accidental nor "poetic," nor, as some of our folklorists would have it, "a figment of the imagination." According to the Greeks, for instance, the nymphs by teaching people apiculture, not only transport mankind from nature to culture, but also help them make another discovery—the weaving of garments which hides their nakedness.[9]

This extensive, and on the surface seemingly unnecessary, argument is provided not only for the determination of the Lithuanian name of *Austėja* but to illustrate the use of the semantic plane in the analysis of mythology. It helps to disclose as well the initial features of the figure of the goddess Austėja: as an industrious weaver, Austėja is both a *bee* and a *woman*. Here again Greek mythology is of help, confirming our inferences based on phrasal stereotypes: during the feast of the earth goddess *Demeter*, called *Thesmophoria*, the married women who participated on that day were symbolically called *melissai*, i.e., bees.[10]

Austėja—Guardian of the Family

Lasicius' text, referring to *Žemyna* and *Austėja* as "fertility" goddesses, continues in this manner:

> ac cum examinantur apes, quo plures in alveos adducant, et fucos ab eis arceant, rogantur.

> When the bees begin to swarm, people pray (to those goddesses) that more of them be brought to the beehives and that they hold back the drones.

Even though there are two goddesses that "promote growth"—*Žemyna* and *Austėja*—and even though both are invoked at the time of swarming, the objective of the entreaty, upon reviewing the text, touches on Austėja, who is introduced here on the apiary plane as the "only true mother of all the bees."[11] Without taking into account how things actually occur in nature—only the ethno-zoologic standpoint is of interest to us—*Austėja* here appears as the idealized mother of the bees, the responsible homemaker figure: first of all, she is not only concerned that the *families* under her guardianship—as all beehive communities are commonly called—multiply and increase, she also protects the maturing youth from the entreaty of the drones. We see that isotopy of the apiculture can be understood without any difficulty as a metaphoric plane with whose help the system of the human family is represented and conceptualized and within which the important role of the mother-housekeeper, responsible for the well-being of the entire family, is to be found. Such a "poetic" mentality corresponds, by the way, to the notion of married women—their place as homemakers—in the ancient society of Lasicius' times: "According to the *Statute*, a larger payment was made for the "head' of the woman than for that of a man. When she married, the woman received the keys to the house, which she carried on her sash, ruled and took care of the entire farmstead."[12]

Austėja and Her Surroundings

Before proceeding to a more extensive analysis of the problems associated with beekeeping, we must emphasize the closeness of the ties between the two goddesses as paired in our text: *Žemyna* and *Austėja*. These relations at first appear "natural": one of the most common epithets of *Žemyna* is "wildflower," and the little bee gathering honey in the green meadow, visits all the blossoms raised by *Žemyna*: *Žemyna* grows the flax and *Austėja* oversees its weaving, and so forth. The personality of *Žemyna* does not enter into the frames of this study: on the contrary, we can expect that a better understanding of *Austėja* will facilitate an analysis of *Žemyna* as well.

On the other hand, even in passing, it is impossible not to record the fact that the introduction of *Žemyna* and *Austėja* in Lasicius' text directly follows the mention of another pair of gods—*Lazdona* and *Babilas*:

> *Lasdona* auellanarum, *Babilos* apum dij sunt.
> *Lazdona* is the god of nuts, and *Babilas*, the god of bees.

We thus are dealing here not with a single bee goddess, but with two deities, who, oddly enough, although in some proximity to one another are not presented together, and are paired with two different goddesses:

bee, "air" deities	Austėja	Babilas
earth deities	Žemyna	Lazdona

Within the framework of this study we will attempt to analyze not only the differences between the two gods of the bees but also the reason for the separate pairings, in one case with *Žemyna*, in another with *Lazdona*.

Bičiuliai

The Auxiliary Kinship Structure

It may be common knowledge even today that "bees are men's work,"[13] that *only men*[14] may engage in beekeeping, and only *adults*.[15] To take up with bees is the same as to take up with women, so thought the ancient Greeks and, most likely, our Lithuanians.

The fact that this does not merely constitute a division of labor between men and women is indicated by the detailed interviews conducted by Petrulis in the regions of Merkinė and Dubingiai. They disclose a new social aspect of beekeeping not noted previously: "In the past and until recent times almost all beekeepers came from families in which there were *several brothers*. It was the *second*[16] who usually took up beekeeping"—such modest deductions are made by our folklorist, without looking for generalizations.

What at first glance appears incomprehensible becomes more apparent when the choice of beekeeper is inscribed in the general frames of social structure. The presence of several sons in a family could not help but raise economic concerns: with their coming of age, it became necessary, according to the historical and geographic context, for the brothers to live together in a fraternal group, or to apportion the land and each live in poverty, or if the older brother was to inherit the farm, for the others to leave home. To take up beekeeping [bitininkauti] under such circumstances meant at the same time to enter into relationships with other families [bičiuliauti] who had or who wished to acquire bees: "From among the group of brothers, the beekeeper soon found a place as a son-in-law."[17]

The rather extensive literature about Lithuanian weddings almost without exception describes this complicated scenario as the bride's entry into her future husband's home. It goes without saying that this is not a realistic but an idealized—even though rather frequent—domestic situation: if every family had only one son and one daughter, a kinship based on the exchange of women would represent a perfect functioning of family structure. The reality, unfortunately, does not correspond to this ideal model. This explains the existence of an auxiliary kinship institution called *užkurystė, žentystė*, or *įsodija* [uxorilocality—entry of the male into the wife's family], an institution which corresponds on the mythic plane to a model of relations which is created with the help of beekeeping. In our estimation, there is no need to search for causal ties between the relations developed on the two planes: beekeeping is not just a means of finding a wife, it seeks to attain, primarily, states of friendship, and from among people who have become "kin through bees,"[18] future sons-in-law can easily be chosen. To repeat: beekeeping, as the ideal model of auxiliary kinship, corresponds to *užkurystė* as the concrete, practical, and, more or less, successful realization of this model.

The correspondence of mythic and social structures is even confirmed by the following ethnographic fact now better understood: the brother-beekeeper, "leaving home to become a son-in-law, *would take the bees as his inheritance*,"[19] just as in ancient Greece the first mythic beekeeper, Aristaeus, having married the eldest daughter of the king of Thebes, consolidates his new kinship by bringing his honey.[20]

The Moral Code

The initial feature of *Austėja's* nature, which became more apparent from the etymology of her name and her brief characterization by Lasicius as a diligent weaver and conscientious housewife, primarily allow one to understand that the relations of the beekeeper [bičiulis, bičiuolis, sebrinas] to the bees, who represent the female sex, are not of a flirtatious nature, but the opposite, bees and their goddess *Austėja* correspond to the portrait of the married, mature revered wife-mother. This can first be observed from the behavior of the beekeeper during the gathering of honey: the Greek *melissa* cannot stand any smell, fragrant or repulsive, reminiscent of a courtesan, thus obligating the Greek beekeeper before collecting honey to shave his head, in order to remove even the smallest hint of smell or aroma.[21] So too is it with our Lithuanian beekeeper: "the bees love but only those with laundered clothes,"[22] and the beekeeper takes care that his "clothes be clean and not full of sweat."[23]

It would be a mistake to think that every man can be a beekeeper: "The bees themselves choose their sebrinas,"[24] and their requirements create not only the *brotherhood code* but represent with it also the *moral world of Austėja*, the guardian of family life. This code of friendship, based on the bees' dislike and rejection of the evil person, is created out of an entire series of definitions of "evil people": with the discovery of the traits of evil, as antonyms, the corresponding traits of the *good person* can be easily ascertained, revealing the ideal image of the bees' husband.

By grouping and summarizing Petrulis' ethnographic findings, we can characterize the *evil person* in this manner:

(1) First, the bees do not like *jealous*, or, expressed differently, *dishonest* people: "bees do not sting honest people, they sting only those that are dishonest; one must not glance at bees from the corners of one's eyes during swarming time."[25] The bees appear here as major opponents of witches and their servants.

(2) "Bees, being wise, cannot stand *angry* people," "especially those who don't get along with their neighbors."[26]

(3) They also cannot stand *stingy* people who violate laws of hospitality and neighborly solidarity.[27]

It is clear that these characteristics involve violations of *social relationships*: the beekeeper's code is based entirely on principles of social bonds and harmony.

The penalty code of the bees is more or less the following:
(1) The bees "do not go" to the evil person (at swarming time).
(2) They sting him (when he is collecting honey).
(3) They "suffocate" and die.
(4) They "do not stay" and fly off.

Greek bees apply this last punishment to the aforementioned *Aristaeus* when he falls in love with another man's wife—*Eurydice*, the wife of *Orpheus*. Here is an example which shows a partial differentiation of two mythological models—Greek and Lithuanian: while the Greek model underscores pure familial morals (the wife's faithfulness and the husband's fidelity), the Lithuanian, as we shall see, organizes the code of social values by developing the primary friendship dimensions of *bičiulystė*.

Bičiulystė

This new dimension of bičiulystė forms, it seems, one of the characteristics of Lithuanian culture. The moral code, which is determined and controlled by the beekeeper's relations with the bees—and with their goddess *Austėja*—is actually the code of social conduct, applied to relations between beekeepers,—it is realized concretely in the contractual form of mutual obligations.

To understand this peculiar interindividual relational form, we must first of all underscore the fact that neither the bees nor the honey they produce enter into commercial capitalism, which is characterized by a generalized system of exchange based on the circulation of money: until the beginning of the twentieth century, neither bees nor honey were bought or sold in Lithuanian society. While excess honey was distributed to friends, neighbors, and women in labor, as well as to beggars[28] on Christmas Eve, sanctions existed against the purchase or selling of bees because of the conviction that it led to failure in beekeeping.[29]

Therefore, the multiplication and circulation of bees was based on entirely different principles. If we consider bees to be wise and able to distinguish a good man from a bad one, it is normal for the swarm itself to choose its new settlement and beekeeper. Such a migration does not differ in essence from the young girl's marriage into another family: "kinship" ties are formed between two families—or between two beekeepers—which cannot be adequately characterized as "joint ownership of the bees,"[30] any more than the departing bride is property "owned" by either family.

In matters of marriage, as well as of swarming, the process of "natural selection" can be improved and ordered, permitting the father or the beekeeper himself to choose—or help choose—the addressee. "One becomes a *bičiulis* by gathering or helping gather a swarm that has left. If one wishes to become friends with someone, one would say, the swarm will soon come, there is a shortage here—get a beehive; if one is interested in becoming a *bičiulis*, one would ask to borrow a beehive, saying: 'Neighbor, let's be friends, lend me your little family.' "[31] We see with what care, with what baroque politeness, these first steps are carried out: the distribution of bees is neither their bequest nor gift; on the contrary, the bees' "owner" acts as if he does not possess the beehive, in that manner turning the giving of bees into a service rendered; if he wants to obtain bees, in turn, he asks "to lend him the family," underscoring with this borrowing the new obligations that are created.

These mutual obligations create "a kinship through bees" called *bičiulystė*: this is an implicit contract formed during the collection of bees at swarming time which obligates the participants to maintain the common moral code (reviewed above) underlying friendly future relations between them. Of course, practically speaking, it can be said that the beekeeper himself from the start chooses a decent person as a friend: thus the act of becoming *bičiuliai* is a contract sanctioned by the bee's passage to another party as a guarantee of its solidity.

Let us backtrack somewhat, recalling that beekeepers, from a social viewpoint, form a separate, independent, social stratum comprised of "second brothers" or "other" sons, who have no claim to the father's inheritance. It is sufficient to imagine that the bipolar beekeeping relations we have noted up to this point expand and increase, forming the entire fraternal network. We will be involved here not with individually paired friends but with larger or smaller beekeeper groups whose members are joined together by close ties of friendship. People say of them, "They are all beekeepers, they all come from one."[32]

The roles played by such groups of "other sons" during the Middle Ages in Western Europe are well known. These young men were ready for all types of adventures and fortune-seeking: the Spanish conquest, the colonization of Eastern Germany, and the Crusades are the most striking examples. The romance novels of Alexandre Dumas have made famous the seventeenth-century Gascon cadets—the Musketeers. The Cadet schools of Imperial Russia were organized on a similar model. It seems that a real basis exists for regarding our *bičiulijas* as the original social forms of Lithuanian feudalism: their existence, explained by the surplus of young men and their close friendship ties, makes it easier to understand what until now has remained an unanswered historical question—the causes and means of expansion of the Grand Duchy of Lithuania, which began with single *campaigns* to the

East and ended with vast territorial conquests. Recalling that Lithuanian "biciulewstwo" is known in the Slavic chancellery language already in the fourteenth century,[33] this hypothesis is supported not only by cultural but also by historical arguments. It is confirmed by a myth recorded by Stryjkowski in which the first Prussian king *Vaidevutis* organized his state in accordance with the example of the bees.[34] The explanation of *bičiulystė* which we offer helps one to understand the significance of the "system of the bees." What is of interest to us, of course, is not the Prussian kingdom and its actual system, but the fact that such a political conception in mythology could be referred to and conceptualized in Lithuania several hundred years ago.

Bandžiulystė

We cannot help but compare the concept of *bičiulystė* with that of *bandžiulystė*: next to *bičiulis* and *bitininkas* [beekeeper]—both synonyms for "friend" [draugas]—the same meaning is used, more or less, even today for the words *bandžius, bandžiulis, bandininkas* [herder], and *susibandžiauti, susibandžiuliauti* means "to become friends."[35] This comparison seems significant: while beekeeping is the "material base" of bičiulystė, the basis for bandžiulystė is considered to be agriculture. The pairing of *Austėja* with *Žemyna*, found in our initial text, is repeated here. This in part corrects our own deviation from the basic theme.

Banda [herd] is one of those ancient Indo-European words used to speak about the common—i.e., similar and different—cultural, social, and economic institutions of Indo-European nations.[36] The present, dominant meaning of this word is the cattle herd—"kaimenė," "keltuva." But *banda* also means "nauda, wealth": these two meanings, common also to the Latin *pecus* is reminiscent of a distant past, the Indo-European nomadic age of animal husbandry. *Nauda*, in turn, is understood as the total product of a man's farm which allows him "to make a living." Another subordinate meaning of *banda* is "loaf of bread," understood in the larger sense as the basic source of sustenance. "To live off a stranger's bread" means to be maintained by others.

Another meaning closely tied to "small loaf" is "pasėlys," referring to "grain or flax sown by the farmer's son or his younger brother or hired hand" from which the forms *bandžius, bandžiulis, bandininkas* are derived.

The structural meaning of *bandininkas* is thus similar to the arrangement of meanings of *bitininkas*: the bandininkas, like the bitininkas, is first of all characterized in terms of his ties with the land or bees, and only after that—according to the reciprocal relations with other bandininkai or bitininkai do the relations acquire the form of friendship. Bonds with land or with bees are not the goal in itself, but only a symbolic means to determine the nature of the contractual relations between two persons: "pasėlys" is neither the land itself, nor compensation in the form of its resources: at the time of the "agreement," these are only mutual obligations which concern the future. However, the difference between bičiulystė and bandžiulystė clears up immediately: while the relations between two *equal* levels of beekeepers who belong to the same social strata are established with the help of bičiulystė, the relations for bandžiulystė are *hierarchical*; they are formed primarily between the master and the herder.

Banda, as the figurative expression of such hierarchical relations, cannot but remind one of *leno, feud* (um), the characteristic concept of feudal land tenure of the Western European Middle Ages on which the entire feudal system of that time was based; the vassal receives land from his suzerain, not as property, but, at least in the early Middle Ages, as a means to feed himself; he is "kept" by his suzerain, taking on certain obligations in return. The noted French historian Marc Bloch has indicated that the structure of such feudal relations is not only characteristic of the ruling aristocratic class, but it organizes and orders all societal relations, especially, the relations between the landlord and peasant.

Bandžiulystė also differs from *bičiulystė* by the inclusion of the friendship bonds: while the bonds of bičiulystė unite men who live in different farmsteads and even other districts,[37] bandžiulystė unites everyone from the same village, even though the young men "belong" to different masters. As we see, these are two different forms of social organization, and it would be a mistake to suppose that all the feudal relations must necessarily be mounted on one spool. These fraternal bonds of *young men* eating the same bread, doing the same work, are reminiscent, for instance, of the Frankish *barons*, the free men of the early feudal period who settled in the villages of the newly-conquered land of Gaul—the future France—belonging to, or rather, obedient to a leader selected by them. The similarities in social structure sometimes are repeated in the lexicon: how can we not help but compare, for instance, our *bandininkai*, that is, "bendraduoniai" [who share bread in common] with the well-known French *compagnons* (a word derived from cum-*pan*-ionem, which also means "bendraduoniai") from Charlemagne's period, who formed permanent military retinues. This, in turn, is reminiscent of another Lithuanian communal institution, *bendros*—the word used in acts of state recorded in the Slavic language to designate the participants of peasant farms who utilized the land communally.[38]

The bond of friendship which united all the young men of one village and their military tradition persisted in Lithuania up to the first half of the twentieth century: in memories of my childhood from the district of Kupiškis, there was still an active traditional rivalry between villages. In the district of Prienai the ritualistic tradition of "battles" between different villages at appointed times—such as Easter morning—still persisted.

The existence of such male societies is verified in the Kupiškis district by the persistence of the *bundyninkų pautienė*[39] on the second day of Whitsuntide. On such occasions, the men of the village would erect their crosses (*Bundinykų kryžiai*); taking into account that such a cross in ancient days was called *krikštas*,[40] and that in the pre-Christian cultural framework this marked the beginning of an event of some sort, we cannot help but be reminded of the well-known "gegužės laukai" of the Middle Ages (i.e., all the rallies that took place between teams of armed men during the month of May [gegužė], when it was determined who was the enemy and which way to go in search of him).

Next to the military traditions of the village youth, and their preparation for the outings of the Bundininkai, we must add yet another of the events preserved and organized in Kupiškiai by the bandininkai-plowmen—the characteristic Lithuanian *corrida*, the bullfight.[41] Even though they are identified with Whitsunday—the date of the holiday for cattle—*bullfights* are nevertheless a test of valor of the men themselves, who utilize bulls especially prepared for such a battle. The course of the bullfight itself, the goal of which is to eliminate one by one the weaker bulls and select the strongest, presenting him as the *leader*, indicates that the bandininkai, in forming a brotherhood of free men, had as well their own hierarchic order and selected their leaders by the same manner.

The case of bandžiulystė, we acknowledge, is far from being definitively organized: historical analysis will undoubtedly enrich it. However, the average nonspecialist reader would be quite mistaken to think that hypotheses of this type are only creations of fantasy, that somewhere in the works of historians, for instance, there is contained a different, a more well-founded truth. It is just not so: historians of the early Middle Ages who attempt to explain the appearance of feudalism, its many forms and developments, find themselves in no better position: the small number of useful written documents, the difficulty of their interpretation, a few archaeological monuments, some dozen words—that is all that forms the foundation upon which historical events and theories are built. While this does not diminish the value of these works, neither should it permit one to look with skepticism when examining cultural traditions or mythological contributions.

Returning to the bandžiulystė, we must state that in both Lithuanian encyclopedias—*Lietuvių Enciklopedija* (Boston) and *Mažoji Enciklopedija* (Vilnius)—there is a confusion of two different social institutions: *brolava*, composed of married brothers, unmarried sisters, and nephews (brothers' sons) living in one place, with *avelinė bičiulystė*, to which we will return later, though briefly, after first becoming acquainted with the ethno-cultural status of the *avis* [the sheep] itself.

Bubilas

Babilas or Bubilas?

The name of the bee god *Babilos*, as recorded by Lasicius, corresponds to the name of Stryjkowski's bee demon *Bubilos*.[42] Both words: *babilas* and *bubilas*, according to *LKŽ*, mean "a fat, corpulent man." Both appear to be of onomatopoeic origin. However, the same consonantal frames: *b- -b*, depending on the vowel, allow for two "sound imitation" variants: *b-a-b* and *b-u-b*. *Babaliuoti* means "to babble," *bābaras*, "a gossip," *būbti*, "to buzz," and *būbauti*, "buzzing":

> Tai kad gražiai *bubia* bitinėlis. *LKŽ* (Rš)
> Viena bitis stipriai *bubauja* aulyje. *LKŽ* (Sr)
> Oh, how the beehive is buzzing.
> A bee is buzzing loudly in the beehive.

This sound imagery allows the selection of an etymon for the explanation of the name of our deity, but it is not sufficient as a base for the meaning of either *babilas* or *bubilas* as a "fat person." Therefore, the fact that *bubinas* is found next to *bubilas*—one can regard them as words having one root with different suffixes—introduces additional information: *bubinas*, first of all, means "a drone" and secondly "a drum" (comp. "His stomach sticks out like a drum" [*bubinas*] [*LKŽ*] Jušk). The coexistence of these two meanings is interesting because the combination of our etymon with the world of bees also explains its passage from an auditory to a visual image: bugnas [a drum] is not only a source of sound, but also a visual—stout, heavy—form.

Furthermore: *bubinas*, *bubilas*, and *bubelis* in folklore are treated as synonyms:

> Ant *bubilo* kalno su geležiniais jaučiais aria. *LKŽ* (Jrg).
> Ant *bubelio* kalno su geležiniais jaučiais aria. *LKŽ* (Ss).
> On the hill [of bubilas—bubelis] ploughing with iron bulls.

These riddles, whose answer is "the sheep is being sheared with scissors on the table," can be compared with:

> Ant *bubino* kalno su geležinėmis akėčiomis akėja. (*LKŽ*) (Jrg)
> On the hill [of bubinas] with iron harrows harrowing.

This is a riddle with the same phrasal structure, whose answer is "to comb hair": all three are based on the same "inflated sphere"—*tertium comparationis*—which in one case corresponds to "sheep" and another to "head."

That this "inflated sphere" can be specified and applied to characterize "a fat person" or rather one with a "paunchy stomach" is indicated by yet another riddle:

> Stovi šakės, ant tų šalių *bubilys*, ant to *bubilio* avilys. (*LKŽ*: LTR Antz)
> There stands a pitchfork, on that pitchfork a *bubilas*, on that bubilas a beehive.

The answer to the riddle is "man."

In our opinion, it is necessary to evaluate *babilas* as a variant of *bubilas* obtained through a contamination of a common auditory base, and accept *Bubilas* as a bee god—without discounting, of course, his "demonic" aspect:

(a) corresponding position of the *drone* in the world of the bees;
(b) manifested by *buzzing* [bubavimu];
(c) marked by *stoutness*, a corpulent trunk or stomach.

Taking into account that corpulence, and especially paunchiness, is even today an external sign of gluttony, of overeating, in our culture, the opposition between the two bee gods—*Austėja*, the producer of material goods and mistress of moderation, and *Bubilas*, immoderate user, hedonist, from whom she must defend her beehive and her bees—becomes quite apparent.

Shagginess

The archaic nature of the lexeme is shown by the fact that *bubilas* appears in *LKŽ* examples only in the figurative sense of "fat person," and, especially, that its nuclear significance can be reconstructed only from its use in riddles—where the meaning of words most often is no longer comprehensible in Lithuanian. This compels us to become more concerned with the comparisons between *Bubilas* and *avelis* [sheep] found in riddles. Next to the examples already presented, we can cite one more riddle of this type:

> Avis bubelė bevedama priėst (verpstė, beverpdama vilnas, pilna stov). *LKŽ* (Pr. LXVII, 34)
>
> Leading the sheep [bubele] to eat (spinning wool, stands full).

Next to the image of "inflated sphere," it is necessary to add one more feature for the comprehension of the figure of Bubilas—shagginess, which corresponds to the general imagery of the bee-drone, especially in that the word drone, along with its significance as a "male-bee," describes a man who "does nothing, lives off others' labor, exploits them" (*LKŽ*), all of which adds to the existing characteristics of *Bubilas*.

Ethnographic facts from our neighboring Latvians are of help here: "If a man's face, chest, arms, legs are hairy, he is called ''the father of the bees' (and) it is said that he is very successful as a beekeeper."[43] Hairiness in a male even today in our own cultural context is supposedly a sign of his sexual prowess. *Bubilas*' shagginess added to his immoderate consumption of food, only confirms a widely constituted mythological phenomenon—the frequent identification of the alimentary with the sexual isotopies, the metaphoric use of one to express the other. Such a correspondence raises no doubts when the issue is centered on the temptations that arise with as ambiguous a product as *honey*.

Sheep and Wool

The determination that sheep and wool can be used as sexual symbols in the Lithuanian context expands considerably the readability of ethnographic texts. Let us take, for example, the following description of an evening gathering: "In the district of Kernavė, as in other regions of Lithuania, women would gather in the evening . . . girls and younger women with their spinning wheels would gather in turn at each other's homes and would spin *only flax* . . . *Wool* was spun mostly by older women since *for some reason* it was 'shameful' for girls to spin wool."[44] The girls' "shame," conversely, appears entirely comprehensible to us.

It is becoming clearer what is meant when during the betrothal the matchmaker calls for the missing bride: "Dear mother, where is the young girl? We need green rue, flax blossoms, *sheep shag!*"[45] It can be understood why in the newlyweds' bed during the nuptials there is "placed a loaf of bread . . . or a *"handful of wool"*:[46] the explanation "so the sheep will propagate" is only a partial rationalization of this ritual. It becomes more apparent why "offerings to house spirits" are made during the wedding ceremony, after the covering with the *nuometas* [see below], that is, the final reception into the family (we would say: the formation of contractual relations between the daughter-in-law and all the actors that enter into her future life). This ritual is fulfilled when the bride is led from one actor-object to another; she drapes a sash or cloth on everyone in turn and similarly "bestows" a gift on the stove, gate, chimney corner, child, omelet, porridge, bread, *sheep*, well, broom, and so on.[47] It is significant that in the circle of all the intimate friends of her future life, only the *sheep* [avis] appears from the animals of the household, thus emphatically ascribing it to the activity sphere of the daughter-in-law [marti]. Therefore, though we do not yet have sufficient documentation, which we trust will be provided by cultural historians, we can ask whether the so-called *avelinė bičiulystė—bandžiulystė*—cannot be explained as a social form of friendship "among women," and not among men.

Bubilas and Lazdona

A return to the Latvian ethnographic sources again allows a comparison of sheep with bees: an official complaint from April 1796, for example, stating "that someone on the second Sunday of Shrovetide had let a *live lamb* into the beehive, in spite of the fact that the fence was sturdy and the gates were closed,"[48] can be understood only when identifying the ewe with the young bee drone [tranas], who threatens to lead out the entire apiary. *Tranauti*, according to Būga,[49] means "novum quaerere domicilium apum examini": thus not only is the concern about protecting young bees from the drones becoming more evident but so is the role of *Bubilas* as "seducer," as one who "leads one from the path."

Everything, of course, depends on the viewpoint chosen. In a rare invocation, a girl tries to persuade the beehive into settling in her rue garden during the swarming:

> Dear bees, come to my garden! Here with the blossoms, *bitinėlis*, come to my little garden. Here there are beds fit for angels, soft covers, you will rest.[50]

It is clear that this does not mean a desire to entice the bees—with whom she has no right to be occupied—but a longing for love.

This portrait of *Bubilas* as voluptuary and enticer—and outwardly, as corpulent and shaggy—appears to be sufficiently distinct to differentiate it from *Austėja*, and at the same time identify it with the *Lazdona* figure, paired to it in the Lasicius text.

The importance of nuts, especially in a community as yet unfamiliar with sweets, is not to be doubted. That it is a special delicacy somewhat comparable to honey, can be understood from one narrative about two gentlemen who argue about which is easier to satiate—a man or a pig. Thus striking a bet, they give some nuts to a pig, who having eaten its fill, refuses to eat more, while the man, even though he has overeaten, upon seeing nuts strewn on the ground, gathers them up and continue to chew.[51] It appears that man differs from animal not only in that he drinks whiskey when not thirsty, but also that he can still continue to nibble on nuts after eating: the nuts protected by *Lazdona* lead man to excess and cannot help but remind us of one of *Bubilas'* basic traits. It should not be forgotten that *Ragana*, kidnapping a child and preparing to eat him, fattens him up with *nuts* and *boiled milk*[52] so that his flesh will be more tender. We will return on another occasion to *Ragana* [the witch] as an authority on Lithuanian gastronomy, underscoring here only her ability to select the most delicious delicacies. Nuts, finally, are not just delicacies but also a means of enticement used, it seems, by the female sex:

> Not for the berries
> Did I ride a hundred miles
> Not for the nuts
> Did I look for you.[53]

According to Daukantas, during the entire matchmaking period "the mother nourishes the bridegroom and the matchmaker with nuts" and only during the engagement does the young couple "eat the nutmeat."[54]

The scope of this study does not allow us to delve deeper into the rather well-documented nut problematic. For our limited goal, it will suffice to note the respective functions of *Bubilas* and *Lazdona*: while *Bubilas* appears as a virile, active and even aggressive enticer and gourmand, the role of *Lazdona* is to provide the female sex with a passive means of enticement—the nut.

Martavimas

Offerings to Austėja

In Juška's *Svotbinė Rėda*, one of the basic wedding episodes is described in this manner:

> After the banquet the bride goes from the table to the middle of the floor. She drinks *mead* or wine and then *tosses the drink toward the ceiling*, after which she dances with the groom. After dancing three times round, they kiss and sit at the table.[55]

The general significance of this ritual is rather clear in the syntagmatics of the wedding, where it is inscribed after the nuptials and after the placement of the nuometas, at which time the bride, surrounded by representatives of both families, crosses from one "state" to another. Thus, the coming out of the bride by herself to the middle of the floor to dance with the groom is the official public announcement of the newly created family to all participants at the wedding—relatives and village community. The ritual drink of mead or wine becomes even more significant (the wine here is a mixture of the juice of apples,[56] whose significance is well-known to us, with mead) as is its tossing toward the ceiling. The commentators of *Svotbinė Rėda*, turning their attention to this "characteristic act," note that "the ritual is peculiar to the newlyweds," and attempt to explain it by comparing the tossing upward with the washing of the bride's feet or throwing beer into someone's eyes during the betrothal. Such an explanation, which searches for a common denominator in the spilling of *liquid*, and not in the semantics of the ritual, tells us nothing. The thoroughness of the commentators, however, is indefatigable: they note in their final observation that "in recent times, the tossing of water or drink from a glass upward occurs before the departure to the wedding or the husband's part of the country."[57] The fact of such a tossing to the ceiling is thus registered not as specific to newlyweds; it is inscribed in another, though similar, place in the wedding text which marks the bride's separation from the family.

Not being content with the wedding rituals only, but reviewing as well the data on childbirth, we find a description of the christening feast in which "the master himself toasts everyone from the first one to the last. And each one, drinking his portion, had to leave a drop in his glass and jumping up *toss it to the ceiling*:

> Vivat, may you live for the next hundred years! And after a hundred years may there be as many children! Vivat, so may it be![58]

The same ritual tossing, accompanied by wishes for a large family, differs from the spilling of the banalized drink—degtinė [a distilled spirit] which starts the wedding dance.

A third similar document encountered by accident describes the same spilling gesture and again in a different context—during *apsėdai*. This is, as we know, one of the late phases in the matchmaking process, at which time "the young girl with her closest friend receives the bridegroom, each one sitting on either side of him" (LKŽ). Again, this ritual has a public character: the matchmaker after reaching an agreement with the parents is speedily dispatched to the neighborhood to invite not only the girlfriend but more witnesses:

> Soon one who is braver tosses the *drink in the glass to the ceiling* and says, "May the bees jump better!!"[59]

Moving from the wedding to the christening, and returning to "the betrothal," we find the same ritual tossing upward to the ceiling: while it appears at the wedding as an isolated phenomenon, by widening the horizons somewhat, it becomes a general stereotypic Lithuanian ritual. Comparing the three descriptions, we lose on the way the aforementioned *mead* at the wedding, which has been changed to a banal distilled spirit, or an unspecified drink: meanwhile we know that the use of mead at these occasions had been diffused throughout Lithuania in the past. Conversely, in the last description we find the mythic intent of this ritual—it is used to urge the *bees to jump*.

Taking into account (a) that all these ceremonies are tied to the young girl's passage to womanhood status, (b) that *Austėja*, as we observed, is the goddess who protects pregnant married women, and (c) that the ritual gesture itself is associated with mead and *bees*, we have some basis for interpreting this ritual spilling as an offering to the goddess *Austėja*.

On the other hand, if we recall the already noted close proximity of *Austėja* and *Žemyna* as "promoters of growth," together with the fact that offerings to *Žemyna*, the "earth" deity, are made in the form of a drink spilled to the ground, we can say with some confidence that it is to *Austėja*, an "air" deity, that offerings are made to the *air*, the ceiling. The participation of this fertility goddess in the festivities explains as well the *jumping* mentioned repeatedly by all the texts: in the first case, the offered mead is spilled before the wedding dance, then during the christening each guest "rising up" tosses the drink, and finally, during the reception of the young girls it is also done so that "the bees jump better." This is one more contribution to the sexual, fertility symbolism.

"When We Were Young Brides"

The close ties we have noted between Austėja and the ceremonies which mark women's change in social and domestic status—betrothal, wedding, christening—compel us to look a little closer at the institution of *martavimas*. The word *marti* in Lithuanian has two separate basic meanings: *marti* refers both to a married woman from the viewpoint of her husband's family (along with šešuras [father-in-law], anyta [mother-in-law], dieveris [brother-in-law], moša [sister-in-law]), and to a member of the female sex who belongs to a certain age group.

The determination of age boundaries for this group will require additional explanation. According to *LKŽ*, the word *marti*, used in this second sense, in turn joins the woman who is called by that name to three separate time periods in her life, one following another.

(a) First of all, a girl is called *marti* when she is of marriageable age, a future bride:

Suaugs dukrelė martaudama, pražydės rutelė kvietkaudama LTR (Pn).

My daughter will grow up while being a *marti*, the rue will blossom while flowering.

(b) *Marti* is also a woman who is already married, spending her first days at her husband's house, still as a guest:

Jau gana apsimartavai, martele, rytoj darban—rugių piauti (MI.)

Enough time as a *marti*, dear daughter-in-law; tomorrow to work—to reap the rye.

(c) *Marti* continues to be used for a married woman up to the time she delivers her first child:

Ji ilgai martavo: apsiženinus per aštuonis metus neturėjo vaikų. (Auk.)

She was a *marti* for a long time; married for eight years without children.

Without taking into account the alternation as to place and time and the presence of various partial synonyms—the meaning of *martavimas* in (a) is *mergavimas* [maidenhood], elsewhere *nuotakavimas* [bridehood]—it can be easily noted that *martavimas* is actually one entire period in the life of a woman, divided into three separate phases, and that the passage from one phase to another is marked by ceremonies into which enters the already mentioned tossing of the mead toward the ceiling as an offering to *Austėja*, in whose final guardianship the woman will be at the end of the period of martavimas, i.e., with the birth of her first child.

This ritual passage from one stage of life to another is stressed even more on the plane of vestimentary culture by changes in the head adornments. Martavimas begins right after the engagement (or after the first banns) and is publicly marked by the wearing of a garlanded *wreath*: "during *mergavimas* the bride-to-be walks about daily with decorations of rue, a wreath and ribbons on her head . . . during the first banns, she does not go to church but remains at home, and during the second and third, going to church with her bridesmaid, decorated with *rue*, a *wreath* and *ribbons*, she prays fervently."[60] In the wedding ritual, as everyone knows, after the removal of the wreath, one of the basic scenes is called *martuotuvės*—it is characterized by the unbraiding of the hair and the placing of the *nuometas*. Finally, the bride enters the status of the female sex when "riding to church for the first time after the christening, the mother places on the marti, not a *nuometas*, that beautifully sewn head-covering with a side veil, but a *mutura* (originally, *moteres* [woman]), which is a billowing linen scarf, with the ends hanging down the back."[61]

Thus, beginning her life as a girl with *braids*, she changes to a garlanded marti wearing a *wreath*, then—to a marti wearing a nuometas, and finally she attains the last significant stage in her life as a woman wearing a *muturas*.

It is noteworthy that such a concept of the development of woman's life is common to both the Lithuanians and the ancient Greeks: the word *numphē*—the marti in Greek which marks the intermediate position between *corē*—girl, and *mētēr*—woman, refers not only to the fully mature girl preparing for marriage as in Lithuanian, but also to the bride up to when she gives birth to her first child, at which point she finally becomes accepted into her new family.[62]

All our observations can be summed up in the form of a chart:

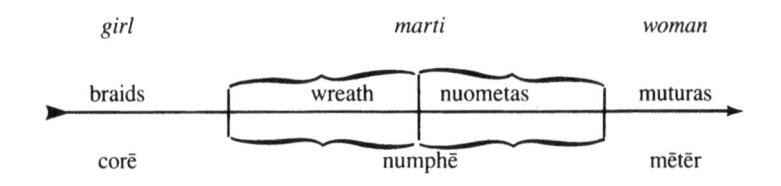

girl	marti		woman
braids	wreath	nuometas	muturas
corē	numphē		mētēr

The Blood of the Marti

There is one more episode recorded in the wedding ceremonies that is of interest to us, and which occurs most often after the placement of the *nuometas* (and rarely before the wreath is removed) widely attested to in Lithuania Minor, and of an unquestionably archaic nature—this is the drinking of the *tears of the marti*[63] or, by another name, the *blood of the marti*:[64] "At midnight when the wreath is removed they drink the tears of the marti. Zuponė ties the mutura on the bride and greets her as a young woman. The husband's mother presents a chestnut full of the tears of the bride."[65] The composition of this drink has changed, it appears, with time: the most modern texts say that it is "a cherry or plum brandy" or "an ordinary mixture of a distilled spirit with sugar and cherry juice," while older sources describe it as a mixture of a distilled spirit and *honey* (Glagau) or a drink composed of a distilled spirit, raisins, and *honey* (Gisevius).

The appearance of honey in the composition of this drink is not surprising since its ritual nature is underscored by the fact that it is drunk not out of goblets or glasses but out of a *bowl* from which every participant at the wedding takes and drinks a *spoonful*.[66] The introduction of such a beverage differentiates it from the other common refreshments and points to the dominant ritual role of honey.

The metaphoric term for the drink as the *tears of the marti* creates no difficulties: it is drunk to mark the bride's passage to a new status, a transformation which is beautifully expressed in the following stanza of the song:

> These dear apples are Sorrows
> But the little nuts are Tears.
> But the little nuts are Tears.[67]

As we see, this is the passage from the guardianship of *Lazdona* to that of *Austėja*.

More interesting is the symbolism of the distilled spirit [degtinė] diluted with honey as the bride's blood: that this is not just an accidental metaphor based, for example, on a similarity in color, is indicated by a document which describes the carrying and distribution by spoonfuls of the blood of the marti to the guests, ending with the final observation: "Tep bov marti papiaut."[68] [Thus the bride was slain]. The honey-blood which the bride brings to the new family not only is given to her future husband, but is distributed among everyone, becomes the property of the whole family. Furthermore, just as the nuts of the *marti* are destined to change to *tears*, so her honey-blood must cease being the object of pleasure and become the means for propagation of the family. We will return to this problematic somewhat later.

The Christening

Similar to the tossing of mead to the ceiling for *Austėja* is the description of the events of the christening day which echo the wedding ritual: on the second day of the christening, one of the godmothers "takes a tin *bowl, full of honey with raisins and distilled spirit,* and accompanied by another godmother goes around the cottage with a song, first addressing the child's godfather (and later in turn the other participants), until they all have received gifts. The presenter gets to taste the *spoon* from the bowl and some cake as well."[69] Just as during the wedding, where the distribution of such a drink is inscribed next to the placement of the *nuometas*, so at christening time this ritual is accompanied by the final step into the female estate—the placement of the *muturas* on the first Sunday after the christening on the way to church, i.e., the first appearance in public. Even though the drink itself is not named—at least in texts known to us—concerning the tears of the bride, or her blood, there is no doubt that it is the same ritual drink, that its significance is similar, that is, on the symbolic plane, a relinquishing of the honey which characterizes the bride and its distribution to the community into which the woman is finally received.

Taking into consideration this drink (together, of course, with *plūdynė*, a mixture drunk during lying-in, composed of distilled spirit boiled with pepper, honey, and butter), it is understandable why, as the date of the delivery approached, the need for honey became so paramount, why "women from families without beekeepers would at such a time, *at any cost*, make every effort to obtain some."[70]

Lalavimas

In order to proceed further with the analysis based on a hypothesis of three thresholds that organize the passage of young girls to womanhood, it will be necessary to attempt to find the ritual of the "tears of the marti"—or rather, some other type of drink associated with honey—which marks her elevation to the ranks of the daughters-in-law at the moment of the "placing of the wreath." This question must not be posed on the individual plane of "crowning" involving a particular girl, that is, on the betrothal plane according to our custom—this is fulfilled by the ritual of the tossing of mead to the ceiling during the reception by the two girls—but at the level of the social acknowledgment of her "suitability for marriage," the introduction of her as a new marti into the social stratum of marčios [pl.].

Since such a ritual should be manifested with the distribution of the drink made with honey, the first analytic step is to review the data concerning beekeeping, searching there for more prominent dates as to the use of honey. There are two such dates: Christmas Eve, when honey is distributed to beggars—a ritual not applicable to any problem in our text—and Easter, about which we know only that, as late as the first part of the twentieth century in Dzukija, something called "Easter mead"[71] was prepared each fall. We have found so far no record of the drinking of Easter mead in any Easter rituals.

Easter, then, insofar as it concerns our theme, is only interesting in that, in the context of the Christian calendar, it marks the end of Lent, a period during which weddings are forbidden. In this sense it echoes Užgavėnės [Shrovetide] as a time appropriate for marriage and representing the last hope for marriage for that year: *atlikti ant rugienių šiaudų, palikti razienoms grėbstyti* [to remain on the rye haulm, to rake stubble] according to *LKŽ* means "not to get married until Shrovetide":

Visos mergos šiemet liks ant rugienių (Rgv.).

All the girls this year will remain [girls] until the rye [fields are] stubble.

Jei šiemet atlikai ant rugienių, tai jau ir nebeapsiženysi. (Rgv.)

If this year you've remained until the rye [fields are] stubble, then you won't get married.

One widely-known Shrovetide custom is the teasing of the old maids; everything takes place as if Shrovetide marked the end of the year by which time an entire marti class—and not individual girls—should have been married.

A conclusion presents itself: Easter is just that starting date which marks the season during which all "suitable" girls must be married; it is a day in whose context one can search for the ritual elements of the "elevation to the ranks of the daughters-in-law." The customs of *lalavimas* [serenading] are suited for this purpose (later partially confused with the customs of *kiaušiniavimas* [egg hunt] and with some of our folklorists additionally confused): "From the first evening of the holiday until the morning of the second day, the singers (mostly *unmarried men*) walked about with a musician, from courtyard to courtyard, greeting the farmers with orations and songs, wishing them good fortune and asking for gifts. *They wished marriage for the unmarried girls.*"[72] This encyclopedic summary, which represents the confusion of two rituals, is supplemented by the description of Skruodenis' research in the district of Merkinė about "lalinkas," i.e., the serenading songs: "They were sung by *male serenaders to maidens* going from cottage to cottage during the evening of the first day of Easter. In the songs, the girl's youth was extolled in symbolic form, along with wishes for her to be wed, and with gifts for the greeting."[73] And indeed, reviewing the songs associated with the serenading, which are not abundant— folklorists naively call them "lyrical songs"—it appears that their subject matter is not varied, which makes it even more significant in our opinion: they sing about a girl whose garland the north wind has blown to the sea but which nevertheless the boy has rescued, receiving for that either an apple, or a blossom, or the girl herself; they sing as well, on a more symbolic plane, about the fallen golden dew, which the girl having gathered brings to her brother. The refrains of the theme are also characteristic:

> "Oh wine, wine, green wine."
> "The greenest wine."
> "Give me wine, green wine."[74]

Transporting ourselves from the twentieth to the nineteenth century and from Dzukija to East Prussia, we find there similar remnants of the festivities of lalavimas. "In the evening, the youths met in a group and went to *another village*, as was the ancient custom, to serenade. They met beneath a window of a landlord and asked permission to sing. When the landlord said 'yes', they started to sing this song: (here an example of a song is provided, whose second stanza, "St. George shook off the dew, ei lalo," is reminiscent of the Dzukai themes as well as the fecundation of the earth on St. George's Day). When they were finished, the master opened the window and gave each serenader some *brandy* and cake *through the window . . .* "[75]

Before making an attempt to offer a conclusion of a more general nature concerning this question, several explanations must be provided to help elucidate one or another detail of the text.

(a) First of all, the East Prussian text underscores the fact that the young men of one village proceed in a group to another village to serenade: this confirms the descriptions of the serenading customs of the Dzukija region.[76] We know from other places that *Laima* blesses the marriages of newlyweds from different villages and, conversely, sends misfortune to the pairs that have come from the same village:[77] the relation between serenading and future marriages is thus unquestionable.

(b) The same text confirms the ritual, indicating that the songs of lalavimas—the Lithuanian serenades—are sung beneath the windows of young maidens, that the "brandy" with which one shows gratitude for the singing, is also distributed through the window. Taking into account the significance of the window as an *opening*, which symbolizes passage from one state to another, we can be confident of the archaic nature of the description.

(c) We observe, finally, that in Dzukija the refrain "some wine, green wine" corresponds to the ritualistic offering of wine in East Prussia. *Lalavimas* [serenading] thus differs in nature from *kiaušiniavimas* [egg hunt]: the former is "repayment" for the young bride's distribution of honey.

By appraising such serenading in the general mythological context, its significance becomes apparent: in conjunction with "valiavimas" and "raliavimas" (comp. valio! ralio! lalo! [toasts]), it belongs to the genre characteristic of all Indo-European cultures, *praise poetry*. Praise, to extol the glory of heroes, military leaders, and princes, is also a mythic operation, through which the person praised acquires additional strength, becomes qualified as a hero or a prince, with the condition, of course, that he accept and appreciate that praise, rewarding the poet-bards, who have distinct social functions in the society. There is the well-known Irish myth, in which *King Bress*, not disposed to reward his bards, lost his throne.[78] This mythic structure is encountered, of course, in all strata of society and in a variety of circumstances. Thus the spring serenade celebrating the beauty of the maiden and forecasting her fortune—her crowning with garlands and marriage—creates the rite of passage, which qualifies and elevates her to the status of daughter-in-law.

Clearly, such a ritual has nothing in common with the Easter of the Christian calendar. It was attached only later, because Easter corresponded with the start of the previously mentioned marriage season. This indicates, on the one hand, the utilization of the lalavimas themes during Joninės [St. John's Day]—into which cosmic marriages are inscribed, manifested by the fall of dew and the fecundation of the earth—and on the other hand, the extension of the Easter serenading into the rituals of Sekminės [Pentecost], especially the customs of *rytagoniai*,[79] which involve all the girls of the village as a group with their characteristic weaving of garlands, mimicking of wedding rituals, and so forth. Beginning with Jurginės—perhaps even earlier—and extending to Joninės—this springtime "martavimas" enacted by the young girls creates a complete ritual cycle which, with the help of individual customs and partial rituals, realizes the cultural model of woman's fate, the fulfillment of her life. These few collected remarks are only programmatic: they are suggestive of the fact that analysis of cultural phenomena of this type do not enter either into calendar festivals or in descriptions of the birth-marriage-death cycle, but form an autonomous cultural dimension.

The Dangerous Marti

In feeling compelled to analyze more extensively the three primary thresholds marking a woman's life—her elevation to the ranks of the daughters-in-law, her marriage, and the birth of her first child—we did not take the opportunity to pause at one very significant episode in her life when she, as *LKŽ* notes, already married, spends her first days as a guest in her husband's house. This period, known to all from a borrowed word as "honeymoon," although brief, is unquestionably quite significant: this is a transitional time when the bride, under the influence of *Bubilas*, having been coaxed from her parent's house, has several days in which to cross over to the guardianship of *Austėja*, who provides her with the abstemious and responsible ideal of the homemaker. This is a time of inner contradiction and destabilization.

This period begins ritualistically with the greeting ceremony of the newlyweds, at which time the parents *anoint the bride's lips with honey*,[80] thus "sweetening" the bride and emphasizing the sexual functions that await her. Therefore, in the final phase of the wedding, which has lasted a few days, when the father-in-law's cake is being eaten, an operation is carried out whose aim is in strict contradiction to it: during the feast "the bridegroom's father *grows leeches* to draw blood from the bride's *passionate place*, and for that reason during the dinner he picks out white veins from the meat and places them on the table."[81] The significance of this ritual need not be explained: in spite of the "blood of the marti" which is distributed and drunk earlier, the danger which she creates for the community is so enormous that a means is found once again "to draw blood." Picking out the sinews from the meat, perhaps, is not enough, because as Praetorius had at one time described, after martavimas the newlyweds were given only food with no fat, and "they were not allowed to eat *any meat* on that day"[82]—this again is a custom which is reminiscent of one of the fasts of the Greek women during the day of *Thesmophoria*.[83]

The Greek mythological context supplements the Lithuanian data and allows for a more complete understanding of their deep meaning: during this "honeymoon" period the danger is that the young bride *numphē* will be not a bee but a drone (*kēphēn*), an *inverted* bee, carnivorous, wild, full of boundless longings, who desires only to gorge on honey, to roll around in that "honey of the drones," which Plato called all the pleasures of the body and the gut.[84] On this occasion one is reminded of the basic meaning of the Orpheus myth: misfortune strikes when the newlywed Orpheus, forgetting that he is Eurydice's legal husband and not her lover, tastes "the honey" beyond all measure, thus transgressing and pulling his wife into his transgression against the laws of gods and men.

The danger for the new daughter-in-law lurks not only in the excess of the newlywed's relations, but with the men in her purview, who cannot remain indifferent in the presence of this excited bride. Therefore *Svotbinė Rėda* clearly states the strict rules of behavior toward her: the placement of the nuometas is a sign of the bride and "from this hour on *no one can touch her.*"[85] We know that in Greece Aristaeus, gazing at the young bride Eurydice, forfeits his bees. It seems, however, that in Lithuania punishment for adultery was considerably more severe. Here is how Daukantas describes the punishment of the guilty for the "violation" of someone else's bees: "Those who had broken into someone else's beehives in the farm or forest had their navels nailed to the hive or hollow, after which they were beaten and driven around until their intestines were all wound around."[86]

In such a context, the presence of two bee deities—*Bubilas* and *Austėja*—becomes apparent and is justified; the differentiation of their functions is based on the contradictions of life itself—the inimical demands of nature and culture. Another pair of gods recorded by Lasicius and connected with wedding rituals corresponds to these bee deities: *Pizius* and *Ganda. Pizius*, as the representative of innate needs, and *Ganda* as overseer of restraint and moderation, correspond completely to the distribution of functions of *Bubilas* and *Austėja*. There is reason to suppose that these are merely the names of epithets of our bee deities expressed on the abstract plane.

Marčios and Laumės

The fact that the ancient Greeks referred to both the marti (*numphē*) and Nymphs by one and the same name cannot help but raise our interest in a question that is of direct concern to us: do the Lithuanian marčios [pl.] and laumės [fairies], even if called by different names, share any similarities between them which would help explain, even in part, the character and behavior of the Lithuanian fairies, or their position in the general mythological framework?

From this standpoint, the pages which we have allotted to the analysis of the age group and social status of the *marčios*, it appears, will be useful: a closer acquaintance with them gives one greater confidence when comparing them with the *laumės*. The perceptible differences can be grouped under two basic points.

(1) First of all, *laumės*, as marčios, are young girls who are "suitable for marriage" but who remain unmarried. As with marčios, their basic preoccupation is the assembling of a dowry. Therefore the cloth they weave and give as gifts is without end, since there is no beginning and, once they have started to weave, they cannot stop. Their assembling of a dowry is without beginning or end, since *laumės* are *eternal maidens*.

(2) On the other hand, *laumės*, like the married but still childless *marčios*, long for children and love them dearly. Just as it is an honor for the *marti* to give birth to her first infant son, so *laumiukai* are the male children of laumės, who differ from the girl children of the witches. However, laumiukai are not "real" children to whom they have given birth, but rather they are created from bundles of straw—in other words, "inverted children." This gives rise to their desire to acquire real chil-

dren, by exchanging new-born infants with their laumiukai, wishing in that manner to end their *eternal state of martavimas*.

Next to the agreement in these two "lifestyles," which appear as characteristic behavioral traits of laumės, one can find additional similarities: laumės are fond of bringing gifts for weddings, they are interested in sheep, and so on. The search for similarities, however, does not enter into the theme of this study.

The attempt to interpret *laumės* as marčios does not in any way diminish their mythic, divine character: laumės undoubtedly are beings associated with water, who most likely belong to the lunar sacred sphere. Neither their glorification nor that of any other deity of a higher class is affected by an explanation based on social structures and institutional models that people wishing to understand the divine world apply to it. Next to the nearly universal application of family structure, the institution of *martavimas* can be utilized as one of the principles of organization from the mythic world.

VI

GODS AND FESTIVALS
VULCANUS JAGAUBIS

Ugnis szwenta, Feuer-Gott[1]
[Sacred fire, Fire-God]

The Labors and Festivals of the Gods

The reaction against romanticism that emerged in the field of mythology at the end of the nineteenth and the beginning of the twentieth centuries was manifested by an extensive verification of "lists of gods," by a search for frequently mentioned "actual" gods historically documented, and by the creation of such gods' official certification. Jonas Balys, who led this "cleansing" process in the area of Lithuanian religion, was successful in reducing the inventory of gods to several serious names which, unfortunately, did not create any religious totality.[2]

At the present time, in this respect, the tendencies in mythological analysis are moving in an entirely opposite direction. While not rejecting philological methods or the criterion of reliability of historical sources, mythologists today are attempting to understand the global structure and significance of a given religion, seeking to determine within it the positions of the gods and their necessity in different sacred constellations, considering their earlier or later mention in historical texts or the phonetic equivalence of their names to be of secondary importance. From this perspective, for instance, the names of the gods and their often repeated conventional attributes carry less weight than their activity spheres and their functions, together with the determination of the cults and rituals associated with them.

One of the urgent tasks for Lithuanian mythology at the present time can be considered to be that of a *new reading* of calendar festivals and of the rituals and customs associated with them. The data collected in this area are abundant, and Balys again indisputably occupies a leading position. However, "to read" etymologically in Latin means "to select," and selection depends, first and foremost, on what one is looking for.

The calendar festivals, as is well known, are tied to seasonal changes, and,

Gods and Festivals: Vulcanus Jagaubis 183

in agrarian communities, to the labors and concerns of the farmer. The work repeated year after year had to be carried out according to given rules and regulations; it had to be blessed and protected; its success was occasion to thank the gods and for them to rejoice in it themselves. Thus the perpetually repetitive cycle of work and festivals cannot be separated from religion: gods participate in them no less than people. Rituals and myths, liturgy and theology are not separable objects.

The degree of religiosity in different communities varies, even individuals who participate in the rituals understand or experience them in different ways. This especially corresponds to a Lithuanian religion which from the fifteenth to the nineteenth centuries—a time period which embraces historical sources and ethnographic data—experienced a constant, even though a comparably slow, process of degradation. The mythologist must act here as an archaeologist, evaluating the nineteenth century records of children's games or traditional pranks of adults as remnants of religious life and attempting to reconstruct their original forms and meaning.

Therefore the new *reading* offered here, by which means we will attempt to reconstruct the ancient figure of one Lithuanian fire god, linking it with the customs of the calendar and of work festivals which often preserve in degraded form basic elements of the cult, in large part is only a somewhat different arrangement of the material gathered by Balys and his collaborators and students. On this occasion, then, we must convey to him our deepest gratitude.

Gabjaujis and Gabjauja

In the section of *Lietuvių liaudies pasaulėjauta* [Lithuanian Folk Worldview][3] devoted to question of fire worship, Balys writes extensively on the cult of the guardian of the family hearth, *Gabija*, succinctly laying out in one paragraph the entire problematic associated with *Gabjaujis*:

(1) The god *Gabjáujis*, "deus horreorum," i.e., "god of the storeroom and granary," is first mentioned in Schultz's Lithuanian grammar (1673).

(2) *Gabjáuja* is mentioned in other sources, verified for the first time by Praetorius in the seventeenth century.

(3) Next to these two forms, the fire god *Jagaubis* is recorded not much later (by Brodowski in 1713–1744, and the Ruhig dictionary in 1747).

Setting aside for the time being the question of this god's masculine or feminine gender (1) and (2), we are in agreement, first of all, with Būga's statement that *Gabjáujis* and *Jagaubis* are two separate forms of the same word, depending on the manner of formation, as in, for instance,

$$\frac{\text{Gab-jáujis}}{\text{*Jau-gabis}} \sim \frac{\text{kali-bóba}}{\text{bob-kalys}}[4]$$

only adding to it, that the compound word later changed through metathesis from *Jau-gabis to Ja-gaubis.

Nevertheless, even though this explanation on the grammatical level appears entirely reliable, it leaves an open semantic problem: *Gab-jáujis* in various sources is characterized as "deus horreorum," while *Jagaubis* is translated as Vulcanus, as Feuer-Gott.

In a recent work,[5] Dumézil attempts to reconstruct the meaning and ritual of the early Roman fall festival called *Volcanalia*. This festival in the Roman calendar is fixed at August 23rd, not long after the gathering of the harvest and during the intense heat of the waning summer. Its aim was to appease the archaic Roman fire god *Volcanus*, by whose command and power fires were often started at that time—the misfortune most dreaded by the farmer.

We find a similar situation in Lithuania. Here, however, under differing climatic conditions, our farmer had to protect the harvested crops not from fires but from early rain by piling them into heated buildings to dry. Lasicius' text, written in the sixteenth century, is comprehensive in this respect: "Since due to the brief summer the harvested grain crops did not have time to dry out entirely, this job is finished inside the building next to the fire. (Due to the vagueness of the theonym, we cite the original.) "Tum vero precandus est illis hisce verbis Gabie deus: *Gabie deuaite pokielki garunuleski kibixstu. Flammam inquit eleua, at ne demittas scintillas.*"[6] The prayer, excerpted here in Lithuanian, is addressed to the god (or goddess?) *Gabija*, asking that he (or she) "raise the vapor," i.e., that the stones of the furnace would steam, increasing the heat, and "not allow sparks," which could start a fire in the crops piled up in the barn.

This text, even if it once again raises the question of the gender of the divinity, is clear and distinct, and we can determine (a) that the god (or goddess) being addressed is a *fire deity* who starts fires, (b) that his dwelling is *jauja* [in the drying barn], or specifically, the kiln, and (c) that one prays to him during the fall, after the harvest.

Other texts, without contradicting this information, supplement our knowledge about the cult of this fire god. According to Praetorius,[7] *Gabjauja* is worshipped at the concluding festivities of threshing, which are called, in later sources, *gabjáuja* (Viduklė, J. Jablonskis, M. Miežinis) or *gabjaujis* (A. Juška).[8]

Gabjauja is a religious ceremony accompanied by a ritual feast. It is thus most probably a religious festival of the village community, corresponding to the Roman *Volcanalia*, slowly changing, with the degradation of the ancient beliefs, into customs and games without religious meaning. At least its partial reconstruction is not difficult: the Praetorius description which preserves the religious meaning can be supplemented by folkloric facts which are not contradictory.

According to Praetorius, on that day, in honor of *Gabjauja*, a rooster was sacrificed and the farmer, raising a ladle of ale, would say: "Lord God, Gabjauja, we offer thanks to you, since we were able to cultivate your good gifts."[9] The text of this prayer confirms the relations of *Gabjaujis* with the people and his activity

Gods and Festivals: Vulcanus Jagaubis

sphere as described by Lasicius: the community, having asked earlier that he hold back his sparks and help dry the crops, now give thanks that he let them work undisturbed. The resources of the earth, whose utilization depends on the favor of *Gabjaujis*, become at the same time his "good gift" to the people.

The festival of Gabjauja, generalizing from the existing—though incomplete—facts, consists of several autonomous elements:

(1) The offering of a rooster.
(2) Meatless dishes composed of vegetarian food.
(3) The carrying of a scarecrow.
(4) The merrymaking of the youth: the dances and games common to festivals of this kind.

The Offering of a Rooster

The offering of a rooster recorded by Praetorius is confirmed by other sources, primarily by Juška, who provides the following example in his dictionary: "A rooster, kept in the barn on the threshing floor, *is killed to honor a deity during gabjauja.*"[10] Balys confirms this obligatory slaughter of the rooster with additional information from an entirely different region—Žiežmariai—citing a song of the harvest mentioned in Donelaitis in which "Laurienė su Pakuliene garbino gaidį"[11] [Mrs. Laurienė with Mrs. Pakulienė worshipped the rooster]. Consequently we must regard the offering of the rooster as a definitive religious fact.

The role of the rooster during the threshing period itself is also noteworthy: according to Juška, the rooster is kept on "the threshing floor of the barn" and "he is fed during winnowing."[12] Consequently the rooster is not just a banal object offered to the gods, he also is a metonym and temporary incarnation of *Gabjaujis* as well: he is cared for during threshing, and grain scattered during winnowing is given to him. It should not be forgotten that the functions attributed to the rooster in all of Lithuania, even in jest, are those of Gabjaujis: "May you burn down," shouts a frightened and angry rooster, or so his cries are explained according to the sounds [13] heard by the people,

Juška cites another custom, thrashing the rooster, whose religious meaning was probably no longer understood: "during *gabjauja*, i.e., after winnowing, the rooster who has been fed on the threshing floor is shoved under a pot; if he dies, all is well, but if he runs away when the pot is banged, then it's the rooster's luck and he will remain alive."[14] The rooster's role as metonym of the fire god here is rather clear: Gabjaujis is the god of the "contained" fire, and covering the rooster with a pot imitates the calm state of the fires during the time of the winnowing; with its end the rooster-fire is liberated since his care and restraint are no longer necessary (similar to the carrying of the scarecrow).

The killed rooster is consecrated to Gabjaujis with the ritual drinking of a ladle of ale and by a prayer directed to the divinity. According to Praetorius' information, the offered rooster has to be black or white and its flesh at the ritual meal is eaten by *men only*.[15]

The Refreshments

Without taking into account the fact that *ale* is a ritual drink, the dishes prepared at the harvest festival are characteristic in that at this time only vegetarian foods from grain using no meat, are prepared. If Gabjaujis is thanked for permission "to cultivate" the crops, then the dishes prepared in his honor make use of his "gift." This explanation, even though it helps us understand how Gabjaujis, being the god of fire, can at the same time be a guardian of the grain storeroom, is not entirely satisfactory. It should not be forgotten that threshing is the final stage in the processing of grain crops, and as such, is associated with the cyclic life of the crops and the deities that guard it. Therefore Balys' reference to the fact that the Lithuanians of East Prussia on the occasion of *gabjauja* would bake a cake in the shape of a woman, called "Bobasuppe,"[16] corresponds completely to the farmer's schema of religiosity: during the festival of Gabjauja there was occasion to thank Gabjaujis and to communicate with the grain deity, now changed in folklore to *Rugių Boba*, who was brought home with the ending of harvest in the last sheaf.

The participation of *Rugių Boba* [Old Woman of the Rye] during *gabjauja* probably reflects this description of an already desacralized custom: "In some Lithuanian regions at the conclusion of threshing, the housewife, having prepared the dishes, would attempt to throw the ladle into the loft or to the threshing floor without being noticed. If she succeeded, she then did not have to serve the helpers; if not, she would be *tied to a bundle of straw* by the reapers and could only be ransomed by promising them food with a keg of ale too."[17] It is clear that this performance in miniature was familiar to everyone from the beginning, that it was impossible not to provide refreshments for the helpers; therefore the mistress of the house bound to a bundle of straw represents no one else but the same *Javų Dvasia* [spirit of the graincrops] who promises to the people ale, which is prepared from the resources of the earth.

It is noteworthy that these vegetarian dishes, this pagan "fast," in the cycle of calendar festivals, is repeated at the beginning of spring, during *Garnio Šventė* (March 25) [Day of the Stork] when, again, only dishes prepared from a variety of grain are eaten.[18] This corresponds completely to the principles developed by Dumézil and applied to agrarian religious festivals, according to which the festivals of the same type or for the same deity are repeated in the annual cycle. The threshing festival and preparation of "goods" for winter, like that of the Romans, is echoed by another involving the "opening" of the seed bin, the inspection and selection of seeds for sowing—Garnio diena.[19]

If the chosen hypothesis is correct, then it should also apply to the case of the fire god Jagaubis: to verify it, we must determine if the figure of Gabjaujis does not emerge anew with the spring, assuming an already forseen position. Such an occa-

Gods and Festivals: Vulcanus Jagaubis

sion could occur, for instance, at the time of Užgavėnės [Shrovetide], which, under the influence of Christianity, became a variable holiday, but which earlier had been celebrated in the latter part of March during the spring equinox,[20] exactly at the same time—as if on purpose—as the now extinct Garnio diena. We will return to this question somewhat later.

The Carrying of Kuršis

Kuršis or *Kuršas* is, as we know, "a scarecrow made from straw and dressed in a man's clothes." It is carried to neighbors who had lagged behind in their work and is thrown at them "to scare and make fun of the reapers; the workers try to catch the pranksters and put them to work."[21] Just as with the housewife bound to a bundle of straw, so too in this custom we can observe a performance, choreographed in advance, as well as the degraded form of a religious ritual. We had just noted that the rooster, tended and fed during the threshing period, can be released alive and free at the end, since his protection of the graincrops is no longer necessary. We can easily imagine the ancient rituals at which time the statue of Gabjaujis was led out in a procession and his guardianship was passed on to the neighbors still in need of it.

Some Observations

The description so far does not offer anything new to the folklore specialist. It is meant to set out systematically the existing ethnographic facts, linking the deity itself somewhat more closely with its cult and at the same time placing itself indirectly against the traditional folkloric manner of tracking, in which the creation of a list of gods is considered a separate task from the description of "customs" and "beliefs." Concerning the examples in Dumézil's analysis of Roman agrarian festivals, we would like to turn our attention not so much to the possibilities of comparing *Jagaubis* and *Volcanus*—although this parallelism is mythologically interesting—as to underscore the importance of the problematic of calendrical festivals in Lithuanian religion. Generally, there is ample interest in these festivals up to the point where they correspond to the Christian calendar, even though it is known that these calendrical holidays—Shrovetide, Easter, St. John, and so forth—are only the most superficial overlays and amalgams of the ancient religion. However, with the start of summer or the approach of fall, these holidays turn into "harvests" and are commonly treated as appendages to the agrarian cycle. The example of the archaic Roman calendar more easily allows one to suppose that the individuation of harvests, their celebration by each farmer on an individual basis, is merely the result of religious degradation and Christianization of the village community, that our description of *gabjauja* could in ancient times have been a festival of the entire community, celebrated together on a predetermined date.

Gawenis

The Second Inhabitant of the Barn

It is odd, at first glance, to find at a different time altogether—in springtime, during Lent—a second mythic being living, it seems, in a dwelling provided for *Gabjaujis*—the *jauja* [barn for storing grain crops]:[22] I have in mind *Gavėnas* (Kupiškis; *Gavanas*, Anykščiai; *Gawenis*, Kossarzewski). It is even more surprising to find that Gavėnas, as we gather, is a spirit living near the furnace. It is said about a blackened, dirty man, "He is a real gavėnas" (Gudžiūnai, Kėdainiai district), "He is sooty, black like gavėnas" (Pagiriai, Kėdainiai district). He is also intimately linked to fire and its radiating light: "Gavėnas will damage your eyes" is an expression in Utėna, used to describe the sun reflected in a mirror; "Gavėnas is sharpening his knife" is said in Dusėtos, if someone reflects light in a mirror.[23] According to Kossarzewski, *Gawenas* is considered to be a "spirit or genie" who, at two or three o'clock in the springtime afternoon, begins to shine through the window (the author, rationalizing, explains this as actually a reflection of a drop of water or an icicle).[24]

We are dealing then with a mythic being, belonging to a sphere of fire deities, who chooses the barn as its dwelling and who raises the interest of the people during the time of Lent. Just like Gabjauja, whose name can be counted among those in the list of gods created by Praetorius called "Namiszki Diewai" [household gods]:

Žempatis, *Žemyna*, *Laumelė*, *Gabjauja*, *Giltinė*, *Drebkulys*, *Bangpūtis*, *Aitvaras*, and *kaukučiai* [pl.].[25]

Gavėnas appears in a similar but separate list, assembled two hundred years ago by Kossarzewski in "Bóstwa domowe Litwinów":

Jargutalis v. *Jurgutalis*, *Giltine*, *Laume*, *Galgis*, *Kukolis*, *Bubas*, *Baužis*, *Babaužė*, *Gawenis*.[26]

Gavėnas of Užgavėnės

The customs of Užgavėnės [Shrovetide] do not enter into the framework of these studies. They pose a very complicated problem. It seems that Christianity, in introducing a moveable period of abstinence and, by extension, a moveable date for the beginning of the fast, gathered into one tangled ball of customs and beliefs an entire set of festivals and rituals converging around two basic poles of ancient customs—the cycle of the new year or *krikštai* and that of the beginning of spring, i.e., the March equinox ensemble.

We will thus attempt to separate from the prominent case of Užgavėnės only the documentation which touches on the appearance and action of Gavėnas.

The Expulsion of Gavėnas

One of the most eye-catching customs of Shrovetide is the ceremonial expulsion of Gavėnas, "Gavano vorymas," long preserved in the region of Kupiškis. "A man dresses in any kind of long plain shirt, puts a sieve on his head, blackens his face with soot, and goes to the farms while others chase him with switches," recounts Balys.[27] What is characteristic about this procession is the fact that Gavėnas, although he is being chased about, is not whipped: his attendants' switches serve to protect Gavėnas from assailants wishing to sprinkle him with water. This ritual changed to a game should be understood as Gavėnas' solemn send off rather than his expulsion.

The second part of the ritual is no less obvious: "After driving through the entire village, Gavėnas undresses, remaining only sooty; then he is driven on a sled through the village: *he sits while others pull the sled*. Having pulled the sled to the edge of the village, they overturn it."[28] Elsewhere, as noted in Mičionys, a variant of the seeing-off of Gavėnas does not mention his overturning, but describes his being driven "to another street."[29]

Elsewhere in Lithuania in place of Gavėnas "a scarecrow made of straw" called *Lašinskas* (Čekiškės, Kaunas district) is driven about; the expression "to defend Lasinskas" in the figurative sense means "to go visiting during Shrovetide" (Barstyčiai, Skuodas district); in Akmėnė it is said that "from Ash Wednesday Lašinskas travels to *Kurša* [Hell]."[30] These citations indicate that the expulsion of Gavėnas is not just a localized custom of the Kupiškis region, but is a custom encountered in all of Lithuania, as much in the upland regions of Aukštaitija as in the lowlands of Samogitia.

Just as Kuršis is carried from the village with the final winnowing, so with winter's end Gavėnas is enticed ceremonially from the village with a retinue, and overturned at the outskirts of the village, or driven to an adjacent village with the hope that this year he himself will go to the place of the "disbelievers," to *Kurša*. In mythology, this often-encountered ritual is best illustrated by the African "dance of the hunt": the hunt carried out in dance acts as the authentic form of its mythic reality, and the "actual" hunt which follows is merely a repetition of the already realized activity.

The Battle of Gavėnas with Mėsinas

The other moment of appearance of Gavėnas is his battle in the *threshing barn on the drying frame*, which lasts an entire hour at midnight from Shrove Tuesday to Ash Wednesday: the duel ends with the victory of Gavėnas, who pushes Mėsinas off the frame (Kvetkai).[31]

This dual is well-known throughout Lithuania, even though the names of the protagonists differ somewhat: one of the fighters is *Kanapinis, Kanapius, Kanapinskas, Kanapickas* [hemp], while his opponent is *Lašininis, Lašinius, Lašinskas, Kumpickas*[32] [bacon, ham] or the already mentioned *Mėsinas* [meat]. The role of Christianity in the selection of names is clear: during the Lenten fast, foods are prepared with hemp oil, since animal fat and meat in general are forbidden. The beginning of Lent thus means the victory of *Kanapinis* and the defeat of *Lašininis*, or at least his temporary removal.

However, in this clearly Christian schema a rather unclear role emerges for *Gavėnas*. One possibility is that *Gavėnas* is associated with *gavėnia* [Lent] and with the mythic being who lives in the threshing barn at this time and who represents Lent. If this is the case then one must identify him with *Kanapinis*, the winner in the battle who remains to rule during the time of Lent: at least this is the explanation provided by Balys of the description from Kvetkai. Another possibility is that *Gavėnas*, ceremoniously driven out during Užgavėnės, is synonymous with *Lašinskas*, who departs for *Kurša*. In that case however, *Gavėnas* not only does not rule over gavėnia [Lent], but his name, one must suppose, has only accidentally been converted to *Gavėnas* due to the chronological correspondence of the festivities of Lent and of this pagan divinity.

Balys' description of the battle of Lašinskas and Kanapinskas indicates that it occurs in the granary [*klėtis*] and not on the threshing floor [*klojimas*] or the mow of the barn [*jauja*]. Thus it would seem that Gavėnas is mixed into this battle without any reason due to the unfortunate similarity of his name with gavėnia [Lent]. We are aware of the importance of the renewal of *flax* in the rituals of Užgavėnės: *Kanapinis* could easily find a place in the non-Christian version of these rituals as a representative of *Vaižgantas*, the god of flax and hemp. And *Lašinius*, using a flitch of bacon, ham, or sausage in place of a weapon, directly echoes the sow's head (or at least its ears) and *tail* which decorate the ritual dish of Shrovetide—šiupinys [hash]. Thus *Lašinius* probably represents another mythic being, in whose sphere of influence are found food products prepared from pork, the basic food set aside by the farmer for the winter.

Gavėnas Tumbles Head over Heals

The manifestation of *Gavėnas* at mid-Lent is more that of a merry pagan festival: "the village youth take an old wooden harrow from the garret and make a cart for him. Seating the funny-looking Gavėnas on the sled, they take him onto the village streets. Coming to a ditch or a deep snowdrift, they overturn poor Gavėnas, and then put him back on the sled again, drive him to another part of the village, shouting happily: ulia, ulia, Gavėnas has tumbled head over heels."[33] These rituals of driving Gavėnas about, as we see, no longer have as their purpose to drive him out, to separate him from the boundaries of the community: just the opposite, everything is done—and repetition of the action only increases its effectiveness—so that Gavėnas would "fall head over heels," so that he would change, or "revert," and, while remaining the same and staying in the same place, show another possible face.

And indeed, in the convictions of ancient people, *Gavėnas* during mid-Lent "turns over on the drying frame in the threshing barn"[34] and leaves there gifts for the children: "pastries and ribbons for the young ladies; for the boys he brings presents 'the Gavėnas cake'" (Kupiškis).[35] Having noted in passing the special care paid by *Gavėnas*—as in the case of *Gabjaujis*—to persons of male gender, we should underscore the fact that the magic act of Gavėnas turning over is not a local-

Gods and Festivals: Vulcanus Jagaubis

ized type of phenomenon but, like the driving-out procession of Gavėnas, a fact of Lithuanian religion: as a basis for that, we can posit Balys' allusion to the overturning of the already Christianized *Silkius* [herring] in the Viduklė district of Western Lithuania.

Therefore, even if we would like to agree with Balys, who perceives in "the expulsion of Gavanas" the driving out of the "winter demon," his overturning on the frame probably indicates his unified, though two-fold, personality. Gavėnas, the monster of the barn, turns head over heels and begins to distribute gifts to the children: we saw that with the approach of springtime he manifests himself as a "rabbit," as a reflection of the stronger rays of the sun, as a "spirit" smiling through the window. Just as *Gaubjaujis* allows sparks and starts fire but also protects the drying crops, so *Gavėnas* can change from a winter monster to a prophet of spring. Thus, his "expulsion" represents only a desire to hasten the process of his "conversion."

The Appearance of the Rooster

In Balys' description of mid-Lent, a rooster unexpectedly appears: "The Samogitians say that at mid-Lent one may eat a rooster without sin. It is also necessary to prepare everything in one hour: to bring in the firewood from the forest, slaughter the rooster, clean it, cook and eat it."[36]

Such a meal "without sin" points to the intrusion of an ancient religious element into the Christian context. Its preparation, however, is realized on an impossible "practical" plane and becomes a "mythic" operation reminiscent of the procedure for the domestication of the kaukai.[37] Just as kaukai with this type of operation are changed from forest beings into household beings, so the rooster during that time most probably is "converted," changing from a "normal" rooster to a mythic being fit for a ritual feast. A rooster appears twice in similar contexts: the first time in relation to *Gabjaujis*, the second time with *Gavėnas*, thus linking these two fiery beings even more.

Although Balys' entire description of Shrovetide is quite condensed, he mentions a rooster two more times in passing. To prolong the festivities of Užgavėnės, after midnight, the rooster was *covered with a trough* so he would not crow.[38] This custom, whose practical explanation cannot obscure the mythic motivations, again is reminiscent of the beating of the rooster in the overturned pot during Gabjauja and his release. As much in the one case as in the other this marks the moment when the functions and duties of the rooster—and of his holy patron—end and a new phase of their life begins.

This same end to the functions of the rooster could be represented by the use of the *rooster's hindquarters* to make the *šiupinys* and eventually to decorate the table: the hindquarters here probably symbolize the coming to an end of the existing season which is within the knowledge of the rooster.[39] The significance of *šiupinys* as the basic dish of the Shrovetide feast has not yet been explained—to my knowledge, analysis of the alimentary or culinary spheres in Lithuanian mythology has barely begun. However, the concurrent use of two meat ingredients in the *šiupinys*—pig's ears and tails and the rooster's hindquarters—is interesting in that it marks the intersection of two rituals and the cults of two separate spheres: the *earth* deity[40] into whose sphere the sow enters, and the *fire* deity to whom the *rooster* belongs.

We must hope that a review of the customs of Shrovetide, in order to find additional facts concerning the rooster, will help to develop and confirm our hypothesis.

Toward a Synthesis

Gavėnas—*Gab-ėnas

The aim of this study will have been long apparent to the reader: to compare and as much as possible attain complete identification between the god of the fall festival—*Gabjaujis-Jagaubis*, and the mythic being of the festival of the approaching spring—*Gavėnas*. From a semantic viewpoint, their essential traits are the same. The rituals and customs associated with them are either similar or uncontradictory. On the historical dating plane, two centuries separate them, a time span during which Christianity finally became established.

There only remains the problem of comparison of their names. Even though *Gavėnas* at first glance appears to be a word created in accordance with the Christian-Slavic *gavėnia*—Kossarzewski even offers to read into it the name of the husband of *Gawiene*[41]—its pagan origins and image do not raise any doubts and are acknowledged by everyone. The question of his actual name is therefore secondary and does not prevent us from considering *Gavėnas* to be the Christian name of the god *Gabjaujis*, thus closing the final page on this argument.

However, one can regard *Gavėnas* not only as a direct formation in accordance with *gavėnia* but also as a distortion of a contaminated authentic name of the god *Gab-ėnas*. Taking into account that the root *gab*, bound to fire deities, not only enters into compound words—*Polengabia, Matergabia*,[42] *Gabjauja, Jagaubis*—but easily takes on various suffixes, nothing stands in the way of our assuming that in addition to the names of the female deity "*Gabija–Gabelė–Gabikė–Gabėta*"[43] there could have existed a male series, "**Gabis–Gabikis–*Gab-ėnas–*Gab-enis*" as well.

The *Gabikis* form—in the sense of "evil spirit"—is verified;[44] the *Gabėnas* or *Gabenis* forms can be found in the deformed *Gavėne* (fricative "b" becoming "v" is a common phonetic occurrence), and *Gabis* (or *Gabys*) is an interpretation offered by Ivinskis of the crop-drying guardian *Gabie* mentioned by Lasicius.[45]

God or Goddess?

There remains one detail that belongs to an even more ancient time: the question of the gender of the deity under analysis here. The fact that there exists only the masculine form of *Jagaubis*, that *Gavėnas*—whatever the phonetic explanation might

Gods and Festivals: Vulcanus Jagaubis 193

be—is undoubtedly a male being, that during the feast of Gabjaujis only men eat the rooster, that "Gavėno pyragas" [cake] is given only to boys, and so on—are all strong, undeniable arguments which confirm his male gender. On the other hand, it is entirely possible that *Gabjauja* in some Lithuanian districts could be described by people as a female *Gabija of the Barn* existing next to the *Gabija of the Ashes*, thus supplementing her with additional guardianship traits. However, this does not change the male status of *Gabjaujis*. These are always secondary problems, which should not overshadow the more important question, namely, that of the representation of the male form of the fire deity.

Comparative Indo-European mythology can be of help here. We have already observed that *Jagaubis*, called Vulcanus in the Roman interpretation, is as much because of his nature, as because of his cult, an equivalent to the archaic Roman *Volcanus*. What is important, however, is not the search for correspondence between individual gods; such a method, conversely, can even be dangerous since chance is often confused with correspondence. Comparative mythology is important in that it clarifies related religious concepts, allowing the analyst to form models of a common underlying nature, which makes it possible to explain the problems of one individual religion.

The Romans, for instance, had two fire deities: *Vesta*, the beneficial fire of the family hearth and the public altar, was strictly separated from *Volcanus*, the destructive fire which elicited entreaties rather than prayer.[46] The opposition of these two deities, as we see, is underscored by their different genders. Indian religious philosophy, as can be expected, is considerably more complicated. Without going into its analysis, for our purpose it will suffice to concern ourselves only with the triple, vertical classification of types of fires which differentiates earthy fire [ours], atmospheric five (Vāyu), and heavenly fire (Saulė [Sun]).[47]

The Lithuanian conceptualization of fire is similar to the Indian classification: next to *Gabija* (earthly fire) and *Saulė* (heavenly fire, with which one communes, for instance, through the help of St. John's Eve bonfire) there is a place as well for *Gabjaujis*, or *Gabėnas*, representing the terrible atmospheric fire—Vėjas—of the Vāyu Kingdom. Kossarzewski's assertion should not be forgotten. He states that *Aeolus Zmudzki* is "dangaus žwieris" [beast of the sky] who—unlike the Greek Aeolus, who blows with his mouth—blows from his fingertips and nails "isz panagių isz nagun, isz pirsztu galun lejd wieja," living "diebesise ant ora"[48] [on the clouds in the air]. This concerns our fire god as well, however, since "Gaweanas pejli galąd, wieja ejn isz panagiun"[49] [When Gavėnas sharpens his knife, the wind comes out from under his nails]. Vedic texts thus help us to understand the windy nature of our **Gabėnas* by approximating him to another, somewhat analyzed, Lithuanian deity—*Aitvaras*.[50]

Matters probably are less simple, however, than they appear on the surface: let us not forget that *Gavėnas*, sharpening his knife, not only lets wind out from under his nails, but light as well, which reflects the rays of the sun: it would seem that with the spring "overturning," it at least in part crosses from the *Vėjas* [wind] sphere into the *Saulė* [Sun] sphere. Our hypothesis thus must be inscribed into the general Lithuanian *fire* problematic, the initial elements of which were assembled long ago by the noted linguist and mythologist K. Būga.[51]

Gabvartai

All sources indicate that *Gabjaujis-Gavėnas* dwells in the *jauja*, that *Gavėnas* turns over on the frame in the *klojimas*, that the mistress of the house prepares the dishes for gabjauja in the *kluonas*. These names for agricultural buildings have not yet been standardized in literary language and change according to dialect. Some of the buildings had disappeared or changed by the end of the nineteenth century. Hearing the names, the reader often has the mistaken impression that he understands the matter. It will be useful to write about the dwellings of our gods in greater detail — such a description could help to explain several mythological details. For this purpose we will utilize I. Butkevičius' *Lietuvos valstiečių gyvenvietės ir sodybos* [Peasant Settlements and Farmsteads of Lithuania (1971)].[52]

Kluonas or *klojimas* (Samogitian: *jauja*) is a building for storing, drying, and threshing the grain crops brought in from the fields. There is in the *interior* of such a building a separate area with a kiln to dry the crops, called *jauja* (Samogitian: *pirtis*). A *kluonas* with *jauja* combination is known in Lithuania at least from the sixteenth century through the mid-nineteenth century, that is, up to the spread of horse-driven threshing machines and until the abolition of serfdom, which forced farmers to give over three or four days of the week to corvée labor on their master's estates, leaving only rainy days or nights for them to harvest their own fields, necessitating the use of a structure into which to bring wet crops in need of drying. Such structures must be considered as corresponding to the ethnographic period that we are studying, whose sources encompass the sixteenth to the nineteenth centuries.

The social significance of the threshing barn itself, the largest building standing nearly empty most of the time, is immense. Not only were a variety of "harvest" dishes prepared there but, during bad weather as well as at mid-Lent, wedding foods were prepared there as well. The *supynės* of mid-Lent and St. George, evenings of dancing and games for the village youth, were also held there. One can imagine then that with the introduction of Christianity from Poland into Lithuania and with the ancient religion taking on a strictly village or familial aspect, the barn became an important center for religious practices: Gabjaujis, of course, was the master of the premises, but in the same place, most notably, a female *Deyve* — a large stone with a flat surface, covered with straw — was also kept.[53] *Javų Dvasia* [spirit of the graincrops] often settled there upon returning from the fields.

The *jauja* itself, as an autonomous structure, was most often situated in the middle of the barn (more rarely, in one of its corners); it measured approximately 6 meters long by 6 meters wide, and 3.5 meters high, with enough ceiling room to accommodate four big carts of grain. The roof of the barn was supported and the dimensions of the walls of the *jauja* were determined by two thick pillars called *pėdžiai*, reinforced with horizontal beams, or *sijai*: the entire barn roof, architecturally speaking, was held up by a construction of two or three pillars reinforced with beams.

Quite surprisingly the fact appears that these pillars, in the Lithuanian region favored by *Gavėnas*, are called by none other than the name of *gavėnai*: "Upon how many *gavėnai* is your barn built?" (Debeikiai, Anykščius district). "Three beams, so we'll need three gavėnai" (Kamajai, Rokiskis district). Not only are the pillars but the beams of the barn are called by the same name: "This year the crops were piled up to the *gavėnai*" (Svedasai, Anykščius district).[54]

The definition in the *Lietuvių kalbos žodynas* [Academic Dictionary of Lithuanian, *LKŽ*] which characterizes the *gavėnas* as a "post" seems to be not entirely accurate: the examples provided, for instance, indicate that for every beam one pillar is not sufficient, that *gavėnas* (or *gavėnai*) means not a one-pillar, but a two-pillar construction. The third example indicates that *gavėnas* (or *gavėnai*) could refer to either the entire combination of two pillars and beam or to one of its crosspieces — the beam.

The same *LKŽ* provides one more word, *Gabvartas*, which, without citing any examples but on the basis of the Schultz grammar, is considered to be a synonym of *Gabjaujis*. The same god — but in the plural — is mentioned by Praetorius: "Es haben auch die Nadraver einige (gods'), die sie *Kaukarus*, item *Gobwartus* et *Gabartus* nennen, selbige aber sind vorige *Kaukuczei* oder Erd-Götter, die ihnen pflegen viel Güter und Segen in die Scheunen und Ställe zu führen."[55] ["The Nadravers also have some gods whom they call Kaukarus, as well as Gabwartus and Gabartus. These same are the previous Kaukuczei, or earth gods, who used to bring them many goods and blessings into their barns and stables."]

The Schultz and Praetorius definitions of *Gabvartai* (or *Gabartai*) are not comparable. Since *Gab*-vartai share a common root with *Gab*-jaujis, we tend to choose the Schultz testimony and to reject the *barn* and *stable* and not the threshing barn [kluonas] as their dwelling. On the contrary, the second part of the compound word -*vartai*, is not used in the singular in Lithuanian: here the testimony of Praetorius and not Schultz (*LKŽ*) is better suited, the more so since *LKŽ* itself provides a separate word *gabartai*, meaning "grate," supported by a citation from Kudirka.

We can attempt to combine into one group the data from the two kinds of sources that concern *gabvartai* [pl.] and *gavėnai* [pl.]. Taking into account the specific construction of *jauja* installed in the threshing barn, *gavėnai* are nothing more than the apertures that are created by the pillars and horizontal beams in which the doors or gates [*vartai*] are placed to separate the *jauja* from the rest of the barn. Since the jauja is the dwelling of *Gabjaujis*, it is separated and guarded by the *Gabvartai*. *Gabvartai* and *gavėnai* are thus either entirely synonymous or two parallel structural elements of the building itself.

The problem of the mythical significance of *Gabvartai* appears to be somewhat different. *Gabvartai* cannot be a synonym for *Gabjaujis* but it is difficult to imagine them as "kaukučiai" [dim. kaukai], as is offered by Praetorius: their place is in the threshing barn and not in the granary.

Here once again comparative mythology can be of help. In the rituals of Volcanalia, Dumézil encounters two secondary female deities associated with the Volcanus cult: one of them is *Stata*, who is responsible for stopping fires, and the second is *Maia*, who takes part in the spread of fires.[56] Thus, taken together, these are helpers of the dual-faced *Volcanus*, and they do both good and evil for people.

In this perspective, the possible secondary role of *Gabvartai* becomes somewhat more apparent: due to their activity, of course, they are similar to the kaukučiai, who guard the crops from fire. The confusion introduced by Praetorius is not surprising. Nevertheless, it is possible to imagine that Gabvartai play a similar role as *Stata* and *Maia*, metonymically expressing the contradictory attributes of *Gabjaujis*: *gabvartai*—the metal grate which both stops and lets the sparks through.

While awaiting additional or alternative facts, the case of *Gabjaujis-Jagaubis-Gavėnas* can be considered accounted for.

VII

GODS AND FESTIVALS
KRIKŠTAI

The Midwinter Festival

Even a cursory glance through *Lietuvių kalbos žodynas* [Academic Dictionary of Lithuanian, *LKŽ*] shows clearly that an ancient festival celebrated in the middle of winter was called *Krikštai*, whose "Christianization," that is, identification with one or another Christian calendar holiday, did not occur without some difficulty. In the *LKŽ* entry on *Kriskštai* we find:
(a) Midwinter: the time around Three Kings' Day or the day itself (January 6).
(b) Day of Revelation (January 25).
(c) Mid-Lent (the fourth Wednesday of Lent—a variable date).
While the entry on Krikštai holds midwinter as "the time around Three Kings' Day," the entry on *midwinter* states that "Grabnyčios [Candlemas] is midwinter itself (Bsg)," while in Lithuania Minor "the 25th of January is midwinter."[1]

Some initial conclusions present themselves: (a) *Kriskštai* in the pre-Christian context is held as a midwinter festival, and (b) taking into account the historical and geographic alternations, an attempt was made to identify this day with one of four church holy days: January 6, January 25, February 2, and the variable date of Mid-Lent. Its complete identification with any of these, however, was possible only with some difficulty, in our opinion, for two reasons. First, the pagan feast day of *Krikštai* followed the Lithuanian lunar calendar, which does not correspond to the Christian solar calendar. Second, the purely "pagan" functions of this festival, which can be explained in the context of Lithuanian religion, did not correspond to the motivations of any of the Christian holidays enumerated above (contrast, for instance, St. George's Day, whose horseman was reconciled with the first herding of the cattle and the Lithuanian spring deity). Our brief study is based on these hypotheses and attempts to corroborate them.

We will therefore utilize the ethnographic data associated with all four Christian dates in attempting to disclose the meaning of this festival, taking into account only their eventual semantic congruence. There is no doubt, for instance, that the figure of the *bear* is associated with midwinter:

"From midwinter on the bear licks her paw" (*LKŽ*, Pc)—her behavior furthermore figuratively signifies the distribution of time into two—old and new—parts of the year:

> "During *Krikštai* the bear turns on her other side" (*LKŽ*, Ls)
> "After *Grabnyčios* the bear turns on her other side." (*Liet. Taut.*, V, 378)

Without investigating in greater depth matters concerning the bear, let us note only that her behavior corresponds in time to both *Krikštai* and *Grabnyčios*.

The Festival of the Beneficent Beginning

There is no explanation for the fact that this midwinter festival, which marks the turning of the year—and the bear—to its other side, is called *Krikštai*. For that purpose, it is useful to examine the semantic domain covered by the entire word family of *krikštas*.

(1) *Krikštinti*, first of all, means "to *start* something for the first time" (*LKŽ*):

> On Sunday we will start to eat [*krikštysim*] the apples. (Smn.)
> Last year, I planted a pear seed, so this year the leaves already are appearing, sprouting [*krikštinasi*] (Ls.)

Narrowing and specifying the meaning of *krykštyti*, it means to *taste* "to touch, to nibble" (*LKŽ*):

> You can't put anything anywhere, the mice will always nibble at it [*krikštija*]. (Trgn.)

Applying it to work in the fields, *krikštyti* means "*beginning* to stack the shocks by binding together four sheaves":

> Whoever will begin to stack [*krikštij*], will bind together three, four sheaves and stack them. (Krs.)

Therefore, *krikštas* is "one or several sheaves bound together into shocks; *boba, tripėdis, jonis*" (*LKŽ*).

(2) The abstract concept of *krikštas* as a "beginning" applied to space provides this root with another parallel meaning—that of an intersection, or the point from which two or more straight lines diverge. This nuclear meaning can be found in the following words:

Krikštas—"corner, the most honorable place at the table," as well as the compound words with the same meaning *krikštasuolė* [corner bench], *krikštastalė* [corner table], *krikštalangis* [corner window].

Krikštkelis or *krikšto kelias*—"crossroads" (N/K).

*Krikštavonė (hibr.)—"that which is put together crosswise, interlocked."

Krikštas—"a cross built to remember the dead or placed by the road" and *krikšto dienos* (SD 119) "The Days of the Cross (before Ascension)."

Gods and Festivals: Krikštai

(3) *Krikštinti* means to *improve*, "to flavor, to make tasty" when preparing something *before its use*:

> We improved [*pakrikštinom*] the pancakes a little; we added an egg, a little milk (Krok.).
> St. Ann improves [*krikština*] apples (around the time when the apples ripen). (Simn.)

Krikštas and Christianity

Such an explanation of the significance of *krikštas* as the beginning of everything, as the inchoative aspect of an activity, often accompanied by an "improvement" feature, supplements the concept of *Krikštai* as a festival: *Krikštai* is not only a midwinter festival, marking the changeover from one year to another, but it refers especially to the year's beginning, the year's turnabout to its better half.

Even a cursory analysis of this semantic field allows one to understand without additional explanation not only the expansion of the concept of *krikštas* ("a beginning," "an improvement") and the application of the word to name the rituals of reception in the doctrines of *Christ*, but also the ambiguity due to contamination of the word *krikščionybė* [Christianity] formed from two roots—the Greek *xrist*—and Lithuanian *krikšt*. *Krikščionybė* signified not only the introduction of "Christianity" but also the beginning of a new era "krikščionėjimas," recorded into the conceptualization of the natural cycles of time, while *krikštas* was understood not only as the beginning of a new year but also as its betterment. Even the basic symbol of the new religion—the cross—was adopted and understood as the sign of a new direction in life, as *krikštas*. This, perhaps, explains in part the comparatively minimal resistance which the thrust of this new faith called forth in Lithuania.

Kirmių Diena

One of the days called *Krikštai*—January 25—whose Christianized equivalent is the commemoration of the "conversion of Paul"[2] has another "pagan" name: *kirmių* or *kirmelių diena* [day of the snakes or worms], or, most commonly, *kirmelinė*, which *LKŽ* identifies as midwinter.

Our information is far from systematized concerning this feast day, whose significance must have been immense—on that day people "would shake the apple trees in the orchard, so that they would be more fruitful; knock on beehives, waking the bees from their winter sleep."[3] Without direct access to folklore archives, we know little about the connection of this day which, it seems, is dedicated to the snake cult, with the snakes themselves. In reading ethnographic texts, we had occasion to encounter the fact, for instance, that snakes in the fall, smelling a certain type of grass and going to hibernate,[4] are revived during *Kirmelių diena* and "come from the forest to the house."[5] On the other hand, sixteenth-century texts which describe the cult of the household serpents [*žalčiai*] and the rituals associated with them, are sufficiently exhaustive, although they do not provide for that cult any calendar date, indicating only that it occurs "at a certain time." A semantic review of one of these texts, as we will see, gives us the right to state what that "certain time" is, namely, either *Krikštai* or *Kirmių diena*.

We have taken the description of the rituals themselves from the Lasicius text[6] even though it is based in its entirety on a previous text of Maletius:[7]

> Praeterea Lituani et Samagitae in domibus sub fornace, vel in angulo vaporarij vbi mensa stat, serpentes fouent, quos numinis instar colentes, certo anni tempore précibus sacrificuli, euocant ad mensam. Hi verò exeuntes per mundum linteolum conscendunt, et super mensam morantur. Vbi delibatis singulis ferculis, rursus discedunt seque abdunt in cavernis. Serpentibus digressis, homines laeti fercula praegustata comedunt, ac sperant illo anno omnia prosperé sibi euentura. Quod si ad preces sacrificuli, non exierint serpentes, aut fercula apposita non delibauerint: tum credunt se anno illo subituros magnam calamitatem.

We present here a translation of the text, correcting somewhat Balys' translation of Maletius and Valkunas' of Lasicius. The basic correction however is in the introduction of the word *krikštinti* in the sense of "tasting," "beginning."

> In addition, the Lithuanians and Samogitians keep the snakes warm in (their) houses, under the stove or in the bathhouse corner (probably steam bath) where there stands a table (that is: a corner table).
>
> Honoring them as deities, *at a certain time of the year* they invite them to the table with a seer's prayers. Crawling out (from out of their sleep) they lie down on the clean cloth (most probably, hand towels) and make themselves comfortable on the table. There, *pakrikštine* (= having tasted a little of) every dish, they slither (to the ground) and return to their hole.
>
> With the retreat of the snakes, the people happily eat the dishes *that have been tasted*, confident that *at that time* (i.e., in the coming year) everything will go well for them. But if, in spite of the seer's prayers, the snakes do not break away (from their lair) or *do not taste* the laid-out dishes—then they believe that in *that year* a great misfortune will befall them.

In the translation we use the word *gyvatė* [snake] following the example of the authors of the past who call this being by its Lithuanian name (sim. *giuoitos* in Lasicius). This means that at that time the word *gyvatė* was used to name both the poisonous and non-poisonous reptiles as well as snakes "gyvatės" and serpents "žalčiai". The modern introduction of the term *žalčiai* would create a new opposition between *gyvatės*, the snakes which come from the forest on that day, and *žalčiai*, the household serpents.

This scene accurately described—whose comprehensive analysis does not enter into the scope of this study—is nothing more than a ritual feast to mark the festival of *Kirmių diena*. Its primary function is to invite the household serpents to taste [*pakrikštinti*] all the foods, one after another, laid out on the table. And *krikštijimas* in the alimentary culture isotopy which is especially important in Lithuanian mythology signifies the marking of the beginning of a new life, guaranteeing as well its successful continuation. There is no doubt as to the significance of a beginning as predestination in Lithuanian mythic thinking: the success of the entire day depends on how it starts (Lasicius rather extensively describes Jogaila [Jagiello], who having unintentionally put on his left shoe first one morning turned in circles for quite awhile on one foot so as to undo the spell of fate for that unlucky day);[8] the first song of the cuckoo establishes the course of the entire year; and so on.

Such an interpretation of *krikštas* allows one to ascertain that the "certain time of the year" (*certo anni tempore*) as indicated by Maletijus and Lasicius coincides with mid-winter and can eventually apply to the Christian January 25: from the blessing of the serpents—or from their refusal to come—depends the fortune and misfortune of the entire coming year (*illo anno*). It can be understood thus why *Kirmelių diena* has the right to be called *Krikštai*.

It is apparent that it would be senseless to talk about the worship of snakes at such a ritual occasion. Household serpents, as was noted by Erasmus Stella as early as 1518, are only "the beloved messengers of god."[9] This is confirmed by ethnographic data:

> Oh, you serpent, dear serpent
> Messenger of the gods
> Take me to the hill
> To the dear little god.[10]

By *tasting* the food, they only fulfill the will of god—or gods—as delegated to them.

It must also be emphasized that tasting the food by no means refers only to the blessing of food or promise of good luck in this specific domain. On the contrary, the food is only that metaphoric plane with which the *forecast* of the coming year is fulfilled, both of fortune and misfortune. This alleviates the need to look for a god in whose name the serpents fulfill this fate. On the one hand, the figure of the snake is combined with one of the primary Lithuanian gods mentioned by Dlugosz, whose Latin name *Aesculapius* corresponds to the Prussian *Patrimpas*. On the other hand, with regard to the function of bestowing fate and fortune, this Lithuanian Aesculapius, it appears, will be none other than *Dievaitis Mėnulis*, the moon diety.[11]

The Christening of the Colt

Another text, recorded some three hundred years later, recounts a different but nonetheless ritual feast:

> The Christening of the Colt [Kumeluko kriksztinos]
>
> Before Candlemas, the maidens pool their money and buy some liquor [arelka] which they stew and mix with poppies, hemp, and honey; they mash these *kamukai* called

cvikinai—boil the liquor with honey—and invite the youth (young men). The youths come on horseback and drink the liquor which is provided by the potful, and they drink all night and into the next day, celebrating the christening of the colt.[12]

This text—an analysis of the culinary isotopy itself would require a separate study—is accounted for with difficulty: besides the mythological explanation, it will be necessary to supplement it with several brief philological commentaries.

(1) The colt [kumeliukas] whose christening [krikštynos] is celebrated is undoubtedly one of the epiphanies of the New Moon.[13] If we keep in mind the non-correspondence of lunar months to the months of the solar calendar, then the fact that the christening is held before Candlemas and not on Kirmelių diena [Day of the Serpents] has no great importance. However, the fact that the feast takes place in the evening and that the merrymaking lasts through the entire night confirms the lunar nature of this festival.

(2) The drink prepared for the christening is composed, as we see, of two parts: a distilled liquor boiled with honey—a peculiar krupnik which is reminiscent of similar lying-in and christening drinks[14]—and kamukai made from mashed poppies, hemp, and honey, which together specify the drink with the peculiar name of *čvikinas*.

(3) These kamukai have a round egg shape, and *kumeliukas* [colt], in turn, is a word used for egg yolk[15] in some Lithuanian dialects: it would follow that kamukas is thus a metonym of kumeliukas, its miniature. If we take into account that kamukai are composed of poppies, hemp, and honey—roughly symbolizing happiness, well-being, and love—these ingredients can be counted as the attributes and signs of the colt and of his divine functions.

(4) The naming of kamukai as *čvikinas* can be explained in terms of the general disposition of the non-Lithuanian origin of this word family: **čvikas* is "the part of the pants where both legs come together" as well as "the pants' fly," and *čvikis* is most commonly known as "the cork."[16] Without further major reasons, it can be understood that the cvikinas composed of kamukai in our context represents the seminal pouch of the colt as the primary noble source of energy. The absorption of such a dish represents a characteristic communication with a potential source of wealth provided by the colt.

(5) It is not surprising then that this type of ritual feast is prepared by the *mergos*, that is, the eligible but unmarried women with whom the community places all the values of the third sacred sphere—love, beauty, well-being. The village youth greet and receive the *New Moon* as befits the youth of the village. These, of course, are only the vestiges, most probably no longer understood, of an ancient, long-forgotten religion. Nevertheless, they cannot help but remind one of some of the religious facts of ancient Prussia: the supervision of the cult of *Patrimpas*, who was represented in the form of a young, happy man, was also entrusted to the *waydolottinnen* (priestesses).[17]

(6) It is probably unnecessary to note that the *Christening of the Colt* legitimately belongs to the rituals of the *Krikštai* festival.

Conclusions

The ambitions of this brief study were somewhat less than the extensive conclusions of some of the explanations would lead one to believe. An attempt was made to reconstruct the ancient Lithuanian New Year festival, called *Krikštai*. It was necessary, first of all, to explain the significance of the naming of the festival itself. However, that was not sufficient: the content of the festival will remain incomplete until it is combined with the rituals customarily associated with it. It appears that the *Christening of the Colt* celebrated by the youth of the community all evening and all night as well as the preparation of the household feast on the day of the festival, attended to by worshippers at which the household serpent-deities taste the dishes and bless the coming year, provide at least a partial portrait of these celebrations. The festival, finally, will be incomplete if it is not consecrated to some deity: the figure of the Moon Deity, *Dievaitis Mėnulis*, whose birth during the month of the horn *ragas* [January] announces the beginning of the new year, takes its appointed place.

NOTES

Foreword

1. Several of Dumézil's works have appeared in English translation; see for example *The Destiny of the Warrior*, trans. Alf Hiltebeitel (Chicago: The University of Chicago Press, 1970); *Archaic Roman Religion*, trans. Philip Krapp (Chicago: The University of Chicago Press, 1970); *The Destiny of a King*, trans. Alf Hiltebeitel (Chicago: The University of Chicago Press, 1973); *From Myth to Fiction: The Saga of Hadingus* (Chicago: The University of Chicago Press, 1973); *Gods of the Ancient Northmen*, Trans. Einar Haugen et al. (Berkeley: University of California Press, 1973); *Camillus: A Study of Indo-European Religion as History*, trans. Annette Aronowicz and Josette Bryson (Berkeley: University of California Press, 1980); *The Stakes of the Warrior*, trans. David Weeks (Berkeley: University of California Press, 1983). For an analysis of his theories, see C. Scott Littleton, *The New Comparative Mythology: An Anthropological Assessment of the Theories of Georges Dumézil*, 3rd ed. (Berkeley: University of California Press, 1982).
2. For a bibliography of works of and about Claude Lévi-Strauss, see François H. Lapointe and Claire C. Lapointe, *Claude Lévi-Strauss and His Critics: An International Bibliography of Criticism (1950–1976), Followed by a Bibliography of the Writings of Claude Lévi-Strauss* (New York: Garland, 1977).
3. Some of Greimas's studies in English translation are *Maupassant: The Semiotics of Text*, trans. and intro. by Paul J. Perron (Philadelphia: John Benjamins, 1988); *On Meaning: Selected Writings in Semiotic Theory*, trans. Paul J. Perron and Frank H. Collins (Minneapolis: University of Minnesota Press, 1987); *The Semiotics of Passions*, trans. Paul J. Perron and Frank H. Collins, with an introduction by Paolo Fabbri and Paul J. Perron (Minneapolis: University of Minnesota Press, 1992); *The Social Sciences: A Semiotic View*, trans. Paul J. Perron and Frank H. Collins, with an introduction by Paolo Fabbri and Paul J. Perron (Minneapolis: University of Minnesota Press, 1990); *Structural Semantics: An Attempt at a Method*, trans. Daniele McDowell, Ronald Schleifer, and Alan Velie (Lincoln: University of Nebraska Press, 1983); and, with J. Courtés, *Semiotics and Language: An Analytical Dictionary*, trans. Larry Crist, Daniel Patte, et. al. (Bloomington: Indiana University Press, 1982).

For a bibliography of Greimas's writings, see Jean-Claude Coquet, "Éléments de Bio-Bibliographie," pp. liii–lxxxv in *Aims and Prospects of Semiotics: Essays in Honor of Algirdas Julien Greimas*, ed. Herman Parret and Hans-Georg Ruprecht (Philadelphia: John Benjamins, 1985). See also *Greimassian Semiotics, New Literary History* 20, 3 (Spring 1989) and Ronald Schleifer, *A. J. Greimas and the Nature of Meaning* (Lincoln: University of Nebraska Press, 1987).
4. Ernst Cassirer, *Language and Myth*, trans. Susanne K. Langer (New York: Harper, 1946), pp. 3–4.
5. A. J. Greimas, *On Meaning*, p. 15.
6. Cassirer, *Language and Myth*, p. 9.
7. For surveys and discussions of theories of myth see Richard Chase, *Quest for Myth* (1949; New York: Greenwood Press, 1969); Percy S. Cohen, "Theories of Myth," *Man* 4 (1969): 337–353; Adrian Cunningham, ed., *The Theory of Myth: Six Studies* (London: Sheed and Ward, 1973); D. H. Monro, "The Concept of Myth," *The Sociological Review* 42 (1950): 115–132; Robert A. Segal, "In Defense of Mythology: The History of Modern Theories of Myth," *Annals of Scholarship* 1 (1980): 3–49; Ivan Strenski, *Four Theories of Myth*

in the Twentieth-Century History: Cassirer, Eliade, Lévi-Strauss and Malinowski (Iowa City: University of Iowa Press, 1987).
    8. See Giambattista Vico, *The New Science of Giambattista Vico*, trans. Thomas Goddard Bergin and Max Harold Fisch (1948; Garden City: Doubleday, 1961), p. 64; Gianfranco Cantelli, "Myth and Language in Vico," pp. 47–65, in *Gaimbattista Vico's Science of Humanity*, ed. Giorgio Tagliacozzo and Donald Phillip Verene (Baltimore: The Johns Hopkins University Press, 1973).
    9. Quoted in Cassirer, *Language and Myth*, p. 85.
    10. Jacob Grimm, *Teutonic Mythology*. 4 vols., trans. James Steven Stallybrass (1883–1888; New York: Dover, 1966).
    11. Jean-Claude Coquet, "Éléments de Bio-Bibliographie," p. liv.
    12. See note 2 above and Vladimir Propp, *Morphology of the Folktale*, trans. Laurence Scott, rev. Louis A. Wagner, Publications of the American Folklore Society, Bibliographical and Special Series Vol. 9, Indiana University Research Center in Anthropology, Folklore and Linguistics Publication 10-, 2nd ed. (Austin: University of Texas Press, 1968); idem, *Theory and History of Folklore*, trans. Ariadna Y. Martin and Richard P. Martin (Minneapolis: University of Minnesota Press, 1984).
    13. See Margaret Hodgen, *The Doctrine of Survivals: A Chapter in the History of Scientific Method in the Study of Man* (London, 1936).
    14. See Don Cameron Allen, "The Allegorical Interpretation of the Renaissance Mythographeres," pp. 201–248 in *Mysteriously Meant: The Rediscovery of Pagan Symbolism and Allegorical Interpretation in the Renaissance* (Baltimore: The Johns Hopkins University Press, 1970).

1. Kaukai

    1. Praetorius, *Deliciae Prussicae*, pp. 29–30, in J. Basanavičius, *Rinktiniai raštai* [Selected Writings] (Vilnius, 1970), p. 362. Divisions in the text are ours. Explanations of the different names for *kaukai* will be presented later.
    2. L. Jucevičius (1848), in Basanavičius, *R. r.*, pp. 365–66. The process itself will be explained later.
    3. E. Gisevius, *Der Kauk-Stein*, in Basanavičius, *R. r.*, p. 377.
    4. Praetorius, in Basanavičius, *R. r.*, p. 362.
    5. J. Lasicius, *De Diis Samagitarum*, Vilnius, 1969, p. 47.
    6. Ibid., p. 48.
    7. L. Ivinskis (1864), in Basanavičius, *R. r.*, p. 366.
    8. Basanavičius, *R. r.*, p. 367 (cites Z. Bruožis, about 1907). This suggests that the *kaukas*' gift in the form of a garment can only be of a later origin.
    9. Only Hartnoch (in the second half of the seventeenth century) indicates that the dwelling of the *parstukai* is under the *linden* tree.
    10. *Bezdukas* also refers to one type of foul-smelling mushroom, *kukurbezdalis* (Lycoperdon); a comparison of *kaukai* to different types of mushrooms was made earlier.
    11. *De Diis Samagitarum*, p. 48.
    12. Compare "Giwi dajktaj, turiedami plauczius, *puszkuj* ir kwiepuj." [Living things possessing lungs, *puszkuj* and breathe.] Kossarzewski, *Lituanica*, 15 a., in K. Būga, *Rinktiniai raštai*, II, p. 527. Compare the words *pukš-eti*, whose root could be the metathesis of the former.
    13. Op. cit., p. 47, in Basanavičius, *R. r.*, p. 361. The Praetorius text, it goes without saying, must be correctly interpreted: it is not a matter of differentiating sorcerers into separate categories, of which there are too many, so that they correspond to reality, but rather of distinguishing between them according to their functional variety and a typology of their magic operations.
    14. Jucevičius, in B. Basanavičius, *R. r.*, pp. 365–66.
    15. J. Banaitis, LTA 982 (56), in *Tautosakos darbai* [Folklore Studies] III, p. 56.

16. Basanavičius, *R. r.*, p. 376.
17. Ibid., pp. 366–67.
18. LTA 2268 (254) in *Taut. darb.*, VII, p. 130; also compare Banaitis, above.
19. Banaitis, LTA 982 (56), in *Taut. darb.*, III, p. 56.
20. L. Geitler, *Lit. Studien* (Prague, 1875), p. 90, in Basanavičius, *R. r.*, p. 367.
21. Banaitis, op. cit.
22. Banaitis, LTA 982 (56), in *Taut. darb.*, III, p. 56.
23. *LKŽ*, compare with Basanavičius, *R. r.*, p. 367.
24. L. Ivinskis (1864), in Basanavičius, *R. r.*, p. 366.
25. Basanavičius, *R. r.*, pp. 370, 372.
26. Ibid.
27. Ibid., p. 369.
28. *Raw vs. cooked* and *naked vs. clothed* are categories which have been thoroughly examined by C. Lévi-Strauss in his monumental work *Mythologiques*, which devotes one volume to each set of categories.
29. Compare with another word or with another meaning of the word *kaukai*: the diminutive *kaukeliai* means literally "a child's night shirt" (*LKŽ*).
30. Basanavičius, *Apie gyvenimą velnių bei vėlių [From the Life of Souls and Devils]* (Chicago, 1903), pp. 106–7, 107–8, 261–63; *Lietuvių tautosaka* [Lithuanian Folklore], III (212), pp. 593–94, and IV (500), p. 204.
31. *LKŽ* (Skr.).
32. *LKŽ* (PPr 287).
33. *Liet. taut.*, II (213), pp. 594–95.
34. See above, no. 30.
35. Compare our analysis of the Lithuanian folktale *La queête de la peur* [The Search for Fear] in *Du Sens*, Seuil, 1970, pp. 231–47.
36. Compare the prayer with which one turns to Vaižgantas during his festival; Lasicius, by way of exception, provides the Lithuanian text: "Vvaizganthos deuaite . . . nie duok mumis *nogus* [naked] eithi. Vaizganthos, inquit . . . neve nos *nudos* incedere premittas." (Ibid., p. 43.) Thus, Vaižgantas is not only the flax god in the narrow sense but he who clothes naked people.
37. *Trakų ir lietuvių, mitologijos smulkmenos* in *R.r.*, and especially pp. 358–80.
38. Ibid., pp. 367–68.
39. Ibid.
40. Ibid.
41. From a mythological perspective, it is unimportant whether the word itself is of Balto-Slavic origin or is an ancient borrowing from the Slavic languages (before the eighth century).
42. Compare the metaphoric use of the *rooster* when talking about *fire*.
43. See Louis Hjelmslev, *Essias linguistiques*, Ed. de Minuit.
44. E. Volteris (1886) in Basanavičius, *R. r.*, p. 371.
45. J. Balys, *Lietuvių Enciklopedija*, XV. p. 467.
46. *LKŽ* (Prng.).
47. LTR (Ls) in *LKŽ*. Compare also Lasicius, according to whom attention is turned to the deity *Ežiagulis* during *Skerstuvės* (p. 44).
48. LTA 1032 (165) Zrs. in *Taut. darb.*, III, p. 189.
49. The frequent confusion of St. George's Day and Easter rituals leads one to think that a single common pre-Christian spring festival may have existed. Compare *Ledų Diena*, which is celebrated on the third day of Easter.
50. Compare Balys' comprehensive study, especially *Pirmoji Perkūnija* [The First Thunder] in *Taut. darb.*, III, pp. 205–14.
51. J. Lasicius, op cit., p. 40.
52. Ibid.
53. "Even though pigs have strong stomachs, they also sometimes get sick when it sleets" (Gr. *LKŽ*).

54. "Susidargnojo kiaulė (t.y., "vem prieš dargna"—the pig vomits when it sleets) (J. *LKŽ*).
55. "Make faces, just like the boar when the sleet comes" (Sin. *LKŽ*).
56. See n. 55.
57. LTA 739 (82) and LTA 757 (81) in *Taut. darb.*, III, p. 207.
58. Kossarzewski, *Lituanica* (1821–1882), in *Taut. darb.*, III, p. 144.
59. *Amalas*, for instance, refers to a parasitic plant (Lat. *Viscum album*), otherwise called *laumšluote*, which grows on oaks, birches, lindens, on which *laumės* [fairies] sit swinging in the evening mist (*LKŽ*).
60. Kossarzewski, in Būga, *Rinktiniai raštai*, III, p. 431.
61. Zem. *LKŽ*.
62. P. Juzulėnas, citing Būga, op. cit., III, p. 431.
63. *LKŽ*.
64. *Liet. Taut.*, VI (legends), p. 645 (718).
65. Kossarzewski 151, in *LKŽ*.
66. Liet. taut., VI (legends), pp. 641ff.
67. Kossarzewski, *Lituanica*, in *Taut. darb.*, III, p. 138. It should be noted that the cloud itself often has the image of the *bull*, and sometimes is even entirely identified with it. In the K. Story, the tale is of a *black hog*.
68. *Liet. taut.*, I, Herding Songs (109), p. 117.
69. Balys, *Liet. tautosakos skaitymai* [Handbook of Lithuanian Folklore], II, p. 34.
70. *LKŽ* (Mlt.).
71. *LKŽ* (B.).
72. *Liet. taut.*, I, p. 116.
73. Balys, *Lietuvių liaudies pasaulėjauta* [Lithuanian Folk Worldview], p. 51.
74. This can most likely be identified with St. George and Pergrubis.
75. This is an earth deity abundantly attested to as much in ethnographic sources as in ethnographic studies.
76. *LKŽ*
77. *LKŽ*.
78. *LKŽ*.
79. *LKŽ* offers them sometimes as separate, independent words, and sometimes only as separate meanings of one word. Taking into account the fact that these words apparently cannot be explained by separate etymologies, we make no artificial distinctions between "words" and "meanings."
80. *LKŽ*.
81. *LKŽ*.
82. *LKŽ*.
83. *LKŽ*.
84. *LKŽ*.
85. *LKŽ*.
86. *LKŽ*.
87. *LKŽ*.
88. *LKŽ*.
89. *LKŽ*

90. *Kaukas* in this sense is somewhat reminiscent of the *sow* (who, without horns, and cloven-hoofed but non-ruminative, is not classified with other *cattle*—it is not certain whether she is even an *animal*), whose nuclear figure is also quite rough. The word "kiaulė" [pig] also means "a pile," "haystack," and "heap."
91. Basanavičius, *R. r.*, p. 381, and Būga, *R. r.*, I, p. 364; II, p. 221 and p. 285, indicate the same site for the recorded example—Salakas.
92. *LKŽ*.
93. *LKŽ*.

94. The noted French historian Marc Bloch has exhaustively analyzed this phenomenon. A large number of the feudal terms from the French Middle Ages are of Germanic origin, even though the structure of French feudalism was created and developed independently from the feudalism of the Holy Roman Empire. Nevertheless, the French terms in question, even though of Germanic origin, do not correspond at all to words with similar meanings in Germany. It would appear that, generally, the borrowing procedure is often used to emphasize only the importance or originality of a concept.

95. "During Shrovetide the boys whittle masks with hooked or long noses out of wood. These have hollowed-out eyes, with long teeth, and after the boys whittle them, they go to search for *bergždines* [barren women] in the farms." (J. *LKŽ*.)

96. Compare to *tranelis* [drone], which is one of the synonyms of "kaukas."

97. The Lithuanian concept of life and death can be represented as three mutually communicating phrases of "life": the "living," the "living-deceased" (or vėlės), and "deceased." Compare our *La quête de la peur* in *Du Sens*, Seuil, 1970.

98. "*Kaukie* sunt lemures," op cit., p. 44.

99. Compare the Kuršaitis [Kurschat] dictionary: "ein ungetauft gestorbenes Kind."

100. The same differentiation of two sacred spheres can be noted in another case: children born between Holy Thursday and Easter (the period during which the Christian God is dead), differ from others. They are "clairvoyant" and can see the vėlės.

101. *LKŽ*.

102. A large number of examples of this activity can be found in Basanavičius, *Apie gyvenimą vėlių bei velnių*, passim.

103. J. Lasicius, op. cit., p. 51.

104. Ibid,, p. 41.

105. *Sikės* or *sikiai*, and *Ilgės* or *Ilgiai* are two separate plural forms. *Ilgi* is a dialect form, recorded by Lasicius. As is the case with the word "Ilgės," the fall festival itself is confirmed by the nature of the payments collected during the fall referred to by this name. Other lexical facts also confirm it.

106. J. Lasicius, op. cit., p. 43.

107. Compare "sikiai, or flaxseed cakes (pressed from flax)," *L* C. 1884, 51, in *LKŽ*. *Kepis*, or *kėpis* is "a flat cake, wafer," according to *LKŽ*.

108. The general organization of these festivals is difficult to reconstruct at this time. According to Lasicius, the first two days were consecrated to *Žemėpatis* (brother of the earth deity *Žemyna*), guardian of the animal herd. The third day was consecrated to *Vaižgantas*, and the following three days to the cult of the dead. Thus there were still four days not consecrated to any specific deity.

109. J. Lasicius, op. cit., p. 43.

110. Ibid. The Lithuanian translator of Lasicius did not understand that vėlės go to the bathhouse and change into clean garments before they sit down at the banquet table.

111. Lasicius records it as *Skierstuvves*. The word, preserved intact up to the present, means, as we know, not only the day of skerstuvės [the butchering] but also the parts of the pig that are eaten immediately, distributed to neighbors, or eaten together by everyone.

112. This holiday is preserved to this day in villages in the Vilnius region, where Polish-speaking people call it by the Lithuanian name "skerdėna" (oral verification).

113. Būga, *R. r.*, I, p. 516.

114. See Basanavičius, *R. r.,* p. 365.

115. Lasicius, op. cit., p. 41.

116. See above, n. 47. "Ežiagulys" in Lithuania is known as the name of a certain wild plant (Lotus). It can be a noun as well as the adjectival epithet. Compare "gargzdenis ežiagulys" [a gravel boundary] (*LKŽ*).

117. Close ties between *Veliona* and water are confirmed not only by the existence of rivers named *Veliuona*, but by folk beliefs—which should be thoroughly analyzed—holding that "the world after death" exists at the bottom of the "sea."

118. Basanavičius is of the same opinion. *R. r.*, p. 276, based on Usener, *Goetternamen*, 1896, p. 104.

119. Compare Basanavičius, *R. r.*, p. 291: "Accompanying (the deceased) to the boundary of the field . . . a small amount of hay is strewn, so the vėlės returning home can sit and rest better by the wayside."

120. Bezzenberger, "Eine neugefundene litauische Urkunde vom Jahre 1578," *Altpreuss Monatschrift*, Bd. 14, p. 459ff. In Basanavičius, *R. r.*, p. 185.

2. Aitvaras

1. Praetorius, *Delicae Prussicae*, pp. 29–30, in J. Basanavičius, *Rinktiniai raštai* [Selected Writings] (Vilnius, 1970), p. 362.
2. J. Bretkūnas, *Postilla*, II, 101, cited in *LKŽ*.
3. Gaigalat, Die Wolfenbutteler Litauische Postillenschrift aus dem Jahre 1575, in *Mitt. der lit. Liter. Gesellschaft*, V, 4, pp. 149–50, cited in Basanavičius, *R. r.*, p. 360.
4. Compare among others, Basanavičius, *Liet. pas yvairios*, [Various Lithuanian Tales] IV, p. 77.
5. Oh—they say—it is aitvaras! He was everywhere—in the apple orchards and the gardens!" LTR 3796 (69), cited in J. Velius, *Senųjų tikėjimų liekanos* [Vestiges of Ancient Beliefs], in *Dieveniškės*, p. 281. It is a region from which aitvaras and the kaukai have finally disappeared, partly changed to manifestations of the devil.
6. *LKŽ*: *Laimykas* s.m. Gdz. "aitvaras."
7. *LKŽ*: *Aitvoras* C17, 3, "A smothering spirit, slogutis." Compare as well Nesselmann in Būga, III, p. 339. *Slogutis* is most often of the female gender, but can be masculine on occasion.
8. See infra, p. 51.
9. N. Vėlius, *Etiudas apie Šaukšteliškių pasakorių Balį Ilgevičų* [A Study of Balys Ilgevičius, narrator from Šaukšteliškiai], in *Dubingiai*, p. 292.
10. See chap. 1.
11. Vėlius, ibid.
12. M. Mažvydas, *Catechismusa prasty szadei* [Simple Words of the Cathechism], Latin introduction, cited in Basanavičius, *R. r.*, 1970, pp. 359–60.
13. Praetorius, *Deliciae prussicae*, ed. W. Pierson, 1871, p. 26. in Basanavičius, *R. r.*, p. 361.
14. See chap 1.
15. "They would bake an omelet [*pautienė*] every day at one farmer's place, but no one would get to eat it (since they would give it to the aitvaras)." Basanavičius, *Liet. pas. yv.*, II, p. 328. Compare to *Liet. taut.*, IV, pp. 529-30 and *LKŽ* (Sl.), *aitvaras*.
16. See Basanavičius, *R. r.*, pp. 358–78. Basanavičius, *Liet. pas., yv.*, II, p. 151.
17. The problem of aitvaras as the provider of coins will be analyzed separately.
18. *LKŽ* (Grk.) *aitvaras*.
19. *LKŽ* (Sl.) *aitvaras*. The obstacle that appears for our interpretation cannot be disregarded because the folkloric texts often speak of the *grain* that Aitvaras brings; it should not be forgotten, however, that *grain* has already been in contact with the heat process during threshing. Besides, the most characteristic reports concerning the provision of grain are about the moment of *milling*, or the use of heat to transform them to *flour* (aitvaras fills the trough placed next to the millstone with grain). See Basanavičius, *Liet. pas. yv.*, III, p. 327. Finally, some texts specify that it is a matter of *dried grains* (id., ibid.).
20. *LKŽ* (Sl.) *aitvaras*. It is possible to add *lard* here (*LKŽ* [Ms.] *Kaukas*), which is prepared by a grinding process just as *flour* is.
21. *Gaidės ir Rimšės apylinkės* [The Regions of Gaidė and Rimšės], pp. 398–99.
22. "Aitvaras sweeps down and starts to *vomit* coins or curds into the trough." *LKŽ* (Grk). Compare the guests who refuse to drink the "ale vomited by the devil." *Gaidės ir Rimšės apylinkės*, pp. 398–99.

23. Compare no. 2; compare also chap. 1.
24. Compare *Die Wolfenbutteler*, p. 360, according to which the Lithuanians believe "ing szemepuszius, Eitwarius, kaukus."
25. Aitvaras is characterized as "Lar pecuniam afferens," Jn Vo2842 (Kp.) in Būga, III, p. 339.
26. "If it is bluish-red, then it is the *monetary* (aitvaras), but if it glows yellow, then it is the grain or milk (aitvaras)." LTR (Kp.) in *LKŽ*. Compare also the statement, "in Prussia, one gentleman used to sell monetary aitvarai," *LKŽ* (Grs.).
27. "The Kaukas brings only material goods . . . in contrast to *pūkys*, who brings coins." Basanavičius, *R. r.*, p. 366 (informant is A. Bruožis, 1907, from Klaipėda). According to data from 1849, the *pūkys* name is characteristic to the Klaipėda region (Basanavičius, *R. r.*, p. 366). It is most probably a German borrowing of the word *Puck* (Balys), even though the contaminated Lithuanian *pūkys* is reminiscent of the bird figure of aitvaras.
28. *LKŽ* (Rom.).
29. *LKŽ* (J.).
30. *Liet, kl. tarmės* [Lithuanian dialects] (Rudiškiai), p. 215.
31 M. Valančius, citing *LKŽ*.
32. Basanavičius, *Liet. pass. yv.*, pp. 76–77.
33. "A bright ball of light rose from the ground (when 'coins were burning')" *LKŽ* (P.). Compare also: "My moja saw the burning (buried) coins" *LKŽ* (Lnkv.).
34. *LKŽ* (Lnkv.).
35. "The Aitvaras is called *Švitelis* in the Žagarai region, in Gruzdžiai, a light along the ground is called *žaltvikša*. Here (Trumpaičiai) I seem to have heard it called *žaltviska*. In Gruzdžiai, J. Staponaitis, from the Račiai village, has said that it is all the same: *aitvaras, švitelis, žaltvikša* (Sl.)" J. Basanavičius, *Liet. pas.*, I, p. 129. Compare K. Būga, I, p. 221, who provides *žaltvikslas* (Ivinskis, 1861) from the meaning of *žaltvykslė* (Mielcke) which is "Irrlicht" [will-o'-the-wisp or ignis fatuus—a flitting phosphorescent light seen chiefly over marshy ground].
36. See Basanavičius, *R. r.*, p. 369, 358–78.
37. Basanavičius, *R. r.*, p. 369; compare *Kaukai*, p. 26.
38. See infra, p. 47.
39. Basanavičius, *Liet. pas. yv.*, II, pp. 181–82 (informant K. Būga).
40. Basanavičius, *Liet. pas. yv.*, pp. 127, 129, 130 (four versions). It must be noted that the reaction of aitvaras is different in these two cases; he reacts cruelly to the "showing of one's rear end," while the opening up of one's nightshirt provokes the aitvaras to stop and offer his services (although aitvaras does not stop being evil because of that).
41. Two versions punish with *sores*, a third changes them to *fleas*, and a fourth writes about *burns*.
42. Basanavičius, *R. r.*, p. 372.
43. Comp. the revenge of Aitvaras: aitvaras thrown into the stove in the form of a *swamp log* not only is combined with the fire of the hearth, but conversely the flame comes out of the stove and sets all the cottages on fire at once (*Gaidės ir Rimšės apylinkės*, p. 397–98).
44. Praetorius in *Mannhardt*, p. 536, in *Taut. darb.*, III, p. 205.
45. See infra, p. 62.
46. "The Aitvarai, it is said, are devils, but they can be seen only in the image of birds (Kalvarija)." Basanavičius, *Liet. pas.*, II. p. 130.
47. See supra, *Kaukai*, p. 18.
48. Basanavičius, *Liet. pas. yv.*, IV, p. 78.
49. Id., ibid., III, p. 326.
50. Id., ibid., II, p. 130.
51. Id., ibid., II, p. 134.
52. Id., ibid., III, p. 328.
53. *Stebuklinga paukštytė* [The wondrous little chick] in *Gaidės ir Rimšės apylinkės*,

1969, p. 362. Compare also two similar versions in Basanavičius, *Liet. pas. yv.,* III, about a forest bird which, when cooked and eaten, leaves under the pillow of the one who has eaten it, a certain number of gold coins every night.

54. Basanavičius, *Liet. pas. yv.,* II, pp. 130–35.
55. Basanavičius, *Liet. pas. yv.,* III, pp. 326–27.
56. *Liet. taut.,* IV, pp. 529–30; other texts mention nine or twelve years (cf. Basanavičius, *Liet. pas. yv.,* II, p. 181). These are magic numbers.
57. Cf. among others, *Gaidės ir Rimšės apylinkės,* pp. 397–98.
58. Basanavičius, *Liet. pas.yv.,* III, p. 274.
59. Basanavičius, *R. r.,* p. 373. Even though the verifications of Wekenstaedt are often suspect, his references concerning the *kelias* [roadway] are confirmed when compared to other texts that mention the riddance of Aitvaras at the *crossroads.*
60. Basanavičius, *Liet. pas. yv.,* III, pp. 326–27.
61. See A. J. Greimas, *Un problème de sémiotique narrative: les objets de valeur* in *Sémiotiques textuelles,* a special issue of *Langages,* no. 31 (Sept. 1973), pp. 13–35.
62. See supra, p. 46.
63. *Gaidės ir Rimšės apylinkės,* p. 396.
64. Ibid.
65. Volter in Basanavičius, *R. r.,* p. 371 and *LKŽ.*
66. *LKŽ* (Bs. *Mt.* I, p. 10).
67. This is otherwise called "karmažinskas pinigas." It is sufficient to put it in the bank, so they would "take away all the money." It is referred to in our times as a hold-up. *Gaidės ir Rimšės apylinkės* (1969), p. 390.
68. Unfortunately, there is no comprehensive study which analyzes the entire separate operations of *sorcery* and *wizardry.*
69. Volter in Basanavičius, *R. r.,* p. 371.
70. Basanavičius, *Liet. pas.,* II, p. 134.
71. Id., ibid.
72. A self-employed servant who, when I was a child in the Kupiškis region, was responsible for removal of dung and was called a "gold carrier."
73. E. Fraenkel in *Archiv für slavische Philologie* (1951), XXI, 1, pp. 140–150.
74. *LKŽ;* cf. Būga, II, p. 99, which in *áite-* identifies a second element of the divine anthroponym *Gardoyts = Gard + aitas;* cf. Būga, III, p. 336, which provides additional examples: "How can you invite such an *aita* to work?"
75. Cf. "*Nuaitavau* the stove (managed to heat it up) so the cake got baked." *LKŽ* (Ls.).
76. Cf., for example, the Hindu deity who, because of her cruelty, is called *Kali the Gentle.*
77. Basanavičius, *R. r.,* p. 358, *LKŽ,* citing N and K, gives the example: "Aitvaras tangled, matted his hair."
78. Būga, III, p. 339 (R II, 187, 250). This polysemy is verified by Nesselmann, according to whom *aitvaras* is, on the one hand, "der Alp, der fliegende Drache, der nach dem Volksglauben Schatze bringt" and, on the other, "den Pferden die Haare zusammendreht, usw. (nicht der Maar, der die Schlafenden druckt)," ibid.
79. *LKŽ* (Lp.).
80. *LKŽ* (Ss.).
81. *LKŽ* (Arm.). This quite distinct personification of *kaltūnas* in this sentence should be emphasized; compare with "Kaltunvėlė would tangle the men's hair" *LKŽ* (Vl.).
82. *LKŽ* (Dplš.).
83. *LKŽ* (Rk.).
84. *LKŽ* (Zp.).
85. *LKŽ* (Kpsl.).
86. *Litauische Zaubersprüche* (Helsinki: Suomulainen Tiedeakatemia, 1929), p. 92.
87. Cf. V. J. Mansikka, op. cit., passim.

88. See supra, p. 48.
89. Basanavičius, *Liet. pas.*, I, p. 128.
90. See supra, p. 52.
91. "If the horse has kaltūnai, it [the mane] must be hacked off with a stone; if cut off with a knife, the horse either becomes *blind* or *lame*," *Taut. darb.* (Lithuania Minor), III, p. 9.
92. *LKŽ* (Kltn.).
93. *Liet. taut.*, IV, p. 539.
94. Basanavičius, *Liet. pas. yv.*, III, p. 327.
95. Recorded by G. Ginken in his published narrative *Žyvaia Starina* [Living Antiquity] (1894), reprinted in Basanavičius, *Liet. pas. yv.*, III, pp. 326–27.
96. *Taut. darb.*, III, pp. 194–95.
97. See supra, p. 47.
98. *Strampas* means "stick" (*LKŽ*). It seems that *aitvaras* is referred to ironically with this word.
99. *LKŽ*.
100. J. Jurginis citing K. Jablonskis, *Lietuviški žodžiai senosios Lietuvos raštinių kalboje* in *Kult. barai*, 1970, 4, pp. 59–60.
101. *De Diis Samagitarum*, 41, and not as a "god of a change in dwelling" (p. 20).
102. J. Jurginis, ibid., p. 60.
103. *Apidėmės* (sf. pl.) means "grave, cemetery" *LKŽ*; compare with *kaukai*, chapter 1.
104. Ibid.
105. "Why didn't I leave that beast on the *road*," laments the man (ibid.).
106. *De Diis Samagitarum*, p. 19. Elsewhere (p. 21) it is said only that he is worshipped in Plateliai.
107. *LKŽ*.
108. *LKŽ* (G. 91).
109. *LKŽ* (J).
110. *Gaidės ir Rimšės apylinkės*, pp. 397–98.
111. LTR 1434 (2) in *Merkinė*, pp. 306–307.
112. *Liet. taut.*, II (Easter songs).
113. *Liet. taut.*, III, pp. 544–47.
114. *Liet. taut.*, III, pp. 551–52.
115. See supra, p. 43.
116. *LKŽ* (Uzp.).
117. Būga, I, p. 135.
118. *LKŽ*.
119. *LKŽ*
120. Basanavičius, *Liet. pas.*, I, p. 28.
121. Id., ibid., II, p. 135.
122. "With the whirlwind's spinning, the little devils celebrate a wedding." Basanavičius, *Liet. pas.*, I, p. 28.
123. *Taut. darb.*, IV, pp. 301–2.
124. *Liet. taut.*, IV, pp. 585–86.
125. Ibid., IV, p. 582.
126. Ibid., IV, p. 583.
127. Ibid., IV, pp. 301–2.
128. Ibid., IV, pp. 585–86.
129. Praetorius, *Deliciae Prussicae*, in Būga, I, p. 148.
130. Kossarzewski, *Lituanica* in *Taut. darb.*, III, p. 137.
131. Id., ibid., p. 145.
132. *Taut. darb.*, III, pp. 185–86.
133. Ibid.

134. *Liet. taut.*, IV, pp. 384–86.
135. Kossarzewski, *Lituanica* in *Taut. darb.*, III, p. 135; the *Brother of the Wind* represented somewhat differently, is identified with the *North Wind*.
136. *Liet. taut.*, III, pp. 230–32.
137. *Liet. taut.*, IV, p. 586.
138. LTA 982 (59) in *Taut. darb.*, VI, pp. 113–14 (the text is recorded in Prussian Lithuania in the Ragainė region according to the Balys study).
139. Id., ibid., p. 113.

3. Aušrinė

1. *Dabartinės Lietuvių Kalbos Žodynas* [Dictionary of Contemporary Lithuanian] (Vilnius, 1972).
2. M. Slančiauskas, *Šiaurės Lietuvos Pasakos* [Folktales of Northern Lithuania]. pp. 184–88.
3. *LKŽ*: "Having cuckooed for barely one month, the cuckoo turns into a hawk." S. p. 187.
4. Cf. J. Basanavičius, *Liet. pas. yvairios* [Various Lithuanian Tales], III, p. 170ff.
5. LTR 1181 (33) and LTR 1134 (81).
6. Basanavičius, *Liet. pas. yvairios*, III, pp. 171–74.
7. *Tautosakos Darbai* [Folklore Studies], III (beliefs), p. 17.
8. Ibid., p. 17.
9. *Liet. Tautosaka* [Lithuanian Folklore], IV, p. 583.
10. M. Davainis-Silvestraitis, *Pasakos, sakmės, oracijos* [Tales, Legends, Orations] (Vilnius, 1973), pp. 162–3.
11. *Taut. darb.*, III, p. 25.
12. Basanavičius, *Iš gyvenimo vėlių bei velnių* [From the Lives of Souls and Devils], p. 21.
13. Id., ibid.
14. "Apie obuolį lietuvių dainose bei pasakose ir vestuvių apeigose" [The Apple in Lithuanian Songs, Folktales and Wedding Rituals], in *Rinktiniai raštai* [Selected Writings], p. 392ff.
15. L. Rhesa, *Dainos oder Litauische Volkslieder* (Königsberg, 1825), p. 266, cited in J. Basanavičius, *R. r.*, p. 402n.
16. A. Juška, *Liet. Svodb. Dainos* [Lithuanian Wedding Songs], p. 823 in J. Basanavičius, op. cit., p. 403.
17. Basanavičius, loc. cit., cites in the footnotes for that occasion the *Nauja lietuviška Ceitunga* [Lithuanian newspaper], no. 84, 1903, describing a case in Tilsit in which "the mail carrier Mielkis confesses that he spent time with Elske Paslatike *obuliavos* [committed adultery]. He would visit during evenings, when the young girls had not yet gone to sleep. Once during the spring he used the ladder, together with Kalvaitis, who carried on with Ida Paslatike."
18. J. Balys, *Lietuvių liaudies pasaulėjauta* [Lithuanian Folk Worldview] (Chicago, 1966), p. 113, cites a series of Latvian "mothers"; jurasmate, vejasmate, ugunsmate, udensmate, laukumate [mother of the sea, the wind, the fire, the fields].
19. Basanavičius, op. cit., p. 397.
20. *Deliciae Prussicae*, ed. Pierson (Berlin, 1871), p. 27, in Būga, *Rinktiniai raštai*, I, p. 148.
21. Basanavičius, *Liet. pas. yvairios*, III, p. 55. The ailing brother is mentioned in *Liet. Tautosaka*, IV, pp. 586 and 584.
22. *LKŽ* (see for these words).
23. *LKŽ* (auštrinis).
24. *LKŽ* (auštrinis).
25. Basanavičius, *Liet. Pas. Yvairios*, III, p. 55. Another text tells about the three sons of *Vėjas*, drowned in the sea: having blown away the water they went too far, "looking at all types of wondrous things" (*Liet. Tautosaka*, IV, p. 587).

26. Slančiauskas, op cit., p. 204.
27. *LKŽ*.
28. *LKŽ*.
29. Davainis-Silvestraitis, op. cit., p. 410.
30. Id., ibid., p. 205.
31. J. Basanavičius, *Liet. Pas.*, I, pp. 143–45.
32. *Lietuvių Tautosaka*, III, p. 590.
33. Basanavičius, *Apie gyvenimą vėlių bei velnių*, p. 282.
34. B. Kerbelytė, *Lietuvių liaudies padavimai* [Lithuanian Folk Legends] (Vilnius, 1970), p. 49, cites folkloric archives: LTR 3289 (105) and LTR 3426 (62) tells of the chopping off of toes; LTR 2268 (174) and LTR 3185 (124) notes that the giant dies from this. In Kerbelytė's book the section devoted to the giants is well documented; her chosen theme—the study of the genre of legends—does not allow her to consider more extensively the problematic of the race of giants.
35. *De Diis Samagitarum* (Vilnius, 1969), p. 40.
36. *Liet. Tautosaka*, I, p. 177.
37. Ibid., p. 175.
38. Davainis-Silvestraitis, op. cit., p. 204.
39. Id., ibid., pp. 89–90.
40. LTR 10a (68).
41. LTR 10b (157).
42. LMD 1 1000 (51).
43. Davainis-Silvestraitis, op. cit., pp. 205–6.
44. The stump—of an unspecified tree—is found in another, parallel text, also on an island of the sea: "Here there is such a *stump,* in that stump a wolf, in that wolf, a pig, in that pig—a duck, in the duck—an egg" (Basanavičius, *Liet. Pas.*, I, p. 142). The egg, to which we will return later, is the dwelling of *gyvastis*.
45. For all these words see *LKŽ*. *Jaučių baubis* is verified as well in the first part of the eighteenth century.
46. Kerbelytė, op cit., devotes a portion of her study to this question.
47. *Liet. Taut.*, V, pp. 463–64.
48. 48. LTR 208 (132), LTR 208 (165), LMB III 73 (93).
49. "La mythologie comparée" in *Du Sens* (Paris, 1970), pp. 117–34; English translation: "Comparative Mythology" in *Mythology*, ed. P. Maranda (Penguin Books, 1972), pp. 162–70 (excerpt).
50. LTR 421 (167), LMD 1 815 (1), LMD I 502 (1).
51. LTR 208 (132).
52. Davainis-Silvestraitis, op. cit., pp. 51–56.
53. *LKŽ* (kumeliukas [the colt]).
54. Basanavičius, *Liet. Pas. Yv.*, p. 178. Cf. also Davainis-Silvestraitis, op. cit., p. 126, where after the sexual act it is said: "thus, he will be mine; I'll be his."
55. Davainis-Silvestraitis, op. cit., p. 163.
56. Id., ibid., p. 206. The other version of this myth is retold by the author in Polish (see p. 421).
57. Lasicius, op. cit., p. 42.
58. Lasicius, *De Diis Samagitarum* (Vilnius, 1969), p. 40.
59. Būga, *Rinkt, raštai*, II, pp. 257–58.
60. Basanavičius, *Liet. Pas. Yv.*, p. 85.
61. Id., ibid., III, pp. 305–6 and 307–8.
62. Op. cit., I, p. 188.
63. *Du Sens*, pp. 231–48.
64. Davainis-Silvestraitis, op. cit., p. 97. *Vokietukas* [the little German], is of course the little devil.

65. *LKŽ* (*kaustyti* [to shoe a horse]).
66. *Lietuvių Tautosaka*, IV, p. 427; compare with another variant in *Dubingiai*, pp. 335–36.
67. Ibid., III, pp. 662–63.
68. Ibid., III, p. 591.
69. Ibid., IV, p. 510.
70. *Taut. Darbai*, III, p. 189ff.
71. *Taut. Darbai*, IV, pp. 301–2.
72. We are thinking here of, among others, the Russian semiotician N. Toporov, who, in our estimation, crosses over too quickly to comparative Balto-Slavic mythological studies.
73. LMD I 815 (1).
74. Also *dūbla* or *dūbliai*—are the entrails of the animal, its intestines (*LKŽ*). Here, most probably, these are the colt's lungs. See in the following segment the analysis of the *lungs* and *liver*.
75. *Liet. Tautosaka*, V, p. 463.
76. Balys, *Liet. Tautosakos Skaitymai* [Handbook of Lithuanian Folklore] (Tübingen, 1948), II, p. 46, correctly notes that Mėnulis—the male Moon—in Lithuanian mythology plays a distinctly larger role than Saulė—the female Sun. Up to now there has been a lack of consistency in the description of the activities of *Saulė* and her worship.
77. See F. Nef et al., *Les structures élémentaires de la signification* (Paris/Brussels, 1975).
78. Davainis-Silvestraitis, op. cit., p. 126.
79. J. Balys, *Liet. istoriniai padavimai*, pp. 36–37.
80. Davainis-Silvestraitis, op. cit., pp. 54–56.
81. Basanavičius, *Liet. Pas.*, I, pp. 117–18.
82. *LKŽ* (Lk).
83. *LKŽ* (Sin.).
84. *LKŽ*.
85. *LKŽ* (O).
86. *LKŽ* (A. Juška).
87. LTR 422 (21).
88. LMD I 540 (1).
89. LTR 422 (21).
90. Basanavičius, *Liet. Pas. Yv.*, I, p. 142.
91. Id. *Liet. Pas. Yv.*, I, pp. 199–204.
92. Cf. "La quête de la peur" in *Du Sens*, pp. 231–48.
93. *Liet. Taut.*, IV, p. 587.
94. Basanavičius, *Liet. Pas. Yv.*, III, p. 157.
95. Id., ibid., III, pp. 169–71.
96. Davainis-Silvestraitis, op. cit., pp. 172–73.
97. Id., ibid., p. 124ff.
98. Basanavičius, *Liet. Pas. Yv.*, III, pp. 75 and 106.
99. Cf. our study in *Du Sens*, pp. 231–48.
100. Basanavičius, op. cit., III, p. 170.
101. Balys, *Liet. taut. skaitymai*, I, pp. 50–70. (The text is Samogitian, recorded by Hugo Scheu around 1875.)
102. Slančiauskas, op. cit., pp. 189–92.
103. Basanavičius, *Liet. Pas. Yv.*, pp. 199–204.
104. Basanavičius, op. cit., IV, p. 153.
105. *Liet. Tautosaka*, III, pp. 230–32.
106. Slančiauskas, op. cit., pp. 83–89.
107. *Taut. Darbai*, IV, pp. 283–84, and *Liet. Tautosaka*, IV, p. 501.
108. Balys, *Liet. Taut. Skaitymai*, I, p. 76.

109. Basanavičius, *Liet. Pas. Yv.*, I, p. 291.
110. Būga, *Rinkt. Raštai*, I, p. 124.
111. Slančiauskas, op cit., p. 220.
112. See n. 74, above.
113. See Balys, *Liet. Taut. Skaitymai*, II, p. 39.
114. Basanavičius, *Liet. Pas. Yv.*, III, p. 75.
115. *Taut. Darbai*, IV, pp. 223–24.
116. *Leit. Tautosaka*, III, pp. 230–32.
117. "Nakviša does not let the man sleep at night, i.e., *takes away his dreams.*" *LKŽ* (nakviša).
118. LTA 832 (437–38) Rsn. [Lithuanian Folklore Archives—Lietuvių Tautosakos Archyvas].
119. LTA 757 (89) Pnv.
120. LTA 828 (202) Mrj.
121. Liet. Taut., IV, pp. 462–63.
122. Cf., for instance, LTR 372 (16) where three horses ask the hero to chop off their heads. Becoming gentlemen, they say, "Don't cry, here we are. We were cursed, *until our heads were chopped off.*"
123. Davainis-Silvestraitis, op. cit., p. 206.
124. LTR 724 (91).
125. J. Puhwel, *The Indo-European Structure of the Baltic Pantheon* (UCLA, preprint).
126. Published in Leipzig in 3 volumes (1876–96), ed. M. Perbach. The historical and philosophical problems of this chronicle do not enter into the frames of this study. We will utilize only the Puhwel citations.
127. Op. cit., p. 77.
128. Op. cit., p. 78.
129. Op. cit., pp. 94–95.
130. Būga, *Rinkt. raštai*, II, p. 77–78.
131. Id., ibid., I, p. 188.
132. M. Stryjkowski, *Kronika*, p. 400.
133. *Deliciae Prussicae*, p. 26; in Basanavičius, *Rinkt. raštai*, p. 361.
134. See Balys, *Liet. Taut. Skaitymai, II. p. 46.*
135. Op. cit., p. 41.
136. Op. cit., pp. 46–47.
137. Op. cit., II, p. 48.
138. Compare *kumeliuko krikštynos [Christening of the Colt]*, Kossarzewski, *Lituanica* in *Taut. Darb.*, III, p. 147.
139. See Būga, *Rinkt. raštai*, I, pp. 149–50.
140. See Balys, *Liet. Taut. Skait.*, II, p. 70.
141. See H. Biezais, *Die Himmlische Götterfamilie der Alten Letten* (Uppsala, 1972), pp. 21–44.
142. Id., ibid., p. 21 passim.
143. Cited in J. Balys, op. cit., II, p. 70.
144. Būga, *Rinkt. raštai*, II, p. 98.
145. H. Biezais, op. cit., p. 26, provides the same etymology for *Aus-eklis*.
146. Davainis-Silvestraitis, op. cit., p. 200.

4. Laima

1. This chapter on Laima is divided into two sections, analyzing first her relations with individual people and, after that, those with all of mankind.
2. J. Basanavičius, *Lietuviškos pasakos yvairios* [Various Lithuanian Tales], IV, pp. 116–17, our italics.

3. An entire bundle of variants can be found in Basanavičius, op. cit.: I, pp. 103–6; III, p. 315; IV, pp. 115–23.
4. Basanavičius, op. cit., I, p. 105; II, pp. 66–67; and Davainis-Silvestraitis, *Pasakos, sakmės, oracijos* [Tales, Legends, Orations] (Vilnius, 1973), p. 283–84.
5. Davainis-Silvestraitis, op. cit., p. 122.
6. Basanavičius, op. cit., IV, p. 115.
7. Davainis-Silvestraitis, op. cit., pp. 283–84. In the footnote (p. 392), the editor notes "This is a rare folktale in Lithuanian folklore. A. T. indicates only Lithuanian variants" (Aarne-Thompson 947 B*).
8. Basanavičius, op. cit., I, p. 105.
9. Id., ibid., II, pp. 66–67.
10. Cf. J. Balys, *Lietuvių Tautosakos Skaitymai [Handbook of Lithuanian Folklore] II*, p. 76.
11. Id., ibid., II, p. 78.
12. E. Gisevius in *Lietuvininkai* [The Lithuanians], p. 143.
13. For example, G. Ostermeyer (1775), cited in Balys, op. cit., II. p. 76.
14. Cf. J. Balys, op. cit., II, p. 79.
15. *LKŽ* (Vs).
16. Snakes or toads, for example, are especially elemental and fitting for medicine before the cuckoo sings. Bathing in water is permitted only after one hears the cuckoo. (*LKŽ*)
17. Numerous examples can be found in the *LKŽ*.
18. *LKŽ* (D20).
19. *Liet. Taut.*, V, pp. 917–18 (Onuškis, 1902).
20. See numerous examples in *LKŽ*.
21. Compare "be quiet, you witch, or you'll cuckoo misfortune up again!" (Ds) and "Gegužė iškukuos bekukuodama," i.e., someone will die (be cursed) (J) in *LKŽ*.
22. *Liet. Taut.*, V (Minkles: 6430).
23. "Having barely cuckooed for one month, the cuckoo turns into a hawk" *LKŽ* (S 187).
24. Basanavičius, op. cit., III, p. 68: A good master, counting his money, becomes rich; and the jealous one, going about his business, sits on it his entire life.
25. Davainis-Silvestraitis, op. cit., pp. 155–57, 216.
26. "Bei der Geburt rufen einige Nadraver noch die *Laime* oder Goettin der Geburt an." Praetorius in Balys, *Liet. Liaudies Pasaulėjauta*, p. 80.
27. Lasicius, *De diis* . . . , *p. 41*.
28. *LKŽ*: KrvP (Mrk).
29. This is a Samogitian humoresque often told by my friend A. Liutkus.
30. Basanavičius, op cit., IV, p. 119.
31. M. Slančiauskas, *Šiaurės Lietuvos sakmės ir anekdotai* [The Tales and Anecdotes of North Lithuania] (Vilnius, 1975), p. 358.
32. Basanavičius, op. cit., IV, p. 119.
33. *LKŽ*.
34. Slančiauskas, op. cit., p. 175.
35. Kossarzewski, Lituanica in *Taut. Darb.*, III, p. 130.
36. Slančiauskas, op. cit., pp. 247–51.
37. *Tautosakos Darbai* [Folklore Studies], IV, pp. 263–64.
38. *LKŽ* (Erz).
39. Basanavičius, op. cit., p. 116-17.
40. Slančiauskas, op. cit., p. 214.
41. *Taut. Darb.*, IV, p. 263.
42. Basanavičius, op. cit., I, p. 104.
43. Id., Ibid., IV, p. 117.
44. *Taut. Darb.*, IV, pp. 263–64; cf. Slančiauskas, op. cit., p. 132.
45. On this occasion one is reminded of the well-known stories about the *Moon* who

pulled the maiden into the well when she was fetching water: they do not differ in essence from the child drowning in the well.

46. Basanavičius, op. cit., IV, p. 115.
47. Id., Ibid., III, p. 315.
48. Id., ibid., I, p. 104.
49. Compare, for instance, the story of a man lost at night, who finds himself in the forest at a wedding arranged by the devils for his neighbor. It appears later that the neighbor had hanged herself. *Dubingiai,* pp. 339–40.
50. Slančiauskas, op. cit., pp. 101–5.
51. Basanavičius, op. cit., IV, pp. 113–15. The significance of cracklings, we will admit, is not clear. Should it perhaps be compared to the cult of the dead and its relation with the pigs?
52. Basanavičius, op. cit., III, p. 58.
53. Slančiauskas, op. cit., pp. 101–4.
54. *Taut. Darb.,* IV, p. 203.
55. Basanavičius, op. cit., I, pp. 123–24, 125–26; II, p. 301; IV, pp. 108–9, 109–10, 110–11, 111–12. an interesting variant appears in *Taut. Darb.,* IV, p. 203, in which *Giltinė* (= death), created by God, gets it into her head to "marry," has a son, and teaches him to be a doctor. From this one variant it is as yet not clear who could be her husband, who is so afraid of her.
56. In place of a *nut,* other variants provide a *barrel,* used earlier as a *valise;* sometimes it is a basket presented by the Old Man God as a gift or even, finally, an *iron coffin.*
57. Basanavičius, op. cit., I, pp. 116–17.
58. Basanavičius, op. cit., pp. 131–32.
59. Id., ibid., II, pp. 262–64.
60. *Lietuvių Tautosaka,* III, pp. 643–45; cf. Slančiauskas, op. cit., p. 191.
61. Balys, *Lietuvių Tautosakos Skaitymai,* II, p. 78.
62. Id., ibid., (Valkininkai).
63. Basanavičius, op. cit., II, pp. 186–87.
64. *Gaidės ir Rimšės apylinkes,* Vilnius, 1969, p. 404; cf. also *Taut. Darb.,* IV, p. 476.
65. *LKŽ.*
66. Slančiauskas, op. cit., p. 253.
67. Cf., along with many others, Basanavičius, op. cit., I, pp. 122–23; IV, p. 78, 113–15.
68. A. Juška, *Liet. Svotbinės dainos* [Lithuanian Wedding Songs), I. p. 46.
69. Id., ibid., I, p. 448.
70. Basanavičius, op. cit., IV, pp. 10–11.
71. Id., ibid., III, p. 117–18.
72. Cf. Slančiauskas, op. cit., p. 124–25.
73. Id., ibid., III, p. 63.
74. A Juška, *Svotbinė Rėda* in *Lietuviškos Svotbinės Dainos,* 1880, II, p. 586 (footnote).
75. Basanavičius, op. cit., IV, pp. 8–9.
76. Id., ibid., IV, pp. 125–31.
77. Id., ibid., I, pp. 116–17.
78. Id., ibid., I, pp. 122–23.
79. Slančiauskas, op. cit., pp. 101–5.
80. Basanavičius, op. cit., I, p. 104.
81. "Perkunas . . . quercus annosae, szermuksznis . . . alibi Akmo, saxum grandivs . . . a rusticulis adhuc . . . colebantur." Rostowski in Būga, *Rinktiniai raštai,* I, p. 144.
82. Rostowski in Balys, *Liet. Tautos. Skait.,* II, p. 22.
83. *Annuae Litterae Societatis Jesu* anni 1600, Antverpiae 1618, p. 550, cited in Būga, op. cit., I, pp. 144–45.
84. Balys, op. cit., II, p. 22.

85. See *Vulcanus Jagaubis*, IV.
86. Cf. G. Dumézil, *Consus et Ops* in *Idées Romaines*, 1969, pp. 293–96.
86a. Būga, *Rinkt. raštai*, I, pp. 144–45.
87. Otto Glagau in *Lietuvininkai* (Vilnius, 1970), pp. 231–32.
88. Balys, *Liet. Liaudies Pasaulėjauta*, pp. 77–78, indicates that the oldest sources of *Laimelės*, other than Praetorius (ca. 1690), are the Latin introduction of the Klein songbook (1666) and the manuscript of the Brodowski dictionary (before 1744).
89. A study recently appearing in Vilnius (N. Vėlius, *Mitinės Lietuvių sakmių butybės* [Mythic Beings in Lithuanian Folktales], 1977, which reached us when this text had already been completed, devotes one section to the analyses of *Laimės* (pp. 56–82). An interested reader can in that manner compare the results of two methodologies which treat one and the same theme at the same time.
90. Davainis-Silvestraitis, op. cit., p. 206.
91. Id., ibid., pp. 205–8. Summaries of texts published in Polish can be found there as well, pp. 420–21.
92. Vilnius, 1976, pp. 110–11; J. Jurginis refers to T. Narbutt, *Dzieje starożytne narodu Litewskiego*, I, Mitologia Litewska, Wilno, 1835, pp. 2–3. We regret that we were not able to make use of the original T. Narbutt text.
93. See chap. 7.
94. Davainis-Silvestraitis, op. cit., p. 205.
95. *LKŽ* (KlvD 185).
96. See supra, p. 113.
97. See supra, p. 82.
98. "Les compagnons de la Fortune" in *Fêtes Romaines* (1975), p. 239.
99. "The sash of Laumė draws the rain from the lakes and rivers," Kossarzewski, Litvanica in *Taut. Darb.*, III, p. 147. The same author in the same text calls it *Laimės juosta*. Compare this to "Laumė draws the water" *LKŽ* (Smn).
100. Būga, *R. r.*, II, p. 323.
101. *Vaivoras* or crowberry (*Vaccinium uliginosum*) otherwise is called *girtuoklė, gervuogė, mėlynė* [intoxicating plant]. See *LKŽ*.
102. Glagau in *Lietuvininkai*, pp. 231–32.
103. According to Būga, both the berry and the sash of Laumė have derived their name from the color *var-, ver-* "žydras" [azure blue].
104. *LKŽ* (Slm). See the word *gaubėti* [contain, encompass].
105. LTR (Pn) in *LKŽ*.
106. See analyses of *Austėja* and *Ganda, Apie Dievus ir žmones*, ch. 5.
107. Slančiauskas, op. cit., p. 124.
108. Basanavičius, *Apie gyvenimą vėliu bei velnių*: sometimes the goddess of the plague *Maro deivė* appears by herself in a chariot with six black horses (p. 39) and other times with "three pretty young maids, dressed in long white robes" (p. 39).
109. *LKŽ* citing Kurschat, II, p. 303.
110. *Taut. Darb.*, IV, p. 225.
111. Kossarzewski in *Taut. Darb.*, III, p. 123.
112. *Liet. Pas.*, I, p. 73.
113. Compare supra, *Aušrinė*, p. 90.
114. The semantic distribution of this word family should be studied separately. Compare *lykuoti* "to count," "to guess even or odd" (*LKŽ*); it is in a certain sense to divine, guess the future.
115. See chap. 5.
116. Citing Balys, *Liet. Liaudies Pasaulėjauta*, 80, p. 11.
117. Z. Slaviūnas, *Sutartinės* [Choral Rounds], II, pp. 649–50. The first was recorded in 1939 (from a 75-year-old informant), the second in 1902 (from an unknown informant).
118. Id., ibid., explanation, p. 735.

119. See supra, p. 78.
120. Such, for instance, is Grunau's assertion concerning the Prussian religion, pp. 94–95 (Puhvel, op. cit., p. 5).
121. See supra, p. 83.
122. J. Balys, *Apie mitologija iš esmės* [Mythology from Essence] in *Naujoji Viltis* [New Hope], 10, 1977, pp. 50–51.
123. *Būdas*, p. 81.
124. Glagau in *Lietuvininkai*, pp. 231–32.
125. Lasicius, op. cit., p. 40.
126. See supra, pp. 42 and 101.
127. We are using unpublished data from the manuscript that the Hellenist J. Jacob read at our seminar, March 8, 1978.
128. S. Daukantas, *Būdas*, p. 29.
129. Slančiauskas, op. cit., p. 124.

5. On Bees and Women

1. J. Lasicius, *De diis samagitarum*, p. 41.
2. B. Savukynas, "Dievai ir jų vardai" [The Gods and Their Names] in *Kultūros Barai*, 6, 1970, pp. 169–73.
3. *Liet. Etnogr. Bruožai* [Features of Lithuanian Ethnography], p. 143.
4. Daina, cited in *Liet. Taut. Apybraiža* [A Survey of Lithuanian Folklore], p. 138.
5. *Liet. Taut.* [Lithuanian Folklore], V, p. 532.
6. *Liet. Taut.*, V, p. 533.
7. *Liet. Taut.*, V, p. 532. Cf. K. Būga, *R. r.*, II, p. 307: *siūti* "korius dirbti" [to sew—"make the honeycombs"], *bitys siuva* "die Bienen tragen.".
8. *Liet. Taut.*, V. p. 532.
9. R. Détienne, *L'Orphée au miel* in *Quaderni Urbinati di Cultura Classica*, XII, 1971, p. 13.
10. Id., ibid., p. 14.
11. Thus S. Daukantas characterizes the mother (*LKŽ*).
12. *Liet. Etnogr. Br.*, pp. 437–38: we have here in mind, of course, *Lietuvos Statutas*. The same mother-housewife role is characteristic of ancient Greek society.
13. So say, at least according to J. Petrulis (*Merkinė*, p. 159), women of the older generation.
14. J. Petrulis, *Dubingiai*, p. 136.
15. J. Petrulis, *Merkinė*, p. 159.
16. *Dubingiai*, pp. 137–38. This fact was confirmed after our lecture in Chicago in December, 1977, by B. Nainys who came from an entirely different corner of Lithuania—Pasvalys.
17 *Dubingiai*, pp. 137–38.
18. Cf. J. Petrulis, *Merkinė*, p. 159: "Sebrinai (i.e., bičiuliai)—kinship due to the bees."
19. *Dubingiai*, pp. 137–38.
20. Détienne, *L'Orphée au miel*, p. 13.
21. Détienne, *L'Orphée au miel*, p. 12.
22. *Dubingiai*, p. 137.
23. *Liet. Etnogr. Br.*, p. 145.
24. *Merkinė*, p. 158.
25. *Merkinė*, p. 159.
26. *Dubingiai*, p. 136.
27. *Dubingiai*, p. 136.
28. Davainis-Silvestraitis, op. cit., p. 278.
29. *Merkinė*, p. 159.

30. *Maž. Liet. Tar. Encik.* (bičiulystė).
31. *Dubingiai*, p. 135.
32. *LKŽ.*
33. *Maž. Tar. Encikl.* [Small Lithuanian Soviet Encyclopedia].
34. B. Kerbelytė, *Kai milžinai gyveno* [When Giants Lived] (Vilnius, 1969), pp. 18–19.
35. All these words can be found in *LKŽ*. The major *Liet. Encik.* notes that *bandininkas* is attested at the beginning of the sixteenth century. The distribution of this word family encompasses all of Lithuania; therefore the ethnographic facts recorded in the Kupiškis region are vestiges of antiquity and not a localized phenomenon.
36. Compare, for instance, the German *Band*, which, among other things, provided for the Italian *bandits* and the ancient French *ban* "all the vassals of one lord."
37. According to J. Petrulis, the bees at swarming time fly as far as 40 kilometers.
38. K. Jablonskis, *Lietuviški žodžiai* . . . , p. 2, cited in J. Jurginis, *De diis*, p. 73.
39. B. Buracas, *Kupiškėnų Sekminės* in *Taut. Darb.*, III, pp. 104–5.
40. See chap. 7.
41. Buracas, op. cit., III, pp. 105–10.
42. Citing the commentaries of Jurginis in *De diis*, p. 72.
43. Ziedonis Ligers, *Ethnographie Lettonne* (Picard, 1954), I. p. 507.
44. Milda Skeirytė, *Audimas* in *Kernavė*, pp. 179–80.
45. Praetorius, cited in *Svotbinė Rėda* [Wedding Laments], in A. Juška, *Liet. Svotbinės Dainos*, II, p. 572, notes.
46. *Svotbinė Rėda*, in op. cit., II, p. 583, notes (Marčinkonys).
47. *Svotbinė Rėda*, in op. cit., II, p. 586, notes.
48. Ligers, op. cit., I, p. 508.
49. II, p. 632.
50. Liet. Taut., V, p. 907.
51. Basanavičius, *Liet. Pas.*, II, p. 326.
52. LMD I 849 (1). Cf. also Basanavičius, *Liet. Pas.*, IV, pp. 84 and 86.
53. Juška, *Liet. Svodbinės Dainos* (St. Petersburg, 1883), facsimile, p. 347.
54. *Budas*, p. 42.
55. *Svotbinė Rėda*, in op. cit., II, p. 343.
56. See supra, p. 73.
57. *Svotbinė Rėda*, in op. cit., II, p. 587, notes.
58. Davainis-Silvestraitis, op. cit., p. 210.
59. *Taut. Darb.*, I, p. 206.
60. *Svotbinė Rėda*, in op. cit., II, p. 293.
61. E. Gisevius in *Lietuvininkai*, p. 146, notes that "this custom now has almost entirely died out, since women can wear the *mutura* not only after childbirth but right after the wedding." And, actually, the ethnographic texts of the nineteenth century most often confuse, or do not differentiate at all, *nuometas* and the *mutura*.
62. Détienne, *L'Orphée au miel*, p. 16. We use conventional French spelling for the Greek words.
63. *Taut. Darb.*, III, pp. 34–35. Cf. Gisevius in *Lietuvininkai*, p. 160, and Glagaw, ibid., p. 247. *Nuotaka* [bride] here is a word used only by the translator. The expression *nuotakos sriuba* [soup of the bride] used in "Lithuanian weddings" (*Lietuvininkai*, p. 192) is only the banalization of the name of the drink. Compare this with *Bobasuppe*, eaten during *gabjauja*, chap. 6, below.
64. *Taut. Darb.*, VII, p. 145 (Klaipėdos kr.).
65. *Taut. Darb.*, III, pp. 34–35.
66. The degradation of the ritual drink can be identified in the description of "Lithuanian weddings" (see n. 63) where a drink made of "degtinė with sugar and cherry juice," called "soup," was spooned out by guests from plates and drunk from glasses by others.
67. *Liet. Taut.*, I, p. 266.

68. *Taut. Darb.*, VII, p. 145.
69. Gisevius, op. cit., p. 145–46.
70. Petrulis, *Dubingiai*, p. 140.
71. Petrulis, *Merkinė*, pp. 162–63.
72. *Maž. Tar. Liet. Encikl.*, II, p. 283.
73. S. Skruodenis, in *Merkinė*, p. 310.
74. *Liet. Taut.*, I, pp. 225–28.
75. C. Cappeller in *Lietuvininkai*, pp. 375–76.
76. "Dzūkų lalauninkai" in *Taut. Darb.*, III, pp. 94–98.
77. See chap. 4, above.
78. Cf. our *La mythologie comparée* in *Du Sens*, 1970, pp. 117–34, where G. Dumézil's descriptive procedures and methodology concerning Indo-European mythology are analyzed.
79. Cf. *Taut. Darb.*, III, pp. 101–4.
80. Lasicius, op. cit., p. 31. The same custom is recorded in Marcinkonys (LTR 4556/176 in *Svotbinė Rėda*, op. cit., II, p. 581, footnote), where the lips of *both* newlyweds are anointed with honey. This is clear degradation of a ritual no longer understood but still preserved.
81. *Svotbinė Rėda*, op. cit., II, p. 345.
82. Praetorius, VIII, pp. 37–38, cited in *Svotbinė Rėda*, op. cit., II, p. 586, footnote.
83. M. Détienne, *Les Jardins d'Adonis*, 1972, p. 155: the fast is accompanied by sexual abstinence.
84. Détienne, *L'Orphée au miel*, p. 17.
85. Juška, op. cit., II, p. 338.
86. Būdas, p. 145. A similar punishment is recorded in Latvia: the guilty one would be tied naked to the tree, in which there was a beehive; having his stomach cut open to the navel and his intestines pulled out and wound around the tree, he would be left there to die. Z. Ligers, op. cit., I, p. 480.

6. Gods and Festivals: Vulcanus Jagaubis

1. Jacob Brodowski, *Lexicon Germanico-Lithvanicum et Lithvanico-Germanicum* (manuscript), cited in K. Būga, *Rinktiniai raštai* [Selected Writings] I, p. 158, footnote 1.
2. J. Balys, *Lietuvių liaudies pasaulėjauta* (Chicago, 1966). See the conclusions he draws in the final pages (pp. 111–16).
3. Ibid., p. 26.
4. Būga, *Rinkt. raštai*, I, pp. 210–11.
5. Georges Dumézil, *Fêtes romaines d'été d'automne* (Paris: Gallimard, 1975), pp. 61–77.
6. *De diis samagitarum* (Vilnius: Vaga, 1969), p. 24 (Lithuanian version) and p. 44 (facsimile).
7. In Balys, op. cit., p. 26.
8. *LKŽ*.
9. In Balys, op. cit., p. 26.
10. *LKŽ*.
11. Balys, *Lietuvių Tautosakos Skaitymai* [Handbook of Lithuanian Folklore] II, pp. 94–95.
12. *LKŽ*.
13. J. Elisonas in *Tautosakos Darbai* [Folklore Studies] VI, p. 325.
14. *LKŽ*.
15. In Balys, op. cit., p. 95.
16. Id., ibid., p. 94.
17. *Mažoji Lietuviskoji Tarybine Enciklopedija*, II, p. 725.
18. *LKŽ* (Geistarai, Vilkaviškio reg.).

19. *Maž. Liet. Tar. Enciklopedija* and *LKŽ* (V. Kudirka).
20. *Maž. Liet. Tar. Enciklopedija* III, (Užgavėnės).
21. *LKŽ* (Kuršis).
22. This is the definition of Gavėnas indicated in *LKŽ*.
23. All the examples are taken from *LKŽ*.
24. A. Kossarzewski, *Litvanica* in *Tautosakos Darbai*, III, p. 127.
25. *Deliciae Prussicae* (Berlin, 1871), p. 26, in J. Basanavičius, *Rinktiniai raštai* (Vilnius, 1970), p. 361.
26. Op. cit., p. 119.
27. Balys, op. it., p. 114.
28. Id., ibid.
29. *Lietuvių Kalbos Tarmės* [Lithuanian Dialects] (Vilnius), p. 303.
30. All the citations are taken from *LKŽ*.
31. Balys, op. it., p. 120.
32. All names are taken from *LKŽ*.
33. Balys, op. cit., p. 120.
34. Balys, op. cit., p. 120, and *LKŽ* (Gavėnas).
35. Id., ibid.
36. Id., ibid.
37. See chap. 1, above.
38. Op. cit., p. 118.
39. Id., ibid., p. 110.
40. See chap. 1.
41. Ibid., p. 117.
42. Lasicius, *De diis samagitarum*, p. 42.
43. *LKŽ* and Balys, op. cit., p. 25ff.
44. *LKŽ*.
45. *LKŽ*.
46. G. Dumézil, op, cit., p. 63.
47. Id., ibid.
48. Op. cit., p. 131.
49. Op. cit., p. 145.
50. See chap. 2, above.
51. See (among other texts) in *Rinktiniai raštai*, I, pp. 210–11.
52. (Vilnius, 1971), pp. 192–98.
53. *Annuae Litterae Societatis Jesu* anni 1660 (Antverpiae, 1918), p. 550, cited in Buga, op. cit., pp. 144–45.
54. Citations taken from *LKŽ*.
55. In Basanavičius, op. cit., p. 362.
56. Dumézil, op. cit., pp. 66–67.

7. Gods and Festivals: Krikštai

1. *Taut. Darb.* [Folklore Studies], III, 37 (LTA 982/24).
2. *Taut. Darb.*, III, 25. It appears that the dominant role of St. Paul in Protestantism helped in the comparison of his "conversion" with the turning of the bear to the other side in Lithuania Minor.
3. *Liet. Etnogr. Bruožai*, p. 539.
4. M. Slančiauskas, op. cit., p. 217.
5. *Taut. Darb.*, III, p. 25 (Lithuania Minor).
6. *De diis*, p. 48 (Latin, p. 30 (Lithuanian).
7. Cf. "Review of analyses" in *De diis*, p. 63, and J. Balys, *Liet. Taut. Skaitymai*, II, p. 67.

Notes for pages 201 to 202

8. *De diis*, p. 20.
9. Balys, *Liet. Taut. Skait.*, II, pp. 66–67, cites his work *Antiquitates Borussicae*.
10. Balys, ibid., citing *Liet. Tauta* [Lithuanian Nation], I, 2, p. 177, indicates that it is a ritual song from the region of Daukšės.
11. Cf. also chap. 3.
12. A. Kossarzewski, *Litvanica* in *Taut. Darb.*, III, p. 147.
13. Compare, among others, the riddle "On a Wednesday, on a Friday, a colt was born with golden horseshoes (the moon)."
14. See chap. 5, above.
15. *LKŽ*.
16. *LKŽ*.
17. See the article *Waidelotte*, in Būga, *Rinkt raštai*, I, pp. 183–87, and S. Grunau, cited in J. Puhwel, *The Indo-European Structure of the Baltic Pantheon*, UCLA, manuscript, p. 5.

NAME INDEX

Aeolus Žmudzki, 61, 193
Aesculap(i)us (Grk. and Lat.), 104, 108, 109, 201
Aitvaras, 18, 19, 21, 26, 28–29, 34, 42–63, 105, 188, 193
Andaj, 104
Angiai, 104
Apidėmė, 53–55, 213*n103*
Aristaeus (Grk.), 163, 180
Audenis, 75
Auseklis (Latv.), 108, 110
Ausschauts (Pruss.), 109–110
Austėja, 118, 150, 158–81
Auszweikus, 109
Aušra, 75, 77, 153
Aušrinė, 9, 64, 74, 77–78, 80–89, 102, 110, 114, 121, 125, 150–57; Servant, 82, 83, 84, 102
Auššveitis, 110–11, 125, 154, 155
Auštra, 75, 77
Auštrinis, 75, 77
Autrimpas (Pruss.), 109

Babaužė, 188
Babilas, 161, 167
Bangpūtis, 75, 105, 188
Barstukas (kaukutis), 20–23, 37, 40, 56, 105, 188
Barzdukas, 18, 20–23
Baubaušis. *See* Jaučių Baubis
Baublys. *See* Jaučių Baubis
Baužis, 188
Bezdukas, 20, 22, 23, 24, 40
Bhaga (Indic), 127, 154
Blessed Virgin, 77, 83, 102, 150
Bog (Slav.), 127, 154
Bress (Irish), 178
Bubalis. *See* Jaučių Baubis
Bubas, 188
Bubilas, 167–71, 179–80

Christ, 199
Cow: of Plenty, 81; Iron, 94; of Laumė, 110

Dalis, 90, 125–33
Demeter (Grk.), 160
Deuotis, 106
Deyve, 134, 194
Dievas, 78, 105, 119–20, 139
Diviriks, 104

Drąsus, 19
Drebkulys, 105, 188
Dwarfs, race of, 136
Dzievaicis, 105

Eglė, 101
Euridice (Grk.), 163, 180
Ežiagulys (Ezagulis), 30, 39, 207*n47*

Fortuna (Lat.), 144

Gabėnas, 192, 193
Gabie deus, 184, 192
Gabija (-elė, -ikė, -ėta), 47, 121, 122, 183, 184, 192
Gabikis, 192
Gabis (-ys), 192
Gabjauja, 105, 183–85
Gabjaujis, 134, 183–87, 190–91
Gabvartai, 194–95
Gaia (Grk.), 154
Galgis, 188
Ganda, 180
Gavėnas (-anas, -enis), 62, 188–92
Gediminas, 142
Gegutė, 116, 117, 201
George, St., 197
Giant: armless, 72; one-eyed, 76, 139; race, 75, 101, 136, 138
Giltinė, 105, 111, 119, 123–25, 133, 152, 157, 188

Indra (Indic), 103, 122

Jagaubis, 12, 13, 183, 187, 192
Jargutalis (Jur-), 188
Jaučių Baubis, 80
Javų dvasia, 12, 186, 194
Jogaila, 201
Joseph, St., 67, 77, 85
Jupiter, 144

Kalvelis, 86–89, 104
Kanapius (-inskas, -ickas), 189
Kaukas (Kaukutis), 10, 18–41, 42, 43, 44–45, 48–49, 56, 105, 188, 191, 195
King of the Crabs, 91
King of the Seas, 62, 95
Kirnis, 55–60
Kumpickas, 189

227

Name Index

Kuršis (-as), 187, 189

Laima (-ė), 59, 74, 95, 101, 111, 112–57, 178
Laima-Dalia, 43, 70, 90, 125–27, 133, 134, 135, 154, 156
Laimelė (Lau-), 113, 135, 156
Laimės (three), 111, 113, 114, 131, 145, 150, 153–55
Laimykas, 43
Lašinius (-ininis, -inskas), 189
Laukpatis, 23
Lauksargis, 43
Laumė, 10, 35, 43, 110–14, 143, 144, 180–81, 188
Lazdona, 161, 170–71, 175
Liubegeldae, 83

Mada (Indic), 196
Maia (Lat.), 196
Man / human race, 136
Marcoppolum, 23
Matergabia, 192
Medeina, 85
Mėnulis, 75, 77, 81, 102, 105–108, 111, 121, 127, 131, 142, 151, 155, 201–202
Mėsinas, 189
Mithra, 51, 59, 69, 71, 103, 105, 122, 127, 142, 156

Namiszki Diewai (household gods), 44, 105, 134, 188
Nelaimė, 125, 126, 157, 176
Nunaday, 104
Nymph (Grk.), 174, 180

Occopiruum, 139
Ops Consiua (Lat.), 134
Orpheus (Grk.), 163, 179

Patrimpas (Pruss.), 102–103, 105, 155, 201, 202
Patulas (Pruss.), 102, 104
Pėleno Gabija (Polengabia), 192, 193
Perkūnas, 31, 33, 43, 47, 54, 61–63, 77, 87, 102, 106, 120–22, 123, 151
Perkunas (Pruss.), 102
Phoenix (Grk.), 46
Pizius, 180
Polyphemus, 76, 139
Praamžius (-is), 138, 139–45, 147
Prakorimas, 138, 139–45, 147, 152, 154, 156, 157
Prakurimas, 137, 139, 140
Prometheus (Grk.), 91
Pūkys, 45, 211$n27$
Pušaitis, 22, 56
Pusčius, 61

Pušetas, 21
Puškaitis, 23–24, 26, 28, 40, 45, 56, 69

Ragana, 74, 85–88, 90, 110, 113, 146, 171, 180
Rugių Boba, 186

Saulė, 33, 64, 76–78, 86, 89, 151, 152, 193; Second Son, 68, 73, 76–77, 82
Sea Maiden, 78–80, 81, 83, 91, 94, 99, 101
Senelis Dievas, 113, 117, 120, 124, 127, 128, 129, 142
Silkius, 191
Slogutė, 43
Sorcerers, 85, 99
Spirit, 112
Stata (Lat.), 196

Šiaurys, 68, 75–77, 79, 81–92 passim, 99
Šventaragis, 6, 104, 142
Švitelis, 45, 211$n35$

Upinis, 33

Vaidevutis (Pruss.), 165
Vaižgantas, 28, 37, 38, 40, 45, 190, 207$n36$, 209$n108$
Vandenis, 75, 79, 80, 138, 139, 144, 147, 154
Vargas, 125, 126
Varuna (Indic), 51, 59, 103, 122
Vāyu (Indic), 61, 193
Vėjas, 61–63, 73, 75, 85, 87, 113, 138, 144, 147, 193
Vejasmate (Latv.), 127
Vėjopatis, 61, 74
Vėjų Motina, 64, 71, 72, 73, 74–76, 97
Vėlė, 37, 38, 90, 91, 209$n102$, 210$n119$; three, 90
Veliona, 38–39, 209$n117$
Velnias (Devil), 27, 43, 48, 53, 61, 62, 76, 80, 86–87, 93, 122, 128, 139, 142, 144, 154
Vesta (Lat.), 193
Volcanus (Lat.), 184, 187, 193, 196
Vulcanus (Lat.), 86, 104, 184, 193

Waydolottinnen (Pruss.), 103, 202
Welina, 42, 43

Žaltviska, 45, 48, 57, 211$n35$
Žemė (Earth), 79, 82, 144, 153, 154
Žemėpačiai, 42, 154
Žemėpatis, 23, 43, 105, 188, 209$n108$
Žemininkai, 101, 104–105, 108, 110, 154
Žemyna, 33, 63, 74, 105, 118, 158–61 passim, 165, 188, 209$n108$
Žynė, 85, 150

SUBJECT INDEX

Acorn, 83
Air, 19, 34, 63, 79, 92, 161, 173, 193
Ale, 13, 44, 186
Altar, 134, 135
Ant, 70
Apple, 72–74, 80, 97, 172, 175
Ax, 126, 139

Ball, 72, 75
Bandininkas, 165–67
Bandžiulystė, 165, 166, 170
Barren woman, 36, 209$n95$
Beads, 88, 97
Bear, 197, 198
Beauty, 74, 78, 80, 92, 94, 106, 155
Bee, 158–81, 199
Beekeeping, 140, 161, 162, 163
Beheading, 100
Bičiulystė, 163–65
Birds (three), 47, 131
Black, 47, 48, 49, 54, 58, 186
Blacksmith, 86, 87, 89
Blindness, 55
Boar, 28, 29, 31, 33, 38, 49
Bobasuppe, 186
Boundary, 112
Boundless, 62, 147
Bread, 21, 165, 166
Bridge, 86, 88
Bridle, 99
Brolava, 167
Brother (second), 161, 164
Bull, 79, 80, 99, 100, 108, 110, 145
Bullfight, 167

Casting a spell, 50
Cherry tree, 56–57
Chick, 47, 54, 58–59
Christening, 150–52; of colt, 201, 202
Christianity, 199
Christmas, 35
Churchyard, 39
Class, 118
Clothed, 26
Cloud, 32, 33, 80
Coal, 25, 26, 45
Coin-bearing aitvaras, 45, 211$n26$
Coins, 26, 45, 59, 211$n53$, 212$n67$; burning, 45, 211$n33$; returning, 50
Colt (of God), 82

Cooked, 19, 21, 44
Corē (Grk.), 174
Cow, 81, 86, 110; iron, 80, 94
Crab, 91, 92
Cradle, 85, 86
Crossroads, 49, 50, 198, 212$n59$
Crowberry, 146
Curds, 44, 210$n22$

Čvikas, 202
Čvikinas, 13, 202

Dalis, 90, 112–31, 135, 142, 146, 154, 157; bedalis, 90–91, 125–26
Daughter-in-law. See Marti
Death, 95, 96, 119, 120
Devil's day, 99
Dew, 80, 88, 97, 153, 177
Dishonesty, 163
Dragon, 19, 94
Dream, 98
Drone, 168, 169, 179, 209$n96$
Drying frame, 189
Dušia (material soul), 90, 95; king without-, 95
Dwindling, 132

Earth, 19, 23–35 passim, 63, 79, 82, 101, 137, 144, 148, 153–54, 173, 192
Egg, 28, 48, 59, 91, 95–96, 202
Egghunting, 177, 178
Elder(berry) bush, 22, 56, 57, 59
Entrails, 88
Evil one, 163
Exchange, 85
Eyes, 52, 53, 58, 106; plucked-out, 58, 92, 97

Fart, 22, 23
Fertility, 158, 173
Find(ing), 49, 83
Fire, 26–29, 34, 44–55 passim, 120, 131, 184, 186, 188, 192–93, 211$n43$
Firewood, 121
Flax, 25, 26, 169, 190; flaxseed, 37
Flood, 76, 136–38, 146, 147, 152
Flour, 44, 210$n19$
Forest, 69, 79, 85, 104, 105
Fortune. See Laimė

Gabartai, 195, 196
Gabjauja (-is), 183, 188

Subject Index

Garden of Paradise, 73
Garnio šventė, 186
Gavėnas, 188, 189; cake, 190, 193; expulsion, 188
Gavėnia, 188, 190, 192
Grabnyčios (Candlemas), 197, 198
Graincrops, 44, 103, 184–86
Granary. *See* Klėtis
Graveyard, 37
Gyvastis, 94–96
Gyvuonis, 92–93, 96

Hail, 30, 31, 32, 39
Hair, 51–52, 69, 70, 77, 83
Ham bones, 30, 37
Hawk, 70–71, 92, 117
Health. *See* Sveikata
Heart, 52
Hemp, 189, 201
Herd, 165, 166; Aušrinė's herd, 80–81, 110
Hobble, 73
Honey, 163, 175, 176, 179, 201
Horn, month of the, 203
Horse, 43, 53, 81, 91, 100, 213*n91*; silver, 81
Horseshoe, 53

Idol, 135
Ilgės, 37, 38
Illness, 52, 92, 94, 112, 155
Island, 79

Jauja, 184, 188, 190, 194–95
Jumping, 172, 173

Kaltūnas, 14, 30, 43, 51–53, 55, 62, 212*n81*, 213*n91*
Kaukas (*Mandragora off.*), 19
Kaukė, 35, 36, 40
Kaukolė, 36, 37
Klėtis, 134, 190
Kluonas, 19, 190, 194
Knife, 61, 87, 97, 188
Knowledge, 75, 81, 85, 115, 145
Krikštai (New Year), 188, 197–202
Krikštas (as beginning), 199
Krikštijimas (as tasting), 140, 200
Krikštinti, 198–99

Ladle, 184
Laimė (Laima), 70, 103, 112–16, 127, 131, 146, 157, 201
Lamb, 129, 130
Lameness, 53
Leader, 167
Leeches, 179
Left (foot), 201
Lerva, 36
Linden tree, 57, 59, 95, 153

Lino kančia, 26–27
Liquid, tossing of, 171–73
Liver, 89–96, 130
Love, 74, 98
Lungs, 89–91, 96, 130
Lyčyna, 36

Mare of the sea, 81–82, 99, 108
Market day, 99
Martavimas, 171–81
Marti, 173–81; blood of, 13, 174, 175; tears of, 175
Material benefit. *See* Nauda
Mead, 13, 172–80
Meat, 44, 179, 185, 189
Melissa (Grk.), 160, 162
Men: groups, 161, 186, 190, 192
Méros (Grk.), 154
Mētēr (Grk.), 174
Mid-Lent, 190, 194, 197
Milk, 21, 44, 86, 97, 103, 110; boiling, 80, 94; spoiling of, 86, 110
Moirae (Grk.), 114, 154, 155
Moon, 43, 105
Muturas, 174, 176

Nails, 52, 62, 193
Naked, 25, 26, 46
Nauda, 18, 22, 44, 110, 118, 132, 134, 155–56, 165
Numphē (Grk.), 179, 180
Nuometas, 174, 176
Nut, 83, 124, 137, 142, 143, 170, 171, 175

Opening, 112, 178
Orchard, 72–74, 76
Overturning: head over heels, 190; drying frame, 191; other side, 198
Ox, 80, 95, 100; blue, 92; oxhide, 121
Ožinis (wind), 75

Pear tree, 49, 56, 58, 59
Pearls, 88, 97
Pestilence, 149
Pig, 30–33, 38–39, 189, 192, 208*nn53,90*; head, 190; tail, 190
Pillar, 54, 195
Plague, 136, 147–49, 152
Poppy (seed), 202
Porridge, 44
Prakorimas (as destiny), 139–40
Prophesy, 112–25, 128, 141, 146, 200

Rain, 31, 39
Rainbow, 33, 137–44 *passim*, 146–48, 153
Raw, 19, 21, 44
Red, 47, 146
Reflection, 84, 154, 155

Subject Index

Riddle, 206
Roadway, 49, 56, 212n59; 213n105
Roasted, 19, 44
Rooster, 29, 47–57 passim, 115, 131, 185–87, 191–92
Rope, 73
Rue garden, 73
Rye, 30
Rye stubble, 176

Saddle, 81, 99
Sash: of favor, 143–45; of harmony, 33
Scarf (fairy), 146
Seas, 75, 79, 91, 95
Serenading, 176–78
Serpent, 47, 199–200
Shagginess, 169, 170
Share. See Dalis
Sheep, 167–70
Ship, 88
Shrovetide, 177, 187–92
Signs, 144, 146, 148
Sikis (flaxcake), 13, 38, 209n105
Skalsa, 21, 44, 45
Skerstuvės, 38–39
Sky, 82, 86, 88
Sleep, 98; kiaulmiegis, 32
Sleet, 31
Smithy, 86
Smoke, 149
Snake, 19, 103–104, 199–200
Sneezing, 95
Snow, 31
Spark, 184, 191
Stallion, 88, 99, 100, 108
Star, 73, 82, 83, 84, 151, 152
Stomach, 88
Stone, 46, 95, 131–35, 146, 153; sparkling, 146
Storm, 30–32, 63, 95
Stump, 57, 80, 211n43, 215n44
Summer lightning, 31, 32
Sveikata, 74, 92, 89–96, 101–107 passim, 152, 155
Swans, 99
Swindler's day, 99

Šermenys (funeral feast), 37, 39
Šupinys, 191, 192

Talent, 118
Taster, 140
Testicles, 28, 34, 38, 48, 49
Thesmophoria (Grk.), 160, 179
Thorn, 83
Three, 156
Three-branched, 131
Three Kings' Day, 197
Threshing barn. See Jauja
Threshing floor. See Kluonas
Throne of the wind, 75
Thunder, 31, 39, 47
Torment of Flax. See Lino kančia
Treasure, 45, 46, 49

Universe, 61, 154
Uprooter, 76
Užkurystė, 162

Volcanalia (Lat.), 184, 196
Vomiting, 31, 45, 210n52

Wages, 25, 131
Waning of the moon, 25
Water, 30–35, 62, 63, 79–80, 82–97 passim, 101, 120, 121, 209n117; golden, 97; healing, 92–93, 96; living, 92–93
Wax (candle), 56
Weaving, 159
Whirlwind, 61, 63, 213n122
Wife, 52, 130, 131
Window, 112, 177, 178
Wine, 171, 177
Wisdom, 129, 142
Wolf, 70–71, 72, 92, 96
Woman, 158–81
Woodchip, 24, 26
Wool, 149, 169, 170
Wreath, 174

Youth, 80, 92, 94, 106, 155

ALGIRDAS JULIEN GREIMAS (1917–1992) was Directeur d'Études à l'École des Hautes Études en Sciences Sociales, Paris. He coauthored (with J. Courtés) *Semiotics and Language: An Analytical Dictionary* and coedited *Essais de sémiotique poétique* and *Introduction à l'analyse du discours en sciences sociales*.

MILDA NEWMAN is a doctoral candidate in linguistics at SUNY/Buffalo and is conducting research on Lithuanian immigrant communities.

Milton Keynes UK
Ingram Content Group UK Ltd.
UKHW041905020923
427856UK00002B/18